# The Assistant Lighting Designer's Toolkit

# The Assistant Lighting Designer's Toolkit

*Anne E. McMills*

**Focal Press**
Taylor & Francis Group

NEW YORK AND LONDON

First published 2014
by Focal Press
70 Blanchard Road, Suite 402, Burlington, MA 01803

and by Focal Press
2 Park Square, Milton Park, Abingdon, Oxon OX14 4RN

*Focal Press is an imprint of the Taylor & Francis Group, an informa business*

*Library of Congress Cataloging in Publication Data*
McMills, Anne E.
The assistant lighting designer's toolkit / by Anne E. McMills.
pages cm
Includes bibliographical references and index.
1. Stage lighting. I. Title.
PN2091.E4M37 2014
792.02'5—dc23
2013041384

ISBN: 978-0-415-71121-0 (pbk)
ISBN: 978-1-315-88470-7 (ebk)

Typeset in Times New Roman PS
By diacriTech

*For my mother, Rose C. McMills*
*—the original "Typewriter"—*

# Table of Contents

# About the Author

Anne E. McMills is a lighting designer and associate lighting designer. Her far-reaching career extends across the many facets of the lighting world—from theatre (including Broadway and the West End) to television and theme parks to architecture, industrials, concerts, award shows, dance, and opera. In addition to designing her own work, Anne has assisted many award-winning Broadway lighting designers, including Ken Billington, Brian MacDevitt, Howell Binkley, Peter Kaczorowski, Jason Lyons, David Lander, Brian Monahan, and others. Anne has also assisted projections designer Elaine J. McCarthy on *Wicked* and *Spamalot*, mounting productions in the United States, the U.K., Japan, Australia, and Germany. Anne is a proud member of United Scenic Artists, Local 829.

Anne achieved her BFA degree in Theatre Design: Lighting from Millikin University in Decatur, Illinois, and her MFA degree in Lighting Design from Mason Gross School of the Arts at Rutgers University in New Brunswick, New Jersey. While pursuing her thesis research, Anne interned at the Royal Opera House at Covent Garden and the Lyric Theatre Hammersmith in London, U.K., as well as the Opéra de Lyon in Lyon, France, in order to analyze the comparison between American, British, and European lighting design practices and technologies.

Currently, Anne is the Head of Design at California State University, Los Angeles, and an adjunct faculty member at Cerritos College in Norwalk, California. In the fall of 2014, Anne will join the faculty of San Diego State University leading the MFA program in Lighting Design.

# Acknowledgments

This book has been a monumental task and could not have come into being without the selfless donation of time from a lot of very busy people. Please forgive me if I miss anyone.

First of all, thank you to my mother, Rose C. McMills, who has always inspired me to be brave and strive for greatness. Thank you for finding time in your busy schedule to be my personal editor and proofreader. Most importantly, thank you for instilling within me your love of books, your passion for prose, your fervor for grammar, and your joy in the beauty of language.

Thank you to my advance readers and information gatherers—Susan Mason, Heather Oliver, Jessica Morataya, Morgan Zupanski, Jennifer Salmeron, Jared A. Sayeg, Jim Milkey, and Rob Halliday as well as the countless others who read excerpts and sections. Your insight and constructive comments helped shape this book for the better. I am grateful for your help.

Thank you to everyone who donated their time assisting with paperwork examples, images, quotes, and edits—Christopher Akerlind, Apollo Design Technology, Inc., Kevin Barry, Ken Billington, Juan Carillo, CAST Software, Richard Crother, Eric Cornwell, Crowood Press, F. Mitchell Dana (whose profound teaching and influence sculpted the career I have today), John Demous, Andrew Derrington, Devin DeVore (for your beautiful cover photo), DHV Productions, Disney Enterprises, Inc., EarthLED, Beverly Emmons, Erin Erdman, ETC, ESP Vision, Bruce Ferri, Cecilia Friederichs and the team at USA829, Matt Gordon, Meredith Greenberg, Rob Halliday, Tony Helinsky, Hevi Lite, Inc., Donald Holder, Jim Hutchison, KB Associates, Inc., Justin Lang, Vivien Leone, Scott Longberry, Jason Lyons, Joan Marcus Photography, Reinhold Meyer, Ed McCarthy, John McKernon, Jim Milkey, Millikin University, Brian Monahan, Samuel Morgan Photography, Jonathan Mulvaney, Nemetschek Vectorworks Inc., Ryan O'Gara, Justin A. Partier, Matt Peel, Anthony Pearson, Charlie Pennebaker, Edward Pierce, Richard Pilbrow, Kenneth Posner, Carol Prendergast, Michael A. Reese and the team at BKA, Landon Roberts, Rosco Laboratories, Philip S. Rosenberg, Jared A. Sayeg, Jen Schriever, Sewell Direct, Steve Shelley, Rick Sorensen, Hugh Vanstone, Andrew Voller, Dave Ward, K.C. Wilkerson, Jake Wiltshire, WMW Reprographics Ltd., WYSIWYG, Michael Zinman, and the Carpenter Performing Arts Center at California State University, Long Beach. It has been a tremendous joy to have so many significant professionals within the field contribute to this project.

Thank you to Jim Milkey, my technical editor and friend. I am so grateful for your observations and careful crafting of my manuscript. Thank you for sticking with me during such a challenging time in your life.

Thank you to my family for their support and input, and to my friends for their constant encouragement (especially those who have traveled with me the longest through this career: Jimmy Babcock, Aaron Jackson, Melissa (Raddatz) Mulvaney, and the always-inspirational, Trillian, who told me to write this book "no matter what.") And, of course, a loving thanks to my four-legged writing partners, Cosette and Sienna, who were always there to make me laugh when I needed it.

Thank you to Focal Press for giving me this opportunity—especially Stacey Walker and Meagan White. Special thanks to Steve Shelley for your guidance and continuing mentorship. And thank you to Jennifer Silva Redmond and Michael Lennie.

Thank you to the faculty, staff, administrators, and students at Cal State L.A. who supported me through my creative leave for this project—especially Meredith Greenburg and John Kennedy.

A special thank you to Ken Billington and his associates. Nothing has affected my career more profoundly than my years working at KBA. There I was taught how to be a great associate *and* a great professional. Without question, this book would not exist without your immeasurable influence and extraordinary training. I am truly honored and humbled to have the legendary Ken Billington write this text's foreword.

And, finally, thank you to my partner, Jonathan Mulvaney, who has supported me throughout this project and every day before and after. Thank you for always listening, giving your brilliant contributions, putting up with my always-busy schedule, and constantly stopping what you were doing to talk me through even the smallest decisions on this book. Thank you for being in my life, supporting my dreams, and always being there for me.

# Foreword by Ken Billington

When Anne McMills contacted me about writing the foreword to this book, I was flattered, but I wondered if she had asked the right guy. After all, the last time I was an assistant was for Paul Sullivan, lighting a Broadway revival of *Lost in the Stars* in 1972.

Much has changed in the past 40 years on Broadway and in the art and craft of lighting. Back then drafting was done by hand, and the hookup was handwritten, using carbon paper to produce copies. There was no channel hookup, just a dimmer hookup, as all the controls were on manual resistance "piano boards." On a Broadway musical, it took three electricians to operate the board. Followspots were direct current, 100-amp, carbon arcs, automated lighting had yet to be invented, and the color scroller was still ten years away. Using a gobo required ordering a Leko with a gobo slot, designing the gobo, and having it cut out of a pie tin or etched into brass—the product of this labor would often burn out almost instantly. Yes, it was the dark ages of lighting design.

What being an assistant taught me, however, was how to be a designer. Back then there was one assistant. We were *not* "associates." Sometimes I did the drafting, but usually I was there to write the focus charts, update the paperwork, write down the cue locations, document the dimmer levels, and keep track of the followspots … also the fun things such as running for coffee and cigarettes and to empty the ashtray at the production table. Yes, everyone smoked at the production tables, even the stage manager at the calling desk. When I was not performing such chores, I was observing the lighting designer and the creative process. I watched the collaboration that created a show, the interactions with the scenic and costume designers, the director, the choreographer, and with management. Keeping up with technology was important, but so were personalities and professional flexibility. The theatre is always a community.

I quickly learned that theatre people, from producer to stagehand, usher to actor, are giving artists. I was young, and they generously showed how things were done and how professionals behaved in the theatre. I could ask questions, of course, and they would be answered, but I had to learn *when* to ask the question. Timing, not just of light cues, was an important lesson. I learned not to question the use of, say, a blue backlight while the director was talking to my boss about a scene. I learned that it might be better to wait until dinner, when things are more relaxed, to voice my thoughts and observations. The lessons I learned still guide my life in the theatre.

Of course, I had the good fortune to work for some of the most successful lighting designers of the day, and luckily I worked extensively as Tharon Musser's assistant. I always say I went to Musser University since my lighting education came from sitting at the production table and observing her professional skill and professional manner.

In the twenty-first century, most designers expect a great deal from an assistant. We have incorporated computers into every aspect of theatrical lighting, automation, and sound. Today's designer does not need to figure out how one man with two arms can execute a cue on a manual board. Today's lighting operator hits a button, and it all happens. The job still starts with a love of lighting, but today's assistant needs to be an expert draftsman, in Vectorworks or AutoCAD, and to have a complete understanding of Lightwright, moving light tracking software, and computer networking. All this technology needs to be integrated, efficient, and in service to the design.

An assistant is there, of course, to support and represent the designer, and this means maintaining a good relationship with the rest of the creative team, being well dressed and articulate, and being a good companion. A lighting team shares long hours, long days, and countless lunches, dinners, and drinks. Some designers I know think that one of most important things an assistant can offer is good dinner company.

Finding that first foothold in the theatre can be rough. How many college students graduate each year with a lighting degree? Working as an assistant offers a sturdy first step towards a professional design career. You get to watch the designer, and if it goes wrong, it's not your fault. You are there to learn the skills and procedures you will need to become your own designer. In another time, it would have been called an apprenticeship, but it is a professional job, and I think Anne has made it very clear what will be expected.

It has been many years since the last time I assisted, and I have a hundred Broadway designs under my belt. I have had many brilliant assistants over the years, and some have become my best friends. Anne's book reminds me of a fact I acknowledge every day; I could not be a good designer without those assistants.

Ken Billington
New York City
September 2011

# Introduction

This is the book I wish I'd had when I was in school. Its goal is to help bridge the seemingly large divide between being a lighting student and becoming a lighting professional—in hopes of making the transition an easier one.

The practice of assisting a lighting designer is a complex topic that is not often covered at length in academic institutions; no matter how hard the professors try to squeeze it in. The result is that students graduate as competent designers, but lack the valuable know-how to break into the business by assisting. Due to this conundrum, the profession has historically remained an apprentice-style or journeyman-like career, requiring most skills to be learned on the job. This book hopes to change that by providing individuals with the skills *before* entering the workforce, thereby making them more valuable assets at an earlier stage in the process and unburdening the designers from constantly training "newbies."

This book aims to unlock insider secrets of the assisting profession. It will help you, the reader, become a better lighting assistant no matter where you are working—whether Broadway or the West End, regional, educational, or while acting as your own assistant. Some concepts discussed may also be useful for assistants in other design disciplines as well as stage managers.

In January 1989, renowned lighting designer Craig Miller published a short article in *Theatre Crafts* magazine called, "A Guide for Assistant Lighting Designers: Some Modestly Proffered Notes." This article was given as a roadmap to generations of future lighting designers assisting Miller at the time—including Broadway greats such as Ken Posner, Peter Kaczorowski, and others. I discovered this article late in the book-writing process—nearly after the completion of my manuscript. If I hadn't, I would have been proud to call that article the forefather of this text. However, as fate would have it, the late discovering of that cherished article further demonstrated how little has truly changed throughout the history of assisting. My laptop might have been his carbon paper, my Vectorworks his plastic lighting template, but the overall sentiment of documenting the lighting design process, being proactive, generous of spirit, and always saying "please" and "thank you" has not changed. The major topics and keypoints of Miller's article, although brief, nearly mirrored this text's concepts. Finding that article further demonstrated to me not only the historical importance of documenting the process of the assistant lighting designer and the profession's staying-power, but also the contemporary need of an updated guide as a staple in our literature and roadmap for future generations to come.

What this book is not: this book is not a book about the fundamentals of lighting design. It assumes the reader previously has that knowledge and should ideally be read by individuals who already grasp the basic concepts of lighting design and the process of tech.

In addition, please note that this book is not intended to provide all of the answers. It cannot, due to the fact that every lighting designer and assistant relationship is different. Within this same vein, the methods described are not considered the *only* way to do things, but instead a distillation of the most common methods used by the top professionals in the field. Also note that the pronouns "he/she" and "him/her" have been alternated within topics when referring to the designer and others. This has been done intentionally to attempt to inject an increased female presence into a historically male-dominated profession. Also note: Quotations found throughout this text without annotations are taken directly from personal interviews and surveys. Terms found within the text in bold font indicate the initial definitive use of the term.

Most of the concepts in this book are based on how the lighting design process works during a professional American production, such as on Broadway, assuming that the fictitious assistant, namely the reader, is working under the constraints, budgets, unions, and amenities that a professional production of high caliber has to offer. Variations on this situation are presented in Part Four of this book, which discusses other systems and styles of production.

This book is broken up into Parts, briefly described here:

- *Part 1: The Profession defines the basics of assisting and covers the qualities and talents needed in order to be successful in the career. Additionally it describes the tools needed to accomplish the daily tasks of the profession, the production personnel dealt with on a typical day, and the unions that they may belong to.*

- *Part 2: The Process covers the phases of the design process from concept to strike and the role and responsibilities of the assistant along each step of the journey.*

- *Part 3: The Paperwork covers tips and techniques for the assistant's documentation process; enabling the reader to learn how to create documents in the professional standard.*

- *Part 4: The Industry details the many and varied organizations and situations that an assistant lighting designer may work within—both domestically and abroad, as well as relevant industries outside of theatre.*

- *Part 5: The Life details what it is like to both start a career and live the life of a freelance assistant lighting designer.*

Overall, this book is intended to fill a void within the literature of the field, which limits the mention of the assistant and their duties considerably. It will elaborate on this extremely complex career and allow new assistants and aspiring designers to begin their careers at a more advanced level. Its goal is to help you, the reader, unlock the secrets that break through the barrier into the professional realm. For more information on *The Assistant Lighting Designer's Toolkit* check out www.ALDToolkit.com.

# Common Abbreviations

**Common Theatrical Abbreviations Used in this Book:**

**Personnel**

- LD—Lighting Designer
- ALD—Assistant Lighting Designer/ Associate Lighting Designer
- PSM—Production Stage Manager
- Carp—Carpenter (usually referring to the Head Carpenter)

**Unions/Organizations**

- IATSE—The International Alliance of Theatrical Stage Employees
- USA—United Scenic Artists, Local 829
- AEA—Actors' Equity Association
- LORT—League of Resident Theatres
- Bway or B'way—common abbreviation for "Broadway"
- CBA—Collective Bargaining Agreement

**Stage Directions**

- US—Upstage
- DS—Downstage
- SR—Stage Right
- SL—Stage Left
- CL—Centerline
- PL—Plasterline
- HR—House Right
- HL—House Left
- CS—Center Stage
- DC—Down Center
- DR—Down Right
- DCR—Down Center Right (sometimes DRC)
- DL—Down Left
- DCL—Down Center Left (sometimes DLC)
- UC—Up Center
- UR—Up Right
- UCR—Up Center Right (sometimes URC)
- UL—Up Left
- UCL—Up Center Left (sometimes ULC)

**Lighting Design Terms**

- HS—High Side
- PE—Pipe End
- HH—Head High
- FOH—Front of House
- EOS—Edge of Stage
- EOD—Edge of Deck
- BK—Backlight
- WM—Warm
- CL—Cool

**Miscellaneous**

- CAD—Computer Aided Drafting
- VW—Vectorworks
- LW—Lightwright®
- ML—Moving Light

# PART 1

# The Profession

An **Assistant Lighting Designer** is responsible for effectively communicating the lighting designer's artistic vision for a production and helping to usher it into physical reality. It takes a special blend of skills—both technical and interpersonal—to succeed in this challenging career.

> *"The big British imports ... turned [assisting] into an occupation. With the mega-musical and the notion of multiple companies, someone could make a living for many years remounting and reconfiguring a show."*
>
> —*Kenneth Posner*[1]

In the past, working as an assistant lighting designer was viewed simply as a stepping stone to becoming a designer. Within the past few decades, things have begun to change. Many young designers still use it as a means to climb the professional ladder, but some are now choosing assisting as a life-long career. Perhaps they find they are particularly good at the unique mix of skills required; perhaps they are not interested in dealing with the enormous pressures of heavy-handed producers, as designers must; or perhaps they find that they prefer the daily interactions with the crew better than with the management types. Whatever the reason, those individuals who choose assisting as a career can become some of most sought-after artisans in the business. After all, having great assistants on a show can make the difference between a smooth process and one that is not.

> *A good assistant needs "to be organized and articulate; they need to have a good eye and be designers in their own right; they have to understand diplomacy and the politics of all of the rest of the people in the theatre; and they need to be someone that you want to spend sixteen hours a day with for months at a time."*
>
> —*Jason Lyons*

## CHAPTER 1

# Understanding Assisting

## DEFINING THE ROLE

The assistant has many responsibilities throughout a production period. These responsibilities may vary considerably depending on the preferences of the designer and on where the assistant is working—Broadway versus educational, for example. Essentially it all boils down to one overarching concept—*the responsibilities of the assistant are anything that facilitates making the lighting designer's vision a reality on stage*. It is up to you, the assistant, to determine exactly what items are required in order to do that. Let this book be your guide.

### ASSISTANTS VS. ASSOCIATES

This book uses both the terms "assistant designer" and "associate designer." When entering the field, you need to know what the distinguishing characteristics are between these two roles.

From an outsider's viewpoint, one might think that the titles of assistant and associate are interchangeable. In some respects they are: both produce paperwork for a production and work in conjunction with the lighting designer making his artistic visions a reality and both are abbreviated as ALD (although sometimes as asst. and assoc.). However, although it may seem like it at first glance, they are *not* the same position. Essentially, the **Associate** designer is the promoted version of an assistant designer. It may take several years to become an associate—a title which commands considerable respect among professionals in the field. While both individuals report to the designer, the assistant may also report to the associate, if there are persons of both titles on the show.

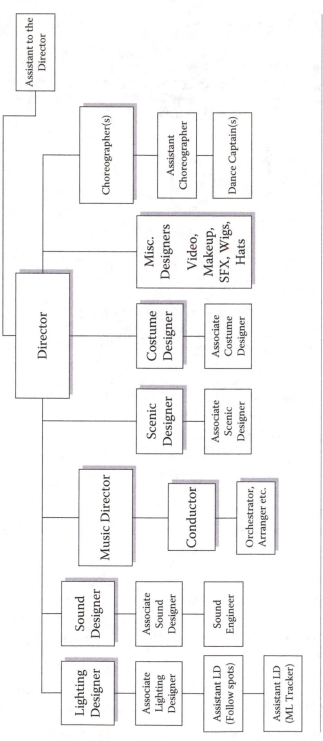

**Figure 1.1** Creative team on a Broadway show.
*Courtesy of: Kevin Barry*

> *"The associate knows when to make judgment calls in the lighting designer's absence, and knows when it's better to wait."*
>
> *—Steve Shelley[2]*

The essential distinguishing factor between these two job descriptions is that the associate, unlike the assistant, is authorized by the lighting designer to make artistic decisions in his absence. The associate can discuss artistic changes with the director and implement those changes in the show—often without discussing the changes with the designer first, depending on the designer-associate relationship. In contrast, if artistic decisions are discussed with the *assistant* in the absence of the designer and/or the associate, the assistant should listen intently and pleasantly, write down the questions (without agreeing or disagreeing to anything), and report them accurately to the designer for direction.

> Please note that for the purposes of this book the term "assistant" has been used universally to include the work of both the assistant and/or the associate depending on the structure of the production. However, if the term "associate" is specifically used, this item relates to associate duties only.

Each relationship is different. Assistants often work with the same designer for several years before they acquire the trust to be promoted to associate. Even after working as an established associate with her regular designers, she may need to start over again with the assistant title when working for any new designers (instead of automatically receiving the associate title).

> *"I expect my associate to be my eyes and ears and my advocate when I'm not in the room: to anticipate problems, to 'put out fires' if necessary until I can arrive, and to continually keep me informed."*
>
> *—Donald Holder*

Some associates focus and cue nearly the entire show without the designer present. Furthermore, when replicating a show, some associates recreate full productions without the designer even showing up.

Not all productions have an associate lighting designer. Typically plays—which are usually considered smaller in scope—will employ only one assistant or one associate. Oppositely, on a large show, such as a Broadway musical, the production may have an associate lighting designer and an additional two or three assistant lighting designers. The number of assistants needed depends upon the scope of the production and which employment situation you are working within. For example, Broadway productions typically employ more assistants than a regional production.

*"Lighting designers are usually spread thin over many different shows at once, so knowing the nitty-gritty of each show is in good hands is invaluable."*

—Jen Schriever

## DIVIDING RESPONSIBILITIES

On shows with multiple assistants, the associate will divide the duties between herself and the other assistants. This can vary greatly depending upon the preferences and working habits of the associate.

Typically the associate will interface with the lighting designer directly and act as his right-hand person. For example, the associate may follow along as the designer cues helping with channels he cannot find or any other needs that he may have, such as taking cue notes. The assistants, then, would take care of any other items required to produce, run, and archive the show, such as work notes, calling followspots, and updating paperwork. In general, assistants are ranked by experience and, therefore, called "**1st assistant**," "**2nd assistant**," and so on.

If a large show has multiple assistants, one model of mapping the responsibilities is as follows: while the associate is working directly with the designer, the 1st assistant (also called the "**Followspot Assistant**") is responsible for the design, creation, and calling of the followspot cues. The 2nd assistant would, then, be responsible for all other items, such as work and focus notes and updating the plot and paperwork. If there is a 3rd assistant, that person is typically in charge of working with the programmer to track and archive the moving lights as needed. This assistant is called the "**ML Assistant**" or "**ML Tracking Assistant**."

**Figure 1.2**  Lighting Tech Table.
*Photo By: Kevin Barry*

Every production situation is different. In situations involving very particular directors, the associate may be the one to design and call the followspots. In other situations, the 1st assistant may take care of all of the paperwork while the 2nd assistant calls the followspots.

All of these guidelines are very loose and depend on the preferences of the team, but overall typically there is one person working closely with the designer (either the associate or the 1st assistant when there is no associate), another doing followspots (if applicable), and another taking care of all the nitty-gritty paperwork. If the show has only one assistant, that assistant is in charge of covering all of these responsibilities.

The idea of a tracking assistant, like an ML tracking assistant, is not a new idea to lighting. Historically, in the days of the old piano boards through the early memory and computer boards, the assistant, or "tracker," would record every level for every fixture in every cue on track sheets. These track sheets would allow the lighting designer to jump easily from cue to cue during rehearsal. (The board operator's cue sheets only recorded changes in level from the previous cues, and therefore only really worked when running cues in sequence.) In the case of early memory and computer boards, the tracking sheets helped to verify the correct levels and reprogram the board if the memory crashed—which happened often.

## ASSISTANT "TO"

*"A young designer coming to New York first off should find an internship. An internship can lead to becoming an assistant in that same studio."*

—*David Lander*[3]

In addition to the lighting design team members mentioned above, sometimes one other individual can be present. This person is titled the **Assistant *To* the Lighting Designer**," and is sometimes referred to as the "intern." The *assistant-to* falls into a gray area because this individual is an intern or personal assistant hired (paid or unpaid) by the lighting designer; not one who is hired through the producers of the show, and, therefore, is not officially considered part of the production. Sometimes the assistant-to may be working for free for experience or internship credit from his university or may be a part of the designer's design office team.

> *"Students [often] study with me and become interns while they're at school, and then they get invited to be the second assistant on a musical and then, eventually, first assistant."*
>
> —*Brian MacDevitt*[4]

Typically this person is non-union, and therefore contractually (on a union show) cannot work on anything specific to the show's implementation in the theatre, like paperwork. However, the assistant-to may run personal errands, such as get coffee, provide tech table snacks, deliver research materials, pick up drawings, or run mail to the post office. This is a great way for advanced students, recent graduates, and budding professionals to be exposed to professional union shows. Working as an assistant-to is a beneficial avenue to gaining exposure to large productions and learning how professional assistants and designers work.

**Figure 1.3** Tech Table with snacks.
*Photo By: Rob Halliday*

*"Getting coffee is not a subservient act; it is an act of mercy."*

*—Vivien Leone*

## QUALITIES OF A GOOD ASSISTANT

*My assistant functions as "frankly a good companion. Lighting design is a lonely, tension-filled life. [I look for] a good companion; one who knows how to be quiet and patient, when to offer support, when to be quietly super-efficient, and how to be able to relax over a nice drink or meal."*

*—Richard Pilbrow*

The first guidelines to being a good assistant are to one, be qualified, and two, be likable. Chances are if you exude an amiable personality (on top of being qualified) you are more likely to get hired quickly and rehired frequently. After all, assistants and designers spend many hours together working side-by-side at the tech table. Many designers believe that the essential skills of assisting can be taught, but personality is the first key that they look for in an assistant.

*"Skill gets you hired the first time, personality gets you hired the second, third, and fourth time!"*

*—K. C. Wilkerson*

*"I am meticulous as to who I choose to work with, and it's not just based on their talent. Their personality and how they are perceived when they walk into a room is also very important."*

*—Howell Binkley[5]*

Of course, no matter how likable you are, you must still prove that you are good enough to keep the job. Being an assistant requires a unique cocktail of talents in order to be successful. For example, you must be the type of person who can keep her head on her shoulders during high-pressure situations and still maintain a pleasant nature. And having a good sense of humor (and the instinct to know when it's appropriate) can break the tension and ease your designer's stress when needed.

*The most important qualities in a good assistant are "passion and dedication, technical competence, [and] a sense of humor."*

*—Richard Pilbrow*

Being good with people overall is a desired quality. You need to be able to navigate between the different attitudes of the people around you. For example, being able to bounce between "the crew guy thing" one minute and interacting with management the next minute can take some practice.

*"The ability to communicate information in the way that people will best receive it (and spur them to take action) can be difficult to master, but it's an invaluable tool."*

*—K. C. Wilkerson*

People-skills make up a large percentage of the essential requirements of a good assistant, which must be maintained even during the final hours of a sixteen-hour day after a full six or seven-day workweek. This may be a challenge, but by achieving it you greatly increase your chances of being rehired on the next show—a constant goal for a freelance assistant.

*"You need the technical skills, the drafting, the paperwork, the organizational skills, etc., but you also need to be a people person ... It's the communication skills that make or break people most."*

*—Jason Lyons*

Some qualities that make up a successful assistant are:

- Detail-oriented
- Easy to get along with
- Flexible
- Quick-thinking
- Deals with change well
- Thick-skinned
- Workaholic
- Tendency towards unrelenting perfectionism
- Ability to stay calm

- Works well under pressure
- Sense of humor
- Pleasant
- Go-getter
- Self-sufficient
- Kind
- Dedicated
- Ready to Learn
- Nurturing
- Meticulous
- Prompt
- Ability to always stay one step ahead of others
- Knowledgeable
- Knows when to speak up and when not to
- Polite
- Good eye for design
- Alert
- Sharp
- Open-minded
- Focused
- Good listener
- Supportive
- Efficient
- Accepts responsibility
- Effective problem-solver
- Works without judgment
- Quick with a smile

Some of these qualities and skills can be discussed in further detail:

### Meticulous

Lighting design is a profession of numbers. The assistant must keep track of channel numbers, cue numbers, dimmer/address numbers, and instrument numbers—just to name a few. Never let even one of them get lost in the shuffle. If a channel cannot be found, it can make your designer very unhappy during a fast-paced moment when that all-important number is required.

> *"If your paperwork isn't perfect then there's no point to any of it. If things are wrong it just becomes impossible to trouble shoot."*
>
> —*Nick Solyom*[6]

It boils down to this—you must write everything down. Period. Even if you have amazing memory retention, multiple numbers and notes from the designer may be thrown at you at once. Better to write them down than to record the incorrect information. Update the changes in their proper place electronically as soon as you can. Do not leave it scribbled on your note pad or typed in the margins indefinitely.

*I can't live without "my notepad and pencil. I write everything down from every-one's names when I first walk into the theatre to every note that needs to happen and anything we change as we go along."*

*—Anthony Pearson*

*"It is the mark of a great assistant that he or she reminds you at 11:30 at night that you said something at 8:10 in the morning."*

*—Kenneth Posner[7]*

*"If you hear the designer agree with the set designer ... take the note without need-ing to be told separately by your designer.... Stay with your designer and keep your pencil moving."*

*—Craig Miller[8]*

The amount of information that changes throughout a typical day of tech can be staggering. Instead of feeling overwhelmed, think of it like a game, like Tetris: you need to keep placing all the blocks (of information) in the most logical places before time runs out. Regarding it more like a fun challenge instead of an oppressive responsibility will keep your attitude positive and encourage you to succeed.

## Working Under Pressure

The job of a lighting designer—and the assistant—is incredibly stressful. Often called "the hot seat," the designer needs to work extremely fast in order to keep the tech process moving.

The lighting designer's job is referred to as "the hot seat" because all other disciplines except for lighting design can be done in advance (rehearsing the actors, building the scenery, making the costumes, etc.). The lighting designer must create her art while everyone else in the theatre is watching and waiting to move on.

During tech, many lighting designers pride themselves on never hearing the PSM say those dreaded four little words, "we're waiting on lighting." (It might as well be a four-lettered word!) In order for this not to happen, the assistant has to be every bit as quick (or quicker) than the designer regarding anything she may need, such as channel and/or cue numbers. The designer may be the one in the hot seat, but it is the assistant who will get burned if the process gets held up.

There are many ways to try to stay on top of your designer's needs. For example, work tirelessly at memorizing the channels for your production. Quiz yourself throughout the day. If you have memorized the channels and your designer is struggling to remember one, you will be able to tell it to her before she even needs to look down at her magic sheet. Or, as another example, if your designer requests a change in the followspots while a musical number is being run, make that change as fast as humanly possible (even if it's messy) so that she can see the implementation of the change onstage before the moment has passed.

### Thick-Skinned

The assistant should "keep a sunny disposition and retain a cheerful attitude regardless of the bloodbath that's being witnessed."

—Steve Shelley[9]

It does not matter if you work for the nicest designer you think you have ever met—there is always a possibility that at some point during the process you will be reprimanded, addressed in a very emphatic manner, or even yelled at. Being a lighting designer is so stressful and full of pressure that it would be unfair to imagine that even the calmest designer would be able to keep his cool at all times. Keep in mind that when this happens it is not typically a reflection on you personally, but often a deflection from the designer during a stressful situation—chances are it is not about you. No matter the reason, try to shake it off, smile, and fix the issue as quickly as you can.

Practice not "taking things too personally. Usually, it is not about you ... unless you make it about you."

—Vivien Leone

In preparation for tense situations, attach a Post-it to your computer that communicates a positive mantra, like "water/duck's back," "this too shall pass," or "just breathe." Repeat this mantra to yourself during stressful moments, take your frustrations out discreetly on a stress ball under the tech table, or take a drink of water and focus on something positive like a photo of your pet, significant other, or an image that makes you laugh. Take a few breaths. Remember that the problem is not personal, fix the issue, and continue with as much positivity, grace, and patience as you can muster. Some designers will apologize later. Some will not. Either way, do not harbor any hard feelings. Just move on as the professional that you are.

## Staying One Step Ahead

Staying one step ahead may be difficult at first when working with a new designer. As you get to know the designer better, it will become more easily achievable.

> A good assistant *"should be capable of identifying problems before they come up and not be surprised by them."*
>
> —*Donald Holder*

The more you try to anticipate issues, the better, but make sure that your designer is comfortable with you taking charge. For example, you notice that a conventional fixture has been knocked out of focus on a boom, but your designer makes no mention of it. If this is the first time you find yourself in this situation with this new designer always ask if it is okay to fix it without him. You might say, "I noticed that channel 82 was kicked during that last transition. Are you comfortable with me touching up the focus after our break?" Chances are the designer will appreciate that you noticed the issue. If he approves, ask the production electrician if she is able to have an electrician focus with you after break. However, if the designer would rather be involved and is not available after the break, add the note to the focus notes. Do not worry if your designer is not feeling comfortable with you focusing on your own yet. Some designers always prefer to focus themselves. Others will develop that level of trust as they get to know you, your artistic eye, and your ability to emulate their techniques and vision.

The incorrect thing to do in this situation would have been racing up on stage, grabbing an electrician, and beginning to focus. Although this may seem like a self-sufficient and go-getter attitude, it is always best to discuss your intentions with your designer first—especially the first time. If the assistant races up onstage, the designer may feel abandoned at an inopportune time or worry that the assistant will focus the fixture incorrectly. As the designer-assistant relationship grows stronger, the designer may allow the assistant a little more rein, but even then tell the designer your intentions before doing something that affects the show.

Keep in mind that the unfocused fixture *could* look like a happy accident that creates interest on a piece of scenery. Your designer may want to keep it and repurpose it instead of refocusing it to its original intent. Keeping the communication lines open will help you to stay on track with your designer's needs.

> *"Anticipate what's needed next … what scenery is needed, when the next break is … Look ahead, assess, and act…. Anticipate the next steps without waiting for direction."*
>
> —*Jen Schriever*

Another method of staying one step ahead is to continually ask yourself, "what notes can we accomplish during the next actor-break?" Can the designer get some cueing notes done?

Or maybe there are a few instruments on the FOH coves that could be easily touched up by an electrician. Is there time to fly in and test that new practical that was hung just before rehearsal?

Again, think of it like a game. Objective: How can you continue to cross things off your list throughout the day to make the least amount of notes possible? The reward at the end of the game may result in a later call-time for you the next morning. Not only that, but your designer will be happier throughout rehearsal as bothersome items begin to disappear.

### Prompt

Don't be late. Ever. Be early—thirty minutes or more is a good rule of thumb. Never let the designer arrive before you do. The assistant is typically the first one of the lighting design team to arrive and the last one to leave.

> *"Assistants are vital. I like to make sure that they know that their input and ideas are welcome. But I do like them to get me a cup of coffee occasionally."*
>
> —*Andrew Bridge*[10]

Arrive early and make sure everything is set and ready for the designer before he enters the theatre. Assure that the tech table is neat and in good order. Bring coffee for your designer if he prefers—extra hot so that it is still warm when he arrives.

Check with the production electrician to assure that she has everything ready for focus notes. Also ask what has been accomplished on the work notes list. Never act pushy or impatient about these items—many notes may not be able to be accomplished for one reason or another. Simply inquire politely so that you can inform the designer what has been completed if he asks.

### Polite

> *"Never lose your sensitivity to the fact that waiting at the top of a 30' ladder is no fun for the focusing electrician."*
>
> —*Craig Miller*[11]

An assistant should always be polite no matter how stressful the situation. As designers, we often make difficult requests of the electricians who sometimes perform nearly impossible—verging on dangerous—tasks for us in order to simply create our art. "Please" and "thank you" should be used even if the electricians are responding in a less-than-generous manner.

> *"Be friendly and kind to other people."*
>
> —*Jen Schriever*

In addition, your production electrician must be treated with courtesy and appreciation. As an assistant, he is your partner, comrade, and, often, savior during the production period. Forge a cohesive relationship based on mutual respect. It can make or break your experience on a show—especially as a new assistant.

## Knowing When To Stay Silent

Learn when to speak up and when to stay silent. Every designer is different. Even different days with the same designer may vary. Pay attention to any subtle clues he may give and try to anticipate his needs.

> *"Sometimes you have to let the designer find something on their own. It is a delicate balance … in the heat of the moment [offering input] can sometimes seem invasive and distracting."*
>
> —*Jason Lyons*

A good rule of thumb is to start off by saying *less* rather than more. Do not begin your working relationship together by saying things like, "what if it was blue?" or "did you try the gobos?" Keep those opinions to yourself. It is not your place as an assistant—especially a new one—to discuss design decisions with your designer. If he asks for your opinion, answer him honestly but do not overdo it with a long discussion on the merits and pitfalls of his decisions. A designer asking for opinions may be feeling insecure and is probably seeking your support and validation more than anything. Delving too deeply and registering (even slightly) negative reactions to any of his design choices may erode your budding designer-assistant relationship in its early stages. Additionally, do not assume after being asked your opinion one time that it gives you free rein to comment on additional moments. Your best bet is to keep your opinions to yourself unless you are asked again.

> Don't *"over-anticipate or second guess the designer—that's rude and unhelpful."*
>
> —*Vivien Leone*[12]

> *"I don't typically look for feedback or positive reinforcement from the people who work with me. I feel it's unfair and perhaps inappropriate to put them in that position."*
>
> —*Donald Holder*

Learn to determine when it is appropriate to ask questions of your designer, such as seeking clarification on a cue note or focus note. The appropriate timing is individual for each designer. For example, you notice your designer sitting and idly staring at the stage. Is it an appropriate time to ask a question? Even if it is just a quick one? You might think it is, but instead, proceed with caution. Your designer may *look* as if he is not doing anything, but actually he may be lost in thought regarding a cueing sequence. If you interrupt with a question, it may throw off his entire solution and make him very unhappy with you. Never assume that your designer is not working.

*"Keep me on track, but do not nag."*

*—F. Mitchell Dana*

Learn to approach your designer in the least obtrusive way possible. Do not launch directly into your question. Instead try using a shorthand-like tactic. Perhaps you say gently, "I have a question" or "when you have a moment" or simply, "question." This may be enough to communicate that you need attention at his convenience. Small changes in approach like this will help build a relationship based on mutual respect. He knows your questions are important and will answer your questions when he is available, and you show respect for the space and time required for his design process.

On the flip side, there are times when it is appropriate to say something regardless of the situation. One of these times is during an emergency—do not be afraid to speak up if you notice that a curtain has landed on a lighting fixture and is beginning to smoke or you see an actor walking towards the pit when you know the designer is about to black out the stage. It is also appropriate to speak up if you see the designer telling the programmer to update the wrong cue, or the programmer is making a typo in the command line. Stop them and diplomatically verify the correct information. Your designer may seem frustrated with you at first, but he will be happy that you saved him from making a grave mistake.

*"Don't answer to the director or producer unless you've already developed that relationship with the designer you're working for."*

*—Jen Schriever*

Additionally, stay reserved when dealing with anyone outside of the lighting team. Always let the designer deal with any top-down communication. If you are approached by the director, producers, or any other higher-ups, politely direct them to speak with the designer or offer to pass on the note. If you fall into a conversation with the director, for example, your designer may feel threatened that you are discussing design decisions without him or a producer may perceive that you committed to a design idea in which the designer is not interested. As the assistant, your interactions should remain internal to the lighting team and other members of the crew.

### Working Without Judgment

As an assistant, you may often have to deliver extravagant work note requests to the electrics crew that seem overwhelming. No matter what the note, deliver it matter-of-factly. Do not complain about it or belittle the note. And never discuss the note in any way that damages the reputation of the designer. It is not your place to judge your designer's design aesthetic and decisions. You are merely the messenger and the facilitator of the note.

### Accepting Responsibility

Take responsibility for any mistakes you have made. Never blame someone else—especially your designer. For example, if you gave the production electrician the wrong note during the previous work session, accept responsibility for it. Do not pretend that the designer changed her mind again. Matter-of-factly state that you had requested the wrong thing, such as hanging the wrong instrument, adding the wrong color, or focusing the fixture incorrectly. Apologize for the mistake and ask politely to rectify it.

### Sense of Humor

A good-natured assistant is usually a well-employed assistant. Try to take life as it comes and enjoy the work even during difficult moments. Chances are your designer will appreciate someone with a kind heart and easy-going attitude sitting beside him.

> *"What do I look for? A sense of humor! ... You sit beside somebody all those hours every day ..."*
>
> *—Tharon Musser*[13]

### Good Eye for Design

Dismiss the myth that assistant designers are "those who cannot do." On the contrary, assistants are incredibly good designers in their own right—partially because they spend countless hours studying the craft of our modern masters at work. Additionally, associates must make creative decisions during the designer's absence while also trying to emulate the designer's style. This can be even more challenging than designing using strictly your own vision.

> *"I want the person next to me looking at the stage too. Or being ready to answer 'what would you do?' ... Pretend that you are the designer (in your head)."*
>
> *—Philip S. Rosenberg*[14]

> *"Put yourself behind the eyes of the designer and be able to go in the same direction, right alongside."*
>
> *—Vivien Leone*[15]

*"I prefer working with assistants who can talk about the work [and have a] love of the theatre … [not] only interested in the latest cool feature of some console or moving light."*

—*Christopher Akerlind*

*"I do not use an assistant … I have a team. [If] I say, 'How the hell am I going to light them up there?' … 'How about 173?' my assistant can say. I want somebody who is a partner. I figure, the more eyes we have working on this, the more problems we're going to catch."*

—*F. Mitchell Dana*[16]

## THE DOS AND DON'TS OF BEING A GOOD ASSISTANT

*"The single most important quality [in a good assistant] is their attitude."*

—*Andrew Voller*

An assistant *"need[s] to pay attention to me, not make me pay attention to them."*

—*Jennifer Tipton*[17]

Many mistakes are made by new assistants when integrating into the business for the first time. Following these tips and tricks can help you minimize mistakes and begin to forge a lucrative career in the assisting world and beyond.

### COMMON "DOS"

• **Look professional.** Dress more like management than you would if working as a stagehand. Don't wear ripped jeans and a t-shirt covered with logos, text, and other pictures—especially controversial or obscene topics. Also, do not wear inappropriately cut items such as extremely revealing low-cut or bare-midriff shirts, extremely low-rise pants, or see-through items. Nice jeans or sensible dress pants and a nice shirt or blouse are encouraged. In contrast, for safety, you must always wear shoes that are load-in appropriate. Steel-toed work boots are not necessary, but good, sturdy-soled, closed-toed shoes that protect your feet are a good choice.

Absolutely no sandals, heels, or skirts. Keep in mind that you are representing your designer and the rest of the design team. Take note of the level at which your designer dresses. If he dresses in an extremely professional manner, match his intention with your style of dress. Remember that you are a professional. Act like it, and dress like it.

- **Use proper headset etiquette.** Often called "Com" or "cans" in the professional community, headsets are connected all over the theatre during tech. You never know who may be listening while you are talking. Rule number one: only speak when required. Extra headset chatter only makes it more difficult for others on your channels to communicate. And rule number two: keep your language clean. Do not curse, use inappropriate language, or ridicule anyone or anything involved in the production. Even if others are doing it, don't engage: it can reflect poorly on you. Extra conversation may also appear to the designer that you are not truly invested in your work and not paying enough attention to her needs.

> *"I can't stand a loud tech table. A lot of shuffling of paperwork, loud talk over headsets, etc. I'm very respectful of the actor's need for concentration."*
>
> —Christopher Akerlind

> *"Keep your comments and questions on the headset to a minimum (unless you're calling followspots on a separate channel). I hate to be interrupted when in the middle of a thought or in the midst of writing a complex sequence of cues."*
>
> —Donald Holder

- **Find good places to eat.** Locate local eateries within walking distance of the theatre for all meals and coffee. The production period on a professional show is spread over many weeks, and the lighting team will often eat at least two meals a day together. Usually after the first few days the team begins to run out of ideas for places to dine, and the repetitive "what's-for-lunch" question begins to arise over headset. Take the opportunity to speak up and propose new options. The team will be grateful you conducted some research and have ideas to suggest.

> *"Never say you're too busy to go to dinner with the designer."*
>
> —*John McKernon*

As you begin to know your designer, pay special attention to items he likes to eat and find a variety of places that carry that type of food. Also take note of any dietary restrictions that he may have (without embarrassing him by asking outright). Is he allergic to seafood or nuts? Is he vegetarian? Is he following any particular weight-loss diet? Research menus and reviews of nearby restaurants that have options he can eat. Gather ideas for a variety of food types to suggest within a moderate price range. In addition, also locate one or two upscale restaurants for nicer dinners during longer meal breaks. (Zagat can be a useful source of curated restaurant reviews for major cities all over the world.)

When working out-of-town, have several options mapped out for the first day. Ask the local crew what nearby eateries they recommend. No matter what the choice, make sure you know how to get there—the group will likely follow you. Also note: have a restaurant app with you that splits up the bill. Often the team will ask for separate checks, but be prepared in case it is needed.

Useful apps for restaurant choices:
- Urbanspoon
- Where To?
- Yelp
- OpenTable
- Wikitude
- Zagat

Useful apps for navigation: (some are city specific)
- Google Maps
- Exit Strategy NYC
- HopStop
- iExit
- TaxiMagic

Useful apps for separating the checks:
- Separate Checks
- Check Ninja

- **Note your designer's preferences.** Some designers are very specific regarding their tech table set-up. On the first day of tech when the designer steps away, discreetly take a photo of the table to use as a reference. At the end of the night clean the tech table, throw away trash, and restore your designer's preferred set-up. Make sure he has everything he needs: Do you need to refill his Post-its or pencil lead? Is the magic sheet in the area that he likes to keep it? Are there enough tech table snacks or do you need to buy more in the morning?

  Another designer preference to note is the all-important coffee order. As a new assistant you may often be asked to go get coffee for the lighting team. Keep the orders in a list on your phone so you always know what your team likes. Who likes cream and sugar? Soy milk? Whipped cream? What size? If not coffee drinkers, what do they want? Tea, juice, or bottled water? Ask the coffee shop for a carrier if there are too many orders to hold with two hands or acquire your own carrier that you keep in the theatre specifically for coffee runs. Bring back plenty of napkins, coffee stirrers, and sugar packets of various kinds. Also, find out if the coffee shop near the theatre gives discounts to those working on the show. Ask your designer if he prefers to have coffee on the table when he walks in each morning. Some designers appreciate—and may expect—this gesture, while others prefer to get their own.

- **Silence all electronic devices.** Silence all your devices during rehearsal—laptop, cell phone, tablet, etc. To avoid mistakes, keep them off permanently during the production process. Not only do noisy devices that interrupt rehearsal reflect badly on you, but they can also embarrass your designer.

- **Memorize the names of your co-workers.** Your designer may be counting on you to feed him names of individuals in the theatre—especially if he needs to grab someone's attention. Try to get to know everyone's name, but pay special attention to electricians, assistant directors, choreographers, sound personnel, the projection design team, assistant stage managers, and anyone else that you may come in contact with daily.

- **Be eager to learn.** Many designers enjoy the energy that a new assistant brings to the table. They appreciate someone passionate about the business and hungry to learn everything that they can. Do not be afraid to ask questions (at the appropriate times) and soak up as much knowledge as possible from the experienced veterans in which you are surrounded.

*When I'm looking for an assistant, I'm looking for "someone whose excitement at being in the room is infectious."*

*—Brian MacDevitt*[18]

*"Know what you don't know, [and] don't be afraid to ask questions. It is so much worse to end up in a bad situation because you had too much pride to ask, then to be embarrassed by having to ask the question."*

—*Jason Lyons*

*"Be a sponge … soak up all the experience you can."*

—*Brian Monahan*

*"A good assistant has to be smart, outgoing, cheerful, well spoken, know when to shut up, and have a wide range of interests outside of theater. And of course, they need to be curious and eager to learn."*

—*John McKernon*

## COMMON "DON'TS"

*"Be confident, but not conceited. People in the theatre can smell both fear and falseness."*

—*Jason Lyons*

- **Don't have a sense of entitlement.** This is probably the most common complaint of today's professional design community. No matter how good your training has been at whatever prestigious university you attended, stepping into your first large professional show makes you a little fish in a big pond. New assistants that act as if they know everything are quickly ignored. Instead, show up willing to learn, open to new ideas, and appreciative of the number of years your new colleagues have worked within the field. The more positive your attitude, the more everyone will be willing to help you succeed.

*"Don't be anxious to show off how much you already know. Be anxious to admit how much you don't."*

—*Peter Kaczorowski*[19]

> *"With an assistant, what I want is a person who comes to me with good basic skills and an open mind to learn what I can teach them. Because by the mere fact that I have hired them, I am saying, 'I will teach you my job. You don't know my job. I don't care what school you go to…. You don't know my field.'"*
>
> —*James L. Moody*[20]

- **Don't text, IM, use social media, or make phone calls.** Unless it directly relates to the current show, texting and social media conveys a sense of apathy, which can quickly damage your budding relationship with your designer. However, some lighting assistants will IM or text each other during tech so as not to disturb the designer on headset. If this is the case, be up-front and explain the situation preemptively to your designer so that she knows you are communicating for work purposes. It will help put her mind at ease, and remind her that the show is your first priority.

> *My biggest pet peeve is when "my assistant is not staying focused … letting them-selves get distracted by cell phone calls, texts, social media, and their personal life."*
>
> —*Brian Monahan*

Freelancers often need to return calls or emails regarding upcoming productions as soon as possible. (More on freelancing in Part Five.) Find the right time to do it—like during a break. (Never leave the tech table during rehearsal.) Let your designer know you are planning to make a call in case she needs anything. If she does, the current show and your current designer is your priority.

> *"Don't talk about your other projects. The most important thing is what's right in front of you."*
>
> —*Kenneth Posner*

- **Don't shop for design jobs.** Even if your career goal is to move away from assisting, do not spend your time "schmoozing" with the director while assisting another designer. Your current job is to be the assistant and your allegiance is to your designer. If it appears that you are constantly undercutting your designer by angling for job opportunities with the director or other designers, there is a strong possibility that the designer will not hire you again. Not only will he begin to feel as if he cannot trust you, but also it may feel to him that you are not invested in his show. Instead, continue to work hard; often designers hand down jobs to their assistants when they are unavailable. If you are dedicated, professional, and likable you will be remembered if any future opportunities are to arise.

> *"Loyalty to me and the lighting team is mandatory."*
>
> —*Richard Pilbrow*

> *"Beware the impulse to create attention for yourself in overt ways. Just being connected to [the] designer is enough."*
>
> —*Christopher Akerlind*

- **Don't sleep or nap on the job**. Sleeping on the job looks unprofessional and may give others a poor impression of you—especially as a new assistant. Also, do not complain or whine about being tired. Chances are that others around you have been working longer hours and arrived at the theatre earlier than you.

> Be *"excited to be there. I can teach someone how to [be a good assistant] as long as they want to be there and are keen to do it. I don't want someone who is going to complain or make more work for me than if they were not there."*
>
> —*Anthony Pearson*

Following the advice in this chapter will help guide you in your journey towards a higher standard of professionalism. The goal is to make your skills as an assistant appear effortless. And the trick is to follow these tips without letting anyone—especially your designer—know that you are doing them. (After all, assistants *are* like the ninjas of the lighting world.)

For example, your designer may actually *like* to be fawned over, but does not like to admit it. If your designer thinks you are handholding him too much, he may feel like he is abusing you as his assistant. However, if you appear to simply be doing a good job, keeping things pleasant, and making his life easier, he will just think you are a naturally fantastic assistant and want to hire you again on his next show.

*"I'm usually looking for the opposite of a showboat; a character who does the work superbly with little fanfare. I like the work to happen as if by magic, seemingly without effort."*

*—Christopher Akerlind*

An assistant has the power to make the process wonderful or miserable for their lighting team—so choose to make things wonderful! In addition, a freelance career depends on your success with each new production. You are only considered as good as your last show—so be *great* on every show you do!

The assisting profession takes a lot of focus, skill, and patience to keep everything organized while still keeping the process moving smoothly forward. Mastering the skills can be tricky, but well worth the confidence you will feel at the end of the day and the success that will follow in your career.

*"Be the best you can be. This is a small business so having a great reputation is paramount."*

*—Brian Monahan*

## CHAPTER 2

# The Tools Required

Many tools are required for success as an assistant lighting designer; these vary from hardware to software to profession-specific specialty items. As an assistant, you are responsible for owning these items and showing up to the job with all tools on hand.

## HARDWARE

### LAPTOP

The most essential tool needed is a laptop—either a PC or Macintosh depending on your personal preference. Purchase the top-of-the-line product available at the time and upgrade to the latest operating system, fastest processor, most RAM, and largest hard drive. Technology outdates itself so quickly that within two years if you did not buy the best, you may be wishing that you had.

When buying a laptop, consider the following:

- Ensure that the computer's hard drive has plenty of speed, reliability, and storage space for storing information from multiple past shows. (You may often refer to paperwork you created in the past as starter templates.) Alternatively, some assistants like to keep this information on a portable hard drive or on the cloud to save space. Consider purchasing a laptop with a solid-state hard drive because it resists damage better during travel.

- A fast enough processor and ample RAM (memory) are also necessary so that the computer can handle several large programs running simultaneously.

- Consider purchasing a laptop with a matte (non-glossy) screen or installing a matte screen protector. A matte screen will help to diffuse the glare of other tech table lights or emergency lighting reflecting on your screen in the dark theatre.

- Purchase an extra mouse, mousepad, laptop lock, and power supply. Write your name on each of them. This allows you to have one set permanently in your home office as well as a set that stays on the tech table or travels in your laptop bag.

> Always connect your lock to a house seat that is permanently attached to the cement theatre floor—not something temporary like a tech table. Never leave your laptop in the theatre overnight. Even though many professional theatres have doormen and other security features, laptops "walk" easily and have done so from many a show.

- The physical weight of the laptop should also be a consideration. It may not seem like much at first, but a few ounces less constitutes a perceivable difference in weight. Your laptop is usually only *one* of the items that you carry daily—this can get heavy, especially when working in a pedestrian city.

- Physical size should also be considered. You may feel you need a larger screen for drafting, but you may discover that it is easier to travel with a smaller item. If concerned about screen size, you can always purchase a large external monitor for your home office and request one in your shop order for the tech table.

- Consider what sort of input/output options the computer has—USB, CD/DVD, SD card? Do you need to purchase additional adaptors or external portable drives? Consider what types of devices you may need to connect with during your show. You may need to communicate with very new devices as well as very old devices. For example, your designer may have a very old computer with which you need to share information. Or he may prefer an archival DVD instead of cloud backup. Theatres still using older consoles may require the use of floppy disks and drives. Make sure your laptop is as flexible as it can be in order to help make these situations simple and efficient.

- Backup options are vital in the cases of theft and total technical failure. Consider purchasing a laptop with included backup software that will automatically back up your information to a physical hard drive or cloud storage. If your computer dies or gets stolen during tech and you have no backup, you put yourself, your designer, and the show in jeopardy.

## CAMERA

Another required tool for the profession is a digital camera/video device. (You can use the camera on your phone if it is of good quality.) Use it for taking photos for focus charts or recording difficult cueing and/or followspot moments during rehearsal.

Make sure your designer gets permission from the director before recording anything during rehearsal. It is against Actors' Equity Association's (AEA) union regulations to capture or record union performers without permission. Assure the director that it will only be used for your internal lighting design purposes and will not be posted anywhere on the internet. If your camera uses cloud technology make sure that you are the only person with permission to see that folder on your cloud. Do not share these items with others or there could be serious consequences.

When considering a camera, look for these features:

- Your camera should be a high-enough resolution to take clear photos and have plenty of memory for storage. Purchase the highest amount of optical zoom available—followed by digital zoom.

- Your camera's flash *must* have the ability to be disabled. Not only is it distracting and dangerous to the performers, but a flash washes out stage lighting thereby rendering your photo useless. A flash also advertises that you are taking photos during an Equity rehearsal, which may upset the union members. Turn off your flash permanently while working on the show and, as an extra precaution, affix a small piece of black gaff tape over the flash. This allows you to be able to remove the tape temporarily if you need the flash for personal reasons but dismisses the worry of accidental flashes in the theatre.

- Multiple resolution settings are recommended. Lower resolutions may be better for some photos such as ML focus chart photos. (More on ML focus charts in Part Three.)

- Purchase a camera with long battery life, the ability to change out batteries, and/or the capacity to work while plugged in. You may need to use the camera for extended periods of time and take hundreds of photos in one continual shoot. Your camera needs to be able to keep up without needing to stop and be charged.

- A camera that accepts an SD card is also recommended in order to hold a multitude of photos without running out of storage space. Purchase additional high-capacity SD cards to use during long photo sessions, if needed. (Assure that your laptop has an SD-card reader. If not, purchase an external one.)

- Photos on stage can be extremely difficult to capture accurately due to the amount of movement, high-contrast lighting, and rich colors. Choose a camera that allows you to adjust exposure, provides image-stabilization to reduce camera shake, and has the ability to take low-light photos. (Some cameras include the option of using interchangeable lenses. Low-light lenses are available, but may be more expensive than standard lenses.)

- Investigate the photo transfer process. If you are purchasing a device that requires a connection to the computer for transfer, buy an extra transfer cable that can be kept permanently in your laptop bag as a spare.

- Purchase a small, adjustable tripod that enables you to set the camera on the tech table to further reduce blurry shots. Some cameras offer a remote trigger option (wired or wireless) that acts as a useful mate to a tripod when battling camera shake. This allows you to place the camera in an ideal location and take photos without physically standing next to the camera or touching it (which may cause it to shake). Other cameras offer a "tethered" option, which enables the camera to be triggered from your laptop and then automatically uploads the images. Tethered cameras can be useful in speeding up the process when using moving light tracking software, such as FocusTrack. (More on FocusTrack later in this chapter.)

## WEBCAM

Like the camera, a webcam can be very helpful to capture a quick photo of a focus or to record a moment in the show that contains a lot of fast cueing and/or followspot changes. Recording this material gives you the ability to return to the saved moments on your own time and step through each different change as needed. Keep the webcam active and discreetly pointed at the stage during rehearsal. If it is already set up, capturing sequences will be a lot easier than trying to pull out your camera.

## PORTABLE COMPUTER SPEAKERS

A set of small computer speakers are useful when cueing a sequence blindly without the band or the cast. Having the ability to play the music (off a demo or recorded video) allows the designer to cue more accurately.

## SMARTPHONE

A smartphone is highly recommended. Not only will it work as your phone, calendar, and your camera/video device, but also there are many apps that can make your life easier as an assistant.

---

Helpful consumer apps: (may not be available on all operating systems)

- Flashlight—helps you navigate through a dark theatre
- JotNot Scanner Pro—scan important documents from others quickly and easily
- YouTube—look up research on the go
- Dropbox—easily access and share your show's information

- Find my iPhone—helps you locate stolen or misplaced Apple devices
- Hangman—when your designer needs a good distraction
- Yahoo Weather—prepare for those few moments you step outside the theatre
- … and so many more!

In the lighting business, one of the best things about owning a smartphone is the variety of lighting-specific apps. (See Figure 2.1.) (On a side note, although not an app, The LightNetwork is also worth mentioning here as a great resource for help, advice, and general discussion.)

Useful lighting apps:
- **Software-Specific Apps**: Software-specific tools
  - LW Touch
  - Nomad
- **Design Apps**: Calculate beam spread and footcandle levels
  - BeamCalc
  - TriangleCalc
  - Lighting Calculator
  - Light Calc
- **Color and Gobo Apps**: Product information and visualizers
  - Swatch
  - Moire
  - myGobo
  - iGobo
- **Equipment Apps**: Fixture information
  - LX Handbook
  - Pocket LD
  - ML Finder Pro
  - DMX Calc
- **Console-Control Apps**: Control of ETC EOS-family consoles and remote cue preview
  - iRFR
  - iRFR Preview

- **Measurement Apps**: Annotate photos with measurements and notes
  - Photo Measures
- **Photo Apps**: Panoramic imaging
  - 360 Panorama
- **Calculation Apps**: Add feet and inches together easily
  - FeetInchesCalc
- **Conversion Apps**: Foreign translations and conversions
  - Theatre Words
  - iPronunciation
  - iConvert
- **Blog Apps**: News and information on the lighting business
  - Jim on Light
  - iSquint

**Figure 2.1** Smartphone lighting-specific apps.
*Logos used with permission*

## TABLET DEVICES

A tablet device, such as an iPad, is becoming more and more necessary to own as an assistant lighting designer. Not only does it typically have all the apps mentioned previously under the smartphone category, but its larger screen size makes viewing plots and paperwork easier. Additionally it is lighter and less bulky to carry than a large binder, allows you to search documents, is readable in low-light conditions, and can double as a flashlight when you are afraid you may fall off the stage.

**Figure 2.2a**   Lightwright Touch.
*Used with permission from Eric Cornwell*

**Figure 2.2b**   Vectorworks' Nomad.
*Used with permission from Nemetschek, Inc.*

One app, **LW Touch** allows you to view a portable version of your Lightwright file in which you can make notes and changes while working away from the tech table. (See Figure 2.2a and 2.3a.)

Similarly, **Nomad** by Nemetschek creates a portable version of your Vectorworks file. (See Figure 2.2b and 2.3b.) You can annotate the drawing with notes and comments as well as take scale measurements from the drawing. Additionally, the mobile app integrates with Vectorworks Cloud Services.

A tablet device can also be useful as a note-taking and communication device—much like a small computer. Apps such as Write 2 are beneficial in taking notes during design meetings and production meetings. From the app, the notes can be stored in a standard folder structure and backed up automatically in Dropbox. PDF apps such as iAnnotate PDF and GoodNotes can be useful when marking up documents sent electronically between individuals.

Most tablet devices also allow for the addition of cases with built-in keyboards for those who find typing on a standard keyboard to be the most productive.

## PORTABLE PRINTER

If you are working in a situation that does not provide a printer, having a small portable one of your own can save you a lot of headaches. Portable printers usually print more slowly than standard printers. Therefore, purchase the quickest printing speed that you can find. Also, buy an additional computer lock or other locking device so that it can be secured to the theatre seats during tech.

## PLOTTER

Some assistants choose to purchase their own plotter (large format printer) to keep at their home. This is a personal, but expensive, choice. Although plotting at home is convenient, the upkeep

| Channel | Position | Unit# | Instrument Type | Wattage | Accessory | Purpose | Gobo | Color |
|---|---|---|---|---|---|---|---|---|
| 83 | SET MOUNT | 3 | PRACTICAL | | | DECK EDGE SL | | LED |
| 87 | SET MOUNT | 1 | PRACTICAL | | | MOON | | LED |
| 91 | SET MOUNT | 6 | PRACTICAL | | | HOSPITAL PRAC | | R87 |
| 92 | SET MOUNT | 4 | PRACTICAL | | | PRACS SR | | N/C |
| 93 | SET MOUNT | 5 | PRACTICAL | | | PRACS SL | | N/C |
| 100 | B PIPE | 1 | S4 PARNEL | 575w | | HSE | | R119 |
| 100 | B PIPE | 3 | S4 PARNEL | 575w | | HSE | | R119 |
| 100 | B PIPE | 6 | S4 PARNEL | 575w | | HSE | | R119 |
| 100 | B PIPE | 8 | S4 PARNEL | 575w | | HSE | | R119 |
| 100 | C PIPE | 2 | S4 PARNEL | 575w | | HSE | | R119 |
| 100 | C PIPE | 5 | S4 PARNEL | 575w | | HSE | | R119 |
| 100 | C PIPE | 7 | S4 PARNEL | 575w | | HSE | | R119 |
| 100 | C PIPE | 11 | S4 PARNEL | 575w | | HSE | | R119 |
| 101 | D PIPE | 9 | S4 PARNEL | 575w | | BAND | | R64 |
| 110 | 4 PIPE | 4 | S4 26 | 575w | | SLASH SR | | L202 |
| 111 | 4 PIPE | 3 | S4 26 | 575w | | SLASH SL | | L202 |
| 115 | 4 PIPE | 1 | S4 26 | 575w | | US PLAT SR | | L202+R132 |
| 116 | 4 PIPE | 2 | S4 26 | 575w | | US PLAT SL | | L202+R132 |
| 117 | 4 PIPE | 9 | S4 26 | 575w | TEMP | WINDOW SL | R77703: DBL WIND | L202 |
| 181 | 5 PIPE | 1 | S4 19 | 575w | | SPEC ICUE SR | | R132 |
| 191 | 3 PIPE | 1 | S4 19 | 575w | | SPEC ICUE SL | | R132 |

**Figure 2.3a**  Lightwright touch screenshot.

**Figure 2.3b**  Vectorworks' Nomad screenshot.
*Lighting by: Bruce Ferri*

and overhead costs can add up. If considering purchasing one, weigh the pros and cons for yourself. The alternative is plotting from your designer's office, using a reprographic service (sometimes still called a "blueprint service,") or using the large-format print services available at select office supply chains.

# SOFTWARE

The software discussed in this section is considered industry standard. Other software programs exist on the market but it is best to use industry-standard software so that interfacing with others is as seamless as possible. Importing and exporting documents between unlike programs may create technical issues or changes in formatting. This can not only slow down the process, but it may also make others frustrated.

Purchase your own professional copies—not educational versions. Using educational versions in a professional setting is against the manufacturer's regulations. In addition, not only do educational versions usually display a large watermark, but they may also infect others' files with the educational stamp when sharing between parties.

The software listed below is by no means exhaustive. Software changes quickly, and frequently new programs appear on the market. With each new software update or new program teach yourself to quickly convert files between older and newer items. You never know from which version you will be receiving important files.

Please note that the paperwork types mentioned here will be discussed in further detail in Part Three.

## DRAFTING AND PAPERWORK SOFTWARE
### Vectorworks

Vectorworks, made by Nemetschek Vectorworks Inc., is largely considered the industry-standard drafting program for theatrical designers in the United States. For lighting designers, it is used primarily to create the drawing package as well as other documents, such as magic sheets. Vectorworks also has the ability to render photo-realistic virtual models, which accurately depict instrument information, colors, and textures (See Figures 2.5 and 2.6.)

Figure 2.4 Vectorworks.
*Courtesy of: Nemetschek Vectorworks Inc.*

Vectorworks is an object-based drafting program that uses symbols, such as lighting instruments, from included content libraries. In addition, it can incorporate instrument data into each individual lighting fixture, such as instrument type, wattage, channel number, unit number, color, gobo, and dimmer number. Vectorworks can automatically sync this information and any changes made between Vectorworks and Lightwright through the use of Automatic Data Exchange.

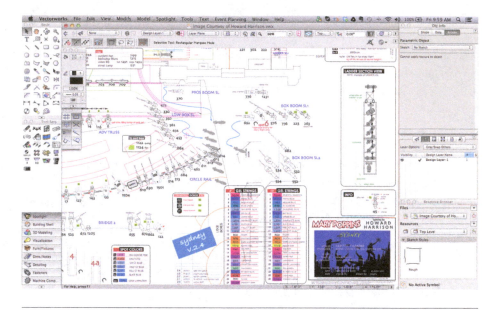

**Figure 2.5**  Vectorworks screenshot.
*Courtesy of: Nemetschek Vectorworks Inc. and Howard Harrison*

**Figure 2.6**  Vectorworks screenshot.
*Courtesy of: Nemetschek Vectorworks Inc. and Michael Helm*

As an additional bonus, Vectorworks has the advantage of some great third party plug-ins created by Joshua Benghiat of Joshua Benghiat Lighting Design and Sam Jones of AutoPlotVW. These plug-ins are created by professional lighting designers specifically to enhance the process of working with theatrical lighting in Vectorworks.

Furthermore, Vectorworks exports directly into lighting pre-visualization program, ESP Vision, to allow for convenient virtual real-time pre-cueing for your production.

Figure 2.7   Courtesy of: ESP Vision.

### Lightwright

Developed by John McKernon and distributed by City Theatrical, Lightwright is considered the professional program of choice for organizing entertainment lighting information.

Lightwright is a hybrid between a spreadsheet and a database, which has been tailored specifically to lighting design. Information for each light can be easily viewed, edited, and sorted. Advanced features are also included such as layouts of DMX addresses for multi-parameter fixtures, color changer strings, and moving light gobo wheels.

As an assistant working on a show you work with Lightwright daily—primarily to create instrument schedules, channel hookups, work notes, and focus charts. The Lightwright file is networked, handed-off, or reconciled between the assistant and the production electrician in order to keep all facets of the paperwork updated. Alternatively, if the copy of the Lightwright file is being passed back and forth *without* the use of networking or reconciling, it is referred to as "the football." The person holding the football is allowed to make changes in the file, but the other person must wait until it is his turn with it. In this situation, keep track of who has the football at all times so that information does not get lost or overwritten.

Figure 2.8   Lightwright.
             *Courtesy of: John McKernon*

### WYSIWYG

WYSIWYG ("what you see is what you get") by CAST Software is popularly used in the concert touring industry. It is also used by the theatrical industry for its pre-cueing

Figure 2.9   WYSIWYG.
             *Courtesy of: CAST Software*

capabilities. WYSIWYG combines the ability to draft plots, produce paperwork, create photo-realistic renderings, and simulate real-time cueing. This powerful software package contains an extensive lighting library full of up-to-date information, which enables the program to produce extremely accurate virtual simulations.

## FOLLOWSPOT AND MOVING LIGHT TRACKING SOFTWARE

### SpotTrack

In 2009, Rob Halliday released SpotTrack and a collective cheer arose from professional lighting assistants around the world. Hungry for a standardized program used to create followspot cue sheets, this program has quickly become a favorite. SpotTrack records important followspot information, such as target name, action items, color frame, intensity, iris size, and more. The program allows you to print master followspot sheets as well as individual sheets for each operator. In addition, page numbers on individual spot sheets can be synchronized by using "gaps" (placeholders for the other operators' moves) so that, during tech, notes and changes can be easily located and discussed.

**Figure 2.10**  SpotTrack.

### FocusTrack

FocusTrack is another time-saving piece of software created by Rob Halliday. It works in conjunction with major lighting console families to record moving light tracking information and moving light focus charts. Depending on your computer, it may even be able to take focus chart photos (of conventionals and moving lights) directly from your laptop using standard built-in camera software.

**Figure 2.11**  FocusTrack.

FocusTrack imports information directly from the console and creates accurate moving light tracking and focus documentation. Information that can be gathered includes focus group names and information, focus chart photos by fixture, a list of which fixtures are in what focuses, which fixtures are not used during the show (so you can avoid paying for items not used when the show remounts), and which scroller colors and gobos are in use in the show file.

The software also creates a cuelist in which scenic needs can be associated with each focus. This allows FocusTrack to group focuses by scenic piece for easy identification later when individual set pieces need focus adjustments.

Other useful functions include: the ability to view similar focuses (so you can decide which ones to merge) and a comparative feature that examines the patch between your Lightwright file and the console for accuracy in your paperwork. In addition, by using a function called FogTrack, the program can help calculate the overall volume of atmospherics cued into the show in order to comply with AEA regulations.

## Moving Light Assistant

Another style of moving light tracking software on the market is Moving Light Assistant created by Andrew Voller. Moving Light Assistant also allows the user to extract moving light information directly from the console to create moving light tracking sheets and moving light focus charts. Photos can be either inserted or taken automatically by a connected camera. Once the photos are imported, the assistant can draw directly on the photos to add any additional notes or information.

**Figure 2.12** Moving Light Assistant.
*Courtesy of: Andrew Voller*

Moving Light Assistant includes a database of moving light configuration information, such as DMX mode, lenses and lamps installed, optional bays items (shutter or iris modules), and each fixture's onboard menu settings. Additionally, you can use the software to create gobo wheel magic sheets and other printouts, such as cuelists.

## FastFocus Pro

FastFocus Pro is another program that works with console data to create moving light tracking documentation and moving light focus charts. It also allows the user to call up

**Figure 2.13** FastFocus Pro screenshots.
*Courtesy of: Matt Peel*

channels and take photos from a laptop. Additionally, this versatile and intelligent program can import 3D fixture information, such as position, directly from Vectorworks as well as convert cuelists from Excel into cue structures within the console, complete with fade time information.

## OTHER LIGHTING-SPECIFIC PROGRAMS

### *Virtual Magic Sheet*

Virtual Magic Sheet (VMS) is a groundbreaking program intended to ease the designer-to-programmer interaction in an artistic and intuitive way. The program allows the creation of an interactive screen that resembles the designer's magic sheet. Real-time data is displayed on this screen to easily inform the designer which fixtures are active, not active, in which color, and at what level. It also displays all information on one page so that flipping through pages of channels on a console becomes a thing of the past.

Creating a VMS template is a fairly intuitive process; virtual buttons and other graphics can be created on the screen in a variety of colors and patterns. This set-up is usually performed by the assistant, and should be complete and tested before the first day of tech.

The concept of VMS has become so popular that console manufacturers are beginning to incorporate this same functionality as a built-in feature within their consoles. Having the feature built-in allows for the information to be shown in both live and blind modes, and incorporates touch-screen capabilities.

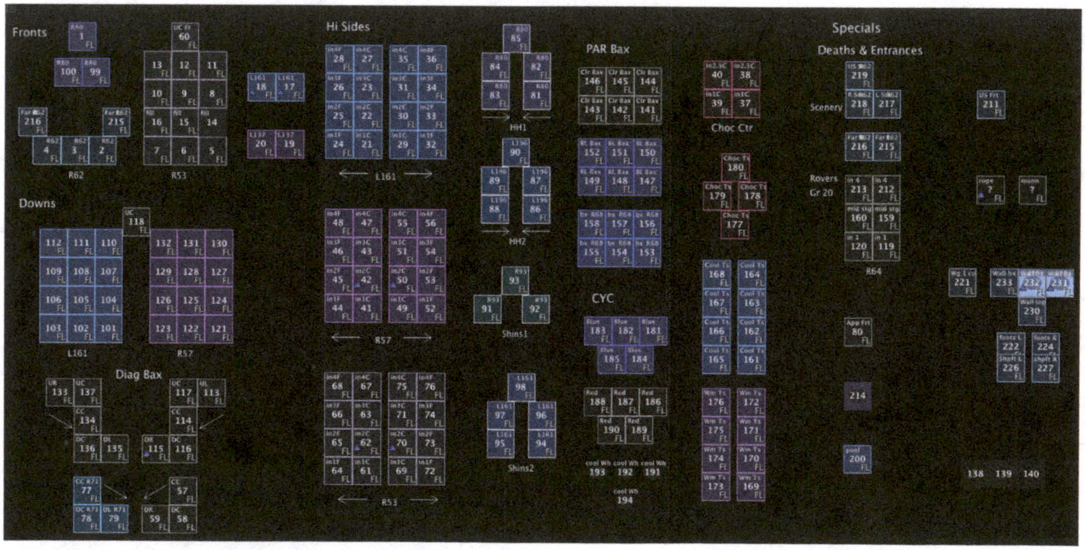

**Figure 2.14**  Virtual Magic Sheet created for the Martha Graham Dance Company, City Center, New York.
*Lighting by: Beverly Emmons*
*Courtesy of: Eric Cornwell*

## OTHER USEFUL SOFTWARE PROGRAMS

Many software programs that are not industry specific can also be useful when working as an assistant. Listed here are a few general consumer software programs that can be useful:

- **Microsoft Word**—used for shop orders and miscellaneous items.
- **Microsoft Excel**—sometimes used for cue synopses, group lists, work notes, and followspot cue sheets as well as financial workbooks and receipt databases (discussed further in Part Five).
- **FileMaker Pro**—database option for cue synopses, work notes, followspots cue sheets, moving light tracking sheets, moving light focus charts, and conventional focus charts. Also an option for receipt databases.
- **Dropbox**—cloud technology used to store show information that can be shared among the lighting team. Also allows syncing across multiple devices (e.g. MacBook and iPad) as well as provides an automatic offsite backup.
- **Parallels and Fusion**—for PC-based offline editors on Macs (needed when working with PC-only consoles).
- **Adobe Photoshop**—for cropping and adjusting focus chart photos and show logos, creating images for custom gobos, and adjusting any other image files needed.
- **GraphicConverter**—a low-cost graphics program that allows for easy batch editing of images, such as adjusting image size on multiple photos simultaneously.
- **Adobe Acrobat and Preview** (built-in for Mac)—for PDFing documents and combining multiple PDFs into a single PDF for archival booklets.

PDF everything that gets "released" (sent out) to prevent others from making changes on your document. The exception to this rule is shared documents that need to be worked on by others, such as sending a shop order to the production electrician. However, a PDF version should also be sent along with the actual file so that a snapshot of the document exists in case there are any technical difficulties on the receiving party's end. This snapshot also creates a record of what was sent in that particular release.

- **PDF Compress**—option for making large PDFs a smaller size for easier emailing.
- **ClickBook** by Blue Squirrel—useful for printing booklets for easier portability. (See Figure 2.15.)
- **Skype and/or FaceTime**—enable face-to-face conferencing (whether professional or personal); great for overseas business travel.

Perhaps, by now, you may be thinking to yourself that assisting is an expensive business. Unfortunately, you are correct. Being an assistant lighting designer requires staying on top of

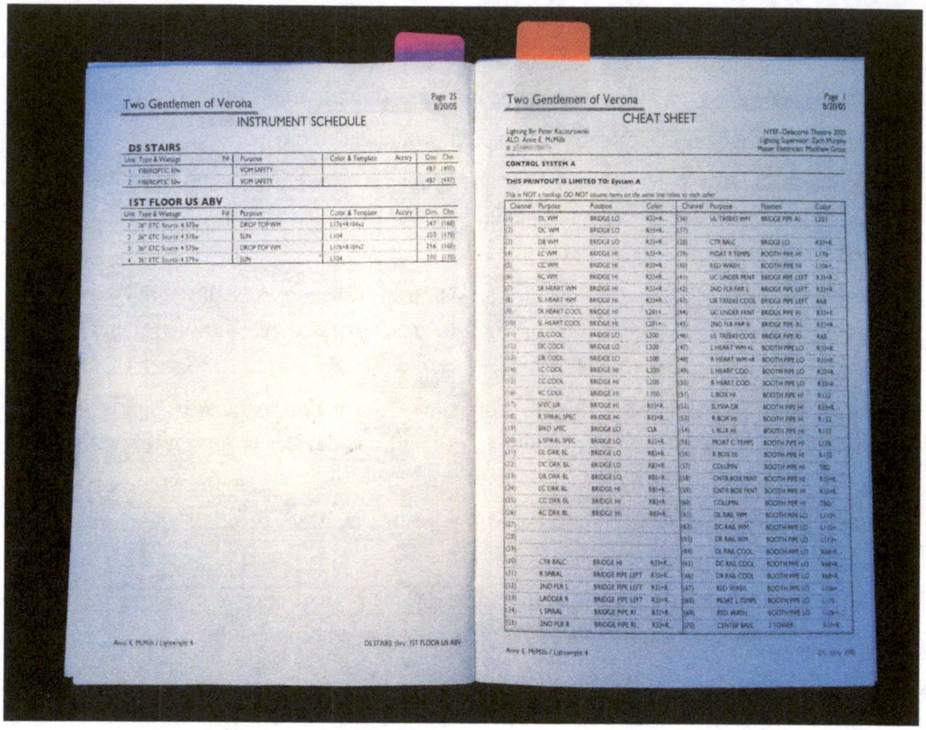

**Figure 2.15** Lightwright printed as a ClickBook booklet.

the latest technology—which certainly can get expensive. Luckily, most of these purchases are tax write-offs, which can help to counterbalance the costs as they begin to add up. (More information on finances and tax write-offs can be found in Part Five of this text.)

## SPECIALTY ITEMS

### ASSISTANT'S KIT

An **Assistant's kit** is a container that holds everything that a lighting design team may use during a production process. Its initial purpose grew from the need to contain the necessary office supplies required. However, it has evolved into something much more complex that holds not only office supplies, but also a variety of other essentials including electronics, snacks, and personal items. This can amount to quite an extensive inventory. A full list of suggested assistant's kit supplies can be found in the Appendices of this book.

An assistant's kit is not something that can be purchased fully assembled but instead is created by each assistant. Create one for yourself by purchasing a sturdy, easy-to-transport container and filling it with supplies. When assembling your kit for the first time, keep in mind that the overall goal is to be able to transform a simple tech table into a comfortable and familiar office space.

*"Be prepared to write on, erase, cut, put back together, attach, measure and hole punch any and every material known to man."*

—*Vivien Leone*

What type of container you choose depends mostly on personal preference and sometimes situation (like travel). Some assistants prefer a large plastic tub or banker's box, while others like using professional roadcases, such as a Pelican case. Another choice is a rolling suitcase—easy to check in as your second bag when traveling by air. No matter what you choose, it is best to find a container that has a lot of integral compartments of varying sizes. This allows for better organization as opposed to lumping everything in one place. The need to dig for items only wastes time during a frantic tech period.

*In my assistant's kit "I have a separate small pencil box that [contains] any razors, knives, or scissors that I could throw in a checked bag if I had to" [for air travel].*

—*Matt Gordon*

In addition to your full kit, create a smaller supplemental kit for yourself. A smaller kit packed with just the essentials can be used on a shorter show, a designer run, or any other more temporary situation.

Use the list in the Appendices of this text as a guide to begin gathering supplies for your kit. Your items may vary depending on the designer you are assisting. Most designers are particular about the office supplies they like to use. In some cases, when working on a show, the designer (or their office staff) may provide you with a specific list of supplies that the designer prefers to use during production. (See Figure 2.17 for an example.) You may even be loaned a fully assembled kit. Choose what makes the most sense for you—use the pre-assembled kit or incorporate the designer's preferred supplies into your own. As long as the supplies are in the theatre, most designers will not care how they arrived.

If you are the first assistant on a show, you are typically responsible for supplying the kit. (If you are the only assistant, you *must* provide it.) If there are multiple assistants on a show, only one well-stocked kit is needed. Ask the associate who will be responsible for bringing it—occasionally it is the assistant, especially if the associate is flying in from out of town.

**Figure 2.16** Multiple sizes of assistant's kits.

KB ASSOCIATES, INC.                                KEN BILLINGTON, *President*

## ASSISTANT LIGHTING DESIGNER
## THEATRE PACKING LIST

*The following list represents what should be included in a "typical" show box. Individual productions may have varying needs, and the show box should be adjusted accordingly.*

**PRODUCTION BOOK:**
- STANDARD TABS:
    - Magic Sheets
    - Instrument Schedule
    - Channel Hookup
    - Focus Charts
    - Followspots
    - Blank (ML, Scenic, etc., as needed)
    - Contact / Schedule
    - Drawings / Notes
- OTHER USEFUL ITEMS:
    - Track Sheets
    - Followspot Sheets
    - ML Sheets
    - Light Plot
    - Lighting Section
    - Set Plans
    - Shop Order
    - Electrical Drawings

**KB SCRIPT:**
- STANDARD TABS:
    - Magic
    - Act I
    - Act II
    - Schedule / Contact
    - Notes

- ALSO INCLUDE:
    - Instrument Schedule (Stapled, not punched)
    - Plastic Sheet Protectors
    - Cheat Sheet (LD)
    - LW Cheat Sheet Printout
    - 12" Ruler / Straightedge
    - White Legal Pad
    - Pencils, #2, Non-Mechanical

**OFFICE SUPPLIES:**
- White Legal Pads (perforated)
- Pencils, #2, Non-Mechanical
- Pencils, #2, Mechanical
- 0.7 Lead Refills
- Pencils, Red
- Pens
- Erasers
- Scale Rule
- 3 Hole Punch
- Post-Its
- Sharpies
- Yellow Highlighters
- Grease Pencil
- Scotch Tape
- Whiteout
- Chalk
- Scissors

**PRODUCTION TABLES:**
- Littlites (If Needed)
- Pencil Sharpener (Battery Operated)
- Power Strip (If Needed)
- Black Contact Paper (If Needed)
- Template Catalogues
- Gel Books
- Profiles List
- TV Color Correction Chart
- Focus Tapes

**COMPUTER:**

- KBA Mac Mini
- Spare USB Flash Drives
- Spare 3.5" Disks (If Needed)

**Figure 2.17** KB Associates' assistant's packing list.

Bring your kit to the theatre the first day you arrive for load-in. Most kits are unwieldy; it would be impractical to carry them back and forth from home every day. Instead, store your kit in the theatre and use a separate bag to carry your laptop and other valuables.

The best place to store your kit is in the row behind the assistants at the tech table or in the seats next to it. (See Figure 2.18.) Both options are easily accessible. When storing it in the row behind, store it across the arms of the chairs and not on the seat cushion. Storing it on the seat's arms allows the seat cushion to stay folded upright and out of the row. This avoids the common (and painful) problem of passersby blindly bashing their knees on the folded-down seat when rushing by in the dark. Similarly, do not store your kit on the floor. This row has frequent traffic—often from the director—and should be kept clear of trip-hazards and obstacles.

Keep frequently used items, like Kleenex, staplers, and pencils, set up like an office on the tech table but keep everything else stored in your kit for use on an as-needed basis. As you begin to use your kit more frequently, you will learn which items can be cut down in quantity (to reduce the physical weight of the kit) and which items need to be kept well-stocked (which may vary by designer).

*The strangest thing I've been asked for that I didn't have in my kit was "an 11×17 envelope, stamps, the New York Times, and Splenda—[all] from the same designer within five minutes."*

*—Justin A. Partier*

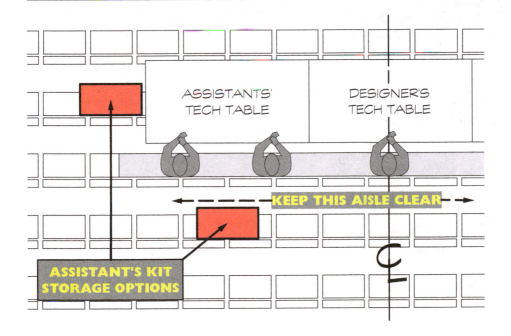

**Figure 2.18** Assistant's kit storage locations.

A few tips on assistant's kits:

- Always store your kit in a dry place. If your kit gets wet, it may ruin all of the paper goods inside. Keep large garbage bags in your kit (that wrap around it completely) for when you get caught walking in the rain.

- Before beginning each new show, check the expiration dates on all of the perishables such as over-the-counter medications and snacks. Change them out as needed.

- Write your initials permanently on EVERYTHING! This means anything from your stapler to your gel books to your computer power supplies. Not only does this help distinguish your items from others', but it also prevents them from being misplaced when the tech table is moved during previews. Sharpies and paint-pens are great for this purpose.

## A SPECIAL NOTE ON PENCILS

**Figure 2.19**  Pencil types.

Many lighting designers (and associate/assistants) are very particular about their pencil choices—probably because of their frequent use. Small frustrations such as pencil leads that break too often can add to the stress of an already stressful day.

The choice depends upon the individual. Some designers prefer standard #2 yellow pencils while others prefer mechanical pencils—in lead weights ranging anywhere from 0.5 to 0.9. Depending on writing habits, the smaller weights may break too easily while the thicker weights may be too smudgy. Most designers can tell you the exact brand and style that they prefer. If your designer gives you these details, write it down or take a picture of the pencil when they are not looking. Purchase several extra for your kit for when they are misplaced.

Also consider purchasing a set of low-cost pencils that can be easily given away when individuals outside of the lighting team ask to "borrow" a pencil from the tech table.

## FOCUS TAPES

**Focus Tapes** are two intersecting strips of fabric marked in 1'-0" increments used during focus to create a grid system onstage for documentation purposes only. One tape is laid on centerline running US–DS, and the other at the plaster or smoke pocket line running SL–SR. The point at which they cross is called 0,0 (pronounced "zero-zero," also written 0'-0"). The grid coordinates are then used to identify the location where the lighting designer stands to focus each light, which are recorded into the focus charts. (More on 0,0 in Part Two and focus charts in Part Three.)

### Fabricating Focus Tapes

Focus tapes are created by the assistant by marking 1'-0" increments on two long pieces of three- to four-inch wide natural-colored jute webbing or white seat belt webbing. These durable materials will not tear easily or stretch over time. Buy lengths long enough to cover the venues you typically work in—at least 30 to 40-feet long is recommended. Create one tape for US–DS and one for SL–SR.

**Figure 2.20** Focus tapes placed on stage.

Some assistants create multiple focus tapes of varying sizes to account for larger and smaller venues.

Making the tapes is fairly simple. Begin with your SL–SR tape. Fold one of the pieces of fabric in half to find the center. Unfold the fabric, and using a black Sharpie or other permanent marker, make a large tick mark and write the number "0" largely and clearly in the center of the fabric. (The numbers need to be large enough to be easily read from several feet away.) After you have located the "0" (centerline mark), lay a tape measure next to the material so that you can mark the SL and SR sides of the fabric. Working out from center, continue marking 1'-0" increments with tick marks and large, clear numbers across the material. Moving SL from center your marks should say "1L," "2L," "3L," "4L," and so forth. Working SR from center your marks should say "1R," "2R," "3R," "4R," and so on. (You can also choose to put tick marks every 1'-0", but only label every other mark.) The text should be oriented so that when standing upstage of the focus tape placed at the plaster line, they can be read right-side up. (See Figure 2.22.) Mark the entire length of the focus tape on each side except for the last six to eight inches at each end of the fabric. In this area write "SL–SR" and your initials on both ends of the tape. This allows you not only to keep ownership of your tapes, but also to easily differentiate the SL–SR tape from the US–DS tape without having to unroll them.

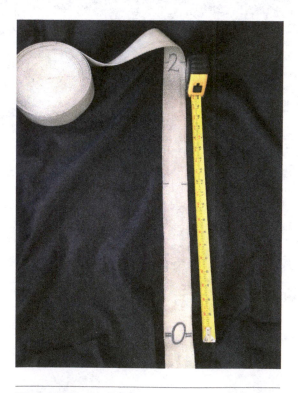

**Figure 2.21**  Creating focus tapes.

You may not have the luxury of having a large space to work in while creating your focus tapes. Don't fret! They can be created in your living room or even your studio apartment—a few feet at a time.

Making the US–DS tape is similar, but slightly different. The "0" for the US–DS tape—when laid onstage—is placed either at the plaster line or smoke pocket line depending on which the set designer used. Therefore, instead of starting at the center of the tape, like you did when marking the SL–SR tape, you will start at one end while accounting for apron space. Because apron areas fall downstage of the plaster line, the numbers are written as negative numbers. Similarly to the SL–SR tape, begin by labeling the very end of the tape with "US–DS" and your initials. Leave a few inches of space and then begin with the negative numbers.

Eight to ten feet of apron space is a good amount. This may not cover the apron spaces of all theatres, but it will be sufficient for many. (You can always use a tape measure added onto your focus tapes in theatres with extreme apron spaces.) Again lay out a tape measure next to the material and mark your increments with "–10," "–9," "–8," "–7" all the way until you get to "0"—orienting the numbers so they can be read while standing upstage looking downstage. After "0," begin your positive numbers—"1," "2," "3," "4" and so forth. (It is not necessary

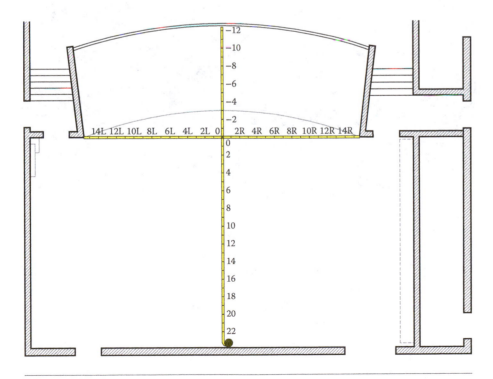

**Figure 2.22** Focus tape numbering layout.

to use a positive or plus sign for the numbers US of the "0" because positive numbers are considered the default.) At the very end of the tape you should again label it with "US–DS" and your initials.

Roll up your tapes to store them. It is easiest to start rolling your US–DS focus tape from the US side. (In some theatres you may not need to completely unroll the upstage side. If the stage is smaller than your tape spans, you can conveniently leave the end rolled while it lays onstage.) As for the SL–SR focus tape, begin rolling from either end—it does not matter which one. Once they are rolled up, secure your focus tapes with a piece of gaff tape, large rubber band, or a piece of tieline so that they do not unroll when stored in your assistant's kit. (See Figure 2.23.)

**Figure 2.23**  Focus tapes rolled up for storage.

The tools listed in this chapter are indispensible to the assistant lighting designer while navigating the needs of a complicated tech process. With the right tools, you can prepare for unexpected situations that may blindside you; the more prepared you are, the more likely you are to be hired back on the next show.

C H A P T E R   3

# Production Personnel

## THE LIGHTING TEAM

Lighting design is a team sport, and many individuals are needed to make a beautiful show come together. Other than the assistants, who else is a part of the team?

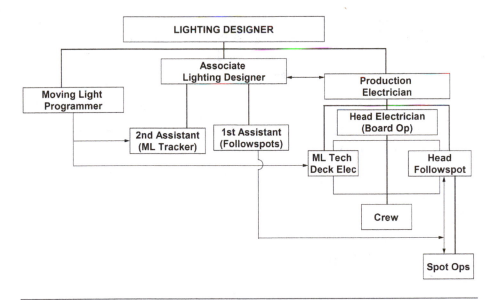

**Figure 3.1** Lighting team flow chart on a Broadway production.
*Created by: Vivien Leone*

## THE LIGHTING DESIGNER

The **Lighting Designer** is the artistic eye that creates the overall look and feel of the lighting for a production.

Designers' relationships with their assistants vary greatly. Associates may be treated by their designers as anything from a trusted partner and loyal companion to merely a worker bee and nothing more. Most designers fall somewhere in the middle of these two extremes.

> *"I expect my assistants to take care of me—and NOT the other way around."*
>
> —*Donald Holder*

> *"I tend to stick to a main associate. We have developed a language; they know how I work, how I organize, and can thus catch mistakes before they become too big."*
>
> —*F. Mitchell Dana*

### Know Thy Designer

Research your designer as soon as you get hired. Begin by talking with his main associates and other assistants. Ask about his preferences, how he likes to work, and his design aesthetic. After that, create a list of unanswered questions to ask the designer directly. Get to know as much as you can before stepping into the first day of tech.

> *"I try and find out all designer preferences ahead of time. Pencils, erasers, markers, flags, etc."*
>
> —*Vivien Leone*

> *"It is the assistant's duty to go to a designer and ask what they need or want.... Know that you have to gather the information."*
>
> —*Philip S. Rosenberg*[1]

Research the designer's style and body of work through articles and photos. What sort of shows does he work on frequently? What color choices does he enjoy? Is his work consistently shadowy and stark or colorful and flashy? The designer's style will vary by show, but pinpointing a career-throughline may help you anticipate designer-appropriate choices later. Useful resources include playbill.com, ibdb.com, newspaper reviews such as *The New York Times*, and articles in trade magazine such as *LiveDesign, Lighting & Sound International,* and *Lighting & Sound America.*

> *"Ask as many questions about how the designer works and their expectations as soon as you as hired."*
>
> —*Justin A. Partier*

## Designer Profile Sheet

Keep a running **Designer Profile Sheet** on each designer you assist—a repository for preferences, items to remember, and pet peeves. (See Figure 3.2 for a basic example.) Review it before each new production as a refresher.

Update the profile sheet regularly. Did her favorite tech table snack switch from gummy bears to almonds? Does she have a new favorite pencil? Did she have another baby since you last worked with her? Keep the designer profile sheet confidential. Do not share this personal information with others.

The following are some suggestions to include on a designer profile sheet:

- **Designer Information:** Designer's name and birthday. How does she like her name billed? For example, does she prefer to use a middle initial? Home and office address—including relevant special instructions such as to which address to send packages or "leave packages on porch."

- **Relations:** Spouse's, partner's, children's, and pets' names—including birthdays and anniversaries. Put birthdays, including the designer's, into your personal calendar as important reminders.

- **USA designer #**, if applicable.

- **Major shows:** Note major shows, awards, and nominations as well as shows you have worked on together (indicated by text in blue in Figure 3.2).

- **Tech Table Needs:** What *must* be present at the tech table for your designer's comfort? Certain pencils? Post-its? Snacks? Hand sanitizer? The daily crossword? When the designer is not watching, snap a quick photo of his tech table set-up to include. (See Figure 3.3.)

- **Favorite Foods and Drinks:** Coffee orders, favorite foods, and tech table snacks. Also add information on allergies and diet-restrictions.

Designer Profile: **DESIGNER'S NAME**

Designer's Bday: **October 12**
Phone & Email:    #917-123-4567 (cell);  myfavoritedesigner@email.com
Home Address:     1234 Cypress Drive, Newport, CT 100XX  (leave packages on back porch)
Office Address:   5678 42nd Street, #9B, New York, NY 100XX

Major Shows:      Show Name A (Tony Award)
                  Show Name B (Drama Desk Award, Tony Nom.)
                  Show Name C
                  Show Name D

Relations:        Wife – Susan (bday Nov 3)
                  Son – Johnny (bday June 6, 2005)
                  Dog -- Pepper

Tech Table Needs:
- 0.7 pencils
- Mini Post-its
- Nuts – almonds (salted)
- Clicky Eraser
- Daily Crossword

Favorite Drinks/Foods:
- Tea w/one sugar and milk
- Loves Thai food and chicken noodle soup

Focus Needs:
- ClickBook of show
- Magic Sheet in sheet protector

Cueing Preferences:
- Label cues "top of scene," "mark," and "block cue"
- All cue notes MUST have dates on them!

Other Notes:
- Channels from SL to SR
- Focus with drafting dots at all areas: mark letters with Sharpie
- Likes personal reminders
- Uses small note pad for previews
- Don't be too helpful, esp when giving cue placements to SM

Remember to:
- Make worklight sub in case stage gets too dark
- Request that electrician buy extra color that is in the scrollers
- Create inhibitive sub for all conventionals; also one for all movers

Important Tips to Remember:
- Followspots – likes the color temperature of the Juliat Korrigan
- Don't forget scrollers on all Autoyokes and haze/smoke on every shop order!

**Figure 3.2**  Designer profile sheet.

**Figure 3.3** Photo of designer's tech table set-up.

- **Focus Needs:** What does he like to have in his hands during focus? Magic Sheet? Instrument Schedule? Does he want the documents stapled, laminated, or in sheet protectors? Which way does he prefer to flip the packet of information? Over the top? Right-to-left like a book? Does he like the focus areas taped out on stage?

- **Cueing Preferences:** Does he have specific patterns that he uses to cue? For example, does he prefer skipping cue numbers within the sequence to leave room for added cues? Or does he always start the second act with a round number? When timing complicated sequences, does he prefer to make part cues (e.g. Q3 part 2, 4, and 6), point cues (e.g. Q3.1, 3.2, and 3.3), or use discreet timing (individual times for individual channels)? If parts, is there a specific pattern, such as moving lights moving in one part, color changers in another, and conventionals in another? Which cues need to be labeled right away? Does he prefer to pre-cue—either virtually or in the theatre? Who takes the cue notes—the designer or assistant? Should the cue notes be dated? Does he generally prefer odd numbered cue timing or even (e.g. time 3, 5, 7 or 2, 4, 6)? Does he have a preferred default cue time (e.g. time 3, 1, 5, 4.9)?

- **Remember to:** Record specific items you dealt with on previous shows with the designer. This list keeps you from making the same mistakes you did before. Some examples are: remember to track color changes in the cuelist; order a hazer for every show; ask to keep chain motors on truss until after one full day of tech; create preset cue 0.5; request extra favorite colors in shop order; add top hats to all FOH units; create an inhibitive sub for all conventionals and movers separately; set default time to 4.9. In this category, record all the designer's idiosyncrasies and pet peeves that you come across—it can save you headaches later.

- **Miscellaneous Preferences:** This is a good catch-all category to store useful information for future shows and keeps you from asking the designer's preferences over and over again. Does he have: Special drawing requirements for drafting? Certain office supplies he can't live without? What channeling patterns does he prefer—SL to SR or SR to SL? Favorite gobos? Favorite colors? Favorite followspots? Are followspots used only in musical numbers or throughout the entire show? Are there times that he doesn't like to be bothered? Does he like getting personal reminders—like upcoming birthdays and anniversaries? Does he prefer to focus or have the associate do it? Specific instructions for magic sheets? Which style of magic sheet does he like best? Does he like to invite people to the gypsy run? Does he want to be cc'd on all emails? Special order for show binder tabs? Is there a specific blend of color correction for a certain followspot that he loves? Review this information before prepping your next show with the designer and incorporate any applicable information.

The designer profile sheet is most successful when recorded privately. No designer wants to know that you are recording information about her throughout the process. It may make her feel uncomfortable and insecure. And, let's face it—it can seem a bit creepy. However, this method is a great magic trick that will make you seem like a rock-star assistant who just happens to remember everything.

### *Design Office Structure*

Some designers run their design business out of an office rather than working from home. They may rent office space and have other employees, assistants, or consultants work there as well.

Get to know how your designer's office works. Is there a main associate that the other assistants answer to, or is it a collective of associate/assistants all working on various shows? Are there any full-time employees, such as an office manager and/or business manager? Are there any other branches or divisions of the office, such as architectural lighting, television lighting, etc.?

Most designers will allow you to work in their design office while prepping their show. This allows you to work closely with the designer and his other associates to get questions answered quickly. You may also be given access to print materials at the office, which saves you personal ink and paper costs.

Work with the associates in the design office to learn the standards in place. What is the preferred organization for show paperwork? How are shows archived? Where are the office supplies kept? How about an electronic starter folder and template files used for beginning a new show? Line weight system? Standard fonts used? Get to know as much detail as you can. The more you become embedded in your designer's world, the more likely you are to become a part of his regular team.

## THE PROGRAMMER

The **Programmer**, also referred to as the "**Moving Light Programmer**," is a designer-technician hybrid who works alongside the lighting designer and programs the lighting console in order to actualize the design. More than simply a "board op," the programmer is a good designer in her own right and furthermore is fully versed in the ins-and-outs of her console of choice.

Programming is a very specialized field. The amalgam of talents needed is unique; it takes the right training, skill, personality, and know-how to succeed. Most designers establish long-standing relationships with their programmers based on mutual understanding and a shared language of design.

---

A good programmer does a lot of work ahead of time in order to anticipate the designer's needs. For example, the scroller color list can give a good indication of the color palette that the designer intends to use for the show. The programmer can use this information as a jumping off point to start building moving light color palettes that may work within the show's context.

---

The programmer translates the designer's vision into the console to create the looks and effects desired. How the designer communicates with the programmer varies by individual. Some designers may communicate their intentions very specifically: "take fixtures 43 and 44, focus them DL, put in the gobo 'lashes,' fuzz them out, and make them red—R27." In contrast, other designers may allow the programmer to have more creative freedom: "I need some deep red texture DL." A good programmer must be flexible and have the ability to work with many different personalities.

During the design prep phase, the assistant communicates with the programmer regarding equipment preferences. What type of console does she prefer? Are there certain fixtures she recommends using? Any specific custom gobos or colors she wants to add to the fixtures? Special items needed for her tech table? What orientation does she want the fixtures hung? During this time, the designer, assistant, and programmer may also visit the manufacturer's showroom to try out any new equipment they are considering for the production.

> Moving lights, or automated fixtures, are also referred to as "movers."

During the tech process the assistant interfaces frequently with the programmer—providing the moving light magic sheets, communicating daily ML (moving light) notes from the designer, and finally, before the production opens, archiving the moving light tracking information and focus charts. (These documents are discussed further in Part Three.)

> A union programmer's day rate is typically based on a 10-hour day with overtime after that. The programmer's contract usually ends on opening night just like the contracts of the designer and the assistants.

The programmer works under very stressful situations and needs to work quickly. Do not interrupt her when she is working on a sequence or it may bring the tech process to a screeching halt.

> Some theatrical shows may utilize two programmers—a "moving light programmer" and a "conventional programmer." In these cases, all moving lights and other multi-parameter fixtures, such as LEDs, are programmed by the moving light programmer and, on a separate console, conventionals are programmed by the conventional programmer—who is often the production electrician or head electrician. In recent years (and especially in the U.K.), as moving light consoles have become increasingly fast to program and shows are using fewer conventional fixtures, on many shows these programmers have merged into one.
>
> On the contrary, extremely large and complex mega-events, such as large concerts and awards shows, have continued to employ multiple programmers simply to divide up the workload—especially if video falls under the jurisdiction of the lighting team. Each programmer works on a separate console and programs his specific sector—e.g. video, FOH movers, overstage movers, conventional fixtures, etc.

During tech, keep a watchful eye on the command line—the area on the console's monitor that displays what the programmer is typing. When the assistant is watching the command line, the designer can keep his eyes on the stage without distraction. If there are any discrepancies between the designer's requests and the programmer's entries, politely speak up. Having two sets of eyes on the command line helps to reduce human error.

> *"During cue making sessions, … watch the screen carefully to confirm that [the programmer] is typing what the designer is asking for. The designer's eyes will be on the stage; he will not necessarily know if the [programmer] is making mistakes."*
>
> —*Craig Miller*[2]

## THE PRODUCTION ELECTRICIAN

The **Production Electrician** is the leader and supervisor of the electrics crew and conducts the physical implementation of the lighting design. The production electrician is considered an equal to the lighting designer, and, by extension, the assistant's partner.

> The production electrician is often called the "master electrician" in regional and academic settings.

During the design prep phase, the assistant should consult with the production electrician on any technical questions that may arise; share a Dropbox folder with him so you can both access the design paperwork. After your prep work is finished, the electrician will prep the technical end of the paperwork, including completing the shop order—adding items to it such as cable lengths, power supplies, lifts, truss, and spare equipment in order to create a complete and working system.

> A good production electrician will order additional colors and gobos that he knows are the designer's favorites—even if they are not specified in the original paperwork. This allows for flexibility when the designer needs to make an immediate change during tech.
>
> One trick he may use is to order extra sheets of gel from the colors used in the show's color scrolls—which may indicate some of the designer's preferred colors. Unused sheets can be stored in his roadbox in preparation for the next time he works with the designer.

During tech and previews the production electrician will work closely with the assistant to achieve completion of the work and focus notes that arise each day. If the show is considered to have "legs," he will also work out a viable maintenance schedule for long-term upkeep.

> **Having "legs":** A production said to have "legs" is presumed to be long-running or is successful enough to move to a progressively higher-profile situation—for example: from regional to Broadway. It can also mean a successful production that will tour and mount in other cities and/or countries.

The production electrician typically stays with the show full time throughout tech and previews, but leaves the show in the capable hands of the head elec after opening. On most Broadway shows, the production electrician continues to receive a weekly fee after opening and throughout the run of the show to help oversee the maintenance of the lighting design. The production electrician may supervise the work on several overlapping shows at once.

## THE HEAD ELECTRICIAN

The **Head Electrician**, or **"Head Elec,"** begins the production process by assisting the production electrician. After opening night, the head electrician stays with the show and becomes the lead point-person for the electrics crew.

During the run of the show she will perform a series of pre-show checks to make sure everything is working properly and runs the console during the performances. She will also take care of problems that need fixing—such as moving light malfunctions, burned out lamps and gel, or conventional fixtures out of focus. In addition, she is in charge of weekly or bi-weekly maintenance calls, which allow extra time in the schedule for large maintenance issues to be fixed, such as swapping out a particularly hard-to-reach moving light. On Broadway, maintenance calls typically take place an hour or two before a regular show-call.

> In the U.S., the standard show-call (meaning the time the technicians show up to work the show) is an hour before "half-hour." "Half-hour" is 30 minutes before the show begins, or "downbeat" for a musical. Therefore, if the show begins at 8pm, the technicians show up for their call at 6:30pm. This gives them roughly an hour to perform all pre-show checks and fix any issues before the house opens and audiences enter. (Because this time is so condensed, the assistant's paperwork must be extremely clear so that the information is available immediately when problems occur.) If these problems are too complex to deal with in this short amount of time and are not crucial to the performance, they will be fixed during a maintenance call.

## FOLLOWSPOT OPERATORS

The **Followspot Operators**, or "**Spot Ops**," are electricians that run the followspots for the production. Typically on a large-scale musical there are two to three spot ops—although sometimes the production may require more or fewer. The designer negotiates the number of operators in the course of contract negotiations.

---

**"Followspot"** is the term used in the professional world for what laymen call a "spotlight."

**"Calling"** means telling each spot operator which move they need to do next, such as pick up a character, change color, etc. (More on followspot in Part Three.)

---

During the tech process, an assistant lighting designer designs and calls the followspot cues. After opening, when the design team is no longer present, one spot op—designated the "lead spot," "contract spot," or "head spot"—will take over calling the show while also running his own spot.

*"On Broadway, the followspot operators take their own cues. In most other situations (opera, ballet, regional theatre), followspot cues are called by the stage manager."*

*—Craig Miller[3]*

The lead spot will also call the show to any replacement operators. Ideally if a replacement is needed, the new person will train for two or three nights—sitting next to the operator that he will be replacing. However, emergencies do happen, and an op may be running followspot for a show that he may also be seeing for the first time. It is the lead spot's responsibility to help him through the process.

If the show is a tour, the lead spot also calls the show to the new operators in each city (who have not seen the show before), while simultaneously operating one spot himself. The assistant should plan the tour so that the lead spot performs all critical and/or difficult pick-ups himself so it is not handled by a new operator in each city who is unfamiliar with the show.

## DECK ELECTRICIAN

The **Deck Electrician**, or "**Deck Elec**," works backstage during the show attending to lighting-related needs during the performances. She may plug in practicals, move rovers into place, or page cable as needed. On some productions, the deck elec may be the same person as the ML tech.

**Practical** = Any lighting fixture on stage that is not inherently theatrical equipment, such as a table lamp or chandelier, or one that is built, such as a marquis lighting effect.

**Rover** = A small, vertical, wheeled lighting position, like a short boom or dance tower, that is rolled into place during the show or out of the way of moving scenery coming offstage.

**Paging Cable** = Moving cable by hand. This includes coiling and uncoiling a length of cable as a piece of scenery is pushed on or off stage.

### MOVING LIGHT TECHNICIAN

The "**Moving Light Tech**," or "**ML Tech**," is tasked with the maintenance and upkeep of the moving lights. Typically a "**ML Hospital**" is sectioned off backstage or in the trap room where broken moving lights, tools, and spare parts are stored. The ML tech works in the hospital during shows testing and fixing the fixtures so that there are always working spare fixtures available and ready to go into the air at a moment's notice.

### HOUSE ELECTRICIAN

Called the "**House Head**," "**House Elec**," or "**House Guy**" (often even when female), the **House Electrician** is the one person who knows the most about the theatre building itself and its electrical capabilities. The production electrician interfaces with the house elec for any questions regarding power needs, house equipment (if any), and location of electrical equipment.

## THE MANAGEMENT TEAM

### PRODUCTION STAGE MANAGER

The **Production Stage Manager**, or "**PSM**," is the lead stage manager on the show. She works closely with the director, design team, and actors to organize schedules, run rehearsals, tech, and performances.

The production stage manager is often called the "stage manager" in academic and regional settings.

During tech and previews, the assistant lighting designer works closely with the PSM to answer questions she may have regarding the designer's cue placements and calling of the show. At the end of each rehearsal, the assistant communicates to the PSM any "SM" (stage manager) notes from the designer.

After opening on long-running professional shows, like Broadway, the PSM monitors the show for consistency. She will train the stage manager (her assistant or ASM) to call the cues for performances so that she can watch the show from the house and give the cast notes if needed. Her intention is to help preserve the director's integrity, initial purpose, and look of the show. She may note incorrect blocking, lines that were dropped or changed, moments that are not working, or help an understudy through a new part.

In some circumstances, part of the PSM's duties may involve working on behalf of the lighting designer. For example, when working on a touring production, the PSM may focus the show in each city; in regional theatre, opera, and dance, the PSM often calls the followspots; and, when working on very low-budget productions, such as Off-Broadway, storefront, or fringe situations, the PSM may run the lighting console for the performances (as well as the sound board, video, and everything else).

## PRODUCTION MANAGER

The **Production Manager**, who may also be known as the **Technical Supervisor**, manages and coordinates the production budget and the overall implementation of the physical production—scenic, lighting, sound, costume, projections, special effects, etc. He oversees the production electrician, technical director, and other department heads as well as organizes the load-in and daily work call schedule.

In some cases, the production manager and the technical supervisor may be two different people. In these cases, the production manager focuses more on budgets and management issues while the technical supervisor deals with production personnel and daily work calls.

Please note that the title of production manager varies wildly depending on the situation. It may be someone like a technical director or a stage manager; sometimes someone managerial who runs budgets; or even, in a road house situation, someone more like a house technician.

## GENERAL MANAGER

The **General Manager** has many duties, but the most pertinent one to know as an assistant lighting designer is contract negotiation. Sometimes the designer will negotiate for the assistant, and sometimes the assistant negotiates directly. After negotiation is complete, the assistant will communicate with general management personnel to coordinate the signing of the contract and other federal payment paperwork, such as W-4s and I-9s.

## COMPANY MANAGER

The company manager deals with billing, company ticket requests, payment of royalties, and the payroll. When working on an out-of-town production or with non-local personnel, the company manager also books travel and housing and arranges weekly per diem. (More on this in Part Four.) In addition, for the out-of-towners and for each tour location, she will create a "welcome packet" containing useful information, such as the location of nearby restaurants, houses of worship, emergency rooms/hospitals, banks, tourist attractions, and more.

## PRODUCERS

The **Producers** are known as "the ones with the money," which is a bit of a misnomer. They are actually the ones who *bring* the money by finding investors to contribute funds to the production—although some may also contribute their own funds.

After acquiring funding, the producers will obtain the rights to the piece and begin to put together the creative team—beginning with the director. They also define the parameters of the production—when and where the production process will begin (e.g. regional, Off-Broadway, etc.).

As the ones holding the purse strings, producers often assume to have decision-making power and may choose to exercise it at any time during a production process. Tensions may elevate when they enter the theatre—especially for the director. As the assistant, always keep an eye out for the producers and inform the designer when they are present.

C H A P T E R    4

# Unions

Depending on where you are assisting, unions can be a very present part of your daily life or not applicable at all. For example, all individuals working on a Broadway production (see Figure 4.2) and within most LORT theatres must be union members, but a typical storefront theatre may not require any union status.

When working in a union house, familiarize yourself with all the unions with which you may come in contact. Pay special attention to things such as daily schedule and break times. If there is ever a question, one person to consult is the PSM. (During tech, part of her job is to work out a daily break schedule based on the union guidelines.)

## UNITED SCENIC ARTISTS, LOCAL 829 (USA)

Union lighting designers and assistants (as well as other theatrical designers) throughout the United States are represented by United Scenic Artists, Local 829 (USA). Local 829 has national jurisdiction and applies to all USA designers no matter where they live; in effect a "national local"—unlike stagehands who have different local numbers for each geographical region.

USA 829 represents many crafts in both live performance and motion pictures. However, the jurisdiction for lighting design is limited to live performance—lighting design for television and film is not covered.

Some USA Agreement terms that affect an assistant lighting designer closely are:

- **Minimum wages/fees are regulated.** If you are a new union assistant starting out, you will probably be offered "union minimum" on your first show—typically as a flat weekly wage. (Flat = You get paid the same on a week you work 40 hours as you do on a week you work 80 hours.) As you become more integrated in the business and/or work with the same producer multiple times you may be able to negotiate a higher rate beyond union minimum.

- **Standard workweeks are regulated.** On Broadway a standard workweek is a six-day week. If you are asked to work seven days in a row (with prior written approval from management) then you must be paid "7th day pay." This only applies if you are called into work at the theatre. If you spend your day off catching up on paperwork, you do not get paid extra for it.

### Collective Bargaining Agreements (CBA)

The union negotiates **Collective Bargaining Agreements** (a contract) with each applicable producing entity or employer group. These Agreements set the minimum terms and conditions of employment, protect those working under the agreement, and have many advantages, including:

- Minimum wage/fee structure
- 7th day additional pay
- Meal penalties
- Day rates
- Employer contributions for health, pension, and sometimes annuity benefits
- Safe and sanitary workplace support
- Protection against non-payment
- Per diem, travel, and hotel expense regulation

The USA national office is located at:

**United Scenic Artists, Local 829**

29 West 38th Street, 15th Floor

New York, NY 10018

Phone: 212-581-0300

www.usa829.org

**Figure 4.1** USA "bug," or logo.
*Courtesy of: United Scenic Artists, Local 829*

- **Meal breaks are regulated.** The Agreement stipulates that you are required to have regular meal breaks throughout a standard workday, no later than by the 5th hour. If, on a rare occasion, the production requires you (with prior approval by the producer) to work over your meal break, then you must be compensated for the missed meal. Another option is that a meal may be provided in lieu of compensation.

- **Day rate minimums are regulated.** When an assistant is hired on a single-day basis or for a partial week, a day rate is negotiated based on the weekly rate divided by the six-day workweek. Those minimums are stipulated in the Agreement as well.

- **Access to health insurance and retirement benefits is provided.** All USA agreements provide for employer contributions to health, pension, and sometimes annuity benefits (sometimes referred to as P&W—Pension and Welfare). Health insurance coverage for individuals who qualify quarterly is provided through the IATSE National Health and Welfare Fund. The Broadway Agreement also requires each company to make contributions (based on a percentage of your gross pay) into the USA 829 Pension Fund and the IATSE National Annuity Fund.

- **Protection against dangerous and unhealthy situations** to support a safe working environment. If you are ever working in a situation that makes you uncomfortable—i.e. asbestos exposure or suspect rigging practices, you can call your union representative to discuss the issue. The representative may visit the theatre to further investigate and work with the producers and/or theatre managers to find a solution.

- **Non-payment protection**. Production companies can be volatile. Shows can close the same night they open, and some even before that. If you are not paid according to contract, the union (through the grievance procedures of the Agreement) will work to assure that you get paid. The union can also file a grievance should you be fired without "just cause" or paid below the contractual minimum. For repeated offenders, USA publishes a list of cautionary employers in its monthly newsletter.

- **Per diem minimums are regulated**. Per diem is additional money paid on top of your weekly wage to cover living expenses while working away from your home city. Although the federal government regulates per diem by city, the union also negotiates a standard rate.

You, your designer, or your designer's agent may conduct the negotiations of contractual terms for the production. (However, no agreement made by the designer limits your contractual right to negotiate for over-scale, as allowed in the CBA.) After an agreement has been reached, you will sign an individual agreement called a "coversheet" that is a required part of the CBA and includes the agreed-upon terms, such as pay scale and number of weeks paid.

Some producers also include a rider, or addendum, attached to the union coversheet. Double-check the rider to ensure nothing contradicts the terms contained within the union's CBA. The CBA always takes precedence regardless of any discrepancies.

USA contracts definitively cover you when working in the United States; when working overseas, it can be a little tricky. If the producers want to use their own contract for overseas employment, make sure that the contract still stipulates essentials like proper wages and per diem. Consult the union before signing anything.

## JURISDICTION

As an USA member, know your jurisdiction and limitations. American unions can be very specialized, depending on the venue. In the strictest situations, crews do not cross over to other disciplines: electrics crews do not move scenery, carpenters do not touch props, riggers do not touch sound, etc.

In a union theatre in the United States, the assistants and the rest of the lighting design team are allowed to touch items that relate to lighting design *only*: not actual lighting or stage equipment. Do not try to help the electricians by picking up a fixture, a gobo, or even a piece of gel. All equipment falls under the stagehand's jurisdiction: even though USA has become an affiliate of IATSE in recent years, the delineation between locals has remained the same.

However, the tech table is a gray area. Sometimes assistants need to rearrange the monitors and other equipment on the tech table to please the designer. Before moving anything the first time, request permission from your production electrician.

## JOINING THE UNION

There are two ways to become a member of United Scenic Artists, Local 829: by exam or by professional membership (commonly referred to as being "bought in"). Once you are inducted into the union, you will be given a union card, stamp, and designer number.

The **Union Exam** is the most common method of joining and is recommended by the union for young designers. Candidates recommended by an exam committee (read: who "pass the exam") are always invited to join. Although at one time the union exam was practical, now it is based largely on experience and portfolio examples. Very specific items are required for the application process. Refer to the union's website for more information: www.usa829.org. The union is discerning. Do not be discouraged if you are not accepted the first time. Add some more experience to your resume and apply again in future years.

Joining as a "professional member" is a process set in place for the lucky few that are hired on a union job before being a member. These potential members are still required to make an application to the union according to the security clause in the Agreement. The producer must verify that he has been hired, the designer must write a strong recommendation in his support, and his resume must be reviewed at a membership meeting. At the meeting, he must still be voted in as an individual rather than as part of the group passing the exam. Acceptance as a professional member is not considered "a given."

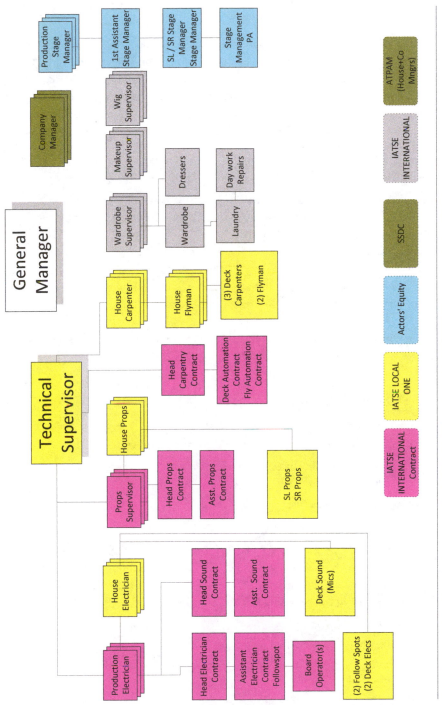

**Figure 4.2** Technical teams and their respective unions on a typical Broadway musical.
*Courtesy of: Kevin Barry*

# IATSE

As an assistant, you will work very closely with the IATSE stagehands when working in a union house. Also known as the "IA," "The Stagehand's Union," or, in New York, "Local One," IATSE is the "largest union representing workers in the entertainment industry. [Their] members work in all forms of live theater, motion picture and television production, trade shows and exhibitions, television broadcasting, and concerts as well as the equipment and construction shops that support all these areas of the entertainment industry."[1] For further information, visit: www.iatse-intl.org.

IATSE stands for "The International Alliance of Theatrical Stage Employees, Moving Picture Technicians, Artists, and Allied Crafts of the United States, Its Territories, and Canada, AFL-CIO, CLC."

IATSE is configured into many different "locals" around the United States and Canada, which have varying memberships and local numbers. A local union directory can be found at: www.iatse-intl.org/member-resources/local-union-directory. Broadway falls under Local One's jurisdiction—arguably one of the most powerful unions on Broadway. A strike from Local One can (and has) shut down Broadway for days on end.

**IATSE break schedule:**
- One-hour meal break required every 4 to 5 hours
- 15 minute breaks required after every 2 hours (also called "coffee")
- 15 minutes required before each meal break or end of night (called "wash-up")

Typical IATSE pay scales:
- After 10-hour day, time and a half
- An additional 4 hours after that, double-time (aka **"golden time"**)
- 8-hour "turn-around" required or next full day is golden time until an 8-hour turn-around occurs (**"Turn-around"** = time between leaving the theatre at night and returning the next morning.)
- Holidays are golden time

Other important things to know about IATSE:
- Minimum number of "heads" required for every call—typically head carp, electrics, and fly
- 4-hour minimum paid for calls shorter than 4 hours

- Different types of workers: "pink contract," "yellow card," etc.
- Meal penalties awarded
- Hotel housing available for short turn-arounds

There is very little wiggle-room in a union break schedule. When a break is called, union stagehands will immediately stop what they are doing and return 15 minutes later to start working again.

Meal breaks are taken every 4 to 5 hours. (Stipulated as 12pm or 1pm and 5pm or 6pm). On a typical day they are taken every four, but hours can be shuffled when needed such as during atypical working hours or "split-lunches."

Split-lunches (called "lunch" even during a dinner break) are when some of the crew take a meal break within the 4-hour block and others during the 5-hour block. Split-lunches allow for one crew to monopolize the stage for an hour without other crews getting in the way—ideal for an hour of dark time or specific scenic focuses that may stop others from working.

The assistant is *not* the person who decides, arranges, or announces these breaks. Typically, for the lighting crew, the production electrician will handle all scheduling issues. However, knowing the break schedule is helpful for your own planning purposes in order to gauge how many notes may be completed within the time allotted.

As an assistant, you should also be knowledgeable regarding staffing stipulations. For example, no matter how short the call is, the stagehands are paid for a 4-hour minimum. Be conscious of this. If you request stagehands for just one hour, you will cost the production money. If a short call is necessary, ask the designer to negotiate.

The same goes for "skeleton crew" calls—calls that need a limited number of crew. Even if you are only lighting, any call still requires the "heads" to be called in: typically the production electrician, the head electrician, the head carpenter, and the head flyman.

Be aware of any additional crew that may need to be added to your skeleton crew. For example, if you are working on cueing a sequence that requires moving an armoire onstage, that would additionally require the head propsman to be called. (The head carp only moves scenery, not props, according to union rules.) Think additional calls through carefully before requesting.

Union members work under different distinctions, or "cards." There are three main types: **Union Card**, **Yellow Card**, and **Pink Contract**. A union card member is an official card-carrying IATSE union member of the local within the production's jurisdiction.

Some stagehands may be what is called a "pink contract." A pink contract, sometimes referred to as a "pink," is a stagehand from another union or local working temporarily under the coverage of the production's local. They pay dues to this local often in hopes of someday being able to join. For example, a stagehand that belongs to ACT, or "Associated Crafts Technicians" (sometimes called the "touring union"), may choose to work a Broadway show under Local One in order to work towards membership.

"**Yellow Card**" members are an important distinction to be aware of when working as an assistant. Simply defined, yellow cards are stagehands working temporarily on the show to help facilitate load-in.

Typically, on a large-scale production, your core team consists of the production electrician, head electrician, followspot ops, deck elec, and moving light tech. However, during load-in, additional electricians will be hired solely to load-in and focus the show. This additional personnel costs the producers a lot more money but is necessary with the amount of work required to mount a large-scale production. Due to this additional cost, the producers are anxious to do what is referred to as "breaking the yellow card"—which means to send those additional stagehands home after hang and focus are complete. According to the IATSE rules, every light must be hung and *every* light must be focused—or at least "touched"—even if this means simply pointing spares onstage.

> **Spare**—a conventional fixture hung and circuited with no foreseen purpose. Intended for later use when a need is discovered.

Finally, be mindful of the pay structures for IATSE members. The IATSE member's regular hourly pay rate is based on a 10-hour day. After 10 hours within a day, they are paid time and a half for the next four hours until they move into "golden time" (which is double their standard hourly rate). After that they *must* have an "8-hour turn-around" before their next scheduled work hour. If that time is breached, they will go into golden time for the entirety of the next working period until an 8-hour turn-around is given. This can be extremely expensive for a large crew. As the assistant, use your crew time wisely and never, ever be the reason that the crew goes into golden time.

## ACTORS' EQUITY ASSOCIATION (AEA)

Another union with which to be familiar is the Actors' Equity Association, also called AEA or simply, Equity. Actors and stage managers belong to this union. The Equity schedule stipulations will dictate the majority of the rehearsal schedule during tech (except in opera, in which case the American Federation of Musicians' union dictates most of the rehearsal times).

**Equity break schedule:**

- Every 5 consecutive hours, there will be a 1½ hour break
- In addition: a 5-minute break after every 55 minutes of rehearsal
- Or a 10-minute break after 80 minutes

One important Equity (and AGMA) contractual term that affects lighting design concerns fog, haze, and other atmospheric substances. In 1997, Equity conducted tests regarding adverse health effects resulting from atmospheric substances used in theatrical productions. As a result, a list was developed of Equity-approved equipment with accompanying usage guidelines.

Based on the height at which your atmospheric is placed and its approximate distance from the actors, the Equity guidelines determine the amount of time allowed for the atmospheric to run while still being safe for the actors' health. This can mean running your atmospheric during specific moments only (such as a fog cue) or programming a long-running effect that turns the machine on and off at timed intervals (for a hazer). If your production uses more than one atmospheric at the same time, Equity may determine that they need to conduct production-specific testing. More information is available on the AEA website within the "Safe and Sanitary" document library at www.actorsequity.org.

The moving light tracking software, FocusTrack, has a useful function called FogTrack, which enables you to calculate the overall fog and haze levels used in a production in order to comply with AEA regulations. (More on FocusTrack in Chapter 2.)

"Equity is part of the Associated Actors and Artists of America (4As), which is a group of performing arts unions that organize under the umbrella of the American Federation of Labor and Congress of Industrial Organizations (AFL-CIO). The other unions that comprise the 4As are the Screen Actors Guild (SAG, representing actors working in film, television, and digital media), the American Federation of Television and Radio Artists (AFTRA, representing actors and announcers working in television, radio, and digital media), the American Guild of Musical Artists (AGMA, representing singers and dancers in opera, dance, and concert performances), and the American Guild of Variety Artists (AGVA, representing entertainers in such areas as variety shows and some job categories at theme parks)."[2]

# AMERICAN FEDERATION OF MUSICIANS (AFM)

In many union theatres, the musicians in the orchestra are affiliated with the American Federation of Musicians (AFM). Similar to IATSE and Equity, knowing the break schedule helps you to forecast the day's schedule during orchestra techs.

**AFM Break Schedule**:

- 5-minute rest period for each hour of rehearsal, except during dress rehearsals
- Standard rehearsal/performance duration is 3 hours
- If rehearsal continues after 3 hours, double-time will be charged in ½ hour increments
- Dinner shall be a 1½-hour break period
- Afternoon rehearsals shall end at 6:30pm and evening rehearsals or performances shall not start before 8pm

Costs associated with orchestra rehearsals and performances can be quite substantial. Due to these large costs, productions watch the clock very carefully when the orchestra is in the pit. Even surpassing the 3-hour limit *by one minute* will put the musicians in double-time. In fact, new musicals may be cut down in order to fit within the 3-hour time block or the orchestra may be asked to leave (and not play) during curtain call. Some shows cut it close enough that extra charges occur even if the house is held for longer than usual or a technical problem occurs that stops the action of the performance.

Because of the expensive nature of union orchestras, any time the musicians are present the rehearsal's focus moves away from the technical elements and towards the needs of the musicians. The lighting team must be careful not to waste time and stall the rehearsal when the orchestra is in the pit or extra charges may occur.

More information on AFM can be found at: www.afm.org.

## OTHER UNIONS TO KNOW

Depending on the theatre, many other unions may be a part of the process. For example, Broadway has a union for practically everyone—even the housekeeping staff.

The following are some other unions found in a Broadway theatre:

- Stage Directors & Choreographers Society (SDC)
- Make-Up Artists & Hair Stylist Union, Local 798, IATSE, AFL-CIO
  - Covers make-up artists and wig stylists
- Theatrical Wardrobe Attendants Union, Local 764
  - Covers wardrobe supervisors and dressers
- The Dramatists Guild Of America
  - Covers playwrights, composers, lyricists, and librettists
- Association of Theatrical Press Agents & Managers, Union No. 18032 (ATPAM)
  - Covers press agents, company managers, and house managers
- Treasurers & Ticket Sellers Union, Local 751
- Ushers, Ticket Takers, and Doormen's Union, Local 306
- Theatre, Amusement, and Cultural Building Service Employees, Local 54
  - Represents elevator operators, cleaners, etc.
- International Union of Operating Engineers, Local 30
  - Represents maintenance personnel—building heating systems, air circulation, fire pumps, and ventilation systems
- Service Employees International Union, Local 32BJ
  - Represents maintenance and cleaning personnel

PART 2

# The Process

Production schedules vary depending on the size and complexity of the show and its design. Large, complex shows may tech for a year or more while others may close even before they open. On average, the assistant lighting designer is contracted for 4 to 8 weeks—typically more weeks for a musical and less for a play.

A typical Broadway production schedule looks like this:
- **Design Prep**—1 to 4 weeks (prep weeks for lighting)
- **Shop Prep**—1 to 2 weeks
- **Pre-hang**—1 to 2 days
- **Load-in/Hang**—1 to 4 weeks
- **Focus/Moving Light Focus**—2 to 4 days
- **Tech**—1 to 2 weeks
- **Previews**—2 to 6 weeks
- **Open**—1 night—with red carpet entrance and opening night party
- **Run**—typically "open run"—no end date

Refer to the Appendices of this text for a complete step-by-step assistant's checklist of responsibilities throughout the production process.

## CHAPTER 5

# Design Prep

## PREP WEEKS

**"Prep Weeks"** are the first phase of the overall design process. During this time, the initial concept for the design and the creation of the initial paperwork are completed. The designer may have been meeting about the project for a long time, but during the prep weeks is when the design begins to be created and documented in a concrete manner. This period is not dictated by a daily schedule and may consist of design meetings, production meetings, lighting meetings, manufacturer demos, and mock-ups as well as paperwork creation.

**Design meeting:** Meetings held between the designers and director only, specifically to talk about the overall design of the show—sets, lights, costumes, sound, projections, etc.

**Production meeting:** Meetings that include the full production team—includes topics such as design coordination and scheduling.

**Lighting meeting:** Internal meetings between the lighting designer, his assistants, and, occasionally, the programmer. Alternatively, it can also be a meeting between the designer, the assistants, and the director to discuss the desired look of the lighting in each scene.

**Manufacturer's demo:** Demonstrations of manufacturer's new equipment being considered for use within a show. Custom items may also be demonstrated in the equipment, such as custom colors and gobos.

**Mock-up:** Roughly assembled full-size part of intended lit piece with integrated fixtures used for experimentation and verification of final product. In theatre, usually a piece of scenery built in full-dimension including a few integrated fixtures to assure the intended lighting look can be achieved as proposed before securing equipment.

Assistants are often paid by the week for prep, and the number of weeks is negotiated into the designer's and assistant's contracts. Two weeks is a typical amount of paid prep time for a Broadway show, particularly a play—although simpler plays may be given only one week. If the show is a large musical, four weeks may be more appropriate to negotiate due to the amount of research, mock-ups, and coordination that may be necessary. A remount or a tour may only be given a few days; regional theatres and others may not pay for prep weeks at all.

Large musicals typically include scenery designed with integral lighting—often called "**practical scenery**." Perhaps it is simply a small fixture mounted on the scenery to light an actor's face, a custom star curtain, LED strips imbedded in a false proscenium, or a set of marquis lights surrounding a featured piece of scenery. Work with the equipment reps and scenic shops to create mock-ups that assure the designer's desired effect can be achieved.

During the design prep process, be aware of all deadlines—usually provided by the production manager. What date is the design package due? When does the production electrician need to begin working with your paperwork? When should bids be finalized? Try to turn things in a day or two early if you can. Be aware that others, such as the production electrician, cannot start their work until you finish yours. (He usually needs two or three weeks too.) Turning your design package in early will not only demonstrate your impressive time-management skills, but will also help out the others who are waiting on you.

A good assistant turns things in on time, but a great assistant turns them in early.

## SITE SURVEY

Before any of the drawings and paperwork can be created, the assistant must gather information about the theatre building itself—even if the designer has previously worked in the venue in case of any permanent remodels or added structural items.

Begin by requesting the electronic architectural drawings of the theatre or pull the information from the scenic designer's drawings. If this information is only available in print, ask to borrow the blueprints, scan them electronically, and trace them in Vectorworks. Specialty reprographic shops and some large office supply chains have the ability to scan and/or print large-format drawings. Call several in your neighborhood ahead of time in case you need this service.

A **Site Survey** is a visit to the theatre ("site") to assure that critical measurements within the architectural drawings received are correct and up to date. Contact the house electrician to set up an appointment, or ask your production electrician to make the call. Print out the theatre plan and section in scale and import copies of the drawings onto your tablet device. Also, bring another assistant from your team—typically your designer will not attend. If you are the only assistant on the show, draft a friend or the production electrician to help—a second set of hands can be helpful.

The site survey will take place on the bare stage long before load-in and usually lasts only an hour or so. This time gives you a chance to verify measurements, take photos, and anticipate any issues that may arise about the space. Be prepared and use your time wisely. It is probably the only time that you will be allowed in the theatre before load-in begins (which is long after you need to finalize the light plot).

Try to think of all of the questions ahead of time that you may need answered and make yourself a list. Here are some examples: Are the box booms located correctly on the drawing? What is the high trim and low trim of the FOH truss? How high is the balcony rail from the stage floor? At how steep an angle is the followspot booth? How far US can the followspots see? And, conversely, can they hit the apron or any forestage being added for the show? What is the best place to locate the tech table? Are there any obstructions, such as an enclosure or centerline support, on the balcony rail that may require special consideration when hanging moving lights?

**Figure 5.1** The theatre, or "site".
*Photo By: Samuel Morgan Photography*

Once in the theatre, to assure the accuracy of the drawings, compare actual dimensions measured within the physical venue to the scaled measurements in the drawing. (A list of recommended dimensions to verify can be found in the Appendices of this text.) Note any discrepancies clearly on the printed drawings or virtually on your tablet—a great place to use Vectorworks' mobile app, Nomad.

Take photos of the overall space and existing structures that you are measuring to create a complete virtual image of the theatre. Also, use an app like 360 Panorama to take panoramic images of the space for further reference. You and your designer will refer back to these photos and images when questions arise during the design process.

If it seems clearer to indicate some of the measurements on the photos of the theatre, the apps Photo Measures or Photo Measures Lite are ideal. (See Figure 5.2.)

**Figure 5.2**  Photo Measures app screenshot with notes.

Bring a small kit of tools with you to the site survey. Helpful items include:

- Pencils and extra lead, erasers, sharpener, etc.
- Highlighters (multiple colors), Sharpies, pens, Wite-Out
- Red pencils
- Notepad
- Tablet device, such as an iPad

- Print-out of the groundplan and section in scale
- Architectural scale rule
- Tape measures (at least two) of long lengths—100'-0" is best
- Disto (laser distance measuring device)
- Camera and/or other device with photo capability
- Another person to help

Using a Disto (also called a laserline or laser measure)—which measures distances using a laser—instead of traditional tape measures will save you time and headaches. It allows you to quickly measure distances to items that you cannot reach without a lift and eliminates the physical limitations of a tape measure. This is wonderful for measuring difficult dimensions such as box boom locations and trim heights. One caveat: to successfully use a Disto you must always block the laser beam with a physical object in order for it to perceive a measurement. This is simple if measuring a dimension such as from centerline to the box boom on a diagonal. However, what do you do if you are measuring the distance from the smoke pocket to the location of the box booms along centerline? The trick is: use your friends! Step 1—you stand at the smoke pocket with the Disto and point the laser along centerline. Step 2—your friend, assistant, or electrician lines himself up with the box booms in the house on centerline. Step 3—the laser beam stops at his belly, hand, or shoe—your pick! (Just don't shine it in his eyes.) And, like a pro, you have verified your difficult-to-measure measurement.

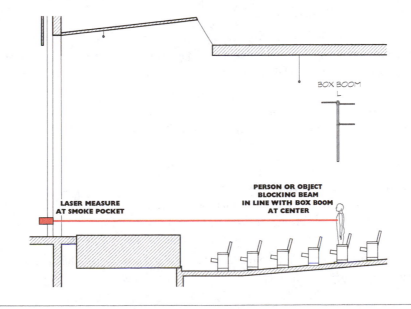

**Figure 5.3** Measuring difficult dimensions with a Disto.

Always use centerline and the plaster line or smoke pocket line (whichever the set design drawings indicate as 0,0) as your standard origin of measure for all dimensions to assure accuracy.

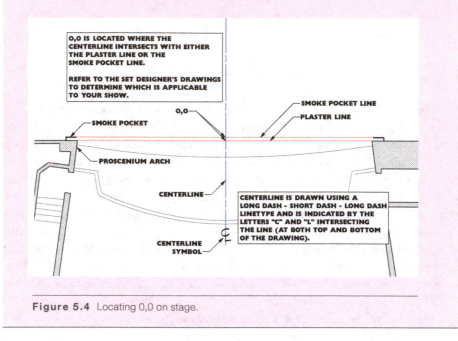

**Figure 5.4** Locating 0,0 on stage.

After returning home from the site survey, update any incorrect items you discovered on the architectural drawings. Save the updated drawings named with a new date and/or REV# (revision number). When finished, upload the drawings and photos to a Dropbox folder to share with your design team. (See the Appendices for more information regarding show folder organization.)

Print out a set of drawings or set up a new drawing for your designer so that she can begin working on the **rough plot.**

## DRAFTING THE PLOT

Once the most up-to-date theatre information is obtained and the scenic design is finalized, the lighting designer can begin working on initial design concepts for the light plot and communicating these ideas to the assistant. Depending on the designer's personal style and relationship with the assistant, this information may be communicated in many different ways:

1. Some designers hand-draft a rough plot and section to scale on vellum, onion skin, or canary paper, then give the rough plot to the assistant to draw into CAD. She may use

squares, dots, or other generic representations of the fixtures and will typically calculate the photometrics herself. The assistant can then transcribe the information directly from the rough plot into CAD and Lightwright.

---

- **Photometrics:** "The data used to describe the performance of lighting instruments—specifically their intensity and beam spread."[1]
- **Vellum:** High-quality paper traditionally used for hand-drafting.
- **Onion skin and canary paper:** Low-quality, thin, and translucent paper used for rough ideas in hand-drafting. Canary paper is the yellow-colored version of onion skin.

---

2. Other designers prefer to hand-draft a rough plot but only detail out a few concrete ideas. With this method, the assistant will need to ask plenty of questions and calculate the photometrics himself to extrapolate the information into CAD.

3. Some designers prefer to work in CAD themselves—creating a skeletal version of the final plot. Before the designer begins her work, the assistant must provide the designer with a base file containing the correct layers, classes, and architectural and scenic drawings. This allows the designer to work freely on the lighting design without worrying about drawing set-up. Once the overall design work is complete, the assistant executes all of the finishing work, such as titleblock, key, notes, instrument numbering, etc.

4. Others may sketch a few ideas down on a napkin or simply have a conversation about the plot. The associate will take notes on what angles, colors, and concepts the designer mentions. The associate (*not* assistant in this case) is then responsible for creating the entire plot from scratch.

After the designer has delivered her concepts, the assistant is responsible for drafting the finished plot and creating all necessary paperwork required for the full design package (discussed further in Part Three of this book). While working on the package, keep a running list of questions to ask the designer and set additional meetings to answer those questions as necessary. Check in with the production electrician and programmer about any technical questions you may have.

---

*"I always... print [the drawing package] before I send it off to make sure I didn't miss anything. It is good practice to see what it will look like, as most people will hang the show from the prints you submit."*

*—Justin A. Partier*

After the full design package is complete, keep a copy of the drawings, paperwork, shop order, and any other items that you submitted in the bid package in a (dated) folder within the "releases" directory in your shared show folder.

## BIDS

Once the design package is finished, the shop order will be sent out for **bid**—an estimate of the overall cost and weekly rental budget from local rental houses, or "**shops**." Usually the production electrician submits the bids, and the designer (or sometimes associate) works with the shop in order to stay within the production budget. Items may be deleted or changed. Once the equipment is finalized and the paperwork updated, the design package is considered ready for load-in.

## DESIGNER RUN

At some point during the design prep (or sometimes during load-in), the designer will invite you, the other assistants, the programmer, and, occasionally, the followspot operators to a

Helpful items to bring to a designer run:

- Show script with tabs delineating acts and scenes
- Magic sheets
- Laptop—with access to show paperwork
- Printed blank followspot cue sheets, if applicable (to rough out the followspot design during the rehearsal)
- Pencils
- Erasers
- Extra pencil leads and/or pencil sharpener
- Highlighters
- Red pencils
- Post-its
- Small ruler or straight-edge
- Small notepads
- Bottled water
- Snacks
- Breath mints and/or gum
- Headache medicine
- Kleenex
- Camera/video device
- Coffee, if requested (extra hot)

**Designer Run**—a rough run-through of the show in the rehearsal studio without any technical elements.

Bring a small kit of essential supplies to the run. Do not bring your full assistant's kit because rehearsal rooms are often crowded. Ask the designer and his past associates what he prefers to have at the table during a designer run.

Show up at least 20 minutes early to the rehearsal room to ensure that there are chairs and table space for the entire lighting design team. If there are not, politely ask the PSM if it is possible to arrange. Make sure that the designer—and hopefully the followspot assistant—is allowed table space even if there is not enough room for the full team. Set up your designer's seat with the script laid out and other items within reach. Try not to interrupt rehearsal if in progress.

Overall the assistant's job during the designer run is to become familiar with the show and take notes on any needed changes conveyed by the designer. However, if you are the assistant in charge of designing the followspots, your job is a lot more intense during this rehearsal.

## THE FOLLOWSPOT ASSISTANT

The followspot assistant designs the followspot action to work in harmony with the overall lighting design and support the intention of the designer. She decides pick-up, color, intensity, fade time, etc. and executes the design by calling the spots to the operators during tech and previews. (Further information in Part Three.)

When working as the followspot assistant, familiarize yourself intimately with the show. Print your own script and make your own binder to use during tech. Read the script several times. Get a copy of the music and listen to it over and over. Calling spots requires that you know the show—and especially its music—inside and out.

When reading the script, try to identify problem scenes, such as scenes with four or five people singing at the same time when you only have three spots with which to light them. (See Figure 5.5.) Mark these scenes in your script to watch carefully during the designer run. Also take note of any scene where you anticipate a character may be hidden by a piece of scenery. (See Figure 5.6.)

Discuss followspot preferences with the designer beforehand. For example, does he like spots used throughout the entire show—even during book-scenes, or just during musical numbers? Does he prefer the spots to stand out in intensity from the rest of the background, or does he want the characters subtly highlighted as if magically glowing? Does he envision frost being used the majority of the time for subtlety, or does he prefer hard-edge spots in certain scenes, like more vaudevillian moments? Does he have a favorite color combination or default iris size that he would like to start with?

During the designer run, most designers prefer that the followspot assistant work semi-autonomously because they are busy with cueing. Try not to bother the designer with too many questions. Follow your instincts and design your best guess.

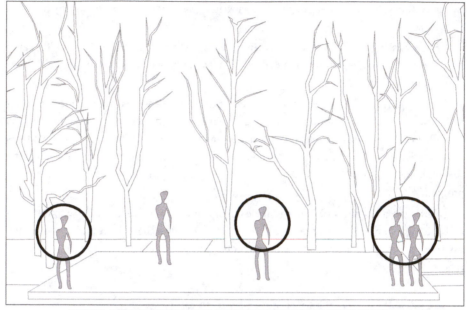

**WITH ONLY THREE FOLLOWSPOTS, HOW DO YOU LIGHT
THE EQUALLY IMPORTANT CHARACTER SINGING UPSTAGE?**

**Figure 5.5**   Example followspot problem scene 1.
*Sketch based on Tom Pye's Fiddler on the Roof*

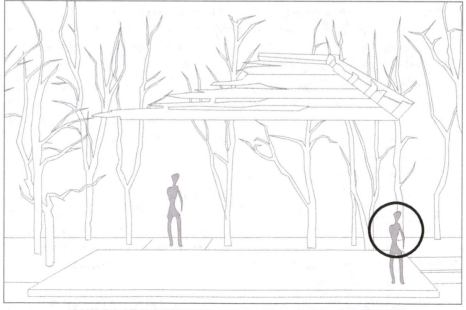

**HOW DO YOU LIGHT THE CHARACTER THAT JUST ENTERED
UNDERNEATH THE FLYING SCENERY THAT BLOCKS YOUR SPOT?**

**Figure 5.6**   Example followspot problem scene 2.
*Sketch based on Tom Pye's Fiddler on the Roof*

Take blocking notes and rough out as much followspot design as possible—either in the edges of your script or on blank followspot cue sheets. Make sure you have some reference for all scenes. Video difficult sequences *only* if permitted by the director.

Keep an eye out for those problem scenes that you flagged when reading the script. If characters are standing too far apart to light properly, alert the designer so that he can discuss the issue with the director at an opportune moment. If the run seems too stressful a time to talk about these issues, flag them for a follow-up discussion.

**How do I deal with problem scenes?**

1. The designer can ask the director if restaging is possible so that some characters stay close enough together to be able to share one spot.

2. If some of the characters stay in one place most of the scene, the designer can light them by using a special or moving light.

3. The director and designer can agree to leave that character only partially in light.

After the designer run, begin making your spot sheets. Work carefully through every move of the show. The goal is to walk into tech with the cue sheets completed. They will change throughout the process, but having the initial framework is key.

**Special**—a fixture with a specific purpose on a singular item or area, such as a chair or DSL. Not part of a lighting system.

**System**—a series of fixtures covering the stage focused at the same angle, for the same purpose, and often in the same color, such as the frontlight system or backlight system.

# Load-In

## SHOP PREP

**Shop Prep** is the time dedicated to preparing and organizing the rental equipment for load-in and hang.

The production electrician and his crew may spend a week or two working in the rental shop organizing the lighting fixtures into roadcases so that they are organized by position when arriving at the theatre. Other things that may occur during shop prep include: pre-hanging fixtures in truss, bundling and labeling lengths of cable, cutting and framing colors and gobos, and loading moving lights with custom items. Shop prep is a very important time for the production electrician. A good shop prep ensures a good and efficient load-in.

If the show is not a rental, prep may happen in-house—cleaning and organizing fixtures pre-cutting color, creating hang cards, etc.

The assistant is not involved directly in shop prep, except by phone for any pending questions.

---

**Hang Cards** (sometimes referred to simply as "cardboards")—Individual lighting positions broken out separately onto their own piece of paper to allow easy reference and portability for the electrician while hanging a position. Typically the production electrician will fabricate the hang cards if he chooses to use them. However, on small shows, the assistant or designer may help create them.

To create hang cards, print out the plot to scale and, using scissors or a paper cutter, cut each lighting position out separately then adhere each position to its own piece of scrap cardboard or foam core for stability.

Attach tie line to both sides of the top of the hang card so that it can be temporarily tied to each lighting position while it is being hung for easy accessibility. Ensure that each hang card is completely dimensioned and contains a lighting key for quick reference.

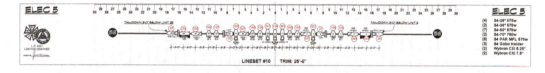

**Figure 6.1**  *Under My Skin hang cards.*
*Lighting By: Jared A. Sayeg*

## SCENIC BUILD

At the same time shop prep is going on for the electricians, **scenic build** is happening in the scenic shop. Once the practical scenery is built and wired, the assistant, the designer, and the production electrician should visit the scenic shop to assure the designer's desired lighting effect has been achieved. If there are any problems or misunderstandings, it is easier to fix them at this stage rather than in the theatre. Take photos of the progress for reference and upload them to the shared show folder.

*"Always go to the shop to look at set electrics. It's a pain to get out there but it's definitely worth getting there and seeing what it looks like before it gets installed in the theatre."*

—Anthony Pearson

## PRE-HANG

**Pre-hang** is sometimes also called "**Spotting Call**." In a four-wall contract house, like Broadway, it is the time before the scenery gets loaded-in that the flys and electrics are "spotted," or measured and marked, by the rigging crew. Pick points are placed to hang the battens and/or truss required for the production. (More on four-wall contracts in Part Four.)

If the house contains an existing fly system, then pre-hang may be more like a standard hang—getting as much hung in the air as possible before the scenery takes up space on the deck. For some productions, there may not be a pre-hang time scheduled at all.

The production electrician may ask the assistant to check in during pre-hang in order to anticipate any problems he may see. Bring your laptop and be ready to discuss any questions that may arise.

> The term "pre-hang" is mostly used on Broadway and in other union houses. Calling the activity "pre-hang" separates it from load-in. Therefore the term exists mainly to keep load-in costs down because non-load-in days do not fall under yellow card rules. (More on yellow cards in Chapter 4.)

## LOAD-IN AND HANG

Load-in is typically the official start date for the assistants to begin to work in the theatre full time. The assistants should be present in the theatre and be available for any questions. The designer will not be present in the theatre during load-in and hang.

### TECH TABLE PLACEMENT

Initially during load-in, the assistant may sit in the house without a table. The electricians will be busy trying to hang the show. They may not be available to set up the tech table for the first few days.

Before confirming the tech table's final location, ask the designer if he would be willing to stop by the theatre during load-in to confirm the placement. Moving the tech table and all its equipment is a time-consuming process, so getting it right the first time is beneficial.

Lighting tech tables (each usually 4'×8' in size) are placed at "**center-center**"—located on centerline and often just in front of the balcony rail (in an average-sized house). The designer's table always splits center so that he has a symmetrical view of the stage. A good rule of thumb is that the stage should encompass the designer's entire point of view. He should not need to turn his head to see the edges of the stage on SR or SL. Be cautious not to block ladder access to the balcony rail for focus. Also, avoid being underneath the balcony because it can block the designer's view of above the stage.

**Figure 6.2**  Disney's *Tarzan* Tech Tables in the Richard Rodgers Theatre.
© *Disney. Photo by: Joan Marcus Photography. Used with permission.*

Additionally, you will need to know where to place the programmer's tech table. Typically this table is placed on centerline in the front row of the balcony—also splitting center so that she has a symmetrical view of the stage floor.  (See Figure 6.3.) Consult with your designer and programmer. Sometimes they will prefer the programmer to start in the orchestra to the right or left of the designer and move to the balcony at a later date in the tech process. If an assistant is assigned to work with the programmer as the ML tracking assistant, add an additional table to the right or left of the programmer's table for him.

Since the designer's table always splits center, the assistants are placed on a separate table either right or left of the designer depending on his preference. Leave the other side of the designer's table open to the aisle, if possible, so that the director can easily reach the designer for discussion.

Some designers like to have a few house seats removed from behind the tech table. Doing this allows a designer the freedom to access the tech table without crawling over the seats or asking others to move. In addition, some designers prefer an entire row of seats to be removed so that they can sit in standard office chairs instead of sitting on "butt-boards" balanced atop the arms of the house seats.

If seats are to be removed, make sure this corresponds with tech table set-up so that all is ready for the designer on the first day of focus. Check for any safety issues from removed seats—sharp objects left over from removed seats can stick out and cause cuts or torn clothing. Ask to have any hazardous items wrapped in foam for the designer's safety. Also, ask the electricians to tape down any cables present in traffic areas.

**Figure 6.3**  Broadway programmer's tech table in the balcony.
*Photo By: Samuel Morgan Photography*

> **Butt-boards** = padded lengths of plywood placed on the arms of the theatre seats so that the design team can sit high enough to see easily over the tech table.

After the tech tables are placed, check that all top surfaces of the tables are matte black—either painted or covered. Black tables reduce the amount of ambient bounce light that may distract the designer during tech. If they are not black, cover them with matte black contact paper or shelf paper. After the tables are blacked, the electricians can begin placing the equipment on the tables.

## TECH TABLE SET-UP

As the assistant you should stay out of the way while the electricians set up your table until they are done. Be available for questions, but do not sit at the tech table until set-up is complete. Keep an eye on the process in case large items need to move. Politely ask to move the item to where the tech table drawing indicates. (Further information on the tech table drawing in Part Three.)

Some designers may also like a downlight or two hung over the tech tables to use as worklight. If this is your designer's preference, ask the production electrician to provide these when possible before the designer arrives on scene. Using the shutters, focus the fixture to only light the tops of the tables, not shine on the design team's heads.

After the tech tables are completely set up by the electricians, the assistants can then "move in." Set up each area with magic sheets, Post-its, pencils, and other items that each individual prefers. Set up communal items from your kit such as a hole punch, stapler, scissors, box of Kleenex, and pencil holders with pencils, pens, highlighters, Sharpies, etc. on the assistant's side of the table. If your department has its own printer, place it on the assistant's side too. Have extra reams of paper and ink available and know the location of the nearest office supply store for replacements.

Set up a pencil holder and other amenities on the designer's table, but keep the clutter to a minimum.

Ensure that each tech table has an adequate number of dimmable Littlites, and each monitor is set to the favorite views that your designer likes to use. Stock your designer's table with non-perishable treats that he likes—perhaps mints, gummy bears, Goldfish crackers, or chocolates—but be mindful that many theatres have rats and/or insect problems. Use a plastic bag or Tupperware container to protect snacks overnight.

If headsets are set up (done by the sound department), test them. If they are not ready yet, remember to test them before tech. Ensure your designer has the type of headset that she prefers—right ear, left ear, featherweight, handset, etc.

When it seems like a good time, ask to get the wireless internet password and printer network set-up information, if applicable. Write this information on a Post-it and secure it to the table so it does not get lost.

Trash and recycle bins should be placed within reach at the ends of the tables.

**Figure 6.4**  Assistant's tech table.
*Photo By: Kevin Barry*

# FOCUS

*"The success of the focusing session will rest largely on your efficiency and your speed."*

—Craig Miller[1]

**Focus,** also called "**Conventional Focus,**" may begin while load-in is still happening. You may be able to focus the FOH (front of house) lighting positions while the set is still being loaded-in upstage. Communicate with your production electrician and inform your designer when focus is anticipated to begin.

Usually the designer's first day in the theatre is focus. However, some designers prefer their associate to focus. The designer may stop by to check in or not show up at all. If this is the case, the associate may focus the entire show.

*A good assistant should have the "ability to step up and take over focus if I have to deal with a client."*

—Bruce Ferri

Before focus, the production electrician should complete the following for all fixtures. Double-check all of this is ready before the designer arrives.

- Hang
- Circuit
- Drop color
- Drop gobos
- Pre-focus (pointing the fixtures in the direction drawn on the plot)
- Patch
- "Flashed out" (working and patched correctly)
- All trims set and on spike for electrics and softgoods (borders and legs)
- Focus table with light is set up for assistant

## PLACING FOCUS TAPES

Before the designer arrives for focus, you must place your set of focus tapes onstage. Be cautious of the politics within the theatre. For one, you do not want to be in anyone's way. Ask the production electrician when the best time is to place your focus tapes. He will discuss this with the other "heads" and let you know.

Secondly, ensure that you will not destroy the painted floor when you tape down the focus tapes. Discuss this issue with the scenic design associate. If he feels comfortable with gaff tape, stick the gaff tape to your jeans once or twice before sticking it to the floor. This will make it less sticky—sticky enough to hold down the tapes, but not enough to pull up any sealed paint. However, if he is uncomfortable with the use of gaff tape you can suggest using blue painter's tape.

When placing the tapes, the US–DS focus tape is always placed on center, but you need to know if "0" is being measured from the plaster line or the smoke pocket line to properly locate it. Refer to the scenic designer's drawings for the answer. Once you have determined the 0,0 lay out both tapes in their proper locations.

Tape down around the 0,0 section on all sides as well as the SL and SR ends of the SL–SR tape. The US–DS tape should be taped down on the DS side (as well as at the 0,0 area), but the US end should be left loose with the excess tape still rolled up. This allows you to easily move or roll up the US end of the tape when tracked scenery or lifts need to roll by while you are focusing.

> Sometimes 0,0 can be measured off of a portal, an edge of a scenic deck, or a flown scenic piece.

## INDICATING THE LIGHTING AREAS

In addition to the use of focus tapes, some lighting designers prefer to have their main lighting areas indicated physically on the stage. Use small pieces of painter's tape or drafting dots to mark each area drawn on the area layout directly onto the stage. (Area layouts described more in Part Three.) Finish by clearly writing the names of the lighting areas on each corresponding piece of tape, such as "A," "B," "C," etc.

Indicating the main lighting areas on stage promotes efficient focusing. The designer can easily locate the main lighting areas (such as Area "A") for repetitive focuses rather than referring to the focus tapes and having to remember exactly where he stood the previous time he focused that area.

> Always consult with the scenic design team before sticking anything to a painted floor.

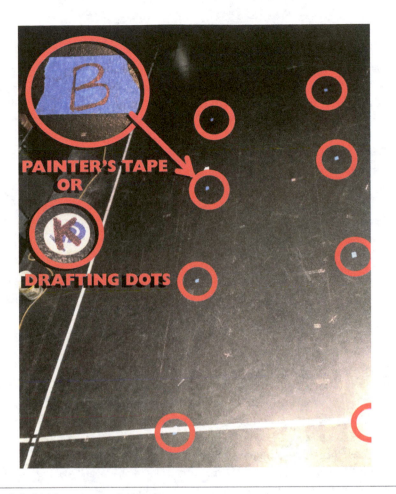

**Figure 6.5**  Lighting areas marked on stage.

Ask your designer ahead of time what method he prefers to use. Some designers may find labeled areas useful while others prefer no demarcation at all. Allow enough time—a few hours to be safe—to lay down focus tapes and areas *before* your designer arrives in the theatre to focus.

## FOCUS TABLE

When setting up for focus, ask your production electrician for a rolling table—a standard theatrical hamper or roadcase works great. This temporary table will act as a small rolling desk on stage for you during focus. (You often need to roll out of the way of a pool of light the designer is focusing. A table without wheels takes a lot more effort.)

On the table, lay out a copy of the plot. Also bring a notepad, iPad and/or small notebook version of the instrument schedule and channel hookup, and focus charts (either in small notebook form or within the show bible). Also have some small Post-its, highlighters (in a few different colors), pencils, erasers, and extra pencil lead on hand. (Keep these smaller items in a small pencil bag to keep them from rolling off the table.)

Ask the electrician for a temporary portable light for the table to keep tripping hazards at a minimum. And finally, ask for a two-way radio or wireless headset that connects you with your production electrician. Assure the radio is tuned to the correct channel. Ask for specific instructions if you are unfamiliar with the style of radio.

It is easy to talk over others or have your first few words cut off when using a two-way radio rendering it useless for you and frustrating for others. Always hold down the talk button for a moment before you begin speaking to keep from being cut off. And if others need to communicate, allow them to finish their conversation before cutting in. Trying to talk while others are talking will cause the radios to allow no one to be heard.

Instead of using radios, wireless headsets can also be used directly through the show's system. Ask the production electrician to check with the sound department to see if the Com system can be used during focus.

## RUNNING FOCUS

The assistant's job during focus is to **"run focus"**—to facilitate the flow of the overall focus session. Duties may include: directing your electricians to the next light or lighting position, requesting channels from the electrician running the remote, requesting scenery to be flown or tracked in, informing your designer of the purpose of each channel, keeping track of which lights have been focused, assuring that the proper color and gobos are in each fixture, writing down any work or focus notes that occur, filling in the focus charts, and making sure that your designer does not fall off the stage while blinded by the lights.

Before focus begins, if you have not met previously take the time to introduce yourself to each electrician individually, as well as the head flyman and the head of deck automation. Shake as many hands as you can. If focus becomes stressful, the more personal the relationship and the more rapport you have with your new allies, the better.

*"Gain the trust of the crew. It's so much easier to get stuff done if the crew trusts and respects you and you can only gain that by earning it. I want the crew to be on my side and want to work with me—not just do it because I told them to."*

—*Anthony Pearson*

Focus can be exhausting for the assistant—like a mental marathon each day—depending on the show's quantity of conventional fixtures. Wear comfortable shoes because your feet will tire quickly from standing for so many hours. Drink plenty of water so that your voice holds up while speaking loudly over the noise of load-in. If there are multiple assistants on the show, divide up the tasks.

Worklights are usually left on at half or a glow during focus. Typically it is never completely dark. Sometimes a large piece of scenery, such as a main curtain or midstage traveler, can be flown in to allow for other teams to work in full light US while focusing happens DS in relative darkness. Make sure that your focus table has a light, and, just in case, carry a flashlight with you at all times. A standard flashlight is more useful than a flashlight app on your phone, in this case. You can turn it on more quickly, and hold it in your mouth if needed.

Typically, an electrician will complete the following on a conventional fixture before the designer begins to focus:

- Pull color (and frost)
- Pull shutters
- Make unit sharp
- Focus hot spot on designer's head and shoulders or face (depending on how the designer works)

After completing focus with the designer, the electrician will:

- Assure the fixture is "locked"
- Drop color (and frost)

You may "run" anywhere from two to four lighting positions at once—alternating your designer's focus between multiple lighting positions and/or electricians. Sometimes a designer will work with two or more lights at once—giving instructions to one electrician, then a second, and returning to check the first electrician's work, then the second.

Use the words "new idea" when the designer changes his mind on a focus. This will assure the crew that the new request—even if a contradiction from the last—is merely a change of heart from the designer rather than something the electrician has done wrong. This can help alleviate any frustrations or misunderstandings.

Your designer may prefer to run lighting positions that "**reverse and repeat**," or "R&R," such as box booms on opposite sides of the stage. These types of positions often include fixtures that focus as mirror images of each other, or "reverse and repeat." It can be helpful to lay the focus charts for these positions side by side for easy reference during focus.

Do not make direct requests of the crew. Funnel your needs through your production electrician. He will announce breaks, direct electricians to move to new positions, and ask for scenery that is needed onstage. (Some production electricians may prefer that you ask for scenic needs yourself—discuss this matter with him ahead of time.)

Keep track of each electrician's name that focuses for you. Write each name on a Post-it and move it in the focus charts each time the electrician moves to a different lighting position. Calling each person's name when directing focus can avoid confusion from the multiple electricians focusing all at once. Inform your designer of each name with each new light.

**Things to remember while running focus:**

- Ask the designer ahead of time how he would like to proceed. Some designers prefer to start with the center front light if the position is easily reachable, like a FOH cove. (Other positions, like overhead electrics, will need to be focused in order from one direction.)

- Try to stay one step ahead at all times. As soon as one light is being focused, get the next one ready while filling out the focus chart at the same time. Never allow the designer to be idle and waiting on you.

- Glow (15–20 percent) the electrician's next light and inform him so he knows where he is going and when he is next in line.

- Tell the designer the purpose of each light as you bring it "up" (turn it on). If lighting areas are taped on stage, point out the relevant spot to your designer before you bring the light up.

- Use Post-its as bookmarks in the focus charts (with focuser's name) when focusing multiple lighting positions.

- Mark fixtures as *halfway* focused and *fully* focused to keep track of completed fixtures. This can be done in Lightwright or with a simple half-an-"x" or "+" symbol written on your printed paperwork. The second half of the "x" or "+" is marked when the light is completely focused. Another method is highlighting the light halfway and fully, or with one color and then another when complete.

- Say each individual's name before speaking directions. Clarifying directly to whom you are speaking avoids confusion and keeps you from repeating yourself. Speak loudly to the electricians focusing so they can hear you over the noise of load-in.

- Do not take fixtures "out" (turn them off) until after the electrician has dropped color and is done touching the fixture to assure that no changes were made accidentally after the designer's final approval.

- When scenery is needed to focus upon, ask for it several fixtures in advance so the production electrician has enough time to ask for the piece.
- Keep a running list of work notes that arise during focus.
- Always say "please" and "thank you" when making requests.

*"Pay attention to the rhythm of the focusing electrician so you can sense when the focus of each lamp nears completion. Have the next channel number on the tip of your tongue."*

—*Craig Miller* [2]

The designer may ask you to focus at the same time as running focus, which takes a lot of skill and multi-tasking ability. If you are focusing and do not have another assistant on the show, you may not be able to keep up on the focus charts. Instead, continue to track which units have been focused, keep asking for channels, and keep focus running smoothly.

Find time later (maybe during a morning work call) to return to your focus charts—preferably a time that does not inconvenience other departments too drastically. When you have that chance, temporarily place your focus tapes, ask to bring up the fixtures, and write down the information. You may need to stand in the light to determine where the hotspot should land.

## MOVING LIGHT FOCUS

**Moving Light Focus** may begin simultaneously with conventional focus. It does not involve the assistant as directly as conventional focus does; generally the programmer will work solo on the majority of the focus needs. However, the assistant should give the programmer an updated set of moving light magic sheets printed out and presented however the programmer prefers: stapled, hole-punched, in sheet protectors, laminated, or loose-leaf.

Ask the production electrician to assure the programmer has a radio on the same channel as you. You may often need to ask the programmer to turn off the moving lights temporarily when conventionals are being focused in the same area as the movers.

During moving light focus, the programmer will test the system, making sure the console and moving lights are working correctly, and set-up the console to her preferences. Many programmers also merge portions of old show files into the new show containing items such as personalized console screen set-ups, favorite palettes, and effects previously created.

After set-up, the programmer will begin to focus the fixtures. She may divide the stage into approximately 12–15 general areas and focus each moving light to each of those areas— such as DR, DCR, DC, DCL, DL continuing that pattern moving US. These positions can be stored in the console for each fixture and easily accessed when the designer requests.

The exact locations of these focus areas can be hard to judge from the programmer's tech table, even if you have marked them onstage. If the programmer prefers, mini traffic cones can be placed on the areas to help identify each location while the programmer focuses. (See Figure 6.7.)

Some designers like to set apart several days of additional time to work on very precise moving light focuses with their programmers, although it is rare that the producers will pay for it.

The programmer may also mix a range of colors for the fixtures—paying special attention to the designer's favorite colors and colors specified within the show's color scrolls, if applicable. And, finally, the programmer will work to create effects or looks that were previously discussed with the designer for specific moments in the show.

**Figure 6.6**  Moving light focus.
*Photo By: Rob Halliday*

## PRE-CUEING

At some point after conventional focus but before the first day of tech, the designer may choose to do some cue writing so that she has cues in the board when tech begins. Because these cues are often very rough they are referred to as "**skeleton cues**." True "**dark time**," or cueing time with the worklights off, is often hard to get while load-in is still going on. Instead the designer may opt to cue while the worklights are still on or dimmed. This does not provide accurate light levels for true cueing but is enough to block in rough ideas.

**Figure 6.7**  Mini traffic cones being used for moving light focus.

Another option for extremely complicated shows, such as concert-style productions, is to cue virtually, or "**pre-cue**," at a pre-visualization studio. These studios, set up specifically for this purpose, display a 3D rendering of the stage, set, and light plot on a large-scale screen in a classroom-like setting. Specialized software is used (such as ESP Vision [Figure 6.8] or

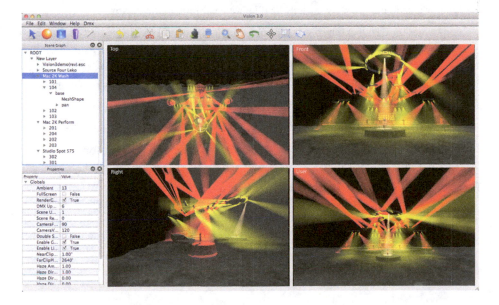

**Figure 6.8**  ESP Vision screenshot.
*Courtesy of: ESP Vision*

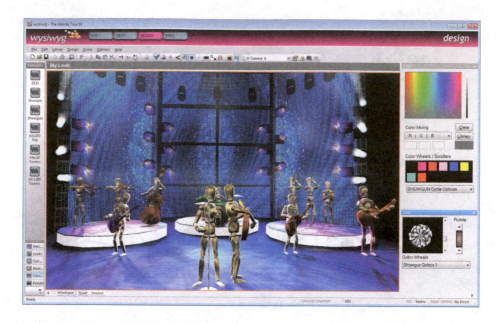

**Figure 6.9**  WYSIWYG screenshot.
*Courtesy of: CAST Software*

Cast Software's WYSIWYG [Figure 6.9]) or a console with a built-in visualizer can be used. A lighting console is hooked up to the system, the music is played (if applicable), and the designer is able to cue the show exactly as if he were working in the theatre.

Sometimes the designer may choose to cue the entire show, and sometimes only a few complicated numbers (depending on how much time has been paid for in the pre-vis studio). The designer may also choose to involve the director in the pre-cueing process. After pre-cueing, the show file is imported into the console at the theatre. It may need a few moving light focus touch-ups, but overall the cues are ready to go!

Some designers will provide a list of colors (a color library) for their programmers that relate to commonly known gel colors. (See Figure 6.10.) (Sometimes they may even provide a list of colors including CMY values recorded when color mixing in a test rig at the shop.) This gives the designer and programmer some common language when working with color. The designer can say, "make it R-26" or "make it color library 28," and the programmer will call up her preset labeled accordingly, which is mixed as closely as she could match it.

**KB Associates, Inc.**

# MOVING LIGHT COLOR PALETTE

## MATCHED TO ARC SOURCE

| STRAW / YELLOW | | SALMON / ROSE | | BLUES | |
|---|---|---|---|---|---|
| 01 | L-103 | 31 | L-153 | 61 | R-60 |
| 02 | R-11 | 32 | L-109 | 62 | R-62 |
| 03 | R-14 | 33 | R-31 | 63 | L-161 |
| 04 | L-104 | 34 | R-34 | 64 | R-64 |
| 05 | R-15 | 35 | L-110 | 65 | R-67 |
| 06 | Custom | 36 | R-36 | 66 | R-68 |
| 07 | G-460 | 37 | L-111 | 67 | R-79 |
| 08 | R-12 | 38 | G-180 | 68 | R-83 |
| 09 | L-101 | 39 | L-113 | 69 | G-905 |
| 10 | Yellow | 40 | R-46 | 70 | Blue/UV |

| LT AMBER / ORANGE | | PINK / MAGENTA | | BLUE / GREEN | |
|---|---|---|---|---|---|
| 11 | R-02 | 41 | R-33 | 71 | R-73 |
| 12 | R-03 | 42 | R-35 | 72 | L-115 |
| 13 | L-176 | 43 | R-37 | 73 | L-116 |
| 14 | R-18 | 44 | R-38 | 74 | R-95 |
| 15 | L-147 | 45 | R-44 | 75 | L-117 |
| 16 | R-21 | 46 | L-128 | 76 | L-144 |
| 17 | Custom | 47 | G-140 | 77 | R-71 |
| 18 | R-22 | 48 | L-126 | 78 | R-69 |
| 19 | R-19 | 49 | G-995 | 79 | R-76 |
| 20 | R-25 | 50 | Magenta | 80 | Cyan |

| ORANGE / RED | | MAGENTA / PURPLE | | GREENS | |
|---|---|---|---|---|---|
| 21 | R-41 | 51 | R-51 | 81 | G-540 |
| 22 | R-24 | 52 | R-52 | 82 | L-138 |
| 23 | L-182 | 53 | R-54 | 83 | L-121 |
| 24 | L-106 | 54 | L-137 | 84 | L-122 |
| 25 | Custom | 55 | L-142 | 85 | R-89 |
| 26 | Custom | 56 | R-57 | 86 | L-124 |
| 27 | G-235 | 57 | R-58 | 87 | G-655 |
| 28 | R-26 | 58 | L-180 | 88 | R-90 |
| 29 | G-250 | 59 | R-59 | 89 | R-91 |
| 30 | Red | 60 | L-181 | 90 | Green |

| N/C & CTO | |
|---|---|
| 200 | N/C |
| 201 | Arc N/C |
| 202 | Tung N/C |
| 203 | |
| 204 | 1/4 CTO |
| 205 | 1/2 CTO |
| 206 | 3/4 CTO |
| 207 | FL CTO |
| 208 | |
| 209 | Black |

**Figure 6.10** Ken Billington's Moving Light Color Library based on the color list created for the Morpheus Color Fader.

## FOLLOWSPOT SET-UP

At some point near the end of load-in, ask your production electrician if your followspot operators can have some time to prep their followspots.

They will need time to situate themselves in the spot booth, set up a note-taking station, and assure that the spots move freely and easily. Also, at this time, they can mark baseline intensities and iris sizes as well as load color and color balance their spots. (More on followspots in Chapter 10.) They should also compare the beams of their spots to assure that the lamps are reasonably matched in color temperature, intensity, and lamp life and sharpen the followspot's focus to "blue sharp." Finally, they can set up their Telrad—a followspot sight that appears to project a bull's-eye target onstage—or other sight to make sure their aim is precise. Find time for them to get all of this done before the first day of tech, if possible.

Most lighting fixtures and followspots can be sharpened to what is referred to as "blue sharp" or "orange sharp" (also called "brown sharp"). These terms describe the color of the edge surrounding the beam when the fixture is in sharp focus. Blue sharp is considered the closest to factory perfect. Which edge chosen is mostly a matter of preference; however, many designers like to focus their fixtures and their followspots to blue sharp before adding frost so that the fixture's optics perform as close to perfect as possible.

C H A P T E R    7

# Tech

"**Tech**," or "**technical rehearsal**," is the time in the process where all technical elements of the production are rehearsed together with the actors onstage. On Broadway and other large professional productions, a typical tech schedule looks like this:

- 8am–12pm: Work, focus, and other technical notes (coffee is taken around 10am)
- 12pm–1pm: Lunch
- 1pm–5pm: Tech with actors onstage (coffee is taken around 3pm)
- 5pm–6pm: Dinner
- 6pm–11:45pm: Tech (break usually around 8:30pm—unless during a run of the show, then it is usually taken at intermission)
- 11:45pm–midnight: end of night production meeting

As per union rules, this schedule can shift slightly. For example, meal breaks may be taken at 1pm–2pm and 6pm–7pm or there may be an extra long dinner for the designers if the actors have to get into costumes, makeup, wigs, and mics. (This time may also be used for catching up on notes.)

If you're counting, that's on average 84 working hours a week—16 hours a day, if you include meals (then, 96 hours a week)—for a 6-day standard theatrical workweek. More if you work 7 days in a row. This is more than double the considered "standard" American workweek of 40 hours in 5 days. These hours can be exhausting, so get as much sleep as possible—especially if you have a long commute to the theatre. If you are working in a city that relies on public transportation, treat yourself to a late-night cab ride home once or twice a week to help with overall fatigue.

Long days of tech (8am to midnight) are often referred to as "**10-out-of-12s**." This term means that the production is rehearsing for 10 hours out of a 12-hour day (including two hour-long meal breaks or one two-hour break). This term can seem misleading because, with the addition of the morning work call, the day equates to much more than a 12-hour day for the technical departments.

## MORNING WORK CALL

*"The attitude you project about the work session will be contagious to the electrical staff. Pace, energy, and a sense of organization for the work call are important."*

—Craig Miller[1]

The morning work call (usually 8am–noon) is a chance for the assistant to get as many notes done as possible that accrued from the day before.

Work notes (that do not need to involve the assistant) are often completed by the crew before the assistant arrives in the morning—such as burn-outs, gel changes, etc. (However, the assistant may choose to come in early to work by herself on paperwork.)

Focus notes, which *do* involve the assistant, are typically accomplished next—sometimes with the designer and sometimes without. Make sure that you have a clear understanding the night before of what needs to happen to the fixture if focusing without the designer.

If there is time, the designer may choose to arrive during the morning work call to complete some cue notes. Occasionally the designer will need you to act as a "**lightwalker**." A lightwalker is an individual who stands onstage so that the designer can see what the light looks like on a person's face to determine the proper light levels. When lightwalking, always be sure to stand still and face DS with your chin up toward the designer at the tech table so that your face can be clearly seen. Minimize socializing with crew, and remove your eyeglasses (if you wear them) to lessen shadows. When you return to the tech table, try to catch up with anything you may have missed in your paperwork.

## STAGES OF THE TECH PROCESS

During a typical day, tech will begin after the lunch break. During tech, the assistant will help the designer with anything he needs, organize notes, and update paperwork.

Depending on what stage of the process you are in, tech can manifest itself in several different ways. Also depending on the style of show, some forms of tech may not be used in the production process. Here are some common stages:

- **Paper Tech**—Paper tech is a meeting before tech begins that includes the designers, the director, and the PSM to discuss the placement and coordination of cues. This meeting may happen in the theatre or elsewhere, but does not include the actual use of any elements on stage. It is purely a discussion.

  Paper tech may or may not exist in your production situation. More commonly in professional situations, before tech the PSM is given a copy of each designer's cue sheets and writes the cues in her calling script, coordinating as necessary. If there are any major discrepancies or questions, she will approach the designers individually to further discuss the issues.

- **Dry Tech**—Dry tech is sometimes called "**Shift Rehearsal**" and does not involve actors. Dry tech is needed if difficult sequences with many set moves are present in the production. Sometimes even the act of getting the curtain out is dry teched depending on the level of complexity "getting into" the show. Transitions may initially be run in worklight before adding in the lighting cues. (Later, when actors are added into the process, this technique may be repeated with the cast watching from the house for the safety of the actors.) If the sequence is dependent on another element, such as projections or sound, those elements will also be included.

- **Cue to Cue**—Cue to cue, sometimes written as "**Q to Q**," involves working through the show with actors and technical elements but skipping acting-only sequences. If there are no light, sound, projection, scenic moves, costume quick-changes, or any other cues during a scene, it will be skipped. Once the desired cues are complete within a scene, the PSM will ask the actors to "hold, please," give a line to jump forward to in the script, and begin again. Cue to cue is an efficient technique for teching plays that do not have many scene shifts or other cues. For musicals, which often have very short scenes and many cues, cue to cue may not be as effective.

- **Tech**—Sometimes standard tech is playfully referred to as "**Wet Tech**"—the opposite of dry tech. The difference being that (wet) tech involves the actors—although still typically in rehearsal costume. At this stage in the process, the full show is teched through methodically without skipping any sections—although the actors may choose to "mark" (hold back or not perform full-out) the choreography and strong emotional moments. Often the PSM will call "hold, please" to the actors and ask that they back up and repeat their lines and blocking to improve the success of the cueing. Full scenic transitions will also be run, but actors are encouraged to stop for any safety concerns.

> Up until dress rehearsal, the actors rehearse in "rehearsal costumes." This can include skirts, corsets, bustles, hats, shoes, or special mock-ups that mimic the costume they will be wear in the production. However, if a show requires a lot of quick-changes, those specific costumes may be included in the tech process.
>
> Some lighting designers—particularly in the U.K.—will insist on teching in costume so that the lighting can be accurately represented on the actual costumes and their true colors.

- **Dress**—Dress rehearsal is the performing of the complete production in full costume, but no audience. Wigs, mics, makeup, masks, and other elements will also be layered in with each consecutive dress rehearsal, if applicable. The show will be performed full-out unless there is the need to stop for train wrecks. The actors are also encouraged to stop if there are problems with costume quick changes.

Occasionally, prior to dress rehearsal, a "**Dress Parade**" occurs. This involves all actors walking onstage to show their costumes in worklight or full stage light. However, in union houses, time in the theatre is so expensive that this element is often skipped.

- **Piano Tech / Piano Dress**—For productions that include an orchestra or band, such as a musical or opera, piano tech and/or dress will be a part of the process. These types of rehearsals are the same as standard tech or dress, but rehearse with a piano instead of the full orchestra. (Rehearsing with the full orchestra or band is called "**orchestra tech**" and "**orchestra dress**." Often abbreviated as "orch tech" or "orch dress" when written.)

- **Sitzprobe**—Sitzprobe, or simply "**sitz**," is a term borrowed from opera (pronounced "zitz PROE beh" or "zitz"). During this rehearsal the actors "sit and sing" with the orchestra prior to the first orchestra tech. Sometimes this happens in the orchestra's rehearsal hall and sometimes on stage. The purpose of the sitz is to give the actors at least one chance to practice the music with the orchestra before having to focus on costumes and tech as well.

  Some designers like to attend the sitz and may ask you to join. If this is the case, bring the same supplies you would bring to the designer run (discussed in Chapter 5) so your designer has everything she needs. Be prepared to take notes and absorb the music.

  If the sitz takes place in the theatre and your designer is willing, the sitz can also be a great time to catch up on work notes, cueing (over worklights), paperwork, or other notes.

- **Wandelprobe**—The wandelprobe, or simply "**wandel**" (pronounced like "von-dul"), is also a term borrowed from opera and is similar to the sitz. The only difference is that the actors will roughly follow their blocking while singing with the orchestra. A common way to remember the difference is, "you sits when you sitz, and wander when you wandel."

- **Gypsy Run / Invited Dress**—The gypsy run is the Broadway equivalent of what most productions call invited dress—the final dress rehearsal performed in front of an invited (nonpaying) audience usually consisting of the company's family and friends. A "gypsy" on Broadway is a performer typically cast in an ensemble, or chorus, who has worked on many Broadway shows. Therefore, inviting one's friends usually consists of inviting gypsies, thereby creating the name "gypsy run." Alternatively, although confusing, some productions may call this type of rehearsal a "preview" (more on previews in the next chapter).

- **Brat Mat**—This type of performance is a matinee performed exclusively for groups of local school children, although sometimes it may include high-schoolers or university students. The brat mat may occur during dress rehearsals, previews, and/or performances. Often a talkback with the actors (and sometimes designers) will be held after the performance. A backstage tour may also be included.

## END-OF-THE-NIGHT NOTES

At the final break before the end of each tech night, ask your designer if you can quickly review the work and focus notes with her so that you can finalize and distribute them. Ask about each note to verify she still wants the task accomplished. You may find that she deletes some items, adds others, and prioritizes many for you. You must distribute these notes before everyone leaves for the night, but do not deliver them before having this conversation.

> *"Be sure you understand which notes are vital and which could wait awhile. If you aren't sure, gently insist that the designer prioritize the list with you."*
>
> —Craig Miller[2]

If there are work or focus notes requiring special requests (such as a longer focus period with a certain piece of scenery or a desperate need for dark time for nit-picky cue notes) write those down additionally on a separate list for your designer. This list of items requires cooperation from other departments and must be discussed during the end-of-night production meeting to work out the next morning's schedule. It may or may not be possible to acquire this additional needed time or scenic element as it may stop other departments from working—your designer or associate will negotiate these items.

Begin printing your notes at least half an hour before the end of the rehearsal, if possible. Print copies of work and focus notes for yourself and the production electrician, cue notes for yourself and your designer (to leave on the tech table), followspot notes for the spot ops, stage management notes for the PSM, moving light notes for the programmer, and any other acquired notes for their respective parties. If there are items added after printing and/or during the meeting, handwrite them on all relevant sets of notes as well as input them electronically.

Although working digitally is efficient, a printed backup in case of technical problems can save the day. At least have a printed copy of work, focus, and cue notes, just in case.

Be cautious if the printer at the tech table is extremely loud. If your printer takes center stage during a poignant moment, it may distract the actors and director, as well as embarrass your designer. You still need to make sure you get your job done, but be cognizant of when you hit that "print" button.

One option is to locate the printer in the theatre lobby or another adjacent room that can help to mask the sound. If using this strategy, check frequently on the printer to circumvent any disastrous paper jams or lack of printing supplies.

## END-OF-THE-NIGHT PRODUCTION MEETING

At the end of each night, the production team has a quick meeting in the house to discuss any emergent issues and the next morning's work schedule. Some designers feel that the assistant should not need to attend the end-of-night production meeting, while other designers will leave and ask the assistants to stay. Other times, the associate or 1st assistant and designer will stay and let the other assistants go home. Each design team dynamic is different. Discuss the designer's preferences with him beforehand. Assume that you are staying unless you hear otherwise.

## STAYING HEALTHY

Tech can be a long and demanding process. Be mindful and take care of yourself. Eating right can be the first key—surviving on coffee, chocolate, and other tech table snacks is never a good idea. One option is to add a well-stocked fruit bowl to the tech table. Although it may be scoffed at initially, a fruit bowl can help everyone's mood and waistline considerably.

Ask if anyone on the crew has a refrigerator that you can use to keep the leftovers in each night. If not, bring the perishables home with you and back the next morning or stock it freshly when needed.

Celebrated lighting designer Gil Hemsley believed in always keeping fresh fruit and flowers at the tech table to promote a good atmosphere. He also liked to have fun items around, such as stuffed animals and toy trains, to ease others' tension during difficult moments.

Try to eat breakfast at home and bring a lunch if you are able. Eating out for all of your meals every day is a pattern that many adopt during tech. Alternatively, you may find that your health and overall mood is generally better when eating familiar foods from home, as well as keeping your calorie-intake and wallet-output in check.

Keep a few cases of bottled water under the tech table to give to the lighting team. Keep these internal or you will run out quickly when the entire company comes looking to you for water.

Try to get some exercise too. Although you may not be able to get up early enough for a jog, try taking a brisk walk during a meal break to clear your head and wake up your body.

Taking care of yourself during tech is essential to being the best assistant that you can be. If you are feeling crabby and unwell, chances are that you will not be providing the best experience that you can for your lighting team. It may begin to erode your relationship with your designer, who may not want to hire you on the next show if you are becoming unpleasant during those long days of tech. You need to be the example and help lead the team in a positive direction each day, even when they are feeling overworked.

*"Keep your crew happy. A happy crew is a productive crew. Your mood affects the crew and the people around you. Stay positive, play like a champion, no excuses."*

—Matt Gordon

*"Be positive. There will always be people who spend far too much time mired in the squalor of negativity. Deny them your energy and stay focused on contributing something positive."*

—K. C. Wilkerson

Most importantly, try to have some fun during tech. This profession can be quite enjoyable and saturated with a lot of wonderful people. Even when things get stressful, keep your attitude positive and find your own joy.

*"If we're not having fun, why are we doing it?"*

—Jason Lyons[3]

**Figure 7.1**   "Glam" Tech Table—complete with mirror ball.
*Courtesy of: Rob Halliday*

# Previews and Performances

## PREVIEWS

**Previews** are (essentially) rehearsals performed in front of a paying audience. During previews, each afternoon changes are implemented in the show, and each evening the show (with the included changes) is performed in front of an audience. Each preview may be a slightly different production.

The production team uses the audience as test subjects to further understand what moments are not "reading" well. These moments may be addressed as changes during the next day's rehearsal. The preview process schedule is the same as tech with morning work calls and afternoon rehearsals, except that performances happen at night (as well as some matinees).

In creative endeavors, like live theatre, things do not always go as planned. *Spider-Man: Turn Off the Dark*, due to a troubled production process, made history for the longest preview period in Broadway history—a whopping 183 previews (as opposed to the usual 30 or so). Opening was delayed so many times that the production team began adopting creative names for each upcoming opening night, such as "faux-pening" and "hope-ening"—terms coined by historic Broadway flops of the past.

## PREVIEW TABLE

Before each preview, the electrics crew will strike the tech table and install a small **preview table** or other custom set-up within the theatre seats at the back of the house for the designer and the associate (or 1st assistant). This may be as simple as a console monitor or tablet device, a powerstrip, a Littlite, and a headset. For previews, this acts as a modified tech table. Check with management to make sure those seats will be blocked off for all previews and not sold to the general public. Other assistants—as well as the assistant's kit and other supplies—will be given temporary locations in the booth or another convenient area.

For all intents and purposes, the lighting team attempts to blend in with the audience during previews and not disturb their experience while watching the show. The assistant will quietly take notes, and the designer may sneak in some small subtle changes.

## PREVIEW REVISIONS

The morning following each preview a pared-down version of the tech table will be set up again in the center of the house—especially if large changes are expected during the afternoon's rehearsal. For example, in a new play or musical, new scenes may be written or rewritten, new songs added or subtracted, and the placement of songs may shift within acts or even between acts. These types of changes will be fully teched in the afternoon and implemented in that evening's show.

The stage management team will hand out new copies of the relevant pages of the revised script, usually on differently colored paper clearly dated on the top. You, the assistant, insert these pages into the designer's script. Transfer any tabs and rewrite any cue placements or notes on the new pages. Try to emulate the designer's style. Keep the old script pages in a safe place (like the back of the show bible—described further in Part Three) as sometimes changes revert.

Besides these script pages, an assistant's duties remain generally the same during previews as they are during tech.

> Be mindful of the time it takes to set up and strike the tech table every day, as well as the time it takes to set up the preview table. This activity can cut into your notes-time considerably. Adjust your expectations for the daily workload accordingly.
>
> To aid the process, strike the lighting design team's items (pencils, binders, laptops, etc.) as quickly as possible to allow the technicians to strike the equipment and tables without delay.

As the preview process wears on and the changes become less dramatic, the designer may choose to handle afternoon notes from the preview table, saving the electricians from having to set up the larger tech table.

## FREEZE DATE

Typically, during previews, there comes a day called the **"Freeze Date"** or **"Lock Date"**—a few days to a week before any important critics are planned to see the show. On the freeze date, extremely large changes, such as new songs and scenes, are no longer allowed. Although small dialogue changes may still be established, the show is then considered frozen. Giving the actors a freeze date allows them to become comfortable in their performances so that the production feels cohesive in time for the big reviews.

For a Broadway show, *The New York Times* is considered the most important review. A review from *The Times* can make or break its success and the future of the show.

As much as they try, sometimes shows are unable to honor the freeze date. Although not ideal, sometimes producers and directors may continue to implement changes well past the freeze date.

## OPENING

**Opening night**, or simply "**open**," is typically the assistant's last day on contract. During the performance, the assistant and designer sit in the regular audience seating instead of a preview table. Check with management to ensure that the entire lighting design team (and their "plus ones") has "comps"—complimentary tickets—for opening night. Also ensure that the entire lighting team (and their plus ones) has a ticket for the opening night party. Spot ops and their dates are usually the first to be forgotten by management, especially since the ops do not have seats allocated for the performance itself.

The assistant's job on opening night is to enjoy the show as if a standard audience member. The only reason changes would need to be made after opening would be for any "lighting emergencies" such as a blackout in the wrong place or a light that tracked through into a blackout.

Additionally, the assistant must deliver all archival paperwork to the show crew before she leaves after opening night. (More on this in Chapter 10.) Better yet, turn it in the day before—the crew will feel more prepared, and you will feel more relaxed to enjoy the fun opening night.

### OPENING NIGHT PARTY

Opening night is considered a huge reason for celebration. For large professional productions, such as Broadway, opening night includes a glamorous opening night party at a fancy location. Everyone dresses up in formal wear and enjoys good drinks and food. Small gifts may be exchanged between the design team and the crew and cast.

### OPENING NIGHT GIFTS TABLE

Although technically off contract, the day following opening the assistant has one last job—stopping by the theatre in the afternoon to collect all the opening night gifts for the designer. Bring a large bag.

Often a table is placed backstage (or somewhere out of the way) specifically for opening night gifts. Sift through to look for items with your designer's name on them. You may even be surprised to see a few nice gifts for yourself. Additionally, retrieve your assistant's kit and other supplies from the theatre to return home.

> Pick up the gifts the day after opening and before that evening's show. Leaving the gifts for too long in the theatre could appear ungrateful (politically).

After gathering the gifts, deliver them to the designer's home or office. Also archive show materials at the designer's office in their proper places. This may involve filing an archival binder on the shelf and/or moving items from cloud storage onto the designer's hard drive.

> "An assistant's [influence] doesn't end on opening night or when the design is frozen. A show needs to be maintained and if it moves, that will need to happen smoothly. An assistant's paperwork and skill are what allow that to happen ... the continuing lives of productions."[1]

After opening, try to relax and recuperate after what was a long and exhausting process. The demanding hours of tech can lead to burnout. Take care of yourself and rejuvenate before your next production so you can continue to be a rock-star assistant.

**PART 3**

# The Paperwork

> *"Paperwork is the language by which the lighting designer's ideas are translated into physical reality."*
>
> —*Vivien Leone*

The "paperwork" (or sometimes the "plot and paperwork") is a term used to generally describe the overall design package documentation that is produced by the assistant lighting designer throughout the production process. It translates the art hidden within the designer's head into a tangible set of technical instructions. The term encompasses many different types of documents, which will be described in detail throughout this section.

Unless otherwise noted (such as with the drawing package), all styles of paperwork mentioned in this text are generally created on 8.5" × 11" paper in the U.S. or A4 in metrically based countries.

Consistency is the key to creating professional-looking paperwork. Each designer and/or design office typically uses a set of standards. Each office may have standard fonts, drafting symbols, and styles that are used exclusively to give its design paperwork a signature look, or brand.

When integrating into a new office for the first time, ask questions regarding any guidelines that may exist and follow them precisely. If these guidelines are not specifically laid out, ask to look through some of their recent production paperwork. Note the fonts, drafting symbols, and other styles that prevail throughout multiple shows and incorporate this information into the current show on which you are working.

Some offices have a starter folder that is organized in the office standard and contains starter documents such as drawing templates to assist you with beginning a new show. Copy the starter folder and rename it to reflect your show name, make it a shared Dropbox folder for the lighting team, and begin creating your documents.

At all times during the process, keep the folder meticulously organized so that the most current file is unmistakable when viewed by others. Keep only the most updated file in the main directory of each folder, while older copies are stored in an "old" or "void" file within that same directory. This prevents mistakes from being made on outdated copies of the documents. (For one possible way to organize your show's electronic folder, see the Appendices of this text.)

For discussion purposes, show paperwork can be divided into two main categories: the pre-production paperwork and the tech process paperwork. In reality, these two categories interlace quite a bit; e.g. all paperwork is created, or "prepped," during the pre-production prep weeks, but some documents may only be empty shells waiting for the information developed during the tech process. And although many documents are primarily created during pre-production, they are constantly updated during the tech process. Neither of these phases lives in isolation.

For the purposes of this book the documents will be discussed in these categories within the next two chapters. Additionally, they are not discussed in any particular order because the creation of the documents overlaps considerably.

- **Pre-production paperwork:**
  - Drawing package
  - Paperwork
  - Magic sheets
  - Shop order
  - Tech table drawing
  - Area layout
  - Groups list
  - Scene breakdown or scene-by-scene
  - Show bible and script

- **Tech process paperwork:**
  - Focus charts
  - Cue synopsis/cue list
  - Followspot cue sheets
  - Work notes
  - Ripple sheet
  - Moving light focus charts and tracking
  - Archival bible
  - Next time sheet
  - Running gifts list

When prepping a new show, work off of a checklist to assure that you complete all items required for the full design package and that nothing is missed. (A design package checklist can be found in the Appendices of this text.) Complete as much as possible during your prep weeks even if it is simply creating base files, or "skeleton files" (files with no content). Sometimes this is nothing other than duplicating an old file, emptying its contents, and saving it with a new file name and show title. By the time the design package is due, you should have all possible paperwork produced, organized, double-checked by another assistant, and ready for tech.

*"The best advice I can give is to double and triple check your work."*

*—Jen Schriever*

Not every show requires the same documentation. For example, you may not have moving lights on your show. If this is the case you would not need to make a moving light magic sheet. Conversely, you may need to create additional items: perhaps your designer requests a special type of magic sheet or maybe a specific detail needs to be drawn for your production. Whatever the case may be, it is your job as the assistant to produce all the paperwork required to fully explain and detail all lighting design needs for the production. If this means that you need to create a custom piece of paperwork for the show, wonderful! The more detail, the better. Just take the time to ensure it is clear, concise, and follows your designer's standards.

Although assisting appears to be a technical job, it actually requires a creative person to do it well. Figuring out precisely what is needed to tell the complete story of a design takes an individual who can problem-solve creatively and effectively.

Before the invention of computers, lighting paperwork was hand-drawn and handwritten. Some wonderful examples of historic lighting paperwork by legendary lighting designers can be found at The Lighting Archive (www.thelightingarchive.org), including paperwork from Ken Billington's original *Sweeney Todd* (1979) and the very first focus charts created by Jean Rosenthal (1948).

Other wonderful examples can be found at The New York Public Library's Theatrical Lighting Database: lightingdb.nypl.org. There you can see original documents from significant productions, such as Tharon Musser's original *Chorus Line* (1975) and Jules Fisher's original *Hair* (1968).

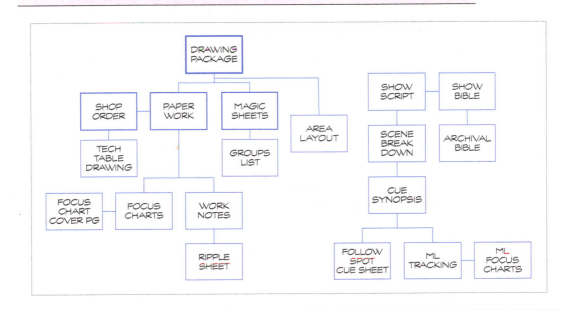

Lighting Paperwork Flow Chart

## CHAPTER 9

# Pre-production Paperwork

Good assistants are defined by many things, but one of the most prominent is the quality, clarity, and professional look of their paperwork. Simple choices that result in beautiful and effective documents consistently separate excellent individuals from the pack. The best assistants excel at combining logical and concise information arrangement with artistic presentation. Nowhere is this principle more prominent than on the light plot.

> *"I don't care if you're a designer, an associate, or an assistant... [we are] all artists and your drafting should reflect that."*
>
> —Matt Gordon

## DRAWING PACKAGE

> *"A light plot is not a light plot until it has coffee stains and cigarette burns on it."*
>
> —Tharon Musser[1]

The **light plot** is part of a larger group of documents that constitute the lighting design drawing package—which is the epicenter that all other documents revolve around within the full design package. The **drawing package** also consists of other plates (or pages) such as the section, FOH, booms and ladders, floor plot, and/or set practicals. (See Figures 9.1a-d.) In the U.S. these drawings are typically made in Vectorworks, although occasionally other programs are used.

The number of plates needed is determined by the scope of the production. If there is not enough information to require an additional drawing, then there is no need to do it.

For example, if the set has only one practical floor lamp, you do not need to create a separate floor plot drawing—simply find an appropriate way to include it in your light plot.

**Light plot**—a drawing of the electrics over stage

**Section**—Typically a centerline section; "cut" view of the stage from centerline to either SR or SL

**FOH**—a drawing of the front of house electrics over the audience

**Booms and ladders**—a drawing in elevation of all verticals: booms, ladders, box booms, rovers, etc.

**Floor plot**—also called a deck plot; a drawing of all floor-mounted instruments and practicals

**Set practicals**—a detail drawing showing the design and technical information of practical scenery and set-mounted fixtures. Depending on the production and level of detail required for proper communication, set practical drawings can range anywhere from one to 20 or more pages.

Consult Vectorworks', or your drafting program's, website for further details on how to proceed with any of the techniques discussed in the following sections.

"Drafting," "drawing," and "plate" are sometimes used interchangeably. A light plot could be considered a plate, a drafting, or a drawing. A section would be another plate, and so on.

## PLATE ORGANIZATION

One typical order (although it varies) in which plates are often numbered and printed for the drawing package is:

1. Light plot [Figure 9.1a]
2. Section [Figure 9.1d]
3. FOH [Figure 9.1c]
4. Booms and ladders [Figure 9.1b]
5. Floor plot (also called deck plot)
6. Set practicals (also called set elex)

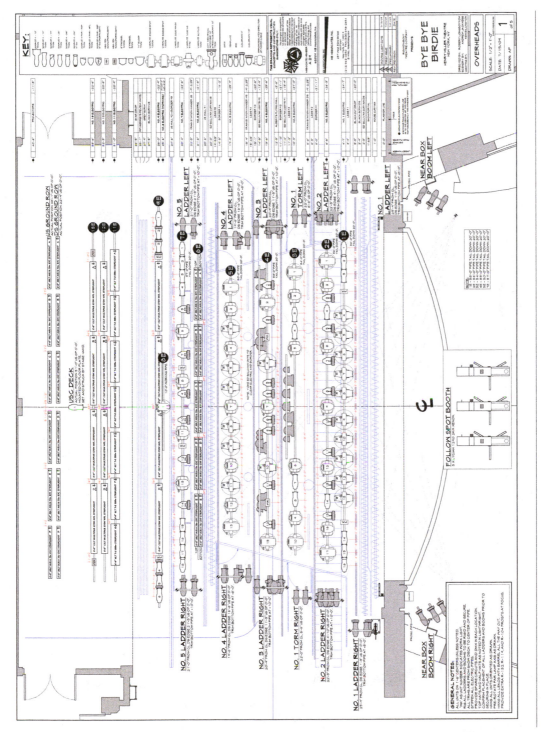

**Figure 9.1a** *Bye Bye Birdie drawing package.*
*Lighting By: Ken Billington*
*ALD: Anthony Pearson*

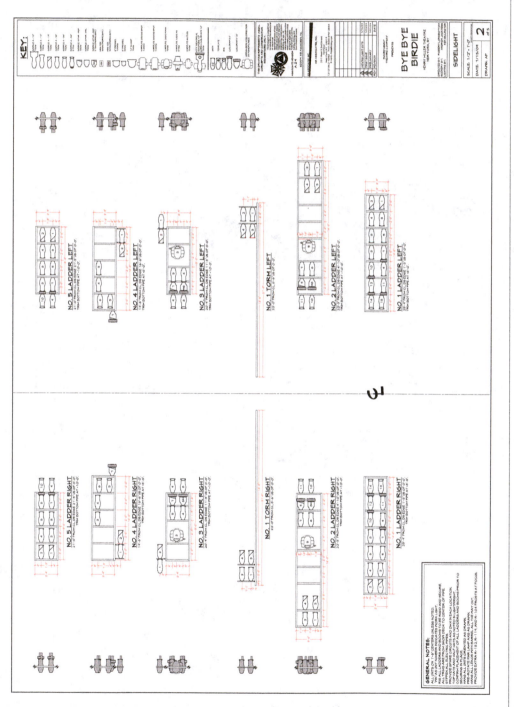

**Figure 9.1b** *Bye Bye Birdie drawing package.*
*Lighting By: Ken Billington*
*ALD: Anthony Pearson*

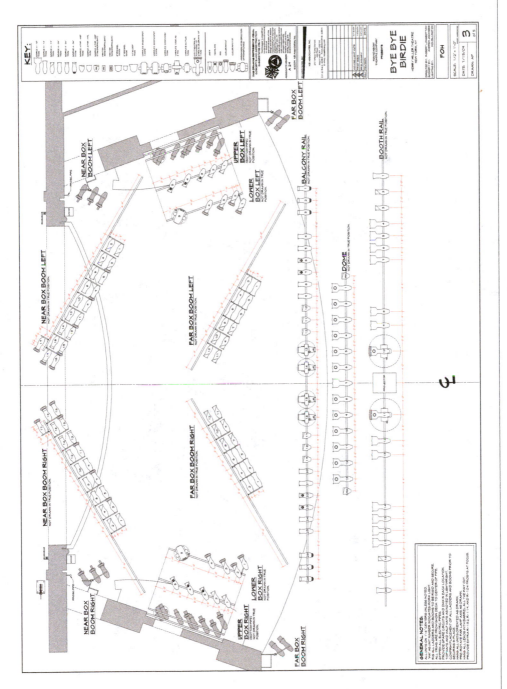

**Figure 9.1c** Bye Bye Birdie drawing package.
Lighting By: Ken Billington
ALD: Anthony Pearson

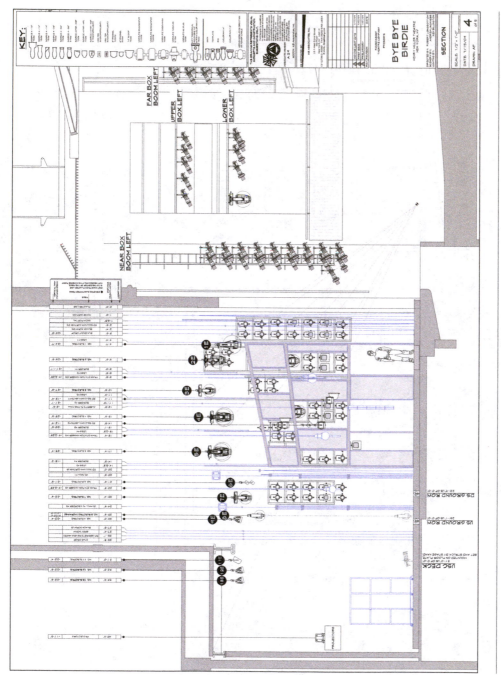

**Figure 9.1d** Bye Bye Birdie drawing package.
Lighting By: Ken Billington
ALD: Anthony Pearson

## DRAWING SET-UP

Begin a new drawing by inserting the architectural drawings of the theatre (that you updated after the site survey) into the starter file that you received from the designer. You may also use your own starter file, or **"tabula rasa"** (blank slate), that you create based on the advice in this chapter.

The next step is to contact the design associates from the other departments working on your production—sets, projection, sound, special FX, automation, etc. You will need copies of their drawings to import (and/or copy and paste) into your light plot so that you can assure the lighting is not going to conflict with any other design elements. (For example, will there be a projector at the center of the balcony rail? Or large speakers in the center of the FOH truss? If so, your designer will have to design around them or negotiate a change with the other department.) Locate exact model types for the equipment specified to verify the items are drawn to the exact dimensions. In the case of projectors, inquire further: is additional clearance required for heat restrictions, access for maintenance, or sound proofing?

After inserting all of the main elements needed, alter the drawing so that it fits into your designer's overall look and organizational framework: all items should be placed into the right classes and layers and be drawn in the correct line weights and attributes proper for its category. Move extraneous items (such as the set designer's text or dimensions) into a "hidden" class so that they are invisible but not deleted in case needed for reference later. Once all elements are properly placed, delete any unneeded classes and layers so that the drawing is completely clean before beginning the lighting. This initial drawing set-up can take several hours of your time, but getting the drawing to be clean and looking professional is worth the effort. Do not skimp on this set-up time by merely importing drawings from the other disciplines without altering them. Take the time to do it right.

Next, carefully inspect the **lineset callout** (also called the **hangplot** or **lineset schedule**), which details items flown above the stage. (See Figure 9.2.) Look for any possible conflicts between lighting and the other departments. Assure that the electrics have least 1'-0" of clearance on either side (US and DS) for fire safety reasons and to allow for proper focus. Additional room may be needed for moving lights. If there are any concerns, communicate with your lighting designer so that he can discuss these issues immediately with the applicable departments.

---

On Broadway, trim heights are typically measured from the scenic deck—not the stage floor. Scenic decks are created to hide the automation equipment used to track scenery. The stage floor is used for trims if a deck is not designed into the show.

Measurements are taken from the scenic deck to the pipe (for electrics) and to the bottom of the softgoods for borders and other masking items.

---

After examining the lineset callout, make any necessary changes and format it like your designer's standard callout. Delineate the electrics with a small dot and "working" (flying) scenery and electrics with bold borders.

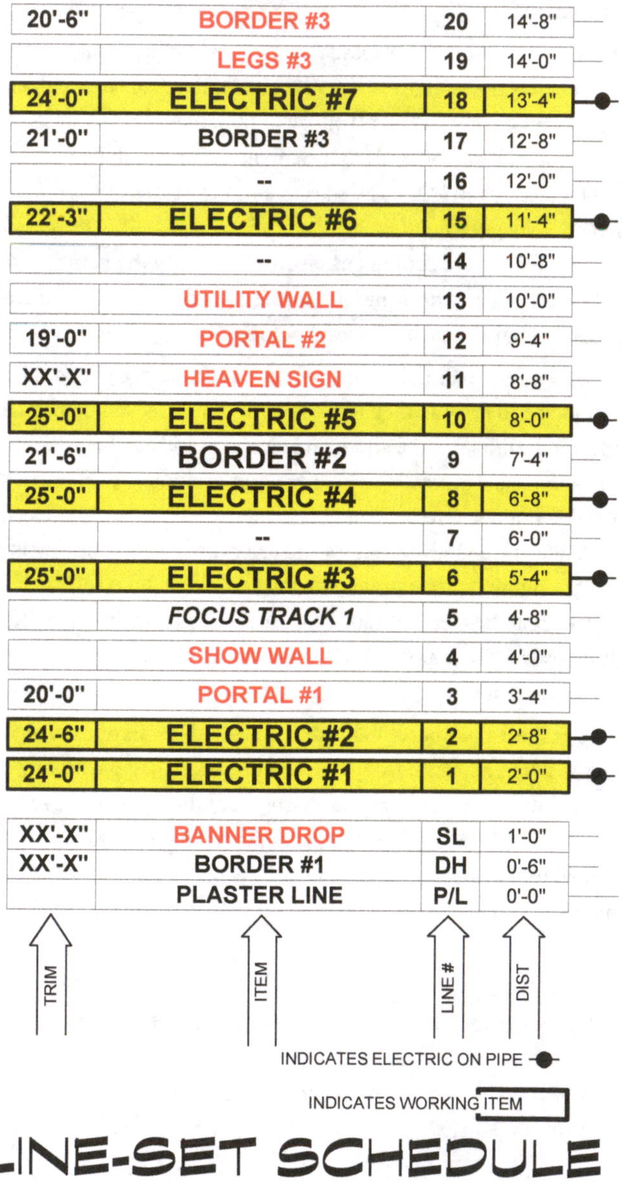

| TRIM | ITEM | LINE # | DIST |
|---|---|---|---|
| 20'-6" | BORDER #3 | 20 | 14'-8" |
|  | LEGS #3 | 19 | 14'-0" |
| 24'-0" | ELECTRIC #7 | 18 | 13'-4" |
| 21'-0" | BORDER #3 | 17 | 12'-8" |
|  | -- | 16 | 12'-0" |
| 22'-3" | ELECTRIC #6 | 15 | 11'-4" |
|  | -- | 14 | 10'-8" |
|  | UTILITY WALL | 13 | 10'-0" |
| 19'-0" | PORTAL #2 | 12 | 9'-4" |
| XX'-X" | HEAVEN SIGN | 11 | 8'-8" |
| 25'-0" | ELECTRIC #5 | 10 | 8'-0" |
| 21'-6" | BORDER #2 | 9 | 7'-4" |
| 25'-0" | ELECTRIC #4 | 8 | 6'-8" |
|  | -- | 7 | 6'-0" |
| 25'-0" | ELECTRIC #3 | 6 | 5'-4" |
|  | FOCUS TRACK 1 | 5 | 4'-8" |
|  | SHOW WALL | 4 | 4'-0" |
| 20'-0" | PORTAL #1 | 3 | 3'-4" |
| 24'-6" | ELECTRIC #2 | 2 | 2'-8" |
| 24'-0" | ELECTRIC #1 | 1 | 2'-0" |
| XX'-X" | BANNER DROP | SL | 1'-0" |
| XX'-X" | BORDER #1 | DH | 0'-6" |
|  | PLASTER LINE | P/L | 0'-0" |

INDICATES ELECTRIC ON PIPE -●-

INDICATES WORKING ITEM

# LINE-SET SCHEDULE

**Figure 9.2** Partial lineset callout.
*Courtesy of: Jared A. Sayeg*

After completing the lineset callout changes, some assistants distribute it as a separate PDF document copied from the light plot onto letter-sized paper. Sending it as a separate document allows easy discussion between parties while working through possible conflicts.

On large-scale productions, fixtures may be hung nearly anywhere to create a good design. They can be hung on the US side of working scenery and used as an electric when the scenery is flown out; hidden in troughs in the deck; hung on flying booms and ladders that move in and out throughout the show; hung on rovers (small rolling booms) that electricians place or remove when necessary; hung discreetly within hidden scenic coves; or integrated into the scenery itself. Work these complicated issues out as early as possible in the design phase.

## DRAFTING STYLES

Overall the design package needs to be neat and clear, but also artistic. You want to clearly communicate important information as well as have a sense of beauty about the drawing. (See Figures 9.3a-h for another example of a professional drawing package.)

Effective methods used to create a pleasing and professional drafting style are:

- Beautiful-looking lighting symbols
- Font choices—typically one style only and always capitalized
- Font sizes—typically three or four different sizes in total
- Line weights—typically no more than five varying line weights

In terms of clarity, some debate exists regarding how much instrument information to display on the plot. Many designers prefer to only include the instrument number and channel number so that the plot stays easy to read. Some include even less. On the contrary, other designers prefer to include nearly all the information such as color, gobo, and purpose. In the U.K. all information is included on the plot because the plot often acts as the sole document for a British production. Before beginning a new drawing with a new designer, ask her preferences on the matter.

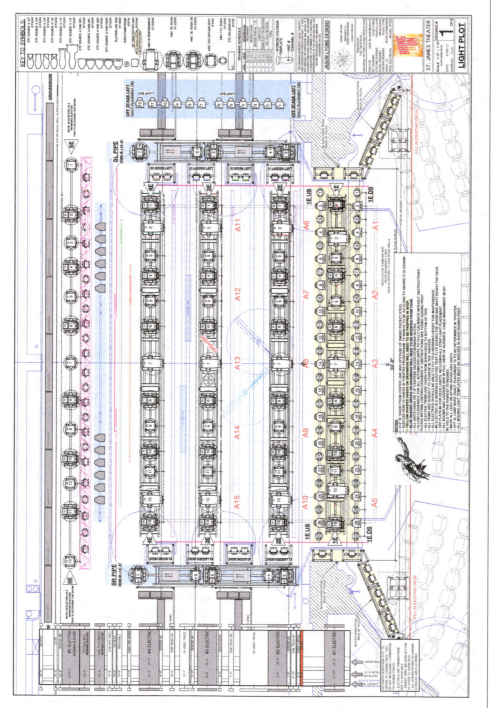

**Figure 9.3a** *Bring It On drawing package.*
*Lighting By: Jason Lyons*
*Assoc. LD: Peter Hoerburger*

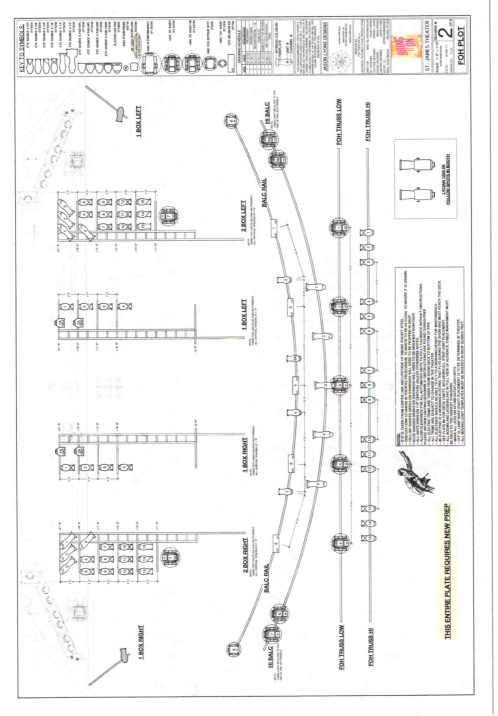
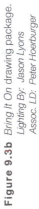

**Figure 9.3b** *Bring It On drawing package.*
*Lighting By: Jason Lyons*
*Assoc. LD: Peter Hoerburger*

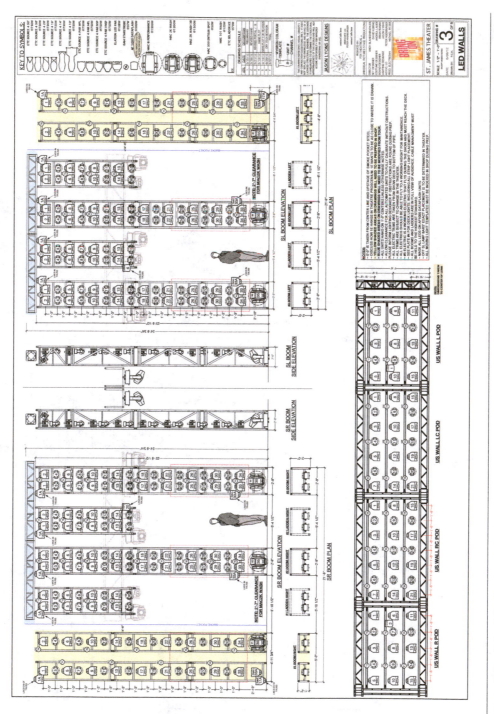

**Figure 9.3c** *Bring It On* drawing package.
*Lighting By: Jason Lyons*
*Assoc. LD: Peter Hoerburger*

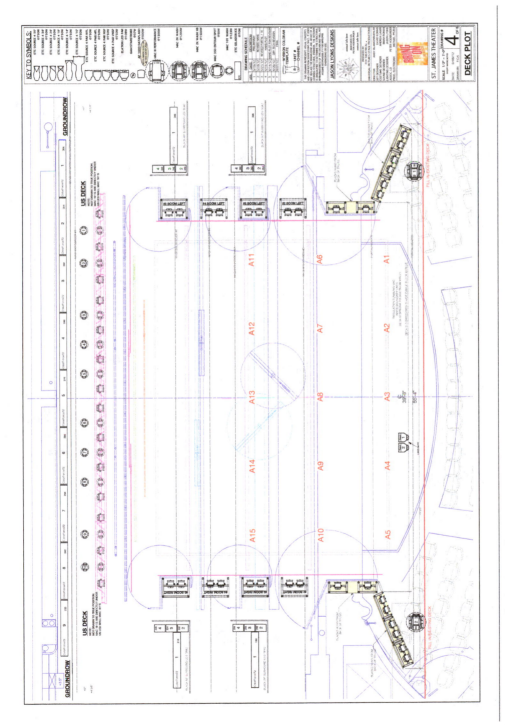

**Figure 9.3d** *Bring It On* drawing package.
*Lighting By: Jason Lyons*
*Assoc. LD: Peter Hoerburger*

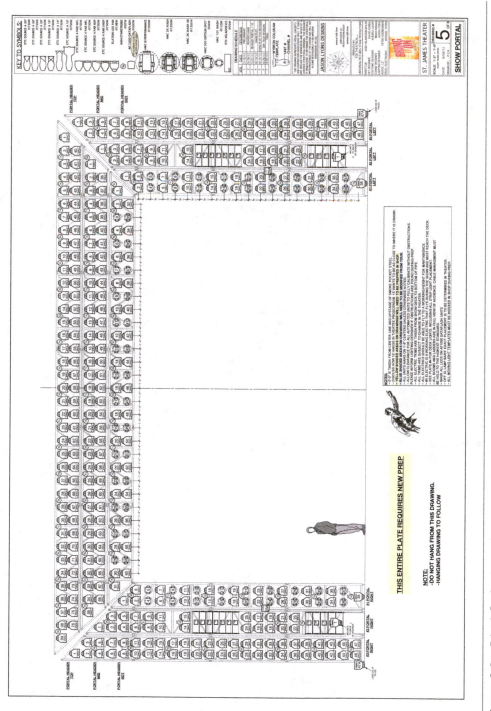

**Figure 9.3e** *Bring It On* drawing package.
*Lighting By: Jason Lyons*
*Assoc. LD: Peter Hoerburger*

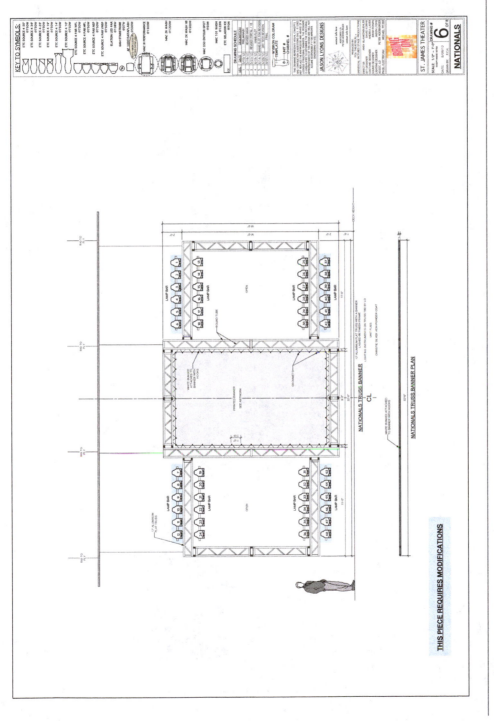

**Figure 9.3f** *Bring It On drawing package.*
*Lighting By: Jason Lyons*
*Assoc. LD: Peter Hoerburger*

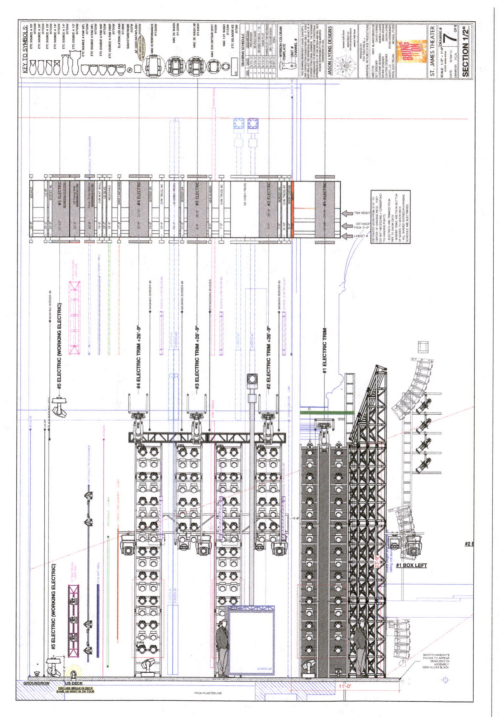

**Figure 9.3g** *Bring It On* drawing package.
*Lighting By: Jason Lyons*
*Assoc. LD: Peter Hoerburger*

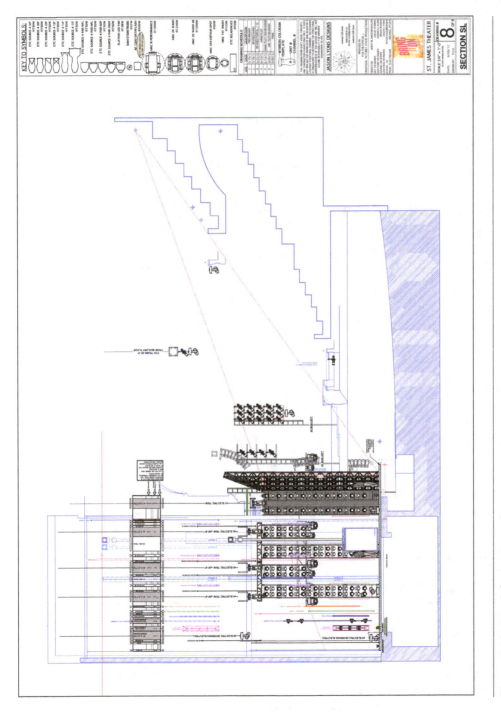

**Figure 9.3h** *Bring It On* drawing package.
*Lighting By: Jason Lyons*
*Assoc. LD: Peter Hoerburger*

## LIGHTING SYMBOLS

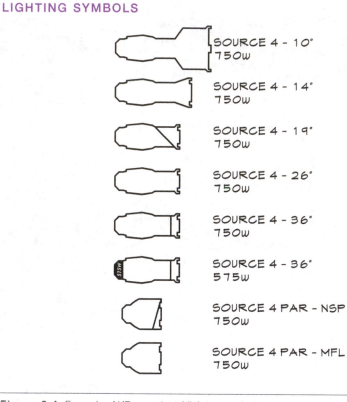

SOURCE 4 - 10°
750w

SOURCE 4 - 14°
750w

SOURCE 4 - 19°
750w

SOURCE 4 - 26°
750w

SOURCE 4 - 36°
750w

SOURCE 4 - 36°
575w

SOURCE 4 PAR - NSP
750w

SOURCE 4 PAR - MFL
750w

**Figure 9.4** Example of KB associates' lighting symbols.
*Courtesy of: KB Associates, Inc.*

Choose good-looking instrument symbols to use in your plot. Many professional design offices choose to use their own set of symbols that have been created by their assistants throughout the years (instead of the standard symbols that come with the software). (See Figure 9.4.) When working with these offices, you will be given access to their library file of symbols for use on their shows. If you need additional symbols, you can download them from the manufacturer's website, Steve Shelley's SoftSymbols™ (Figures 9.5a-b), or create your own.

**Figure 9.5a** SoftSymbols.
*Courtesy of: Steve Shelley*

If you pull a symbol from the manufacturer's website and it seems too complicated or increases your file size too much, use it to create your own symbol. Download a technical drawing in PDF form (such as a spec sheet or dimensional diagram) from the

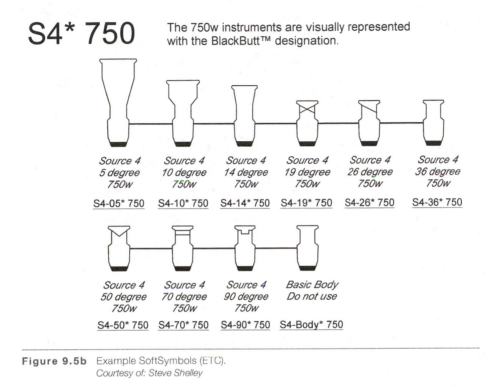

# S4* 750

The 750w instruments are visually represented with the BlackButt™ designation.

| Source 4<br>5 degree<br>750w | Source 4<br>10 degree<br>750w | Source 4<br>14 degree<br>750w | Source 4<br>19 degree<br>750w | Source 4<br>26 degree<br>750w | Source 4<br>36 degree<br>750w |
|---|---|---|---|---|---|
| S4-05* 750 | S4-10* 750 | S4-14* 750 | S4-19* 750 | S4-26* 750 | S4-36* 750 |

| Source 4<br>50 degree<br>750w | Source 4<br>70 degree<br>750w | Source 4<br>90 degree<br>750w | Basic Body<br>Do not use |
|---|---|---|---|
| S4-50* 750 | S4-70* 750 | S4-90* 750 | S4-Body* 750 |

**Figure 9.5b**  Example SoftSymbols (ETC).
*Courtesy of: Steve Shelley*

manufacturer's website. You can then (in a separate file from your light plot) import the PDF, trace that diagram in a separate layer, set your preferred line weights, and create a new symbol using your tracing.

## SYMBOL PLACEMENT

When placing your lighting symbols into your plot, align them to face US, DS, SR, or SL only. (See Figure 9.8.) Even if the instrument focuses 45 degrees in one direction, insert it closest to the angle it will face. This technique keeps the plot neat and clean looking and gives the production electrician a quick way to communicate the prefocus of the fixtures to his crew.

> A good production electrician will **"prefocus"** all fixtures during hang to help expedite the focus process. Prefocus means pointing the fixture roughly in the direction it is drawn on the plot.

In directional fixtures, insert arrow symbols to indicate the direction the unit should face (striplights) and to indicate the predetermined bottle direction (PARs). (See Figure 9.6.) These small details aid in prefocus and, therefore, streamline the focus process in general.

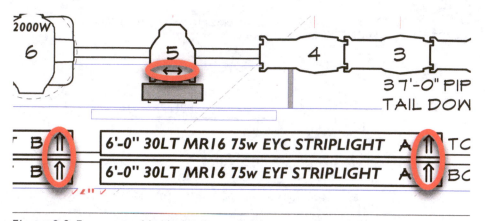

**Figure 9.6**  Focus arrows & bottle direction symbols.
*Courtesy of: KB Associates, Inc.*

Also, use arrows on moving light symbols to indicate the orientation of the fixture as hung on the electric (see Figure 9.7). (Ask your programmer and production electrician their preference.) The arrow usually indicates the direction of the cable as it leaves the fixture and may be different for each fixture type in your plot. Hanging the fixtures all in the same orientation not only allows for easier programming, but may also turn the function display menus US and away from the audience's view.

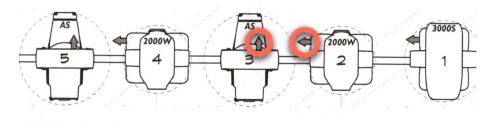

**Figure 9.7**  Moving light symbols with arrows.
*Courtesy of: KB Associates, Inc.*

Moving light fixture orientation becomes extremely critical when touring or replicating a production. Orienting the fixtures the same direction as the original production avoids the need for additional programming and focusing time to correct an incorrect physical orientation.

## DIMENSIONING

Place your instruments at regular intervals and dimension the distance between the centers of each fixture (see Figure 9.8). Begin at centerline and dimension outwardly across the electric. Stop at the last fixture—no need to dimension all the way to the end of the pipe or to the wall of the building unless for a specific purpose.

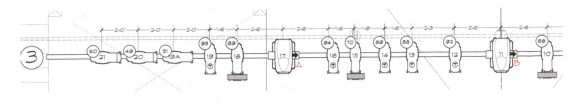

**Figure 9.8** *Pacific Overtures* excerpt showing correct instrument orientation and dimensioning.
*Lighting By: Brian MacDevitt*
*Assoc. LD: Anne E. McMills*

Correct instrument spacing is necessary to developing a light plot that can be successfully focused in real-world conditions. The standard spacing for conventionals facing US or DS is 1'-6" (or 18") **"on center"**—meaning from c-clamp to c-clamp. No two fixtures should be closer than 1'-6" on center or you run the risk of the fixtures' physical bodies conflicting during focus. The exception: two fixtures can be hung on 1'-0" centers if the two fixtures have the same exact focus (such as two front lights focused to the same area in different colors). Standard spacing for conventional sidelights facing SR or SL is 2'-0" on center.

For moving lights, specifically moving head fixtures, leave enough room for the head to be able to swivel completely in all directions. A safe bet is to leave 3'-0" of total clearance around the fixture (1'-6" on either side from center). Also account for added accessories to your moving lights such as top hats or spill rings. If you need to place moving lights in a particularly tight space, consult your programmer and production electrician.

For booms, ladders, and other verticals, 2'-0" vertical spacing is standard between conventionals hung on sidearms. For moving lights, vertical space depends on the overall fixture height. Check the manufacturer's specifications to assure there is enough total clearance for the moving head to hang straight down safely.

When placing fixtures on the electrics, space them apart using only round, sensible increments of no less than 0'-3". For example, do not place instruments 4'-2 ½" apart. This sort of number makes sense for, say, a scenic designer whose drawings need to be extremely exact, but for a lighting designer it is impractical. An inch or two will not have a significant impact on your fixture's focus so nudge the instruments on the drawing to the closest round number available and dimension accordingly. Use increments of 0'-0", 0'-3", 0'-6", or 0'-9" only.

Also note that dimensions in the U.S. should be written using a dash symbol between the feet and inches (i.e. 1'-0", 2'-6", 3'-9", and so on). This dash helps delineate more clearly between the feet and the inches—assuring that, for example, 1'-0" does not get mistaken for 10".

## FONT CHOICES

Limit your use of fonts to one style of font only: a standard version and a bold version.

If the designer does not have a favorite font, choose one that is a hand-drafted style. Some Broadway favorites include: Graphite Light, Heavy Hand, Mr. Hand, and City Blueprint. (See Figure 9.9.) Type all text in capital letters to retain the hand-drafted look.

# GRAPHITE LIGHT
# MR HAND
# HEAVY HAND
# CITY BLUEPRINT

**Figure 9.9** Hand-drafted style fonts.

The only place that a different font should be used is within the show logo. The logo should be imported into the title block fully intact without any worry about the font used.

> *"I like to use the same fonts on all my paperwork so it looks like a 'set' of paperwork not just a plot, Lightwright, and spot sheets, etc."*
>
> —*Justin A. Partier*

## FONT SIZES

Use no more than three or four font sizes throughout the entire drawing package. Use one main size font for the majority of the items, and larger or smaller sizes for specific items. Be consistent. (See Figures 9.10a-b.)

Example font size guidelines by category:
- Plate title ("Light Plot," "Section," etc.)—36 point in bold typeface
- Lighting position labels ("#1 Electric")—18 point in bold typeface
- Instrument #s, channel #s, and notes—12 point
- Dimensions—6 or 8 point

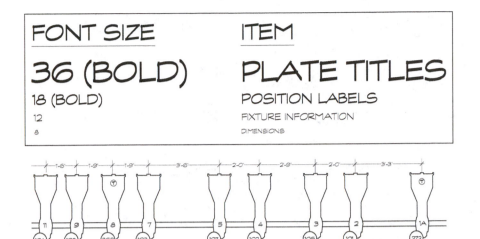

**FONT SIZE**

**36 (BOLD)**

18 (BOLD)

12

8

**ITEM**

**PLATE TITLES**

POSITION LABELS

FIXTURE INFORMATION

DIMENSIONS

BOOTH PIPE

NOT SHOWN IN ACTUAL POSITION

**Figure 9.10a–b**  Sample font size guidelines.

## LINE WEIGHTS

Use consistent line weights to make your plot look professional.

> *The most important thing to remember when creating a professional-looking light plot is "line weight!! I want to see immediately what information is the most important on the drawing."*
>
> —*Vivien Leone*

Break your drawing items down into 3 to 5 main line weight categories and be consistent. Here is one example of a successful way to manage line weights (shown in mils):

- 40 = title block and border
- 25 = architectural walls (hatched)
- 15 = all lighting fixtures, lighting positions, and centerline
- 7 = scenic groundplan (in a medium grey) or scenic details on the section (in black)
- 1 = dimension lines

| ITEM | LINE WEIGHT | |
|---|---|---|
| TITLE BLOCK & BORDER | 40 MILS | ▬▬▬▬▬ |
| ARCHITECTURAL WALLS | 25 MILS | ▬▬▬▬ |
| LIGHTING FIXTURES & CENTERLINE | 15 MILS | ─────── |
| GROUNDPLAN (GREYED OUT) | 7 MILS | ─────── |
| DIMENSION LINES | 1 MILS | ─────── |

**Figure 9.11**    Sample line weight guidelines.

**Line weights** (how heavy the lines are drawn) direct focus to the items that are most important. At first it may be easy to think of a drafting as just a bunch of lines on a page, but actually every drawing tells a story—after all it's called a light "plot." If you think of it that way, it makes creating the light plot a more artistic experience and result.

For example, think of a light plot as having characters just as a play does. The main characters, our protagonists in the story of our light plot, are the lights; the supporting characters are the set pieces. The antagonists in our story—or the objects that cannot be avoided and block our main character's progress—are items such as the architecture and the title block and border. Thinking of the plot in this manner helps translate these items into line weights—our main characters get dark and prominent lines so they stand out among the crowd; our supporting characters get lighter and grayed-out lines so they don't upstage our protagonists; and our antagonists get very thick and dark lines to block the way of our protagonists. (See Figure 9.11.)

## DRAWING ORGANIZATION

Symbols, fonts, sizes, and line weights are the key to a beautiful-looking light plot and drawing package. It is what produces a professional end-result. However, it is the properly *organized* plot that further elevates a beautiful light plot to professional-grade. Pay attention to detail and make sure every object is created in its proper class and layer. The more organized your plot, the easier it is for others to work with.

Every designer and design office will have a different set-up regarding layers, classes, and so forth. If receiving a starter file from the designer's office, these defaults should be provided. However, if you are starting from scratch, see Figures 9.12 a-b for one way to organize your drawings.

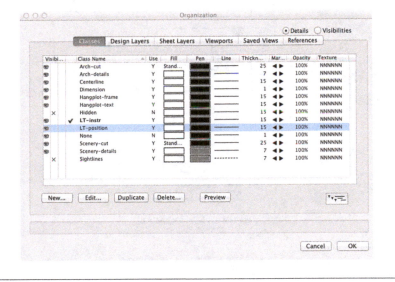

**Figure 9.12a–b** Example layer and class organization—Vectorworks.

Shortened layer and class names can help you be concise. For example, "Arch" can be used for "architecture" and "LT" for lighting. Group like items together using a dash, such as LT-instr and LT-pos for "lighting instrumentation" and "lighting position."

## TITLE BLOCK

**Title blocks** run along the right-hand side of the page and contain all of the basic information regarding the show, the plot, and the designer. The main information—show name, logo, location, theatre name, date, scale, etc.—should appear in the lower right-hand corner of the drawing. See Figure 9.13 for an example of a professional title block.

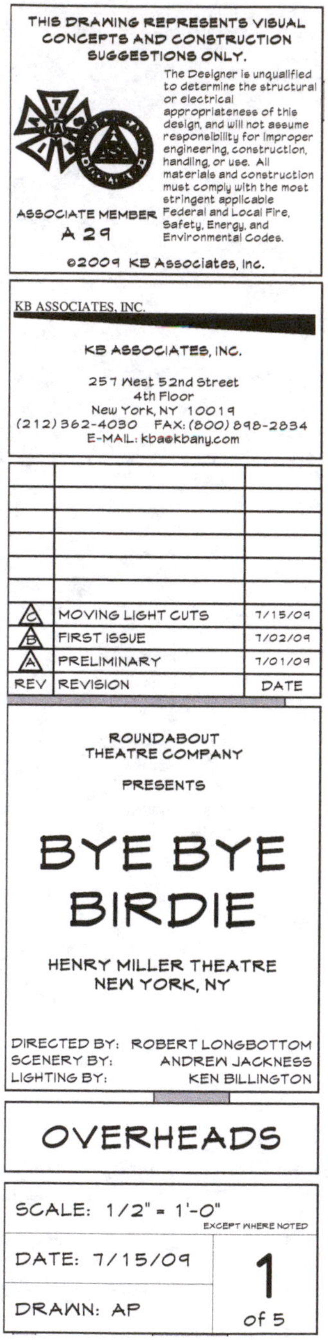

THIS DRAWING REPRESENTS VISUAL
CONCEPTS AND CONSTRUCTION
SUGGESTIONS ONLY.

The Designer is unqualified to determine the structural or electrical appropriateness of this design, and will not assume responsibility for improper engineering, construction, handling, or use. All materials and construction must comply with the most stringent applicable Federal and Local Fire, Safety, Energy, and Environmental Codes.

ASSOCIATE MEMBER
A 29

©2009 KB Associates, Inc.

KB ASSOCIATES, INC.

KB ASSOCIATES, INC.

257 West 52nd Street
4th Floor
New York, NY 10019
(212) 362-4030   FAX: (800) 898-2834
E-MAIL: kba@kbany.com

| | | |
|---|---|---|
| | | |
| | | |
| | | |
| | | |
| | | |
| ⬡C | MOVING LIGHT CUTS | 7/15/09 |
| ⬡B | FIRST ISSUE | 7/02/09 |
| ⬡A | PRELIMINARY | 7/01/09 |
| REV | REVISION | DATE |

ROUNDABOUT
THEATRE COMPANY

PRESENTS

# BYE BYE BIRDIE

HENRY MILLER THEATRE
NEW YORK, NY

DIRECTED BY:  ROBERT LONGBOTTOM
SCENERY BY:       ANDREW JACKNESS
LIGHTING BY:       KEN BILLINGTON

## OVERHEADS

SCALE: 1/2" = 1'-0"
EXCEPT WHERE NOTED

DATE: 7/15/09

DRAWN: AP

1
of 5

**Figure 9.13**  Example title block.
*Courtesy of: KB Associates, Inc.*

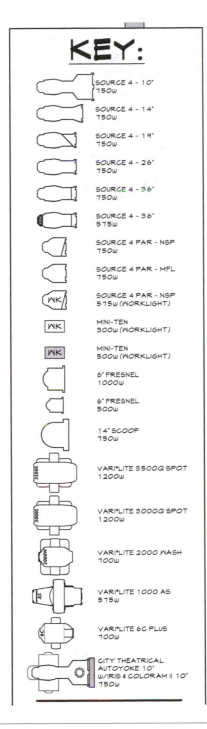

**Figure 9.14** Example lighting key.
*Courtesy of: KB Associates, Inc.*

Title blocks also include the **lighting key** and the **lighting legend**. The key shows all the fixtures and their wattages used on the plot, and the legend shows every accessory. Tailor each of these items specifically to your show instead of using a stock symbol. See Figures 9.14 and 9.15 a-c for examples of a professional-style key and legends.

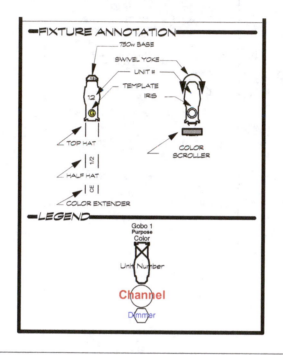

**Figure 9.15a**  Example lighting legend.
*Courtesy of: Jared A. Sayeg*

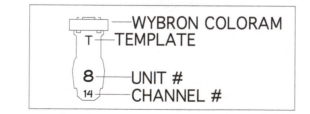

**Figure 9.15b**  Example lighting legend.
*Courtesy of: Jason Lyons*

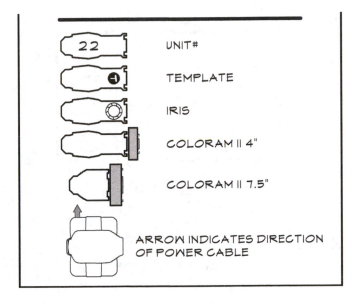

**Figure 9.15c**   Example lighting legend.
*Courtesy of: KB Associates, Inc.*

The title block should also be connected to a full border that surrounds the entire drawing in a very dark line weight (i.e. 40 mils). A border visually delineates the scope of the project.

A standard lighting title block should include the following information:

- Show information:
  - Show logo
  - Theatre name and city
- Technical information about the drawing:
  - Title of drawing, or plate title—i.e. "Light Plot," "Section," etc.
  - Scale
  - Date
  - Drawn by
  - Drawing # of #
  - Drawing schedule—version, date, description—i.e. "Rev1," "08-16-12," "Revision #1" (See Figure 9.16.)

| | | |
|---|---|---|
| F | FINAL | 12/3/10 |
| E | REVISION #3 | DATE |
| D | REVISION #2 | DATE |
| C | REVISION #1 | DATE |
| B | LOAD-IN | 11/16/10 |
| A | PRELIMINARY | 11/8/10 |
| REV | REVISION | DATE |

**Figure 9.16** Sample drawing schedule.
*Courtesy of: Jared A. Sayeg*

- Personnel information:
  - Produced by:
  - Director, set designer, costume designer, lighting designer
  - Production electrician
  - Production manager or technical director
- Lighting designer's information:
  - Lighting designer's name, phone number, email, etc.
  - USA "bug" (logo) with designer's USA number and signature, if applicable
- Legal disclaimer (see below)
- Legend
- Key
- General notes—optional—sometimes shown in separate box within drawing

The purpose of a legal disclaimer in your light plot is to help cover the lighting designer in case of any accident, injury, or emergency that happens onstage. Although this information does not replace actual legal counsel, here is one example of a disclaimer:

"This drawing represents visual concepts and construction suggestions only. It does not replace the knowledge and advice of a licensed structural engineer. The designer is unqualified to determine the structural or electrical appropriateness of this design, and will not assume responsibility for improper engineering, construction, handling, or use. All materials and construction must comply with the most stringent applicable federal and local fire, safety, energy, and environmental codes."[2]

## GENERAL NOTES

**General notes** are notes that apply to the drawing as a whole. There are no concrete standards on what needs to be included. If there are unusual circumstances for the hang that need special explanation, general notes can help to clarify the situation.

Some common general notes are[3]:

- All units hang on 1'-6" centers unless otherwise noted.
- Provide spare circuits and DMX at all locations.
- Discuss all units mounted on scenery with designer.
- Hang all units and pre-rotate PAR axes in orientation as shown.
- Note clearances for all automated units.
- All electric trims are taken from show deck to pipe.
- All border trims are from show deck to bottom of goods.
- All trims are subject to change in the theatre.
- Boom measurements are taken to the boom pipe, not the instruments.
- Confirm placement of all ladders and booms on site with designer prior to securing in place.
- All booms and ladders to be rigid and secure.
- Stiffen all electric pipes.
- Barrels with R-132 should be run sharp before adding the frost.
- Hang all Fresnels with lamp at full spot.
- Provide extra R-132, R-119, R-104, and other frosts during focus.

## VERTICALS

Locate vertical lighting positions, such as boom, ladder, and rover placements, on your light plot by placing a footprint (a shaded or hatched plan view) of the boom and its highest instruments in its actual location. Include the orientation of the instruments and any hardware used, such as sidearms. After placing the footprint, label it clearly with its position name and coordinates measured from centerline and 0'-0" DS. (See Figure 9.17.) All other information regarding the verticals should appear in elevation on the Booms & Ladders drawing.

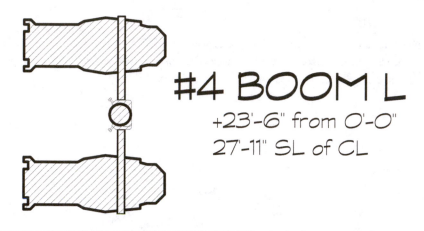

**#4 BOOM L**
+23'-6" from 0'-0"
27'-11" SL of CL

**Figure 9.17**    Boom footprint.

## SECTION

The purpose of the **centerline section** is to be a working drawing for the lighting designer when determining photometrics as well as an accurate side-view picture of the theatre during the production.

Accurately portray all fixtures as best you can with proper trims, yoking, spacing, and placements—including set, floor mounts, and all verticals. Use lighting section symbols and elevation symbols (Figure 9.18) when displaying the fixtures and include accessories such as top hats, barndoors, sidearms, c-clamps, and other items that take up physical space. Ensure that your symbols for all equipment are scaled properly, and verify correct dimensions of auxiliary equipment such as foggers and hazers. Being as accurate as possible will help determine appropriate clearances needed for working scenery and actor entrances to help anticipate any future issues.

## SET ELEX

**Set Elex**, or "elecs" or "electrics," also called the **Set Practicals** plate in the drawing package, requires a lot of intricate information to adequately communicate the design intent. (See Figure 9.19.) This may include technical details, such as lamp type, lamp specification (or "spec"), lamp spacing, wattage, manufacturer, etc. Work directly with your production electrician and arrange mock-ups with your designer to test the equipment before committing the design ideas to paper.

> *"Technically, the most challenging and interesting situation is any show with a lot of set electrics because that adds another layer of coordination between the lighting designer, director, set designer, scenic shop, etc."*
>
> —*Vivien Leone*[4]

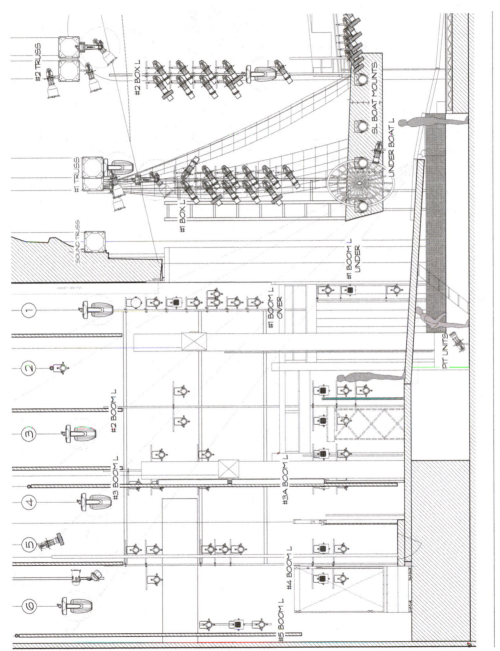

**Figure 9.18** *Pacific Overtures section (close-up).*
*Lighting By: Brian MacDevitt*
*Assoc. LD: Anne E. McMills*

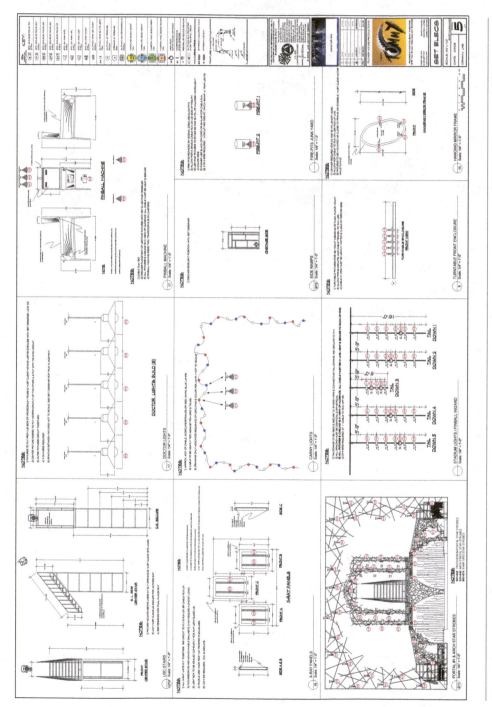

**Figure 9.19** *Tommy* set electrics.
*Lighting By: Jared A. Sayeg*

## PRINT SIZES

Once the drawings are complete, ask another assistant to double-check your work against the supporting paperwork before printing. When ready, print the number of copies the production electrician asks for and one full set for the lighting team. If your designer does not have a plotter to print full-size drawings, find a local reprographics, print shop, or office supply store that can print large format. Black and white printing (which is less expensive) is usually fine for most plots, although some designers prefer to use color.

Typical light plots are drawn in 1/2" = 1'-0" or 1/4" = 1'-0" scale imperial (1:25 or 1:50 in metric). Determine which scale best fits your drawing on the paper size you wish to use. In the U.S., most lighting drawings are printed on "**ARCH D**" size paper (24" × 36") and occasionally "**ARCH E**" (36" × 48") for larger venues. In metrically based countries the most common paper size used is "A1" (59.4cm × 84.1cm) with the occasional use of the larger size "A0" (84.1cm × 118.9cm).

## METRIC

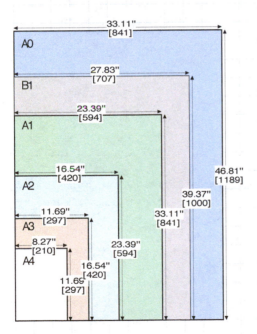

The metric "A" series is based upon an A0 sheet being one square metre in area. Although the B1 sheet is in the "B" series, it has come to be commonly accepted.

## ARCHITECTURAL

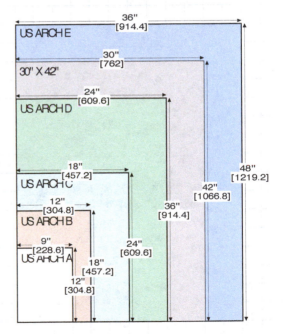

Architectural sheet sizes are based upon a 36" x 48" sheet, and proportionally smaller sizes. In addition to the above, the 24" x 42" sheet size is commonly accepted as a standard size.

**Figure 9.20** Standard paper sizes.
*Courtesy of: WMW Reprographics Ltd.*

## FOLDING DRAWINGS

Once drawings are printed, they should be folded, unless your designer and/or production electrician prefer them to be rolled. Folded copies allow your drawings to be easily carried and stored in the show bible. (If rolling drawings, roll them printed side out so they lay flat when unrolled. Assure that the title block information is displayed on the outside of the roll.)

Follow these instructions to properly fold a drawing:

1. Fold both short sides to each other, with the drawing inside.
2. Fold both short sides back again towards the centerline fold.
3. Fold horizontally to display the title block on the front of the folded drawing.[5]

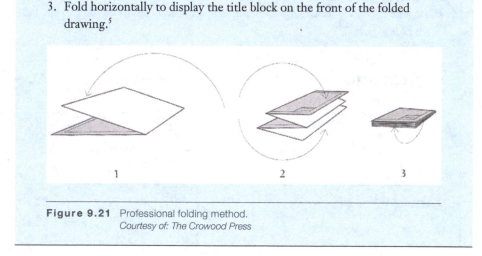

**Figure 9.21** Professional folding method.
*Courtesy of: The Crowood Press*

Step 3 (above) can also be altered by folding the drawings in thirds or quarters (instead of in half) to better fit in a binder. Since the major title block information falls in the lower right-hand corner of the drawing, it will form a basic cover page showing the logo, designer's name, and other essential information directly on top when folded.

# PAPERWORK

Although the term **"paperwork"** often refers to the overall design package, it is also used specifically to mean the organizational lighting documentation—namely the instrument schedule, channel hookup, etc.

In the U.S., Lightwright is used as the industry standard for the creation of this paperwork. In the U.K. and other countries, often the plot acts as the sole source of information on a show and paperwork may not be used. (In fact, if paperwork is used, some theatres in Europe still prefer it to be handwritten.) This section will focus mainly on paperwork creation in Lightwright. Nevertheless, many of the concepts are universal no matter what method you choose.

Lightwright is a powerful tool to use as an assistant and one of the most important. Following the tips listed in this section is only the beginning. Other features include tools such as gobo and color wheel set-up for moving lights and live inventory counts. Lightwright will help you to keep all of your information neat, clean, and organized—a sure sign of a professional assistant.

Data is exchanged between Vectorworks and Lightwright by using the automatic data exchange feature. After completing the initial work on the plot and paperwork, begin to clean-up the Lightwright file to assure that your naming conventions are consistent throughout the document. A simple way to do this is by using the maintenance menu. (Consult www.mckernon. com for questions regarding the following procedures.)

## MAINTENANCE

Maintenance is a great way to stay organized. It helps you to check for consistency, delete unused items, and delineate in what order items are shown and printed. By using the maintenance menus, revising information results in convenient global changes.

Once the maintenance menus are organized (as discussed below), remember to "remove all unused." This function keeps your list organized by displaying only the items in use within the production.

- **Purpose:** Capitalize and alphabetize your purposes. Capitalization gives the paperwork a sense of "drafting hand" like the fonts used on the plot. Alphabetization makes searching more efficient. Confirm that purposes with "like" titles are named so that the common

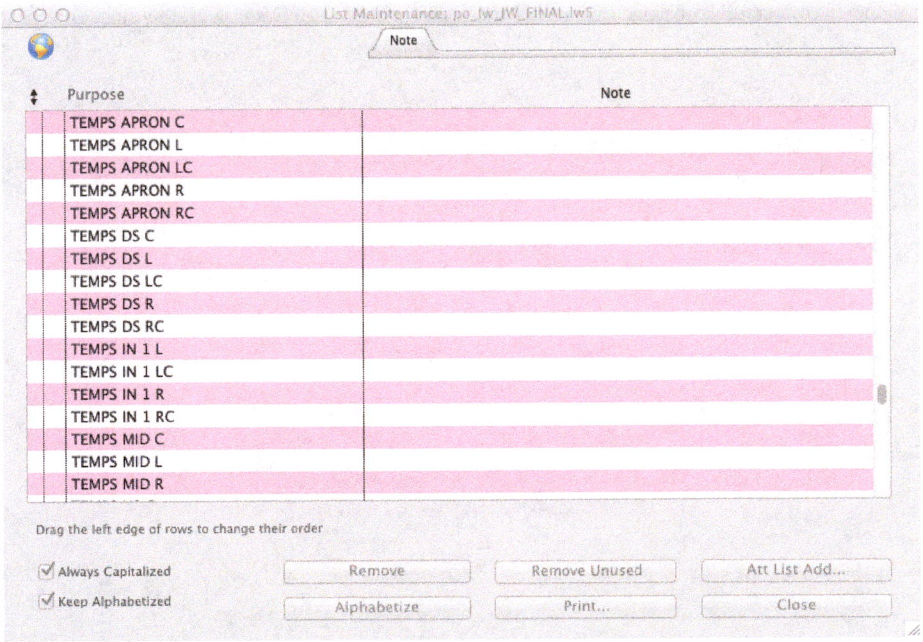

**Figure 9.22** Lightwright maintenance: purpose.

term is the first word in the purpose. For example, a DR apron special and a DL apron special should be named as follows: APR SPEC L and APR SPEC R (as opposed to naming them R APR SPEC and L APR SPEC). Naming these items correctly alphabetizes them next to each other—making searching easier. (See Figure 9.22.)

- **Position:** Position should be capitalized, if desired, but not be alphabetized. Instead, order the positions in a logical fashion. One common method is to order the positions from DS to US and from top to bottom. For example: start with FOH (beginning with the furthest DS, including box booms); then overhead electrics (from DS to US); booms and ladders next (from DS to US); floor fixtures and groundrow (from DS to US); set practicals and mounts; and, finally, miscellaneous items such as atmospherics (foggers/hazers), fans, etc. Group "like" positions together so that #2 Boom R is followed by #2 Boom L, and be consistent when alternating between left and right. (See Figure 9.23.)

  In addition, when naming positions always place the numbered part of the name (#1, #2, #3 or 1st, 2nd, 3rd) on the front of the name and the stage directions (L or R) on the end, i.e., #1 Box Boom R or 2nd Electric (as opposed to Box Boom R #1 or Electric #2). Using this convention avoids confusion when addressing the instrument number. For example, if you are discussing the 5th instrument on the 3rd Box Boom on SR the instrument would be identified as #3 Box Boom R #5. It would be too confusing to call it Box Boom R #3 #5.

- **Instrument Type:** Like position, capitalization for instrument type is a preference, and alphabetization should not be used. Instead, move similar fixture types together and order them from smallest beamspread to largest. (See Figure 9.24.) Begin with the most common

**Figure 9.23** Lightwright maintenance: position.

fixture type used in the plot, such as Source 4s, and continue through various main fixtures types ending with miscellaneous items, such as set practicals. Also, assign categories (such as Light, Moving Light, or practical) to your fixtures, designate attributes (such as Pan, Tilt, and Color) if applicable, and add in any stock equipment from which you may be working. Furthermore, allocate which fixtures should and should not be displayed in the focus charts. (Items such as practicals and moving lights are not conventionally focused, and, therefore, should not be shown as a focusable item.)

One possible example of an instrument type ordering system:

- Conventional ellipsoidals such as ETC Source 4s from lowest degree to highest degree
- PARcans or Source 4 PARs (from VNSP to VWFL)
- LED fixtures (ellipsoidals then wash fixtures)
- Striplights
- Effects items, such as strobes
- Moving lights (spot then wash)
- Miscellaneous, such as star curtains, etc.
- Scrollers and other devices
- Practicals

**Figure 9.24** Lightwright maintenance: instrument type.

Additionally within instrument type, verify that you have used consistent and concise naming conventions for your fixtures, such as ETC S4 19 or S4-19. Using full names, such as spelling out "Source Four" in this case, will result in lengthy wrapped columns when printed and produce an inefficient and unwieldy paperwork package. Include enough information so that the fixture is unmistakable, but be concise enough to save space. (Please note, some information may be extracted from Vectorworks' light info record attached to each symbol. Keep those naming conventions concise, if needed.) Collapse any duplicate entries that may contain additional spaces or wrong characters.

On a related note, accessory names should also be shortened. Some examples are: Barndoor as BD, template (or gobo) holder as Temp, top hat as TH, and halfhat as HH. When using data exchange, Lightwright displays the symbol name—not the light info record information—for static accessories from Vectorworks. Therefore, to keep your accessories' names concise, you must change their symbol name in Vectorworks.

- **Color and gobo:** Begin by alphabetizing the color and gobo maintenance categories, and then drag the items into numerical order if needed. Ensure that "like" groupings are listed together, such as Rosco and LEE, and that your most prominently used company for the production is listed first—e.g., if most of your color is Rosco, drag these colors to the top of the list. (See Figure 9.25.) For color, simply the color number, such as R02, is sufficient. For gobos, however, write the number as well as the name to avoid any ordering mistakes. For example, Rosco's 77806 Leaf Breakup Large might be written as: R77806: Leaf Brkup Lrg. This prevents any typos in the number resulting in

**Figure 9.25**  Lightwright maintenance: color.

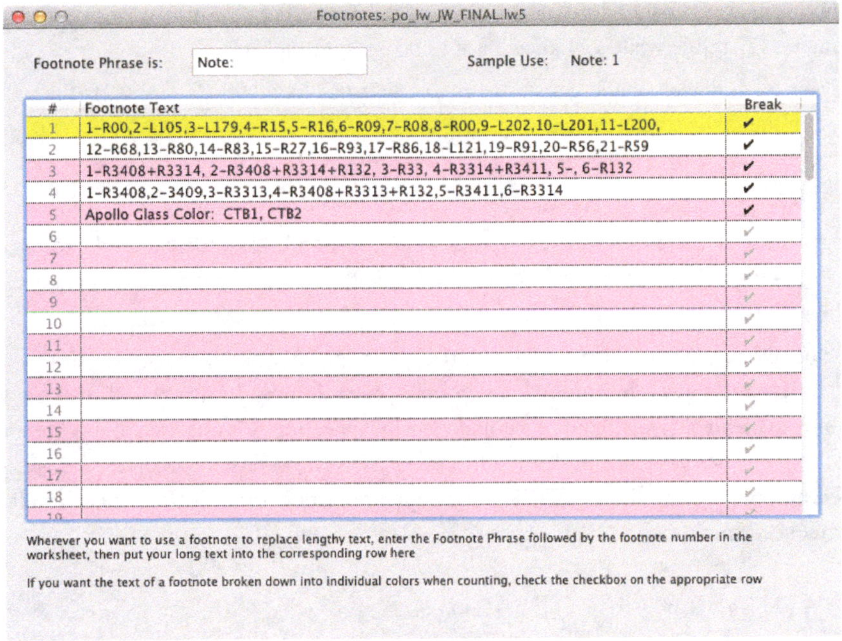

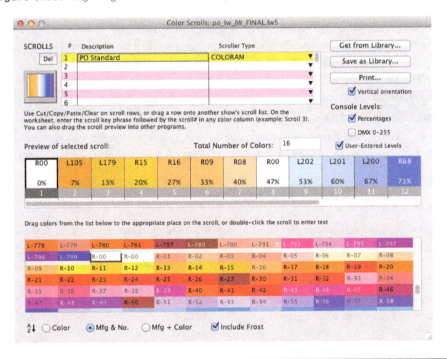

**Figure 9.26a**   Lightwright footnotes screenshot.

**Figure 9.26b**   Lightwright color scroll screenshot.

the unexpected cost of ordering a full set of the wrong gobos. Shorten the name as much as possible while still allowing it to be easily deciphered.

Color for followspots and gel strings can be listed as footnotes (Figure 9.26a) or called out in the color scrolls feature (Figure 9.26b).

## LAYOUT

Using a neat layout in Lightwright makes your paperwork easy to read and professional looking. If the design office does not provide you with a Lightwright layout template, create your own.

Under the layout tab, construct columns that group the information in logical pairings, such as "instr type & watts," "position & unit #," and "color & gobo." Add vertical lines between columns to create a layout that is clear and visually appealing. Also be sure to use the proper font that your design office prefers. Gill Sans or Helvetica are good choices if there is no preference. See Figures 9.27 and 9.28 for examples of layouts for an instrument schedule and channel hookup.

## SHOW TITLE AND PAGE HEADER

Under the set-up menu, access the show title and page header option. Enter the necessary show information in this window. See Figure 9.29a for a sample header layout and the information that is ideal to include.

When you have finished entering the information, use the layout tab to format it. Ensure that none of the information overlaps. Lightwright places the date automatically, as well as the paperwork title (such as "Instrument Schedule" or "Channel Hookup"), but these items can be shifted within the layout if desired. (See Figure 9.29b.) The contact phone number listed should be the main associate's number (used in case any questions arise from others).

Also, access the options under the layout menu. Check the box "long headers only on pg. 1." This will show all the show title and page header information only on the first page and short headers on the subsequent pages. When printed, it can save a lot of paper (and trees!) in the long run.

## REGISTRATION

Registration information can be found in the Lightwright preferences menu and should always be considered before printing. Lightwright can store up to five different registrations. This allows you to store not only your own registration information, but also information for the designer or designers with whom you are currently working. Ensure that the correct registration is selected for the production's designer before printing so that the correct name appears on the bottom of each page.

**LIGHTING BY HUGH VANSTONE**
ASSOCIATE LD: PHILIP ROSENBERG

SHUBERT THEATRE: NEW YORK
PROD. ELECTRICIAN: MIKE LOBUE

**Note: This printout does not show atttributes attached to units**

| Unit | Chn | Dimmer | CktN | C# | Type, Accessories, Watts | Color & Template | Purpose |
|---|---|---|---|---|---|---|---|
| **BOOTH** | | | | | | | |
| 1 | | | | | LYCIAN 1290 2kw | Note 1 + L206 | FOLLOWSPOT 3 |
| 2 | | | | | LYCIAN 1290 2kw | Note 1 + L206 | FOLLOWSPOT 1 |
| 3 | | | | | LYCIAN 1290 2kw | Note 1 + L206 | FOLLOWSPOT 2 |
| **SPOT PLAT SL** | | | | | | | |
| 1 | (440) | H1/193 | R1A | 5 | 26°S4 750w | | CONFETTI |
| 2 | (440) | H1/193 | R1A | 6 | 36°S4 750w | | CONFETTI |
| 3 | (440) | H1/193 | R1A | 5 | 26°S4 750w | | CONFETTI |
| **SPOT PLAT SR** | | | | | | | |
| 1 | (440) | H1/194 | R1B | 5 | 26°S4 750w | | CONFETTI |
| 2 | (440) | H1/194 | R1B | 6 | 36°S4 750w | | CONFETTI |
| 3 | (440) | H1/194 | R1B | 5 | 26°S4 750w | | CONFETTI |
| **2BBL** | | | | | | | |
| 1 | (208) | H1/1 | PS-01 | 1 | RAM 10°w/TH 10w | Note 2, HS | CC BXBM |
| 1 | (208) | H1/102 | R1A | 2 | 10°S4w/10"CC 750w | R132 | BXBM CC<L |
| 2 | (208) | H1/2 | PS-01 | 2 | RAM 10°w/TH 10w | Note 2, HS | CC BXBM |
| 2 | (208) | H1/102 | R1A | 2 | 10°S4w/10"CC 750w | R132 | BXBM CC<L |
| 3 | (202) | H1/103 | R1A | 3 | 19°S4w/TH 750w | L201 | BXBM<L 201 |
| 4 | (202) | H1/103 | R1A | 3 | 19°S4w/TH 750w | L201 | BXBM<L 201 |
| 5 | (204) | H1/104 | R1A | 4 | 19°S4w/TH 750w | CLR | BXBM<L CLR |
| 6 | (204) | H1/104 | R1A | 4 | 19°S4w/TH 750w | CLR | BXBM<L CLR |
| 7 | (206) | H1/105 | R1B | 1 | 19°S4w/TH 750w | L143 | BXBM<L 143 |
| 8 | (206) | H1/105 | R1B | 1 | 19°S4w/TH 750w | L143 | BXBM<L 143 |
| 9 | (542) | H1/150 | R1B | 3 | 19°S4w/TH 750w | L201, T:R77774(A) | BXBM<L 201 |
| 10 | (542) | H1/150 | R1B | 3 | 19°S4w/TH 750w | L201, T:R77774(A) | BXBM<L 201 |
| 11 | (544) | H1/157 | R1B | 4 | 19°S4w/TH 750w | CLR, T:R77774(A) | BXBM<L CLR |
| 12 | (544) | H1/157 | R1B | 4 | 19°S4w/TH 750w | CLR, T:R77774(A) | BXBM<L CLR |
| 13 | (546) | H1/404 | R4A | 4 | 19°S4w/TH 750w | L143, T:R77774(A) | BXBM<L 143 |
| 14 | (546) | H1/404 | R4A | 4 | 19°S4w/TH 750w | L143, T:R77774(A) | BXBM<L 143 |
| 15 | (548) | H1/401 | R4A | 1 | 19°S4w/TH 750w | L008+R132 | BXBM<L 008 |
| 16 | (548) | H1/401 | R4A | 1 | 19°S4w/TH 750w | L008+R132 | BXBM<L 008 |
| 17 | (550) | H1/402 | R4A | 2 | 19°S4w/TH 750w | R57+R132 | BXBM<L R57 |
| 18 | (550) | H1/402 | R4A | 2 | 19°S4w/TH 750w | R57+R132 | BXBM<L R57 |
| 19 | (552) | H1/403 | R4A | 3 | 19°S4w/TH 750w | R59+R132 | BXBM<L R59 |
| 20 | (552) | H1/403 | R4A | 3 | 19°S4w/TH 750w | R59+R132 | BXBM<L R59 |
| W1 | | | R1B | 2 | S4PAR MFLw/TH 750w | | WORKLIGHT FoH |
| X | | | R1B | 5 | SPARE CIR | | |
| X | | | R1B | 6 | SPARE CIR | | |
| X | | | R4A | 5 | SPARE CIR | | |
| X | | | R4A | 6 | SPARE CIR | | |

NOTES:
1. L206,G105+,L202,L161,L137,R44,R132
2. R00,R371,R69,R68,R76,R79,R81,R21,R49,R346,R56,R23,R25,R15,R01,R09,R95,R83,R26,R90,R382

Philip S. Rosenberg / Lightwright 4

BOOTH thru 2BBL

**Figure 9.27**  *Spamalot* instrument schedule.
*Lighting By: Hugh Vanstone*
*Assoc. LD: Philip S. Rosenberg*

CHANNEL HOOKUP

Page 5
3/23/05
SpamalotNYC-PR91Final.lw4

Note: This printout does not include all attributes attached to units

| Channel | Dimmer | CktN | C# | Position | Unit# | Type, Accessories, Watts | Color/Temp | Purpose |
|---|---|---|---|---|---|---|---|---|
| (119) | H1/178 | R1W | 5 | 1E | 18 | 26*S4w/HH 750w | L201+R132 | AREA LC>R |
| (120) | H1/173 | R1V | 5 | 1E | 13 | 26*S4w/HH 750w | L201+R132 | AREA DL>R |
| (121) | H1/143 | R1M | 2 | BOX RAIL R | 2 | 19*S4w/HH 750w | L201+R132 | X/LT>R FoH PUNCH |
| (122) | H1/141 | R1L | 2 | BOX RAIL L | 2 | 19*S4w/HH 750w | L201+R132 | X/LT<L FoH PUNCH |
| (123) | H1/142 | R1M | 1 | BOX RAIL R | 1 | 19*S4w/HH 750w | R132 | X/LT>R FoH PUNCH |
| (124) | H1/140 | R1L | 1 | BOX RAIL L | 1 | 19*S4w/HH 750w | R132 | X/LT<L FoH PUNCH |
| (125) | H1/284 | R2L | 4 | 2 BM R | 11 | 19*S4w/TH 750w | L201+R132 | X/LT>R MS |
| | H1/284 | R2L | 4 | 2 BM R | 12 | 19*S4w/TH 750w | L201+R132 | X/LT>R MS |
| (126) | H1/258 | R2S | 4 | 2 BM L | 11 | 19*S4w/TH 750w | L201+R132 | X/LT<L MS |
| | H1/258 | R2S | 4 | 2 BM L | 12 | 19*S4w/TH 750w | L201+R132 | X/LT<L MS |
| (127) | H1/315 | R3F | 4 | 3 BM R | 7 | 19*S4w/TH 750w | L201+R132 | X/LT>R US |
| | H1/315 | R3F | 4 | 3 BM R | 8 | 19*S4w/TH 750w | L201+R132 | X/LT>R US |
| (128) | H1/269 | R2U | 4 | 3 BM L | 7 | 19*S4w/TH 750w | L201+R132 | X/LT<L US |
| | H1/269 | R2U | 4 | 3 BM L | 8 | 19*S4w/TH 750w | L201+R132 | X/LT<L US |
| (129) | H1/325 | R3H | 3 | 4 LAD R | 3 | 26*S4w/TH 750w | L201 | CASTLE WALL SCRAPE |
| (130) | H1/441 | R4N | 3 | 4 LAD L | 3 | 26*S4w/TH 750w | L201 | CASTLE WALL SCRAPE |
| (131) | | | | | | | | |
| (132) | | | | | | | | |
| (133) | | | | | | | | |
| (134) | | | | | | | | |
| (135) | H1/168 | R1U | 3 | 1E | 6 | 26*S4w/HH 750w | CLR, T:DHA406(A) | TEMP WASH |
| | H1/168 | R1U | 4 | 1E | 7 | 26*S4w/HH 750w | CLR, T:DHA406(A) | TEMP WASH |
| (136) | H1/179 | R1X | 3 | 1E | 20 | 26*S4w/HH 750w | CLR, T:DHA406(A) | TEMP WASH |
| | H1/179 | R1X | 4 | 1E | 21 | 26*S4w/HH 750w | CLR, T:DHA406(A) | TEMP WASH |
| (137) | H1/205 | R2A | 3 | 2E | 6 | 26*S4w/HH 750w | CLR, T:DHA406(A) | TEMP WASH |
| | H1/205 | R2A | 3 | 2E | 7 | 26*S4w/HH 750w | CLR, T:DHA406(A) | TEMP WASH |
| (138) | H1/206 | R2C | 4 | 2E | 9 | 26*S4w/HH 750w | CLR, T:DHA406(A) | TEMP WASH |
| | H1/206 | R2C | 4 | 2E | 10 | 26*S4w/HH 750w | CLR, T:DHA406(A) | TEMP WASH |
| (139) | | | | | | | | |
| (140) | | | | | | | | |
| (141) | H1/374 | R3B | 5 | 1 BM R | D1 | 4'3" MINISTRIP 20LT/2CKT EYF 750w | L201, HS | |
| (142) | H1/295 | R2Q | 5 | 1 BM L | D1 | 4'3" MINISTRIP 20LT/2CKT EYF 750w | L201, HS | |
| (143) | H1/375 | R3B | 6 | 1 BM R | D2 | 4'3" MINISTRIP 20LT/2CKT EYF 750w | CLR | |
| (144) | H1/296 | R2Q | 6 | 1 BM L | D2 | 4'3" MINISTRIP 20LT/2CKT EYF 750w | CLR | |
| (145) | H1/285 | R2L | 5 | 2 BM R | 13 | 19*S4w/TH 750w | R79+R132 | X/LT>R MS BL |
| | H1/285 | R2L | 5 | 2 BM R | 14 | 19*S4w/TH 750w | R79+R132 | X/LT>R MS BL |
| (146) | H1/259 | R2S | 5 | 2 BM L | 13 | 19*S4w/TH 750w | R79+R132 | X/LT<L MS BL |
| | H1/259 | R2S | 5 | 2 BM L | 14 | 19*S4w/TH 750w | R79+R132 | X/LT<L MS BL |
| (147) | H1/316 | R3F | 5 | 3 BM R | 9 | 19*S4w/TH 750w | R79+R132 | X/LT>R US BL |
| | H1/316 | R3F | 5 | 3 BM R | 10 | 19*S4w/TH 750w | R79+R132 | X/LT>R US BL |
| (148) | H1/270 | R2U | 5 | 3 BM L | 9 | 19*S4w/TH 750w | R79+R132 | X/LT<L US BL |
| | H1/270 | R2U | 5 | 3 BM L | 10 | 19*S4w/TH 750w | R79+R132 | X/LT<L US BL |
| (149) | | | | | | | | |

Philip S. Rosenberg / Lightwright 4

(119) thru (149)

**Figure 9.28**  *Spamalot* channel hookup.
*Lighting By: Hugh Vanstone*
*Assoc. LD: Philip S. Rosenberg*

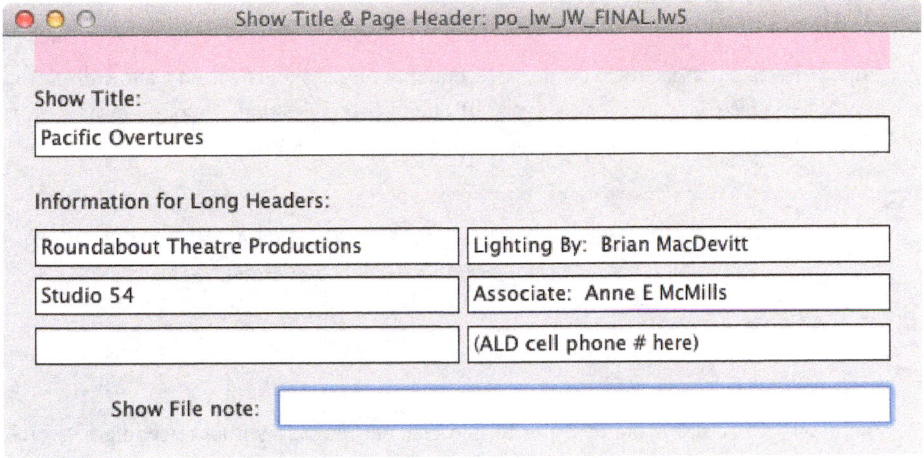

**Figure 9.29a**   Sample page header set-up.

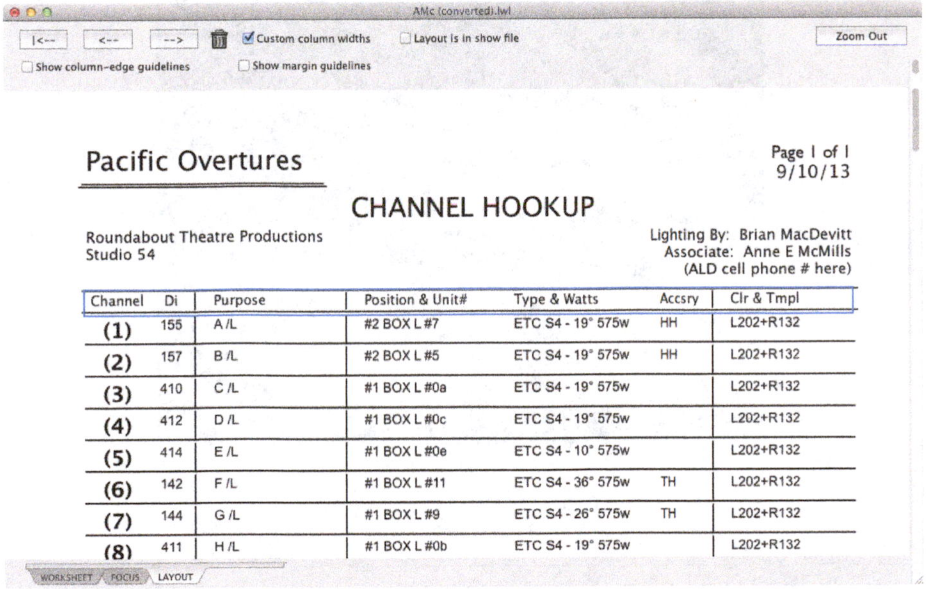

**Figure 9.29b**   Sample page header layout.

## MAGIC SHEETS

A **magic sheet** is an associative visual representation of all channels within a show displayed on only a few pieces of paper—an average of one to two pages and a maximum of four, if possible. (However, extremely large shows may have more than four.)

> *"If the pertinent information will legibly fit on one page, do not put it on two; and do not orient written information on a page so that constant head turning is required to read it."*
>
> —*Vivien Leone*

The magic sheet allows the designer to find channels quickly without needing to search lengthy items such as a plot or channel hookup. Generally, the magic sheets are internal documents for the lighting design team only.

In the U.K., the light plot itself is used as a magic sheet. All information is added on the plot so that it becomes one main resource.

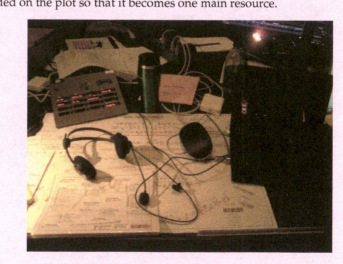

**Figure 9.30**   A light plot / magic sheet on a tech table.
*Courtesy of: Kevin Barry*

In addition to acting as a quick reference, the magic sheet also can serve as a cross-check to the plot and paperwork before submitting the design package. By visually laying out the designer's channeling structure, it is easier to notice deviations from set patterns. For example, you may discover a system that is channeled SL to SR, although all other systems are channeled SR to SL. If so, you may have found a mistake—politely ask your designer to verify.

**Channeling Structure**—a pattern used by lighting designers in order to channel all the fixtures in a light plot logically. For example, frontlight channels 1–18, backlight 11–28, sidelight 21–28, and so forth.

**System**—a series of fixtures covering the stage focused at the same angle, for the same purpose, and often in the same color, such as the frontlight system or backlight system.

Some individuals use the word "magic sheet" and "cheat sheet" interchangeably, although magic sheet is more common. "Cheat sheet" usually refers specifically to certain types of magic sheets—described further in this chapter.

## MAGIC SHEET PREFERENCES

Of all the paperwork types used in the assistant world, none is more varied, personal, and customizable than the magic sheet. It is also one of the most vital—often acting as the designer's sole reference.

The scope of the show and your designer's preferences will determine which types or styles of magic sheets you need to create for your production. For example, if your show uses conventional fixtures only, you may simply need a conventional style magic sheet. However, if your show contains a large amount of moving lights, you additionally need to create moving light magic sheets. Think carefully about the entire show and consider what information needs to be made clear. This will help you determine which different styles of magic sheets you may or may not need to create.

*"Magic sheets are extremely personal, and should work for the individual using them."*

—*Vivien Leone*

While most designers prefer their assistants to create the magic sheets, some may prefer to make their own. If this is the case, still create one for yourself. It will help you to learn the show better and make you faster at helping your designer find channels.

*"There's no point in having an assistant who only finds [the channel] I'm looking for after I've found it."*

*—John McKernon*

Magic sheets are created within a variety of different software programs. Some assistants prefer to use Vectorworks, while others use Microsoft Excel or Adobe Photoshop. It may depend on what seems the most appropriate for the style of each magic sheet.

## MAGIC SHEET STYLES

Typically magic sheets are created to print on 8.5" × 11" (or ANSI "A") size paper in the United States and A4 standard paper size in metrically based countries, if applicable. At the top of each page, include title information such as the show title and logo, theatre and city name, lighting designer's name, associate/assistant designers' names, and an "as of" date in preparation for revisions. The body and orientation of the magic sheet depend on the style. The following are several common styles produced in the industry.

### *Conventional Magic Sheets*

- **System-style magic sheet**—One typical (and maybe most common) style of magic sheet for conventionals is the system-style magic sheet. It involves laying out channels by system in small boxes across the page. (See Figures 9.31a-c.) Each box represents the stage as seen from the house, and each displays a different lighting system. If desired, small not-to-scale groundplans (or representations of the groundplan) can also be placed within the boxes in a grayed-out color. Label each box with the system name and color for easy identification. Some designers also prefer to add arrows indicating the direction from which each system is focused.

  The channel numbers for each system are located in roughly the area the lights are focused on stage (*not* where the instruments are physically hung). Group numbers may also be indicated by using differently colored fonts, a highlight effect, or circling the group number.

- **Groundplan-style magic sheet**—A groundplan-style conventional magic sheet begins by filling the page with a not-to-scale groundplan as a background. The channel numbers (for all systems and specials) are laid on top of the groundplan where they focus on the set. (See Figures 9.32a-b.) Small arrows are often used to represent the direction from which the light is focused. Color-coding is also used to provide more clarity between similar systems of different colors (warm and cool, for example). This style of magic sheet is also popular in the television lighting industry.

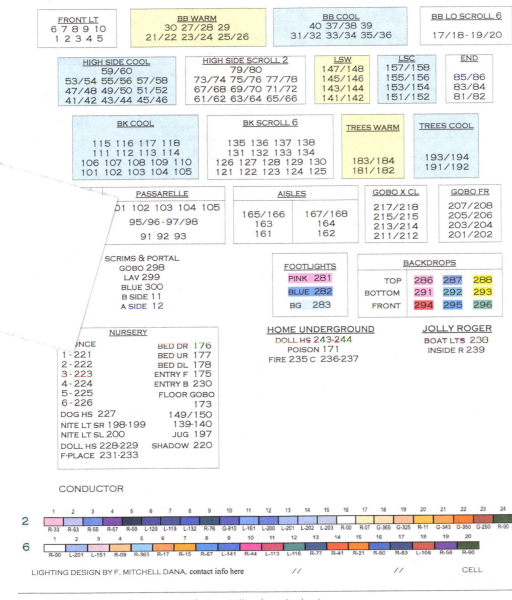

**Figure 9.31a**  *Peter Pan* system-style conventional magic sheet.
Lighting By: F. Mitchell Dana
Assoc. LD: Brenda Veltre

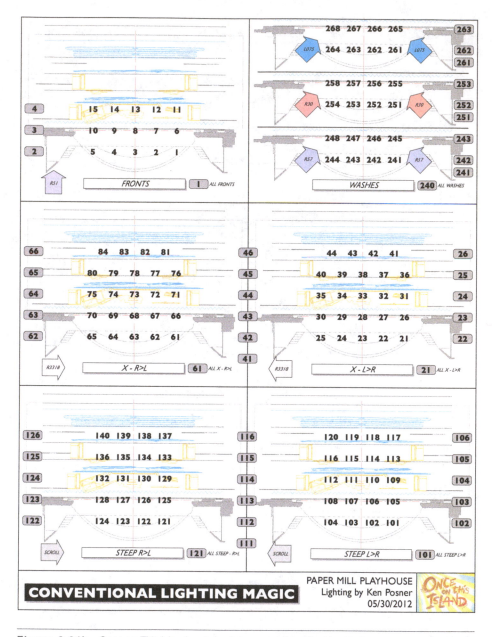

**Figure 9.31b** *Once on This Island* system-style conventional magic sheet.
*Lighting By: Kenneth Posner*
*Assoc. LD: Anthony Pearson*

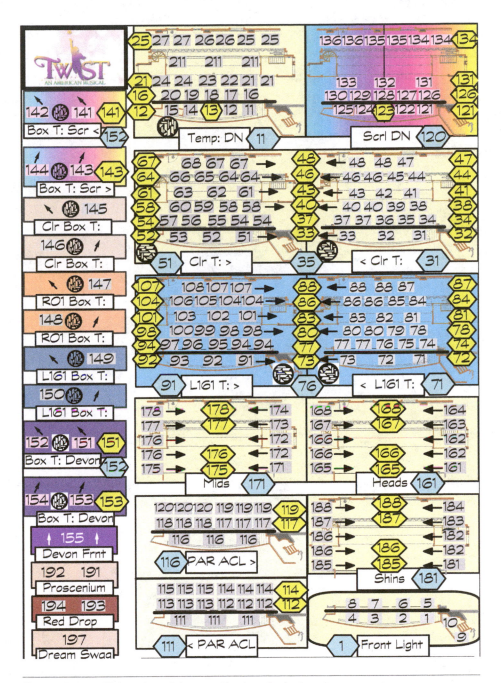

**Figure 9.31c** *Twist* system-style conventional magic sheet.
*Lighting By: Howell Binkley*
*Assoc. LD: Ryan O'Gara*

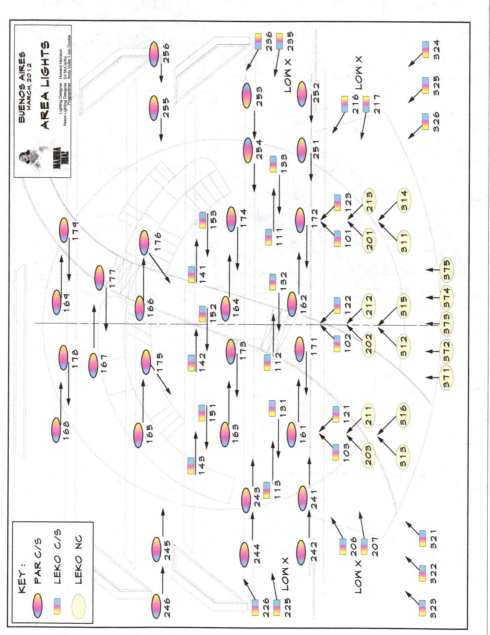

**Figure 9.32a** *Mamma Mia groundplan-style conventional magic sheet.*
*Lighting By: Howard Harrison*
*Assoc. LD: Ed McCarthy*

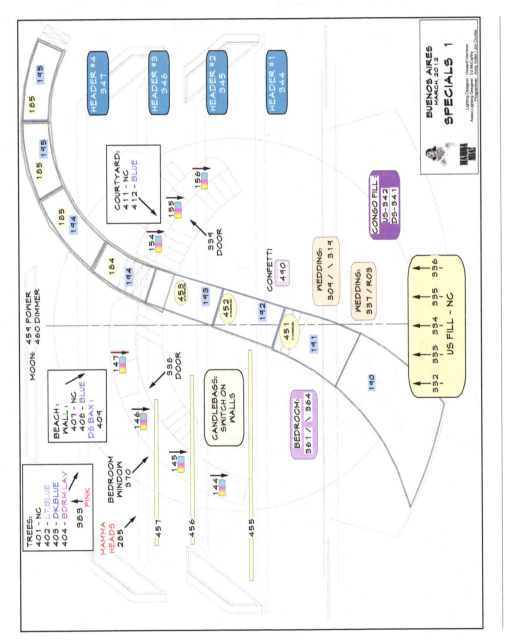

**Figure 9.32b** *Mamma Mia groundplan-style conventional magic sheet.*
*Lighting By: Howard Harrison*
*Assoc. LD: Ed McCarthy*

- **Scenic magic sheet**—On large productions, such as a Broadway musical, many scenic pieces are practical—meaning electrified. When a practical scenic piece is so detailed that it does not fit well into a standard conventional magic sheet, then a separate scenic magic sheet should be made. This type of magic sheet focuses solely on one or two intricate pieces of practical scenery usually shown in elevation with the corresponding channel numbers placed accordingly. (See Figures 9.33a-b.)

## Moving Light Magic Sheets

- **Moving light magic sheet**—The moving light magic sheet varies from its conventional counterparts because, due to the moving light's variable focusing ability, it shows where the moving lights are physically hung instead of where they are focused

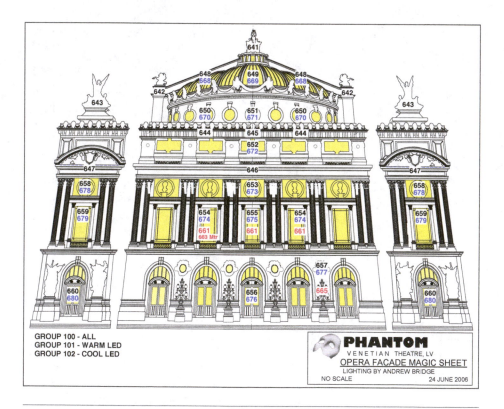

**Figure 9.33a**  *The Phantom of the Opera*, Las Vegas, scenic magic sheet.
*Lighting By: Andrew Bridge*
*Assoc. LD: Vivien Leone*

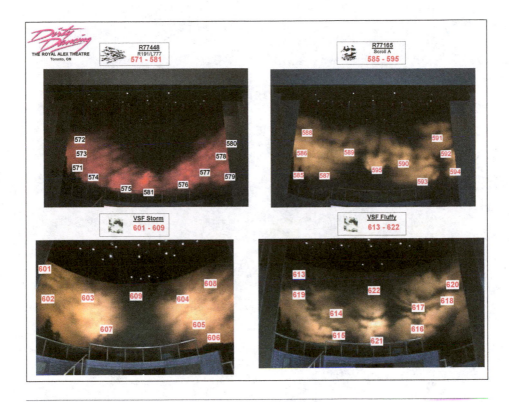

**Figure 9.33b**   *Dirty Dancing* scenic magic sheet.
*Lighting By: Tim Mitchell*
*Assoc. LD: Vivien Leone*
*Custom Cloud Gobos Designed By: Jon Driscoll*

(like a conventional magic sheet). Moving light magic sheets look somewhat like a small, simplified, not-to-scale light plot, but only displaying moving lights. (See Figures 9.34a-c.)

When creating this magic sheet, position the groundplan to cover the full page and draw it in a lighter, grayed-out line weight. On top of the groundplan, place simplified versions of moving light symbols and the electrics or truss in approximate positions over the stage. Scale the fixture symbols to a larger size so that they are easy to read. Space the fixtures apart roughly in the same manner that they are hung. Write the channel numbers boldly inside each fixture. Color-code the fixtures in clearly different colors so that it is easy to distinguish visually between wash and spot units and/or different manufacturers. (Include a key for reference.) Choose colors that do not obscure the readability of the channel numbers. If you choose to use dark colors for the fixtures, typing the channel numbers in white can sometimes be easier to read.

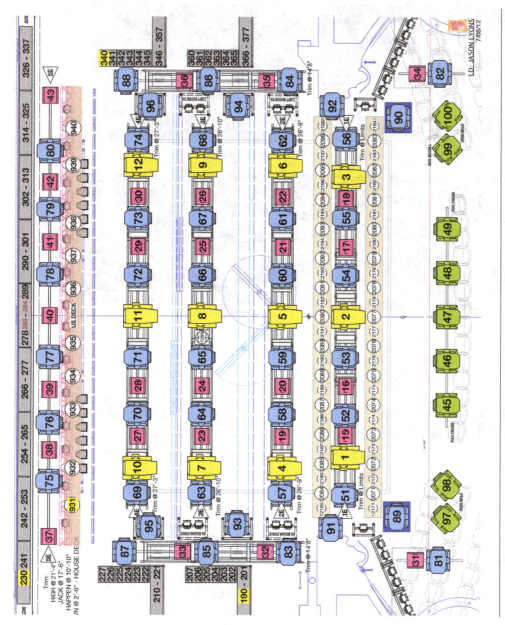

**Figure 9.34a** *Bring It On moving light magic sheet.*
*Lighting By: Jason Lyons*
*Assoc. LD: Peter Hoerburger*

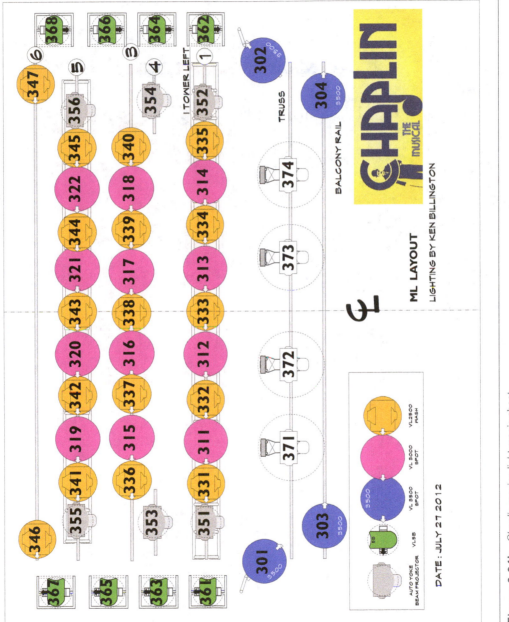

**Figure 9.34b** *Chaplin moving light magic sheet.*
*Lighting By: Ken Billington*
*Assoc. LD: John Demous*

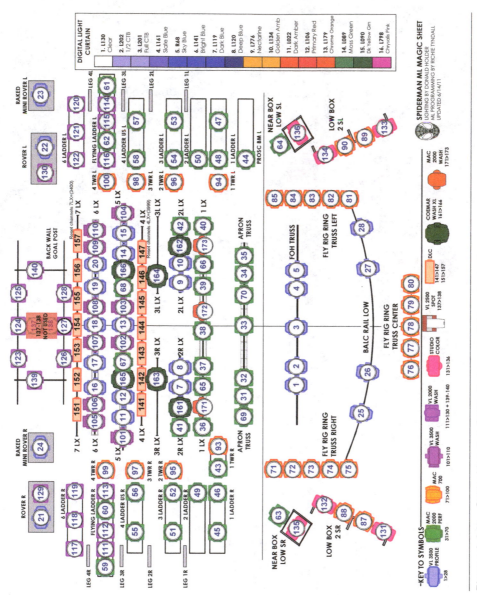

**Figure 9.34c** *Spider-Man: Turn Off the Dark moving light magic sheet.*
*Lighting By: Donald Holder*
*Assoc. LD: Vivien Leone*

- **Gobo wheel magic sheet**—Most moving lights have anywhere from one to four wheels contained within each fixture. These wheels may be referred to as "color wheels," "gobo wheels," or "effects wheels." The gobo wheel magic sheet shows what gobos, colors, and other effects (stock or custom) are loaded in each wheel within each type of fixture in your production. (See Figures 9.35a-b.) Look for the following information in the fixture's manual found on the manufacturer's website: number of wheels contained in each fixture, what default items are loaded, which slots rotate and which do not, effects wheels that come standard, and if any slots are not customizable.

To create the magic sheet, download the images of each gobo, color, and/or effect wheel that will be used in your production. (Download the images in a fairly large resolution so when scaled down a distinguishable pattern is still visible.) Assemble all of the items in a circular or linear pattern on the page in the same order as located in the fixture. Label each image with its corresponding gobo/color number, name, and either "stock" or "custom." Also indicate which gobos can rotate. Repeat the process for each fixture type.

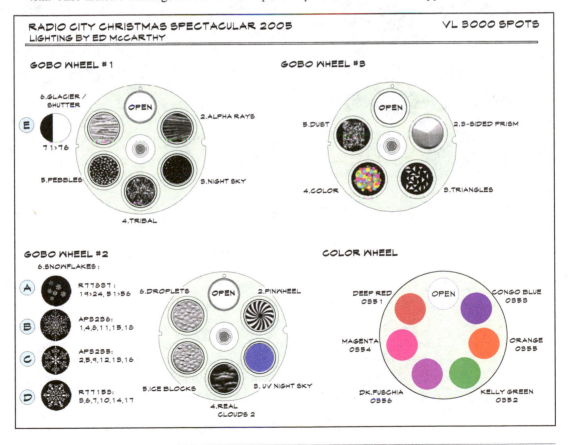

**Figure 9.35a**   *Radio City Christmas Spectacular* gobo wheel magic sheet.
*Lighting By: Ed McCarthy*
*Assoc. LD: Anne E McMills*

MOVING LIGHT MAGIC SHEET

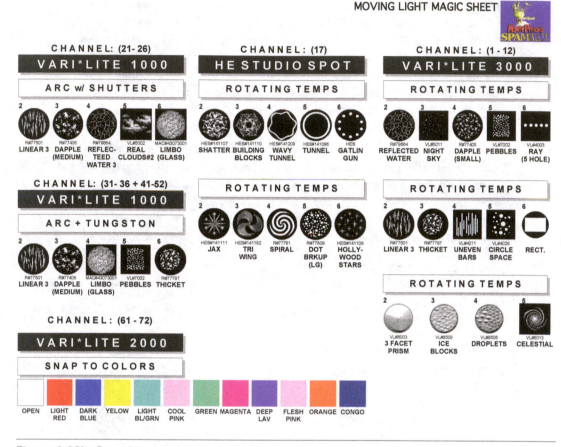

**Figure 9.35b** *Spamalot* gobo wheel magic sheet.
*Lighting By: Hugh Vanstone*
*Assoc. LD: Philip S. Rosenberg*

## Other Equipment-Specific Magic Sheets

• **Scroller color cheat sheet**—A scroller color cheat sheet is simply a list of gel colors in the gel string of the scrollers (color changers) in your production. (See Figures 9.36a-b.)

List the scroller colors, corresponding color names, and frame numbers in descending order. (For example, Frame #1 may be "R00: clear," Frame #2 may be "R02: bastard amber," and so forth.) You may also choose to color code the information according to gel color or cut small pieces of gel out of a gel book and adhere them next to the color name after printing. If there are varying scrolls used in different systems within the light plot, repeat the process for the second set of scrolls and delineate them clearly on your magic sheet—such as "Scroll A: Frontlight" and "Scroll B: Sidelight." Some designers like to tape the scroller color cheat sheet to the side of their tech table monitor for easy reference.

# LINCOLN CENTER THEATER
# THE NANCE

# SCROLLER LIST

| FRAME | AUTO/ REVOLUTIONS | |
| --- | --- | --- |
| | NUMBER | NAME |
| 1 | R00 | Clear |
| 2 | G105 | Antique Rose |
| 3 | G106 | 1/2 Antique Rose |
| 4 | R3208 | 1/4 Blue |
| 5 | R3204 | 1/2 Blue |
| 6 | R3203 | 3/4 Blue |
| 7 | R3202 | Full Blue |
| 8 | L103 | Straw |
| 9 | R08 | Pale Gold |
| 10 | R4315 | CalColor 15 Cyan |
| 11 | LHT079 | Just Blue |
| 12 | G250 | Medium Red XT |

| FRAME | BAX / FRONTS | |
| --- | --- | --- |
| | NUMBER | NAME |
| 1 | R00 | Clear |
| 2 | G105 | Antique Rose |
| 3 | R3208 | 1/4 Blue |
| 4 | R3204 | 1/2 Blue |
| 5 | R3203 | 3/4 Blue |
| 6 | R3202 | Full Blue |
| 7 | L103 | Straw |
| 8 | R21 | Golden Amber |
| 9 | R23 | Orange |
| 10 | G250 | Medium Red XT |
| 11 | L126 | Mauve |
| 12 | R56 | Gypsy Lavender |
| 13 | LHT120 | Deep Blue |
| 14 | LHT079 | Just Blue |
| 15 | G847 | City Blue |
| 16 | R3220 | Double Blue |

AS of 7/27/13

Lighting Design: Japhy Weideman

**Figure 9.36a**   *The Nance* scroller color cheat sheet.
*Lighting By: Japhy Weideman*
*Assoc. LD: Justin Partier*

# SPIDERMAN COLOR STRINGS

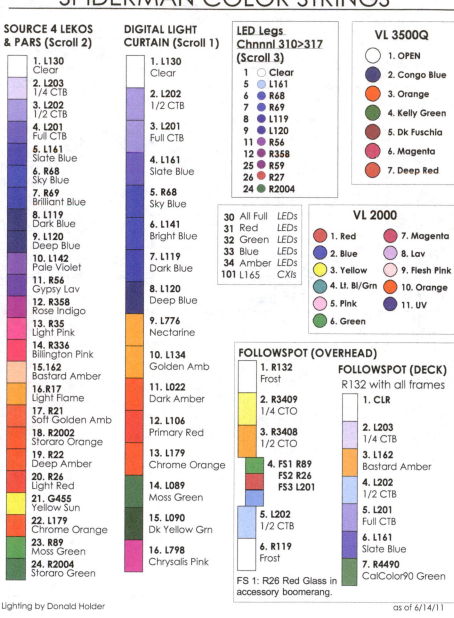

**SOURCE 4 LEKOS & PARS (Scroll 2)**

1. L130 Clear
2. L203 1/4 CTB
3. L202 1/2 CTB
4. L201 Full CTB
5. L161 Slate Blue
6. R68 Sky Blue
7. R69 Brilliant Blue
8. L119 Dark Blue
9. L120 Deep Blue
10. L142 Pale Violet
11. R56 Gypsy Lav
12. R358 Rose Indigo
13. R35 Light Pink
14. R336 Billington Pink
15. 162 Bastard Amber
16. R17 Light Flame
17. R21 Soft Golden Amb
18. R2002 Storaro Orange
19. R22 Deep Amber
20. R26 Light Red
21. G455 Yellow Sun
22. L179 Chrome Orange
23. R89 Moss Green
24. R2004 Storaro Green

**DIGITAL LIGHT CURTAIN (Scroll 1)**

1. L130 Clear
2. L202 1/2 CTB
3. L201 Full CTB
4. L161 Slate Blue
5. R68 Sky Blue
6. L141 Bright Blue
7. L119 Dark Blue
8. L120 Deep Blue
9. L776 Nectarine
10. L134 Golden Amb
11. L022 Dark Amber
12. L106 Primary Red
13. L179 Chrome Orange
14. L089 Moss Green
15. L090 Dk Yellow Grn
16. L798 Chrysalis Pink

**LED Legs Chnnnl 310>317 (Scroll 3)**

1   Clear
5   L161
6   R68
7   R69
8   L119
9   L120
11  R56
12  R358
25  R59
26  R27
24  R2004

30  All Full  LEDs
31  Red       LEDs
32  Green     LEDs
33  Blue      LEDs
34  Amber     LEDs
101 L165      CXIs

**VL 3500Q**

1. OPEN
2. Congo Blue
3. Orange
4. Kelly Green
5. Dk Fuschia
6. Magenta
7. Deep Red

**VL 2000**

1. Red
2. Blue
3. Yellow
4. Lt. Bl/Grn
5. Pink
6. Green
7. Magenta
8. Lav
9. Flesh Pink
10. Orange
11. UV

**FOLLOWSPOT (OVERHEAD)**

1. R132 Frost
2. R3409 1/4 CTO
3. R3408 1/2 CTO
4. FS1 R89
   FS2 R26
   FS3 L201
5. L202 1/2 CTB
6. R119 Frost

FS 1: R26 Red Glass in accessory boomerang.

**FOLLOWSPOT (DECK)**
R132 with all frames

1. CLR
2. L203 1/4 CTB
3. L162 Bastard Amber
4. L202 1/2 CTB
5. L201 Full CTB
6. L161 Slate Blue
7. R4490 CalColor90 Green

Lighting by Donald Holder

as of 6/14/11

**Figure 9.36b**  *Spider-Man: Turn Off the Dark* color strings cheat sheet.
*Lighting By: Donald Holder*
*Assoc. LD: Vivien Leone*

- **Followspot color cheat sheet**—A followspot color cheat sheet is made in the same way as the scroller color cheat sheet only it lists the colors loaded in the followspots instead. Also like the scroller color cheat sheet, if there is a different load in one of the followspots, delineate it clearly. Color code as desired and tape it to the tech table monitor—although this one is best served in front of the followspot assistant instead of the designer. (See Figure 9.37.)

- **LED magic sheet**—Due to the nature of LEDs, there can be many channel numbers within a close proximity to each other. Having a magic sheet showing the specific layout can be helpful with complex designs. However, if LED information is covered on another magic sheet, such as a scenic magic sheet, there is no need to create an additional document. (See Figures 9.38a-b.)

**Figure 9.37** Followspot color cheat sheet taped to tech table monitor.

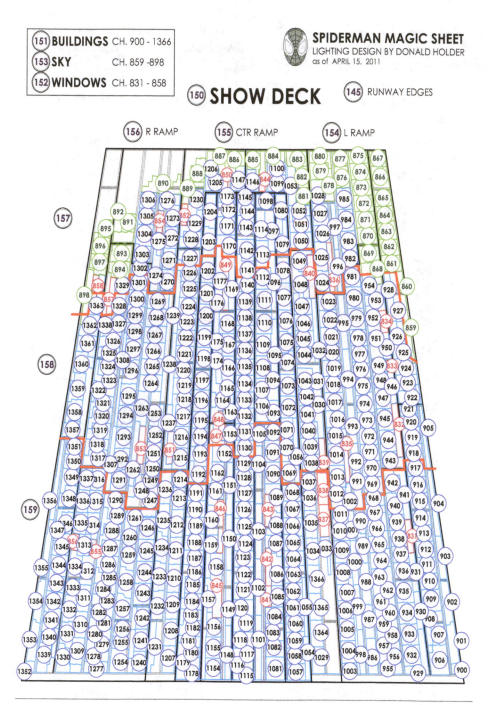

**Figure 9.38a**  *Spider-Man: Turn Off the Dark* LED magic sheet (in this case also a scenic magic sheet).
Lighting By: Donald Holder
Assoc. LD: Vivien Leone

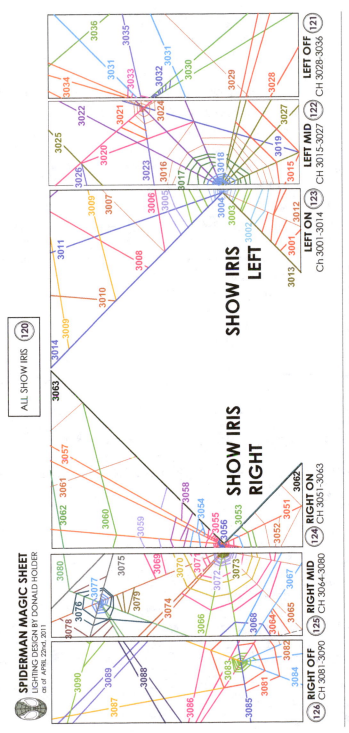

**Figure 9.38b** *Spider-Man: Turn Off the Dark* LED magic sheet (in this case also a scenic magic sheet).
Lighting By: Donald Holder
Assoc. LD: Vivien Leone

## Other Cheat Sheets

- **20-across**—A "20-across" is a style of cheat sheet laid out like a console monitor displaying multiple rows of 20 channels. You can also alter it to be a "25-across" or "Flexi-across" depending on the console layout your designer prefers. It provides a quick reference for determining purpose when looking at the console monitor.

  Lay out the channel number columns and rows in the same configuration as the console monitor. Underneath each channel number, identify its purpose and color. Leave unused channels blank. Abbreviate long names: for example, use "HS DR" instead of "High-Side Down Right." Use arrows to indicate focus direction of each system and color-code by system color, if desired. (See Figures 9.39a-c.)

- **Cheat Sheet**—A standard cheat sheet simply lists the channel number, purpose, and color of every used channel in a numerical listing—an abridged version of the channel hookup. (See Figures 9.40a-b.) Because a cheat sheet is not a visual reference, be specific when entering the purpose for each fixture. Do not use blanket system names such as "BK CL" (cool backlight), for example. Instead, identify each channel separately: "BK CL DR," "BK CL DCR," BK CL C," etc. or "BK CL A," "BK CL B" (which refers to the focus areas on your area layout). Cheat sheets can be created or printed out from Lightwright.

## CHAPLIN

2012 BARRYMORE THEATRE — CONVENTIONALS — Date: 9/4/12 — Lighting by Ken Billington

| 1 | 2 | 3 | 4 | 5 | 6 | 7 | 8 | 9 | 10 | 11 | 12 | 13 | 14 | 15 | 16 | 17 | 18 | 19 | 20 |
|---|---|---|---|---|---|---|---|---|----|----|----|----|----|----|----|----|----|----|----|
| DL | DL/C | DC | DR/C | DR | L | ↘C | R | | | | | | | BIRDIES | L | C | R | FOOTS | FOOTS |
| L203 / R-351 AREA | | | | | | | | | | | | | | L-203 | | L-203 | | L-106 | G-845 |

| 21 | 22 | 23 | 24 | 25 | 26 | 27 | 28 | 29 | 30 | 31 | 32 | 33 | 34 | 35 | 36 | 37 | 38 | 39 | 40 |
|----|----|----|----|----|----|----|----|----|----|----|----|----|----|----|----|----|----|----|----|
| DL | DL/C | DC | DR/C | DR | L | C↗ | R | | | | WASH L to L | WASH L to C | WASH L to R | WASH L to L | WASH L to C | WASH L to R | WASH | KICK | UV |
| L203 /R-351 AREA | | | | | | | | | | | (261) | (262) | (263) | (264) | (265) | (265) | L-137 | G-160 | D146 |

| 41 | 42 | 43 | 44 | 45 | 46 | 47 | 48 | 49 | 50 | 51 | 52 | 53 | 54 | 55 | 56 | 57 | 58 | 59 | 60 |
|----|----|----|----|----|----|----|----|----|----|----|----|----|----|----|----|----|----|----|----|
| DL | DL/C | DC | DR/C | DR | L | L/C | C | R/C | R | Mid L | Mid L/C | Mid C | Mid R/C | Mid R | UL | UC | UR | US | |
| (241) | (242) | (243) | (244) | (245) | (246) | (247) | (248) | (249) | (250) | (251) | (252) | (253) | (254) | (255) | L-201 | L-201 | L-201 | (259) | |

| 61 | 62 | 63 | 64 | 65 | 66 | 67 | 68 | 69 | 70 | 71 | 72 | 73 | 74 | 75 | 76 | 77 | 78 | 79 | 80 |
|----|----|----|----|----|----|----|----|----|----|----|----|----|----|----|----|----|----|----|----|
| SL Wall | Back Wall L | Back Wall L | Back Wall R | Back Wall R | SR Wall | MID | MID | US Wall | Truss | Hang Lamp | Karno | Studio | Lamp | | Flicker On Air | | Flicker 1 | Flicker 2 | Flicker 3 |
| | | | | | | L-203 Temp | | | | | WDS | WDS | 1913 Projector | | | | Chaplin Face N/C | | |

| 81 | 82 | 83 | 84 | 85 | 86 | 87 | 88 | 89 | 90 | 91 | 92 | 93 | 94 | 95 | 96 | 97 | 98 | 99 | 100 |
|----|----|----|----|----|----|----|----|----|----|----|----|----|----|----|----|----|----|----|----|
| Ends US | Ends US | Sky Drop | Door Back | | | | | Fresnel L | Fresnel R | Lamp | | Rope | Fspot | Fresnel L | Fresnel R | Shaft DS | Shaft US | Fresnel L | Fresnel R |
| 8E L-702 | | L-201 | L-201 | | | | | 5K 5E | | 1939 Projector | | N/C | Deck | WDS Deck | | GRID Fresnel | | 5K 4E | |

| 101 | 2 | 3 | 4 | 5 | 6 | 7 | 8 | 9 | 10 | 11 | 12 | 13 | 14 | 15 | 16 | 17 | 18 | 19 | 20 |
|-----|---|---|---|---|---|---|---|---|----|----|----|----|----|----|----|----|----|----|----|
| X FAR | X CTR | X NEAR | X FAR | X CTR | X NEAR | X FAR | X CTR | X NEAR | X FAR | X CTR | X NEAR | X FAR | X CTR | X NEAR | DS | In I | In II | In III | in IV |
| DS L-702 | | | ← IN I | L-702 | | ← IN II | L-702 | | ← IN III | L-702 | | ← IN IV | L-702 | | (271) | (272) | (273) | (274) | (275) |

| 121 | 22 | 23 | 24 | 25 | 26 | 27 | 28 | 29 | 30 | 31 | 32 | 33 | 34 | 35 | 36 | 37 | 38 | 39 | 40 |
|-----|----|----|----|----|----|----|----|----|----|----|----|----|----|----|----|----|----|----|----|
| X FAR | X CTR | X NEAR | X FAR | X CTR | X NEAR | X FAR | X CTR | X NEAR | X FAR | X CTR | X NEAR | X FAR | X CTR | X NEAR | DS | In I | In II | In III | in IV |
| DS L-702 | | | → IN I | L-702 | | → IN II | L-702 | | → IN III | L-702 | | → IN IV | L-702 | | (276) | (277) | (278) | (279) | (280) |

| 141 | 42 | 43 | 44 | 45 | 46 | 47 | 48 | 49 | 50 | 51 | 52 | 53 | 54 | 55 | 56 | 57 | 58 | 59 | 60 |
|-----|----|----|----|----|----|----|----|----|----|----|----|----|----|----|----|----|----|----|----|
| X FAR | X CTR | X NEAR | X FAR | X CTR | X NEAR | X FAR | X CTR | X NEAR | X FAR | X CTR | X NEAR | X FAR | X CTR | X NEAR | DIAG L | DIAG L | Dict Spec | Shin← | Shin |
| DS L-161 | | | ← IN I | L-161 | | ← IN II | L-161 | | ← IN III | L-161 | | ← IN IV | L-161 | | L-702 | (269) | N/C | L-203 | L-203 |

| 161 | 62 | 63 | 64 | 65 | 66 | 67 | 68 | 69 | 70 | 71 | 72 | 73 | 74 | 75 | 76 | 77 | 78 | 79 | 80 |
|-----|----|----|----|----|----|----|----|----|----|----|----|----|----|----|----|----|----|----|----|
| X FAR | X CTR | X NEAR | X FAR | X CTR | X NEAR | X FAR | X CTR | X NEAR | X FAR | X CTR | X NEAR | X FAR | X CTR | X NEAR | DIAG L | DIAG L | Dict Spec | Shin→ | Shin |
| DS L-161 | | | → IN I | L-161 | | → IN II | L-161 | | → IN III | L-161 | | → IN IV | L-161 | | L-702 | (270) | N/C | L-203 | L-203 |

| 181 | 182 | 183 | 184 | 185 | 186 | 187 | 188 | 189 | 190 | 191 | 192 | 193 | 194 | 195 | 196 | 197 | 198 | 199 | 200 |
|-----|-----|-----|-----|-----|-----|-----|-----|-----|-----|-----|-----|-----|-----|-----|-----|-----|-----|-----|-----|
| ILL 1 | ILL 2 | IILL 1 | IILL 2 | IIILL 1 | IIILL 2 | US Par | | | | ILL 1 | ILL 2 | IILL 1 | IILL 2 | IIILL 1 | IIILL 2 | US Par | | | |
| BP2 Studio X L-201 | | | | | | | | | | BP2 Studio X L-201 | | | | | | | | | |

**Figure 9.39a**  20-across, *Chaplin.*
*Lighting By: Ken Billington*
*Assoc. LD: John Demous*

# "MEN'S LIVES" – Bay Street Theatre

As of 6/22/12

Lighting Design © 2012 John McKernon

Magic sheet (25-across). Each cell shows a channel number and its focus/position label. Section names are indicated in the grid.

| Ch | Pos | Ch | Pos | Ch | Pos | Ch | Pos | Ch | Pos | Ch | Pos |
|----|-----|----|-----|----|-----|----|-----|----|-----|----|-----|
| 1 | DC | 2 | DRC | 3 | DLC | 4 | SR | 5 | Ctr | 6 | SL |
| 7 | UR | 8 | UC | 9 | UL | 10 | DC | 11 | DRC | 12 | DLC |
| 13 | SR | 14 | Ctr | 15 | SL | 16 | UR | 17 | UC | 18 | UL |
| 19 | SR (DUNES) | 20 | SL | 21 | ↑ | 22 | ↑ | 23 | ↑ (UPPER LEVEL) | 24 | ↓ |

| Ch | Pos | Ch | Pos | Ch | Pos | Ch | Pos | Ch | Pos | Ch | Pos |
|----|-----|----|-----|----|-----|----|-----|----|-----|----|-----|
| 25 | DC | 26 | DRC | 27 | DLC | 28 | SR | 29 | Ctr | 30 | SL |
| 31 | UR | 32 | UC | 33 | UL | 34 | DC | 35 | DRC | 36 | DLC |
| 37 | SR | 38 | Ctr | 39 | SL | 40 | UR | 41 | UC | 42 | UL |
| 43 | SR | 44 | SL | 45 | ↗ | 46 | ↓ | 47 | (SLOPE) | 48 | ↓ |

| Ch | Pos | Ch | Pos | Ch | Pos | Ch | Pos | Ch | Pos | Ch | Pos |
|----|-----|----|-----|----|-----|----|-----|----|-----|----|-----|
| 49 | DC | 50 | DRC | 51 | DLC | 52 | SR | 53 | Ctr | 54 | SL |
| 55 | UR | 56 | UC | 57 | UL | 58 | DC | 59 | DRC | 60 | DLC |
| 61 | SR | 62 | Ctr | 63 | SL | 64 | UR | 65 | UC | 66 | UL |
| 67 | SR (DUNES) | 68 | SL | 69 | (BOAT GAPS) | 70 | — | 71 | (PATH) | 72 | — |

| Ch | Pos | Ch | Pos | Ch | Pos | Ch | Pos | Ch | Pos | Ch | Pos |
|----|-----|----|-----|----|-----|----|-----|----|-----|----|-----|
| 73 | DC | 74 | DRC | 75 | DLC | 76 | SR | 77 | Ctr | 78 | SL |
| 79 | UR | 80 | UC | 81 | UL | 82 | DC | 83 | DRC | 84 | DLC |
| 85 | SR | 86 | Ctr | 87 | SL | 88 | UR | 89 | UC | 90 | UL |
| 91 | SR | 92 | SL | 93 | ↗ | 94 | ↗ (DUNE NOOK) | 95 | ↗ | 96 | ↓ |

| Ch | Pos | Ch | Pos | Ch | Pos | Ch | Pos | Ch | Pos | Ch | Pos |
|----|-----|----|-----|----|-----|----|-----|----|-----|----|-----|
| 97 | SR | 98 | US | 99 | DS | 100 | Fog | 101 | (WINDOWS) | 102 | ↑ |
| 103 | ↗ | 104 | Day | 105 | Storm | 106 | Grey | 107 | Moon | 108 | Pool (NATE) |
| 109 | Iris | 110 | Pool (POPEYE) | 111 | Iris | 112 | — | 113 | — | 114 | — |
| 115 | ↙ | 116 | ↙ | 117 | ↗ | 118 | ↗ | 119 | ↗ (VOMS) | 120 | ↗ |

CYC: 104 Day, 105 Storm, 106 Grey, 107 Moon

| Ch | Pos | Ch | Pos | Ch | Pos | Ch | Pos | Ch | Pos | Ch | Pos |
|----|-----|----|-----|----|-----|----|-----|----|-----|----|-----|
| 121 | SR | 122 | Ctr | 123 | SL | 124 | Ctr | 125 | Ctr | 126 | SL |
| 127 | SR | 128 | Ctr | 129 | SL | 130 | SR | 131 | Ctr | 132 | SL |
| 133 | SR | 134 | Ctr | 135 | SL (CYC BOTTOM) | 136 | SR | 137 | Ctr | 138 | SL |
| 139 | SL | 140 | DRC | 141 | DC | 142 | DLC | 143 | DRC | 144 | DLC (FAR DOWNSTAGE) |

CYC TOP: 121 SR, 122 Ctr, 123 SL

| Ch | Pos | Ch | Pos | Ch | Pos | Ch | Pos | Ch | Pos | Ch | Pos |
|----|-----|----|-----|----|-----|----|-----|----|-----|----|-----|
| 145 | SR | 146 | Ctr | 147 | SL | 148 | Ctr | 149 | Ctr | 150 | SL |
| 151 | SR | 152 | Ctr | 153 | SL | 154 | SR | 155 | Ctr | 156 | SL |
| 157 | SR | 158 | Ctr | 159 | SL | 160 | SR | 161 | Ctr | 162 | SL |
| 163 | DRC | 164 | DC | 165 | DLC | 166 | DRC | 167 | DC | 168 | DLC |

SPARES (152–159); HAZERS SR (164–168); FAR DOWNSTAGE (163–168)

| Ch | Pos | Ch | Pos | Ch | Pos | Ch | Pos | Ch | Pos | Ch | Pos |
|----|-----|----|-----|----|-----|----|-----|----|-----|----|-----|
| 169 | SR | 170 | Ctr | 171 | SL | 172 | DL | 173 | SL | 174 | SR (ColorSpots) |
| 175 | SL | 176 | — | 177 | — | 178 | — | 179 | 4P | 180 | 5P |
| 181 | BP | 182 | DP | 183 | 8P | 184 | 9P | 185 | — | 186 | — |
| 187 | Power | 188 | Pump | 189 | Fan | 190 | Pump | 191 | Fan | 192 | — |

MOVERS: 169 SR, 170 DR, 171 Ctr, 172 DL, 173 SL  
STARS: 1, 2, 3, 4, 5, 6  
HAZERS SR: Power, Pump, Fan, Pump, Fan

**Figure 9.39b** 25-across, *Men's Lives.*
*Lighting By: John McKernon*

**PHANTOM - Las Vegas**  —  **CHEAT SHEET - (201 > 400)**  —  6/24/2006

| 201 | 202 | 203 | 204 | 205 | 206 | 207 | 208 | 209 | 210 | 211 | 212 | 213 | 214 | 215 | 216 | 217 | 218 | 219 | 220 |
|---|---|---|---|---|---|---|---|---|---|---|---|---|---|---|---|---|---|---|---|
| AREA - G-8 | | | | | AREA - G-7 | | | | | | AREA - G-3 | | | | | | | | |
| BOOTH - L203 / FORESTAGE | | | | | COVE - L203 / STAGE | | | | | | BALCONY - Warm | | | | | | | | |
| DL | DLC | DC | DRC | DR | DL | DLC | DC | DRC | DR | UC | L | LC | C | RC | R | | | | |

| 221 | 222 | 223 | 224 | 225 | 226 | 227 | 228 | 229 | 230 | 231 | 232 | 233 | 234 | 235 | 236 | 237 | 238 | 239 | 240 |
|---|---|---|---|---|---|---|---|---|---|---|---|---|---|---|---|---|---|---|---|
| G-6 | G-5 | | G-6 | G-5 | | | | | | G-2 | G-1 | | G-2 | G-1 | | G-4 | | | |
| BxBm R | | | BxBm L | | | | | | | BxBm R | | | BxBm L | | | 1LX | | | |
| DL-C | L | C | DR-C | C | R | | | | | DL-C | C | L | DR-C | C | R | UL | UC | UC | UR |
| L202 | L202 | L202 | L202 | L202 | L202 | | | | | L103 | L103 | L103 | L103 | L103 | L103 | L103 | L103 | L103 | L103 |

| 241 | 242 | 243 | 244 | 245 | 246 | 247 | 248 | 249 | 250 | 251 | 252 | 253 | 254 | 255 | 256 | 257 | 258 | 259 | 260 |
|---|---|---|---|---|---|---|---|---|---|---|---|---|---|---|---|---|---|---|---|
| G-10 | | | | | G-13 | | | | | G-11 | | | | | G-14 | | | | |
| BOOTH - C/C | | | | | BOOTH Gobo - C/C | | | | | BxBm - C/C | | | | | BxBm Gobo - C/C | | | | |
| L | LC | C | RC | R | L | LC | C | RC | R | L | C | C | R | | L | C | C | R | |
| | | | | | | | | | | BBmR | | BBmL | | | BBmR | | BBmL | | |

| 261 | 262 | 263 | 264 | 265 | 266 | 267 | 268 | 269 | 270 | 271 | 272 | 273 | 274 | 275 | 276 | 277 | 278 | 279 | 280 |
|---|---|---|---|---|---|---|---|---|---|---|---|---|---|---|---|---|---|---|---|
| G-15 | | | | | G-16 | | | | | | | | | G-17 | | | | G-39 | |
| TRUSS - C/C | | | | | | | | | | Gobo X - C/C | | | | | | | | Dancer | |
| DL | DC | DR | | | | | | | | 2LX | | | | 3LX | | 2LX | | L | R |
| | | | | | | | | | | DL | DLC | DRC | DR | DC | C | ULC | URC | | |

| 281 | 282 | 283 | 284 | 285 | 286 | 287 | 288 | 289 | 290 | 291 | 292 | 293 | 294 | 295 | 296 | 297 | 298 | 299 | 300 |
|---|---|---|---|---|---|---|---|---|---|---|---|---|---|---|---|---|---|---|---|
| G-12 | | | | | | | | | | G-19 | | G-20 | | G-22 | | G-21 | | | |
| DOWNLIGHTS - C/C | | | | | | | | | | BACKLT - C/C | | | | | | | | | |
| DL | DLC | DC | DRC | DR | L | LC | C | RC | R | Bay1 <L | | Bay1 >R | | Bay2 | | Bay3 | | | |
| | | | | | | | | | | Near | Far | Near | Far | Near | Far | Near | Far | | |

| 301 | 302 | 303 | 304 | 305 | 306 | 307 | 308 | 309 | 310 | 311 | 312 | 313 | 314 | 315 | 316 | 317 | 318 | 319 | 320 |
|---|---|---|---|---|---|---|---|---|---|---|---|---|---|---|---|---|---|---|---|
| G-24 | | | | | G-26 | | G-28 | | | | | | | G-30 | | | G-32 | | |
| X/L >BOOMS L - C/C | | | | | | | | | | | | | | | | | | | |
| Fstage | | | | R | C | C | L | XDR | XDC | XDL | XR | XC | XL | XR | XC | XL | XR | XC | XL |
| Balc | Part | | | Aprn | Aprn | Aprn | Aprn | 1BmL | 1BmL | 1BmL | 1BmL | 1BmL | 1BmL | 2BmL | 2BmL | 2BmL | 3BmL | 3BmL | 3BmL |

| 321 | 322 | 323 | 324 | 325 | 326 | 327 | 328 | 329 | 330 | 331 | 332 | 333 | 334 | 335 | 336 | 337 | 338 | 339 | 340 |
|---|---|---|---|---|---|---|---|---|---|---|---|---|---|---|---|---|---|---|---|
| G-23 | | | | | G-26 | | G-27 | | | | | | | G-31 | | | | | |
| X/L >BOOMS R - C/C | | | | | | | | | | | | | | | | | | | |
| Fstage | | | | L | C | C | R | XDL | XDC | XDR | XL | XC | XR | XL | XC | XR | XL | XC | XR |
| Balc | Part | | | Aprn | Aprn | Aprn | Aprn | 1BmR | 1BmR | 1BmR | 1BmR | 1BmR | 1BmR | 2BmR | 2BmR | 2BmR | 3BmR | 3BmR | 3BmR |

| 341 | 342 | 343 | 344 | 345 | 346 | 347 | 348 | 349 | 350 | 351 | 352 | 353 | 354 | 355 | 356 | 357 | 358 | 359 | 360 |
|---|---|---|---|---|---|---|---|---|---|---|---|---|---|---|---|---|---|---|---|
| G-32 | | | | G-49 | | G-44 | G-48 | | | | | | | | | | | | |
| PROSC - C/C | | | | | | | | | | | | | | | | | Gas Globes | | |
| KK-Rail | | Truss | | KK-A.Bm | | KK-Pit | | Angl U/L | | Angl | Harp | Harp | | Soff | Eyes | | Top | Mid | Bott |
| Pros | Angl | L | R | L | R | Wm | Cool | Wm | Cool | Pins | Pins | U/L | | it | | | | | |

| 361 | 362 | 363 | 364 | 365 | 366 | 367 | 368 | 369 | 370 | 371 | 372 | 373 | 374 | 375 | 376 | 377 | 378 | 379 | 380 |
|---|---|---|---|---|---|---|---|---|---|---|---|---|---|---|---|---|---|---|---|
| G-41 | G-34 | | | | | | | G-48 | | G-45 | | G-42 | | G-43 | | | | | G-46 |
| O.BOX - C/C | | | | | | O.Box | | DUSTCOVER | | | | | SIDE BOXES - Wm | | | | | | Pros |
| KK-Rail | | Truss | | | Side | Pit - Wm | | Pros | Box | Pros | Side | Rail | | Tech Box | | | | | Top |
| L | R | L | R | | Box | L | R | Truss | Pit | Pit | O.Box | Box | 1 | 2 | 1 | 2 | 3 | 4 | CS |

| 381 | 382 | 383 | 384 | 385 | 386 | 387 | 388 | 389 | 390 | 391 | 392 | 393 | 394 | 395 | 396 | 397 | 398 | 399 | 400 |
|---|---|---|---|---|---|---|---|---|---|---|---|---|---|---|---|---|---|---|---|
| DS FOOTLTS | | | | | | | | | | | | | | | | | Worklt | | MD |
| PIT | | MR16 | | | Bulb | Relay | | | | | | | | | | | Gas | Elec | |
| L | R | L | C | R | L+R | L | R | ON | | | | | | | | | | | |

**Color Code**
- Unit with Scroller
- Unit with Twin Spin
- Unit with TS+CS
- Units not used in Show

**Figure 9.39c**  20-across, *The Phantom of the Opera,* Las Vegas.
*Lighting By: Andrew Bridge*
*Assoc. LD: Vivien Leone*

*THE SOUND OF MUSIC*          CHEAT SHEET          Page 1 of 14

contact info here                                 7/28/13
PMP SOM LW FINAL112512.lw5                        contact info here
PAPERMILL PLAYHOUSE                               LD: F. Mitchell Dana
ALD: Brian Barnett          Master Electrician: Drew Kawczynski

This is not a hookup or instrument schedule. Do not assume items on the same line relate to each other.

| Channel | Purpose | Position | Color | Channel | Purpose | Position | Color |
|---|---|---|---|---|---|---|---|
| (1) | Area 1 DR | FAR COVE | CL | (40) | HSL | 1 PIPE LS# 5 | CL |
| (2) | Area 2 DRC | FAR COVE | CL | (41) | HSR | 1 PIPE LS# 5 | CL+ |
| (3) | Area 3 DC | FAR COVE | CL | (42) | HSL | 1 PIPE LS# 5 | CL |
| (4) | Area 4 DLC | FAR COVE | CL | (43) | HSR | 3 PIPE LS# 21 | CL |
| (5) | Area 5 DL | FAR COVE | CL | (44) | HSL | 3 PIPE LS# 21 | CL+ |
| (6) | Area 6 R | NEAR COVE | CL | (45) | HSR | 3 PIPE LS# 21 | CL |
| (7) | Area 7 RC | NEAR COVE | CL | (46) | HSL | 3 PIPE LS# 21 | CL |
| (8) | Area 8 CC | NEAR COVE | CL | (47) | HSR | 3 PIPE LS# 21 | CL+ |
| (9) | Area 9 LC | NEAR COVE | CL | (48) | HSL | 3 PIPE LS# 21 | CL |
| (10) | Area 10 L | NEAR COVE | CL | (49) | HSR | 6 PIPE LS# 50 | CL |
| (11) | BBR W >DR | 1 PLATFORM... | L153 | (50) | HSL | 6 PIPE LS# 50 | CL |
| (12) | BBL W >DR | BOX BOOM L | L153 | (51) | HSR | 6 PIPE LS# 50 | CL |
| (13) | BBR W >DC | PLATFORM R | L153 | (52) | HSL | 6 PIPE LS# 50 | CL |
| (14) | BBL W >DC | PLATFORM L | L153 | (53) | HSR | 6 PIPE LS# 50 | CL |
| (15) | BBR W >DL | BOX BOOM R | L153 | (54) | HSL | 6 PIPE LS# 50 | CL |
| (16) | BBL W >DL | 1 PLATFORM... | L153 | (55) | HSR | 7 PIPE LS# 58 | CL |
| (17) | BBR W >UC | PLATFORM R | L153 | (56) | HSL | 7 PIPE LS# 58 | CL |
| (18) | BBL W >UC | PLATFORM L | L153 | (57) | BLUE FILL | FAR COVE | R80 |
| (19) | BBR W >UL | PLATFORM R | L153 | (58) | BLUE FILL | FAR COVE | R80 |
| (20) | BBL W >UR | PLATFORM L | L153 | (59) | BLUE FILL | FAR COVE | R80 |
| (21) | BBR C >DR | 1 PLATFORM... | R64 | (60) | BLUE FILL | FAR COVE | R80 |
| (22) | BBL C >DR | BOX BOOM L | R64 | (61) | LSW DR | FAR TORM R | L153 |
| (23) | BBR C >DC | PLATFORM ... | R64 | (62) | LSW DL | FAR TORM L | L153 |
| (24) | BBL C >DC | PLATFORM L... | R64 | (63) | LSW 1R | 1 LADDER R | L153 |
| (25) | BBR C >DL | BOX BOOM R | R64 | (64) | LSW 1L | 1 LADDER L | L153 |
| (26) | BBL C >DL | 1 PLATFORM... | R64 | (65) | LSW 2R | 2 LADDER R | L153 |
| (27) | BBR C >UC | PLATFORM ... | R64 | (66) | LSW 2L | 2 LADDER L | L153 |
| (28) | BBL C >UC | PLATFORM L... | R64 | (67) | LSW 3R | 3 LADDER R | L153 |
| (29) | BBR C >UL | PLATFORM ... | R64 | (68) | LSW 3L | 3 LADDER L | L153 |
| (30) | BBL C >UR | PLATFORM L... | R64 | (69) | STEEPLE ... | 3 LADDER R | R64 |
| (31) | HSR | TRUSS US | CL | (70) | SP | 3 LADDER L | CL |
| (32) | HSL | TRUSS US | CL | (71) | LSC | FAR TORM R | R67 |
| (33) | HSR | TRUSS US | CL | | | | R67+... |
| (34) | HSL | TRUSS US | CL | (72) | LSC | FAR TORM L | R67 |
| (35) | HSR | TRUSS US | CL | (73) | LSC | 1 LADDER R | R67 |
| (36) | HSL | TRUSS US | CL | (74) | LSC | 1 LADDER L | R67 |
| (37) | HSR | 1 PIPE LS# 5 | CL | (75) | LSC | 2 LADDER R | R67 |
| (38) | HSL | 1 PIPE LS# 5 | CL+ | (76) | LSC | 2 LADDER L | R67 |
| (39) | HSR | 1 PIPE LS# 5 | CL | (77) | LSC | 3 LADDER R | R67 |

**Figure 9.40a**  *The Sound of Music* cheat sheet made in Lightwright.
*Lighting By: F. Mitchell Dana*

OBSESSION  DESIGN  
VIDEO  AUSTIL

SONDHEIM ON SONDHEIM.

STUDIO 54  
MARCH 2010'

| | AREAS | | | | DOWN | | | | SCRIM | |
|---|---|---|---|---|---|---|---|---|---|---|
| 1 | BY | DL | G-105 / R-54 | 201 | 1P | L | 361 | 80 | TOP | | R-83 |
| 2 | | DL/C | | 202 | | L/C | 362 | 81 | G ROW | L | R-83 |
| 3 | | DC | | 203 | | C | 363 | 82 | | C | |
| 4 | | DR/C | | 204 | | R/C | 364 | 83 | | R | |
| 5 | | DR | | 205 | | R | 365 | 85 | | L | 161 |
| 6 | | UL | | 221 | | L | R-79 | 86 | | C | |
| 7 | | UL/C | | 222 | | L/C | | 87 | | R | |
| 8 | | UC | | 223 | | C | | 88 | | L | 137 |
| 9 | | UR/C | | 224 | | R/C | | 89 | | C | |
| 10 | | UR | | 225 | | R | | 90 | | R | |
| 31 | | PLAT | | 231 | 5P | UL | | 91 | 3P | L | R-83 |
| 21 | BY R | DL | | 232 | | UL/C | | 92 | | C | |
| 22 | | DL/C | | 233 | | UC | | 93 | | R | |
| 23 | | DC | | 234 | | UR/C | | | | | |
| 24 | | DR/C | | 235 | | UR | | | SCENERY | | |
| 25 | | DR | | | | | | 94 | #1 LEGS ⊤ | | R-79 |
| 26 | | UL | | | BAND | | | 95 | #2 LEGS ⊤ | | |
| 27 | | UL/C | | 41 | ENDS LEFT | | G-107 | 96 | #1 + #2 LEGS ⊤ | | |
| 28 | | UC | | 42 | | RIGHT | 136 | 97 | #2 BORD ⊤ | | |
| 29 | | UR/C | | 43 | DOWN | | R-83 | 98 | BY #2 BORD ⊤ | | |
| 30 | | UR | | 44 | DOWN | L | 137 | 99 | #2 BORD LOW ⊤ | | |
| 32 | | PLAT | | 45 | | C | | 100 | SLIDER LEGS ⊤ | | |
| 11 | TRUSS | DL | 136 | 46 | | R | | | | | |
| 12 | | DC | | 47 | SYNT DN | | 203 | | WORKS | | |
| 13 | | DR | | 48 | WOODWIND | | | 264 | HOUSE STEPS | | 25% |
| 14 | | UL | | 49 | WOODWIND | | | 269 | VOM. HSE LTS | | |
| 15 | | UC | | 50 | HORN | | | | | | |
| 16 | | UR | | 51 | PIANO | | | | SPECIALS | | |
| | | | | 52 | VIOLIN | | | 18 | DOORS | L | N/C |
| | | | | 53 | BASS | | | 19 | " | C | N/C |
| | WASH | | | 54 | CELLO | | | 20 | " | 12 | N/C |
| 34 | BY L TO L | | 351 | 56 | MUSIC | | 203 | 211 | SUNDAY SPEC | | N/C |
| 35 | | C | | 57 | SYNT MUSIC | | | 212 | " LESLIE | | N/C |
| 36 | | R | | 58 | PIANO MUSIC 30 | | | | | | |
| 37 | BY R TO L | | 352 | 59 | CONDUCTOR 50 | | R-79 | | | | |
| 38 | | C | | 60 | " 20 | | 203 | | | | |
| 39 | | R | | 55 | MUSIC STAND LTS | | 70% | | | | |
| 40 | RAIL KICK | | DUNB 146 | | | | | | | | |

**Figure 9.40b** *Sondheim on Sondheim* cheat sheet.  
*Lighting By: Ken Billington*

After the creation of your magic sheets, print and group them back-to-back in logical pairs. Protect them by using heavyweight sheet protectors or, if preferred by your designer, laminating them. Before placing the documents in the protectors, consider your designer's preferences on paper turning—does he prefer to flip the page over along the long side or the short side? If you are unsure, ask him—especially before laminating.

## SHOP ORDER

The **shop order** is an itemized list of equipment that needs to be rented or purchased for the production. It usually does not cover "house" (stock) equipment. The shop order, along with the plot and paperwork, is considered the core of the design package.

Once the shop order is received, the rental house, or shop, will calculate the cost of the overall lighting equipment rental or purchase for the production's run. Rentals are often given as a weekly rate. Once a final cost is agreed upon, the shop order, which was originally "for bid only," will be turned into a **"pull list"** from which the shop can "pull" the finalized equipment to be shipped to the theatre.

> *"Always check your shop orders—mistakes are all too often made, and they can be very painful."*
>
> —*Hugh Vanstone*

The shop order is a joint document—created initially by the assistant lighting designer and finished by the production electrician. (An example shop order can be found in the Appendices of this text.)

### TITLE PAGE

The shop order begins with a title page. This page should contain the following information:

- Name of show
- Theatre name and address or touring company name
- Date issued
- "For Bid Only"—if the shop order is being sent out for bids and is not finalized yet
- Lighting designer's name and contact information
- Associate lighting designer's name and contact information

- Producer's name and contact information
- General manager's name and contact information
- Production electrician's name and contact information
- Dates: Shop prep, pre-hang, load-in, open, close date (if applicable), as well as location of load-in if a touring production

## GENERAL NOTES

Typically the second page of the shop order lists some general notes applicable to the overall production.

Some common shop order general notes are as follows[6]:

- All units to come with lamp, c-clamp, pin connector, black (both sides) color frame, and safety cable.
- All ellipsoidals are to be aligned.
- All units, barndoors, color frames, doughnuts, safety cables, top hats, iron, truss, and any other hardware and accessories to be painted flat black (both front and back).
- Provide 10 percent spare lamps for each type of unit, as per electrician.
- All electronics are to have the latest software installed unless otherwise specified.
- All hardware, perishables, cable lengths, dimmer rack types, and power distribution requirements to be specified by production electrician.
- All safety cables, chesboros, pipe, and other iron are to be considered part of the rental package.
- Any revisions or substitutions must be fully disclosed at time of bid.
- Bidder assumes responsibility for delivery of any additional materials that are required on site due to rental shop oversight or error.
- Color scrolls to be made and loaded by shop. All color changes to be calibrated for synchronization across all units.
- For automated units that are not brand new: included in the price of the rental, the shop should expect to replace 30 percent of all fixture lamps during the first two weeks of tech to match the color temperature of all units.

- All automated fixtures must be available to be turned on and checked with the designer and programmer in the shop at least one week prior to shop load out.

- Please provide 10 percent spares for all automated units.

- Absolutely no substitutions without written permission from the designer and production electrician.

- Entire package to be made ready by supplier and to include all connectors, cables, controls, etc. so as to comprise a complete system.

- All equipment shall be available on the first day of shop prep unless alternative plans have been arranged with the production electrician.

- The implementation of this lighting design must comply with the most stringent applicable federal and local safety and fire codes. All light plots, drawings, and the equipment list represent design intent and visual concepts only. The lighting designer is unqualified to determine structural appropriateness of the design and will not assume responsibility for improper engineering, construction, handling, or use of the lighting equipment that implements this design.[7]

## EQUIPMENT

After this initial information, an equipment list follows. Include all applicable details, such as quantity numbers, exact manufacturer and model names, and wattages. No abbreviations should be used on this document. For example, do not simply list "Source 4," instead write "ETC Source 4–10° 750w" with a quantity number.

When specifying quantity numbers, include 10 percent spares for each major fixture type. Having spares accounts for any changes that may happen during the production process as well as any replacements needed.

On the shop order, group equipment into categories. Here are some examples:

- Conventional units

- Automated units

- Accessories—such as scrollers, template holders, top hats, hazers and other effects units

- Hardware—such as lifts, pipes, truss, sidearms, and rigging hardware
- Cable—standard cable as well as DMX, breakouts, two-fers, feeder, and adaptors
- Dimmers—conventional dimmers as well as control modules for automated units and LEDs
- Control—lighting consoles, monitors, remotes, and any other system control needs
- Perishables—templates, gel, blackwrap, haze and fog fluid
- Tech table—any items that will be returned after opening night including the tables themselves, Littlites, remote monitors, and printers. (Fast-printing laser printers are best if you can get one.)

The assistant begins the shop order by laying out the basics—units (both conventional and automated fixtures), accessories (what size template holders needed and custom colors and gobos for the moving lights), basic control (like consoles), and tech table needs. Then he hands it off to the production electrician who fills in the rest of the nitty-gritty technical details—cable needs and lengths, lifts, dimmers, power supplies, truss, pipe, and even specifics on perishables such as gel and gobos. Inform your production electrician of any additional color or other items your designer prefers to have on hand so that it is accounted for in the shop order. If custom gobos are to be fabricated for your production, include high-resolution drawings of the intended gobo in the format required by the fabrication company.

If you are working in a smaller venue, you may be working as a designer-assistant-electrician-crew hybrid. In this case, it is your responsibility to fill in all of the details on a shop order before sending it out for bids.

If the production includes a large amount of practical scenery, the shop order may also need to be accompanied by a set electrics list. (See Figure 9.41.) This type of spreadsheet breaks down which pieces of scenery light up, and what lamp sources are used including quantity and wattage. It may also include details about the nature of the electrical wiring, which should be further detailed diagrammatically on the set elex plate in the drawing package.

# Little Miss Sunshine – SET ELECTRICS

| Set Element | Fixture | Voltage | Wattage | Qty | Circuits | Lamp Color | Wireless | Notes |
|---|---|---|---|---|---|---|---|---|
| SL Panel 1 - DS (For Broadway Only) | iColor Fuze Powercore (10'x60") - 1ft | 120v | 12w x 62 | 62 | N/A | RGB | No | Color Kinetics Item Number: TBD. Around Perimeter of Light Box. Focuses at US face of Light Box |
| | Data Enabler - DMX | 120v | 744w | 1 | | N/A | No | Color Kinetics Item Number: 106-000003-04. For Power and Data |
| SL Panel 2 - US (For Broadway Only) | iColor Fuze Powercore (10'x60") - 1ft | 120v | 12w x 60 | 60 | N/A | RGB | No | Color Kinetics Item Number: TBD. Around Perimeter of Light Box. Focuses at US face of Light Box |
| | Data Enabler - DMX | 120v | 720w | 1 | | N/A | No | Color Kinetics Item Number: 106-000003-04. For Power and Data |
| SR Panel 1 - DS (For Broadway Only) | iColor Fuze Powercore (10'x60") - 1ft | 120v | 12w x 62 | 62 | N/A | RGB | No | Color Kinetics Item Number: TBD. Around Perimeter of Light Box. Focuses at US face of Light Box |
| | Data Enabler - DMX | 120v | 744w | 1 | | N/A | No | Color Kinetics Item Number: 106-000003-04. For Power and Data |
| SR Panel 2 - US (For Broadway Only) | iColor Fuze Powercore (10'x60") - 1ft | 120v | 12w x 60 | 60 | N/A | RGB | No | Color Kinetics Item Number: TBD. Around Perimeter of Light Box. Focuses at US face of Light Box |
| | Data Enabler - DMX | 120v | 720w | 1 | | N/A | No | Color Kinetics Item Number: 106-000003-04. For Power and Data |
| US MT Profile Ground Row | TPR Polymer Fiber Optic Cable - 0.75mm Fiber Optic Illuminator (incandescent) | 120v | 150w | 300 | 3 | N/C | No | TPR Fixtures Code: CK-30. As Single Fibers and Groups of 2, 3 & 5 Fibers as per drawing to follow. 590 Fibers Total. TPR Product Code: TPR-FI-150 - 120 - TWBLA - PC3. (Twinkle Black 3 Plugs). [Feeds from Center] |
| MT Profile Light Box Drop #1 | ETC Source Four MultiPAR - 12 NSP (3 Cir) | 120v | 2300w x 15 | 5 | 15 | Clear | No | Hung on Pipe as per Drawing. Hang as tight to pipe as possible. Light Box Top - DS |
| | ETC Source Four MultiPAR-3 NSP (3 Cir) | 120v | 575w x 6 | 2 | 6 | Clear | No | Hung on Pipe as per Drawing. Hang as tight to pipe as possible. Light Box Top - DS |
| | 6'-0" 3CKT MR16 75w EYF Striplight | 120v | 750w x 21 | 7 | 9 | Clear | No | Hung on Pipe as per Drawing. Hang as tight to pipe as possible. Light Box Top - US |
| | 6'-0" 3CKT MR16 75w EYF Striplight | 120v | 750w x 18 | 6 | 6 | Clear | No | Hung on Pipe as per Drawing. Hang as tight to pipe as possible. Light Box Sides - SL & SR |
| MT Profile Light Box Drop #2 | ETC Source Four MultiPAR - 12 NSP (3 Cir) | 120v | 2300w x 15 | 5 | 15 | Clear | No | Hung on Pipe as per Drawing. Hang as tight to pipe as possible. Light Box Top - DS |
| | ETC Source Four MultiPAR-3 NSP (3 Cir) | 120v | 575w x 6 | 2 | 6 | Clear | No | Hung on Pipe as per Drawing. Hang as tight to pipe as possible. Light Box Top - DS |
| | 6'-0" 3CKT MR16 75w EYF Striplight | 120v | 750w x 21 | 7 | 9 | Clear | No | Hung on Pipe as per Drawing. Hang as tight to pipe as possible. Light Box Top - US |
| | 6'-0" 3CKT MR16 75w EYF Striplight | 120v | 750w x 18 | 6 | 6 | Clear | No | Hung on Pipe as per Drawing. Hang as tight to pipe as possible. Light Box Sides - SL & SR |
| VW Bus - Full Size | Head Lights - S6 Lamp | 2v | 21w x 2 | 2 | | Clear | Yes | Fitted inside VW Bus Head Light Housing behind 7" PAR Type Lens. |
| Battery Running Time - 45min/Show | Brake Lights - S8 Automotive Lamp | 2v | 21w x 2 | 2 | | Clear | Yes | Fitted inside VW Bus Break Light Housings. |
| | Turn Indicator Left - S8 Automotive Lamp | 2v | 21w x 2 | 2 | | Clear | Yes | Fitted inside VW Bus Turn Signal Housings. |
| | Turn Indicator Right - S8 Automotive Lamp | 2v | 21w x 2 | 2 | | Clear | Yes | Fitted inside VW Bus Turn Signal Housings. |
| | Dashboard Dials - Rosco LitePad HO (3"x12") | 2v | 12v | | | | Yes | Fitted behind dashboard instrument dials translucent panel. |
| | City Theatrical - ShowDMX 3x10A Dimmer | 2v | 120v x 3 | 2 | | | | Must be inter-changable between shows. Run time per show TBD. |
| | City Theatrical - ShowDMX Receiver | 2v | | | | | | Built into vehicle base. |
| | Batteries as Needed | 2v | | | | | | Built into vehicle base. |
| | Battery Charger | 2v | | | | | | Must last 2 shows on one charge. Built into vehicle base. Run time per show TBD. Built into vehicle base to re-charge must be easily accessible. |
| VW Bus - 30" Remote Control | Head Lights - S6 Lamp | 2v | 6w x 2 | 2 | | Clear | No | Fitted inside VW Bus Head Light Housings. |
| (All Lamps operated by Single Switch) | Brake Lights - S6 Lamp | 2v | 6w x 2 | 2 | | Clear | No | Fitted inside VW Bus Break Light Housings. |
| Battery Running Time - 5min/Show | Interior Fill - Rosco LitePad HO (3"x12") | 2v | 12w | 1 | | Clear | No | Mounted inside of bus. Should not be easily visible from outside of bus. Run time per show TBD. |
| | Batteries as Needed - Double Set | 2v | | | | | | |
| | External Battery Charger | 2v | | | | | | |
| CS Roof and Sign | "24 HOURS" LB - Westflex SHD Coremax X-WP | 120v | 2w x 18 | 18 | | White | No | 18 x 1'-0" runs on 2/3" centers in light box. TPR Code: FL-SHD-CHX-W-WP. |
| | "GAS" Sign - Neon w/Transformer | 120v | TBD | 1 | | Cobalt Blue | No | Design as per Drawing. Color: Tecnolux Cobalt Blue (n.16). Transformer mounted to back of hanger. Must be Dimmable. |
| | "FOOD" Sign - Neon w/Transformer | 120v | TBD | 1 | | Ruby Red Neon | No | Design as per Drawing. Color: Tecnolux Ruby Red Neon (n.118-N). Transformer mounted to back of hanger. Must be Dimmable. |
| | Neon Tubes - Rose Brand NeoFlex Diffused | 120v | 2.5w x 2 / 5w x 4 / 7.5w x 1 | 7 | 7 | Cool White | No | 2 x 1'-6" runs, 4 x 3'-0" runs and 1 x 4'-6" run of Rose Brand - NeoFlex Diffused 120v (Cool White). All individual Circuits. Might require dummy loads on dimmers. |
| | City Theatrical - WDS DMX 15A Dimmer | 12v | 180w | 1 | | | | For Dimming TPR Westflex LED product. Mounted to back of hanger. |
| | Transformer - 12v | 120v | 50w | 1 | | | | For Powering TPR Westflex LED product. Mounted to back of hanger. |
| Motel/Hospital Night Stand 1 | A19 Lamp | 12v | 50w | 1 | | Soft White | Yes | Night stand lamp with 12v Lamp. |
| Battery Running Time - 10min/Show | City Theatrical - WDS DMX 15A Dimmer | 12v | 180w | 1 | | | | Built into night stand. |
| | City Theatrical - ShowDMX Receiver | 12v | | | | | | Built into night stand. |
| | Batteries as Needed | 12v | | | | | | Must last 2 shows on one charge. Built into night stand. Run time per show TBD. |
| | Battery Charger | 12v | | | | | | Built into night stand. Power cable to re-charge must be easily accessible. |
| Motel/Hospital Night Stand 2 | A19 Lamp | 12v | 50w | 1 | | Soft White | Yes | Night stand lamp with 12v Lamp. |
| Battery Running Time - 10min/Show | City Theatrical - WDS DMX 15A Dimmer | 12v | 180w | 1 | | | | Built into night stand. |
| | City Theatrical - ShowDMX Receiver | 12v | | | | | | Built into night stand. |
| | Batteries as Needed | 12v | | | | | | Must last 2 shows on one charge. Built into night stand. Run time per show TBD. |
| | Battery Charger | 12v | | | | | | Built into night stand. Power cable to re-charge must be easily accessible. |
| Motel/Hospital Night Stand 3 | A19 Lamp | 12v | 50w | 1 | | Soft White | Yes | Night stand lamp with 12v Lamp. |
| Battery Running Time - 10min/Show | City Theatrical - WDS DMX 15A Dimmer | 12v | 180w | 1 | | | | Built into night stand. |
| | City Theatrical - ShowDMX Receiver | 12v | | | | | | Built into night stand. |
| | Batteries as Needed | 12v | | | | | | Must last 2 shows on one charge. Built into night stand. Run time per show TBD. |
| | Battery Charger | 12v | | | | | | Built into night stand. Power cable to re-charge must be easily accessible. |
| Motel Sign | "MOTEL" Sign - Neon w/Transformer & Dimmer | 12v | TBD | 4 Ltrs | | Emerald | Yes | Design as per Drawing. Color: TecnoLux Emerald (n.35B). Transformer mounted in crate. Must be Dimmable via DMX. |
| Battery Running Time - 10min/Show | "...-E" Sign - Neon w/Transformer & Dimmer | 12v | TBD | 1 Ltr | | Emerald | Yes | Design as per Drawing. Color: TecnoLux Emerald (n.35B). Transformer mounted in crate. Must be Dimmable via DMX. |
| | "CABLE TV" LB - Westflex SHD Coremax X-WP | 12v | 2.66w x 5 / 3w x 4 | 9 | | White | Yes | 5 x 1'-4" runs and 4 x 1'-6" runs on 2/3" centers in light box. TPR Code: FL-SHD-CHX-W-WP. |
| | "VACANCY" LB - Westflex SHD Coremax X-WP | 12v | 2.33w x 8 | 8 | | White | Yes | 8 x 1'-2" runs on 2/3" centers in light box. TPR Code: FL-SHD-CHX-W-WP. |
| | "NO" LB - Westflex SHD Coremax X-WP | 12v | 0.66w x 8 | 8 | | White | Yes | 8 x 0'-4" runs on 2/3" centers in light box. TPR Code: FL-SHD-CHX-W-WP. |
| | City Theatrical - WDS 15A Dimmer | 12v | 180w x 3 | 3 | | | | For Dimming TPR Westflex LED product. Built into scenic crate. |
| | City Theatrical - ShowDMX Receiver | 12v | | | | | | Built into scenic crate. |
| | Batteries as Needed | 12v | | | | | | Must last 2 shows on one charge. Power cable to re-charge must be easily accessible. |
| | Battery Charger | 12v | | | | | | Built into scenic crate. Power cable to re-charge must be easily accessible. |
| Hospital Soffit with Steer Curtain | Neon High - Rose Brand NeoFlex Diffused | 120v | 42.5w | 1 | | Cool White | No | Rose Brand - NeoFlex Diffused 120v (Cool White) 25'-6". Individual Circuit. Might require dummy load on dimmer. |
| | Neon Middle - Rose Brand NeoFlex Diffused | 120v | 45w | 1 | | Cool White | No | Rose Brand - NeoFlex Diffused 120v (Cool White) 27'-0". Individual Circuit. Might require dummy load on dimmer. |
| | Neon Low - Rose Brand NeoFlex Diffused | 120v | 47.5w | 1 | | Cool White | No | Rose Brand - NeoFlex Diffused 120v (Cool White) 28'-6". Individual Circuit. Might require dummy load on dimmer. |
| LHS "Sun" Stage | G18 Lamps (Individual E26 Sockets) | 120v | 25w x 39 | 39 | 3 | Clear | No | 3 Circuit Chaser. Unit trails cable. Prod Electrician to confirm length, type and location of power feed. |
| Wireless DMX Transmitter | City Theatrical - ShowDMX Transmitter | 120v | | | | | | |

**NOTE:** 7 x City Theatrical WDS 15A Dimmers from La Jolla Playhouse Stock. 1 x City Theatrical ShowDMX Transmitter, 5 x City Theatrical ShowDMX Receivers & 2 x City Theatrical ShowDMX Dimmers (3 x 10A) from Lighting Shop as part of Rental Package.

**Figure 9.41**  Little Miss Sunshine set electrics spreadsheet.
Lighting By: Ken Billington
Assoc. LD: Anthony Pearson

# TECH TABLE DRAWING

A **tech table drawing** is a not-to-scale, simplified block drawing of the layout of equipment requested for the tech table. Often considered part of the shop order, the tech table drawing details individual set-ups for the designer, assistants, and programmer—things like remote monitors, headset channels, and task lights. Having this drawing not only helps to ensure the desired equipment is ordered, but also saves time during the tech table set-up while loading-in.

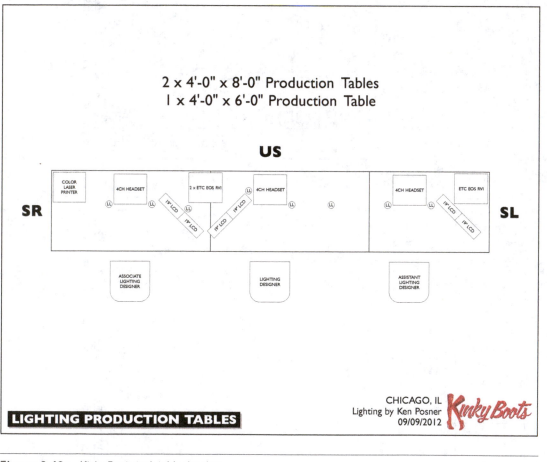

**Figure 9.42a**  *Kinky Boots* tech table drawing.
*Lighting By: Ken Posner*
*Assoc. LD: Anthony Pearson*

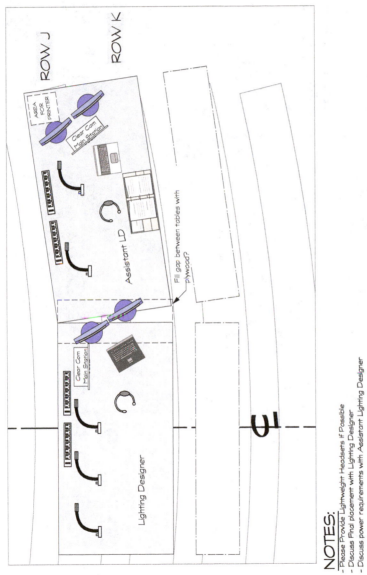

ROW J

ROW K

AREA FOR PRINTER

Clear Com Main Station

Assistant LD

Fill gap between tables with plywood?

Clear Com Main Station

Lighting Designer

Lighting Tech Table Layout
Scale: 1/2" = 1'-O"
Drawn: JP

NOTES:
- Please Provide Lightweight Headsets if Possible
- Discuss Final placement with Lighting Designer
- Discuss power requirements with Assistant Lighting Designer

**Figure 9.42b** *33 Variations* tech table drawing.
*Lighting By: David Lander*
*Assoc. LD: Justin A. Partier*

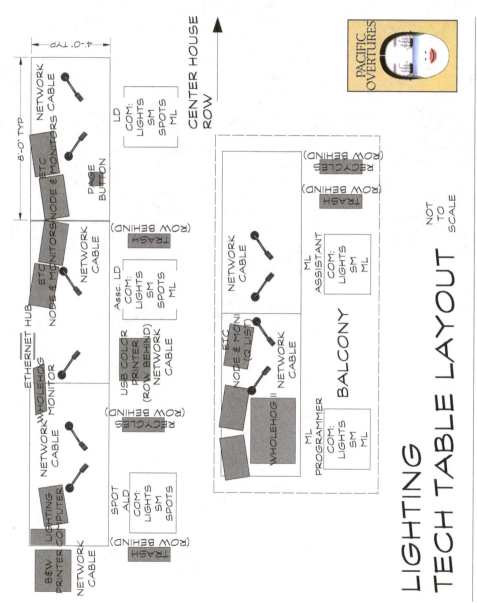

**Figure 9.42c** *Pacific Overtures tech table drawing.*
*Lighting By: Brian MacDevitt*
*Assoc. LD: Anne E. McMillis*

A tech table drawing should contain the following information:

- Show name and/or logo
- Lighting designer's name
- A title such as "Lighting Tech Table Layout"
- "Not-to-scale" notation
- Tech table size—4' × 8' tables are considered standard. Depending on the level of production, you may need anywhere from one to five tables for the lighting team (with an average of two to three). Ideally the designer and the programmer should each have their own table.
- Placement of tech tables in house. Refer to Chapter 6 for further discussion on this topic.
- Placement and quantity of remote tech table monitors desired for each table. Accompanying equipment, such as RVI nodes—which allow user-defined views on the monitors—should also be placed. Ask your production electrician what equipment is best to include.
- Placement and quantity of dimmable Littlites, or other task lights, on each table.
- Placement of console and monitors on programmer's table.
- Butt-boards and/or special seating requests (detailed further in Chapter 6).
- Trash and recycle bin placements.
- Printer placements—not applicable for remotely networked printers placed elsewhere in the theatre.
- Headset, or "Com" information assigned to each individual in the lighting team. On large professional productions, multi-channel headsets are often used, which allows each channel to be muted separately and set at an individual volume. Common channels used for the lighting department on a large production are as follows:
  - "Lighting Private"—used only for the lighting design team to talk among themselves without disturbing other departments. Great for cueing.
  - "SM"—connects the lighting design team with the production stage manager to discuss the calling of cues and other SM-related needs.
  - "Spots"—used specifically for the followspot assistant to discuss and call cues to the followspot operators.
  - "ML Private"—additional private channel between the lighting team and the programmer, if desired. Traditionally used on shows that have used two separate programmers for conventionals and moving lights.

Your designer will choose which channels he prefers to listen to and turn off the others. As the assistant, you need to listen to all available channels at all times and respond when needed.

In addition, some designers prefer to use a handset instead of a headset. A **handset** is an old-fashioned corded telephone handset, which has been modified for use with a Com system. It has a button on the handset that is push-to-talk when the designer wants to use it. Indicate the need of a handset if this is your designer's preference. For complicated shows, create a **headset specification spreadsheet** to clarify who-gets-what-channels and what types of headsets. (See Figure 9.43.)

## AREA LAYOUT

An **Area Layout** visually describes the location of the designer's main focus areas on stage. (See Figure 9.44.) **Focus areas**, also called lighting areas or acting areas, are imaginary divisions of the stage imagined by the lighting designer and used in order to create an even wash of light across the entire playing area. The designer decides on these areas while designing the light plot, and then uses them again as a guide during focus.

A focus area is typically 8'-0" to 12'-0" in size and overlaps the adjacent areas by approximately 20 percent or more.

Begin the area layout by filling the page with a simple grayed-out groundplan. Then lay the focus areas on top in a bold line weight. In the center of each area, assign an alphabetical letter. (The letters should follow the same pattern as the designer's channeling structure—SR to SL or SL to SR whichever is appropriate.) Dimension how far these areas are from 0,0 both SR/SL and US/DS.

If desired by your designer, these areas can be labeled on stage for focus (as described in Chapter 6). They can also be included with your focus charts as part of your focus chart cover page (more information in the next chapter). That way you can simply record, "to Area A" in your focus charts instead of recording duplicate location coordinates every time a main area is focused.

# Kinky Boots - HEADSETS

07/22/2012<br>Lighting by Ken Posner

| NAME | POSITION | LOCATION | TYPE | HEADSET | CHANNEL | LABEL | ACCESSORIES | NOTES |
|---|---|---|---|---|---|---|---|---|
| Ken Posner | LD | Center of Orchestra | 4CH | Telex Lighweight Single Muff | A | Stage Manager | Headset Extension | Please ensure box is as low profile as possible. |
| | | | | | B | Lighting Private | | |
| | | | | | C | ML Private | | |
| | | | | | D | Spot Private | | |
| Anthony Pearson | Associate LD | SR of LD | 4CH | Telex Lighweight Single Muff | A | Stage Manager | Headset Extension | Please ensure box is as low profile as possible. |
| | | | | | B | Lighting Private | | |
| | | | | | C | ML Private | | |
| | | | | | D | Spot Private | | |
| Keri Thibodeau | Assistant LD | SL of LD | 4CH | Telex Lighweight Single Muff | A | Stage Manager | Headset Extension | Please ensure box is as low profile as possible. |
| | | | | | B | Lighting Private | | |
| | | | | | C | ML Private | | |
| | | | | | D | Spot Private | | |
| Aland Henderson | ML Programmer | Center of Orchestra behind LD (TBC) | 4CH | Telex Lighweight Single Muff | A | Stage Manager | Headset Extension In-Line Mic On/Off Switch | Please ensure box is as low profile as possible. |
| | | | | | B | Lighting Private | | |
| | | | | | C | ML Private | | |
| | | | | | D | Spot Private | | |
| Matt Taylor | ML Tracker | SR of ML Programmer | 4CH | Telex Lighweight Single Muff | A | Stage Manager | Headset Extension | Please ensure box is as low profile as possible. |
| | | | | | B | Lighting Private | | |
| | | | | | C | ML Private | | |
| | | | | | D | Spot Private | | |
| Randy Zaibek | Production Electrician | Back of Orchestra (TBC) | 4CH | Telex Lighweight Single Muff | A | Stage Manager | Headset Extension | Please ensure box is as low profile as possible. |
| | | | | | B | Lighting Private | | |
| | | | | | C | ML Private | | |
| | | | | | D | Spot Private | | |
| Michael Brown | Conventional Console | Back of Orchestra (TBC) | 4CH | Sennheiser Dual Muff | A | Stage Manager | Headset Extension In-Line Mic On/Off Switch | Please ensure box is as low profile as possible. |
| | | | | | B | Lighting Private | | |
| | | | | | C | ML Private | | |
| | | | | | D | Spot Private | | |
| | Lighting Operating Position | Back of Orchestra SR of Sound | 4CH | Sennheiser Dual Muff | A | Stage Manager | Headset Extension In-Line Mic On/Off Switch | Please ensure box is as low profile as possible. |
| | | | | | B | Lighting Private | | |
| | | | | | C | ML Private | | |
| | | | | | D | Spot Private | | |
| | Spot 1 | Booth SL | 2CH | Sennheiser Dual Muff | A | Stage Manager | | |
| | | | | | B | Spot Private | | |
| | Spot 2 | Booth Ctr | 2CH | Sennheiser Dual Muff | A | Stage Manager | | |
| | | | | | B | Spot Private | | |
| | Spot 3 | Booth SR | 2CH | Sennheiser Dual Muff | A | Stage Manager | | |
| | | | | | B | Spot Private | | |
| | Dimmers | SR High Jump | 2CH | Sennheiser Dual Muff | A | Stage Manager | | |
| | | | | | B | Lighting Private | | |
| | Deck Elec / ML Tech | Deck | 2CH Wireless | Telex Lighweight Single Muff | A | Stage Manager | | |
| | | | | | B | Lighting Private | | |

**Figure 9.43** *Kinky Boots* headset specification.
*Lighting By: Kenneth Posner*
*Assoc. LD: Anthony Pearson*

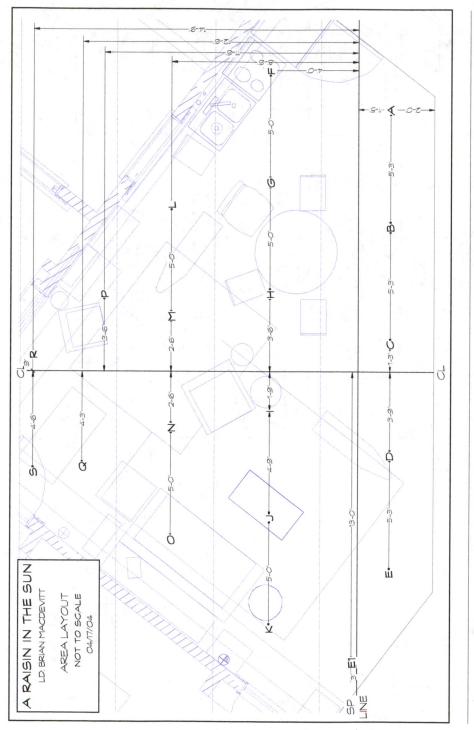

**Figure 9.44** *A Raisin in the Sun area layout.*
*Lighting By: Brian MacDevitt*
*Assoc. LD: Anne E. McMills*

# GROUPS LIST

A group is a set of channels programmed together so that several channels can be illuminated together at once without having to type each in separately. A **groups list** is a simple inventory of these groups. (See Figure 9.45.) Give your groups list to your programmer before load-in so that the groups can be programmed into the console before the designer begins to cue.

**RADIO CITY MUSIC HALL CHRISTMAS SPECTACULAR 2005**

LIGHTING BY ED McCARTHY

**GROUP LIST**

OBSESSION

| # | DESCRIPTION | # | DESCRIPTION | # | DESCRIPTION |
|---|---|---|---|---|---|
| 1 | ALL LANDING <L PINK | 140 | ALL X LEFT AMBER | 700 | ALL BLUE HOUSE |
| 2 | ALL PIT WASH PINK | 141 | X AMBER IN 1 | 701 | BLUE A COVE |
| 3 | ALL WOOD WASH PINK | 143 | X AMBER IN 2 | 702 | BLUE B COVE |
| 4 | ALL LANDING <L CC | 145 | X AMBER IN 3 | 703 | BLUE C COVE |
| 5 | ALL PIT WASH CC | 147 | X LT.PINK IN 4 | 704 | BLUE D COVE |
| 6 | ALL WOOD WASH CC | 150 | ALL X LEFT DK.PINK | 705 | BLUE E COVE |
| 7 | ALL WOOD WASH BLUE | 151 | X DK.PINK IN 1 | 706 | BLUE F COVE |
| 10 | ALL FRONTS | 153 | X DK.PINK IN 2 | 707 | BLUE G COVE |
| 11 | ALL PIT FRONTS | 155 | X DK.PINK IN 3 | 708 | BLUE H COVE |
| 14 | ALL WOOD FRONTS | 157 | X BLUE IN 4 | 709 | BLUE SOFFITS |
| 21 | ALL LANDING <R PINK | 160 | ALL X RIGHT AMBER | 710 | BLUE URNS |
| 24 | ALL LANDING <R CC | 170 | ALL X RIGHT DK.PINK | 800 | ALL RED HOUSE |
| 32 | ALL MEZZ CC | 181 | ALL KICKS <L CC | 801 | RED A COVE |
| 37 | ALL UV WASH | 186 | ALL SIDES <L CC | 802 | RED B COVE |
| 40 | ALL DK.BLUE DOWNS | 191 | ALL KICKS >R CC | 803 | RED C COVE |
| 41 | DK. BLUE DOWN IN 1 | 196 | ALL SIDES >R CC | 804 | RED D COVE |
| 42 | DK. BLUE DOWN IN 2 | 201 | ALL BANDCAR PINK | 805 | RED E COVE |
| 43 | DK. BLUE DOWN IN 3 | 211 | ALL BANDCAR LAV | 806 | RED F COVE |
| 44 | DK. BLUE DOWN IN 4 | 401 | ALL BLUE FOOTS | 807 | RED G COVE |
| 45 | DK. BLUE DOWN IN 5 | 404 | ALL BLUE BORDER | 808 | RED H COVE |
| 60 | ALL CC DOWNS | 421 | ALL RED FOOTS | 809 | RED SOFFITS |
| 61 | CC DOWN IN 1 | 424 | ALL RED BORDER | 810 | RED URNS |
| 62 | CC DOWN IN 2 | 441 | ALL GREEN FOOTS | 900 | ALL GREEN HOUSE |
| 63 | CC DOWN IN 3 | 444 | ALL GREEN BORDER | 901 | GREEN A COVE |
| 64 | CC DOWN IN 4 | 461 | ALL AMBER FOOTS | 902 | GREEN B COVE |
| 65 | CC DOWN IN 5 | 464 | ALL AMBER BORDER | 903 | GREEN C COVE |
| 80 | ALL ENDS <L | 481 | ALL CLEAR FOOTS | 904 | GREEN D COVE |
| 81 | | 492 | ALL DROP FRONTS CC | 905 | GREEN E COVE |
| 82 | ALL ENDS IN 1 | | | 906 | GREEN F COVE |
| 83 | ALL ENDS IN 2 | 504 | ALL CC LANDING <L | 907 | GREEN G COVE |
| 84 | ALL ENDS IN 3 | 506 | ALL CC WOOD | 908 | GREEN H COVE |
| 85 | ALL ENDS IN 4 | 512 | ALL CC 2 MEZZ | 909 | GREEN SOFFITS |
| 86 | ALL ENDS IN 5 | 518 | ALL CC 2 DROP FRONTS | 910 | GREEN URNS |
| 90 | ALL ENDS <R | 524 | ALL CC LANDING >R | 950 | ALL AMBER HOUSE |
| 100 | ALL X LEFT LT.PINK | 532 | ALL CC 3 MEZZ | 951 | AMBER A COVE |
| 101 | | 538 | ALL CC 3 DROP FRONTS | 952 | AMBER B COVE |
| 103 | X LEFT LT.PINK WOOD | 540 | ALL CC DOWN | 953 | AMBER C COVE |
| 104 | X LEFT LT.PINK IN 1 | 541 | CC DOWN IN 1 | 954 | AMBER D COVE |
| 106 | X LEFT LT.PINK IN 2 | 542 | CC DOWN IN 2 | 955 | AMBER E COVE |
| 108 | X LEFT LT.PINK IN 3 | 543 | CC DOWN IN 3 | 956 | AMBER F COVE |
| 110 | ALL X LEFT BLUE | 544 | CC DOWN IN 4 | 957 | AMBER G COVE |
| 111 | | 545 | CC DOWN IN 5 | 958 | AMBER H COVE |
| 113 | X LEFT BLUE WOOD | 581 | CC KICKS <L | 959 | AMBER SOFFITS |
| 114 | X LEFT BLUE IN 1 | 586 | CC SIDES <L | 960 | AMBER URNS |
| 116 | X LEFT BLUE IN 2 | 591 | CC KICKS >R | 961 | BLUE/RED STRIPE |
| 118 | X LEFT BLUE IN 3 | 596 | CC SIDES >R | 962 | RED/GREEN STRIPE |
| 120 | ALL X RIGHT LT.PINK | | | 963 | SUNSET |
| 130 | ALL X RIGHT BLUE | | | 995 | ALL SCROLL B LAMP |
| | | | | 996 | ALL SCROLL B SCROLL |
| | | | | 998 | ALL SCROLL A LAMP |
| | | | | 999 | ALL SCROLL A SCROLL |

**Figure 9.45** *Radio City Christmas Spectacular* groups list.
*Lighting By: Ed McCarthy*
*Assoc. LD: Anne E McMills*

If your designer does not provide you with her preferred groups, create your own. The designer can choose whether or not to use them, but it is better to have them already programmed. Use a logical method. One popular way is using the first number of channels to name the group number. (See Figure 9.46.) An example of this method would be grouping all of the frontlight channels (channels 1–20) into group "1," and all of the backlight channels (channels 21–40) into group "21," and so on. To get more advanced, you can then group the "in 1" items from the same system together, the "in 2" row together and onward moving upstage using the last channel number in the series. Therefore, to continue with our example, if channels 1–5 are the DS frontlight "in 1," then they would be both in group 1 (which contains all of the frontlight) as well as group 5 (which would only bring up channels 1–5 as the "in 1" frontlight). Continuing on, group 10 would bring up channels 6–10 as the "in 2" frontlight and so on.

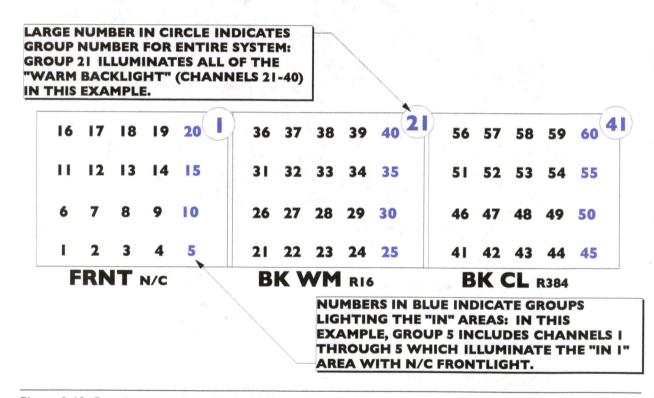

**LARGE NUMBER IN CIRCLE INDICATES GROUP NUMBER FOR ENTIRE SYSTEM: GROUP 21 ILLUMINATES ALL OF THE "WARM BACKLIGHT" (CHANNELS 21-40) IN THIS EXAMPLE.**

**NUMBERS IN BLUE INDICATE GROUPS LIGHTING THE "IN" AREAS: IN THIS EXAMPLE, GROUP 5 INCLUDES CHANNELS 1 THROUGH 5 WHICH ILLUMINATE THE "IN 1" AREA WITH N/C FRONTLIGHT.**

**Figure 9.46** Example grouping method (excerpt from a conventional magic sheet).

"In 1," "in 2," etc.—In a proscenium theatre, the corridor of stage space running SR to SL between the legs. "In 1" would fall DS between the proscenium and leg #1; "In 2" occurs between leg #1 and leg #2; and so on.

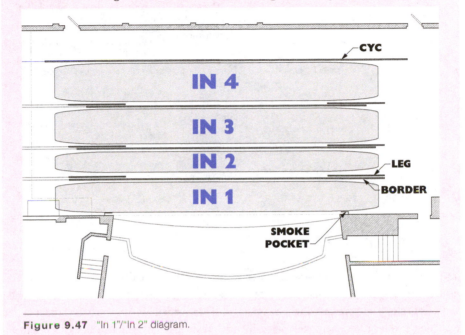

**Figure 9.47**  "In 1"/"In 2" diagram.

## SCENE BREAKDOWN AND SCENE-BY-SCENE

Scene breakdowns and scene-by-scenes are quick reference documents that display the scenic state of each moment in the production. They may also include intended time of day.

The **Scene Breakdown**, also known as a **Scene List,** is a simple spreadsheet listing act/scene number, page number, location/scenery onstage, time of day, and notes. (See Figure 9.48.) Comb through the script and include any lighting indicators that you find. Having these notes readily available helps the designer to stay within the playwright's overall concept, if so desired.

The **Scene-by-Scene,** also called the **Transition Plan** or **Transition Breakdown,** displays scene names and numbers, locations, small groundplans, and photos from the model within each new moment in the show. It is a valuable resource during a multi-set musical but is usually unneeded during a small play with no scenic changes.

| Scene | Page # | Location | Time of Day | Notes |
|-------|--------|----------|-------------|-------|
| **ACT I** | | | | |
| 1-1 | 1 | Narrator | Dawn | "The dawn came, but no day." "In the morning, the dust hung like fog" "film of dust" |
| 1-2 | 1 | Oklahoma - Roadside | Day / Afternoon | "hotter than hell on this road" "i hate to hit the sun -- but it's better now" (pg6) |
| 1-3 | 6 | Joad's Front Yard | Evening / Dark | "...come in here with a flashlight..." |
| 1-4 | 10 | Car Sales Lot | Day | salesmen at work |
| 1-5 | 11 | Uncle John's Front Yard | Late Afternoon Sunset / Suppertime | "Connie come just in time for supper" "have some supper..." |
| 1-6 | 26 | Uncle John's Front Yard | Just before dawn into dawn | "getting along towards day." "what are you doing now... so early?" |
| 1-7 | 28 | Musicians / Truck Travels | Dawn into next night | grandma sleepin |

**Figure 9.48** *Grapes of Wrath* scene breakdown.[8]

Conveniently, the scene-by-scene is often created by the scenic department. Once received, print each scene as an individual letter-size (or A4-size) page, insert the pages into heavyweight sheet protectors, and organize them chronologically in a small binder. Place the binder on the tech table in a location where you can easily reach them and the designer can easily see them. That way you can help by flipping pages while the designer is cueing.

## SHOW BIBLE AND SCRIPT

The show bible, also called the "lighting bible" or simply "bible," is a binder used to store printed lighting design documentation. The show bible is usually a large 3-ring binder (in the U.S.)—typically 2" or 2½" in width depending on preference and size of show. A view binder—one with a clear front pocket—is useful to hold a cover page, and a "D"-ring binder will hold more pages than traditional "O"-ring binders. Additionally, the show bible can become the archival bible after opening.

When providing printed archival documents for your designer, you may find you need an additional binder simply to hold the moving light focus charts and tracking information.

In addition to the show bible, you also need to create a show script for your designer. A show script is a separate small 3-ring binder (usually 1" wide) containing the script and only items that the designer may need on a daily basis.

**Figure 9.49**   Example binder cover.

## BINDER COVERS AND SPINES

Create binder covers and spines for your bible and script. (See Figure 9.49.) Include the following information on your covers:

- Title of show
- Show logo
- Name of lighting designer
- Title of binder (such as "Lighting Bible" or "Lighting Script")
- Name of theatre and location

Spines should include the same information as the cover, except for the show logo—usually there is not enough room. Instead, simply type in the name of the show.

Cut the spines neatly and straight using a paper cutter. (Small, consumer-grade paper cutters can be purchased at your local office supply store.) Insert the spines so that the show title can be read right-side up when the binder lays down on a table.

## TABS

Use page dividers with tabs to delineate between categories of paperwork. As with all paperwork preferences, ask your designer and their design office how many tabs and what kind are preferred. For example, do they like 8-tab styles or 5-tab styles? Blue? Clear? Multicolored? And how many do they need? Also ask what categories are desired and in what order they should appear.

If no preference is given, choose a style with sticky printable labels. Individual paper labels (that do not adhere) can easily fall out and get lost.

One possible way to organize your binder tabs is as follows:

**Show Bible**

- Magic sheets and area layout (placed on top in heavyweight sheet protectors—no tab needed)
- Contact sheet (stapled and hole-punched)
- Calendar (always keep current date on top—stapled and hole-punched)
- Instrument schedule
- Channel hookup
- Focus charts
- Cue synopsis
- Followspot cue sheets

- ML focus charts
- ML tracking
- Shop order
- Act 1
- Act 2
- Drawings (may contain small versions of scenic drawings or lighting drawings in sheet protectors)
- Notes and misc.

**Script**
- Magic sheets (placed on top in heavyweight sheet protectors—no tab needed)
- Contact sheet (stapled and hole-punched)
- Calendar (always keep current date on top—stapled and hole-punched)
- Act 1
- Act 2
- Notes and misc.

Print a script for the lighting bible, lighting script, and your followspot assistant, if applicable. Prepare the scripts by using small Post-it flags or tabs to indicate act/scene breaks and/or songs. Use different tab colors for each act.

When the binders are complete, hole-punch and insert the paperwork. Some items, such as magic sheets, may be better kept in heavyweight sheet protectors to safeguard against heavy daily use. Other frequently accessed multi-page items, such as the contact sheet and calendar, may need to be stapled as well as hole-punched.

Additional items may also be included in the show bible. For example, if the design office prefers archival materials to be copied to a flash drive, CD, or other storage device, include printed labels and a holder for the device that secures it to the binder. Furthermore, some assistants include the instrument schedule and channel hookup printed in small booklet form and a small notepad with pencil in the front of the binder.

For the script, the designer may prefer a small ruler or straight-edge to be included (used to neatly write cue placements in the script) and a small notepad with pencil.

Additionally, download a copy of each user manual for all electronic equipment such as moving lights, LED fixtures, and consoles. Save these files in a "literature" folder in your shared Dropbox. You may need to refer to them in case of technical difficulty.

C H A P T E R   1 0

# Tech Process Paperwork

Lighting paperwork is a living thing continually evolving throughout the production process until opening night. Unlike the pre-production paperwork discussed in the last chapter, tech process paperwork begins its life as an empty shell, or **skeleton file**, and becomes complete day by day as the lighting design matures; exactly the opposite of something like a light plot (a pre-production item) that begins the tech process as a complete document and gets altered when changes occur.

## FOCUS CHARTS

**Focus Charts**, sometimes called "conventional focus charts," diagram the focus for every conventional light within the show. Their purpose is to enable the head electrician (or sometimes the PSM) to be able to refocus a fixture without the designer or assistant present.

Focus charts are also used when moving a show to another city—whether on tour or for a new company. The focus charts from the original show will be used as a jumping off point for replicating the production in the new theatre.

The focus chart document is a template consisting of individual fields intended to describe the aspects of each focus—including where the designer stands while she is in the hot spot, how fuzzy or sharp the edge of the beam is, and what shutter cuts are used, if any. (See Figure 10.1.) During focus, the assistant will observe the designer focusing each light, and record each choice in the focus charts.

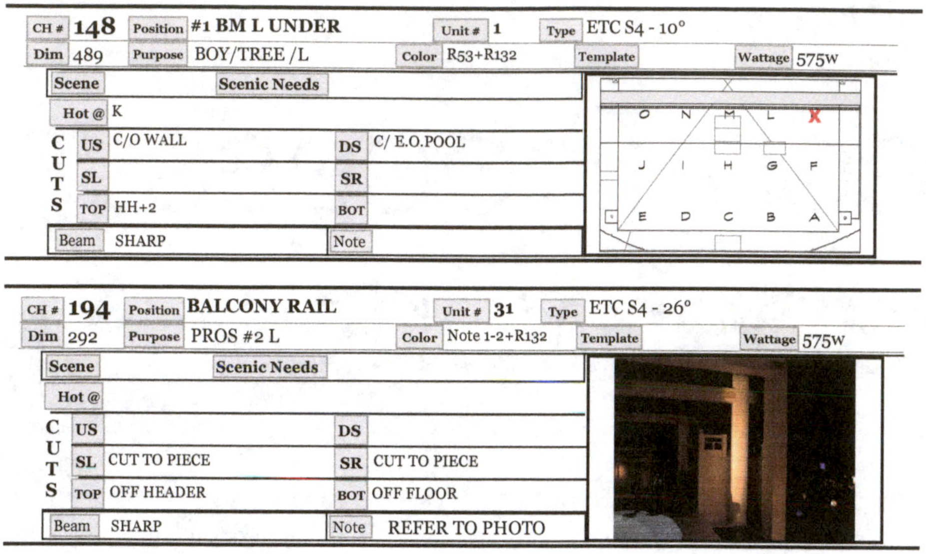
CH # 148 | Position #1 BM L UNDER | Unit # 1 | Type ETC S4 - 10°
Dim 489 | Purpose BOY/TREE /L | Color R53+R132 | Template | Wattage 575W
Scene | Scenic Needs
Hot @ K
CUTS: US C/O WALL | DS C/ E.O.POOL
SL | SR
TOP HH+2 | BOT
Beam SHARP | Note


CH # 194 | Position BALCONY RAIL | Unit # 31 | Type ETC S4 - 26°
Dim 292 | Purpose PROS #2 L | Color Note 1-2+R132 | Template | Wattage 575W
Scene | Scenic Needs
Hot @
CUTS: US | DS
SL CUT TO PIECE | SR CUT TO PIECE
TOP OFF HEADER | BOT OFF FLOOR
Beam SHARP | Note REFER TO PHOTO

**Figure 10.1** *Pacific Overtures* focus charts made in FileMaker Pro.
*Lighting by: Brian MacDevitt*
*Assoc. LD: Anne E. McMills*
*Database Created by: Charles Pennebaker*

Focus charts can be created by using Lightwright or developed through the use of other software, such as FileMaker Pro. If using a program other than Lightwright, the instrument information should be imported into the focus charts so that channel, color, barrel type, and all other information is integrated into one document.

## LIGHTWRIGHT FOCUS CHARTS

In Lightwright, focus charts can be formatted under the "layout" tab—in one column or two depending on preference. (See Figure 10.2.) Import a drawing to be your default image—typically a groundplan or your area layout. The input fields can also be moved around if you like a different visual organization than the default.

Once the layout is complete, fill out each chart under the "focus" tab. If needed, the groundplan you imported may be drawn on directly to visually represent the way the light falls onstage. (See Figure 10.3.) For unusual or hard-to-describe focuses, import a digital photo of the fixture.

*CHAPLIN*

## FOCUS CHARTS

**IV LADDER LEFT**

| U# | Purpose | Instrument Type & Accessory & Wattage | Color & Gobo | Dim | Chan |
|----|---------|----------------------------------------|--------------|-----|------|
| 1 | Studio X | Source 4-Par NSP+7.5" Top Hat 575w | N/C | 1/321 | (187) |

**10R** @ **+18**   FNote:

| | | |
|---|---|---|
| Scy: | US: Land Off Wall | DS: |
| Beam: In/Sp - - + - - Out/FI | SR: | SL: |
| Axis: \| — / \ L/R US/DS | Top: | Bot: |

| U# | Purpose | Instrument Type & Accessory & Wattage | Color & Gobo | Dim | Chan |
|----|---------|----------------------------------------|--------------|-----|------|
| 2 | Red Drape Slash | Source 4-26° 575w | L-106 | 1/322 | (217) |

**SL** @ **Drop**   FNote: **Broadway Slash**

| | | |
|---|---|---|
| Scy: Academy Red Drop | US: | DS: |
| Beam: In/Sp - - + - - (Out/FI) | SR: | SL: |
| Axis: \| — / \ L/R US/DS | Top: | Bot: |

| U# | Purpose | Instrument Type & Accessory & Wattage | Color & Gobo | Dim | Chan |
|----|---------|----------------------------------------|--------------|-----|------|
| 3 | Studio X | Source 4-Par NSP+7.5" Top Hat 575w | N/C | 1/321 | (187) |

**CL** @ **+18**   FNote:

| | | |
|---|---|---|
| Scy: | US: Land Off Wall | DS: |
| Beam: In/Sp - - + - - Out/FI | SR: | SL: |
| Axis: \| — / \ L/R US/DS | Top: | Bot: |

| U# | Purpose | Instrument Type & Accessory & Wattage | Color & Gobo | Dim | Chan |
|----|---------|----------------------------------------|--------------|-----|------|
| 4 | Back Wall Slash L | Source 4-36° w/Temp+Temp+Donut+ColoRam 575w | (282), T:R-77448A | 1/323 | (63) |

@   FNote: **Top**

| | | |
|---|---|---|
| Scy: Back Wall | US: | DS: To Wall |
| Beam: In/Sp - - + - (·) Out/FI | SR: | SL: Off SL Pilaster |
| Axis: \| — / \ L/R US/DS | Top: Land At Scenic Truss | Bot: |

| U# | Purpose | Instrument Type & Accessory & Wattage | Color & Gobo | Dim | Chan |
|----|---------|----------------------------------------|--------------|-----|------|
| 5 | X to Far | Source 4-19°+6.25" Half Hat 575w | L-702 | 1/324 | (113) |

**10R** @ **+18**   FNote:

| | | |
|---|---|---|
| Scy: | US: Off Wall | DS: +12 |
| Beam: In/Sp - - + - - (Out/FI) | SR: | SL: |
| Axis: \| — / \ L/R US/DS | Top: HH @ 16R | Bot: |

| U# | Purpose | Instrument Type & Accessory & Wattage | Color & Gobo | Dim | Chan |
|----|---------|----------------------------------------|--------------|-----|------|
| 6 | X to Far | Source 4-19°+6.25" Half Hat 575w | L-161 | 1/325 | (153) |

**10R** @ **+18**   FNote:

| | | |
|---|---|---|
| Scy: | US: Off Wall | DS: +12 |
| Beam: In/Sp - - + - - (Out/FI) | SR: | SL: |
| Axis: \| — / \ L/R US/DS | Top: HH @ 16R | Bot: |

| U# | Purpose | Instrument Type & Accessory & Wattage | Color & Gobo | Dim | Chan |
|----|---------|----------------------------------------|--------------|-----|------|
| 7 | Back Wall Slash L | Source 4-36° w/Temp+Temp+Donut+ColoRam 575w | (282), T:R-77448A | 1/323 | (63) |

@   FNote: **Bottom**

| | | |
|---|---|---|
| Scy: Back Wall | US: | DS: To Wall |
| Beam: In/Sp - - + - (·) Out/FI | SR: | SL: |
| Axis: \| — / \ L/R US/DS | Top: | Bot: |

KB Associates, Inc. / Lightwright 5   IV LADDER LEFT

**Figure 10.2** *Chaplin* focus charts made in Lightwright.
*Lighting by: Ken Billington*
*Assoc. LD: John Demous*

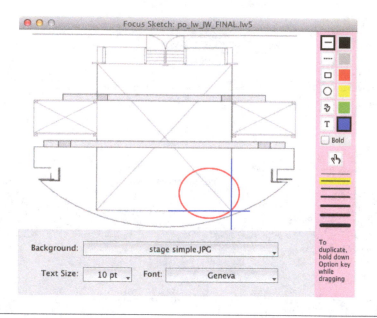

**Figure 10.3**  Focus sketch screenshot in Lightwright.

Note: If you are having trouble with your focus chart photos appearing too dark, try taking the photo again with the worklights on or at half. The ambient light will give your camera more visual reference, which allows it to balance the contrast better. Also, never use a flash when taking photos for lighting purposes. The flash will wash out all of the lighting and render the photo useless.

**Figure 10.4**  Taking focus chart photos.
*Courtesy of: Rob Halliday*

The following are some examples of common information recorded in the focus charts:

- **Location**—Where the designer stands for the hotspot to hit his face or back of his head or, alternatively, where the beam of light lands on stage. Whichever method the designer prefers, note the method in the focus chart cover page (discussed below).

  Most designers stand so that the hotspot hits his face or the back of his head (depending if he faces the light or faces away from it). Wherever he chooses to stand, the assistant records the position of the designer's feet (from 0,0) within the grid created by the focus tapes (discussed further in Chapters 2 and 6). For example, if the designer is standing at 2'-0" SR of centerline and 8'-0" US of the smoke pocket, write down 2R@+8. Alternatively, if the fixture is lighting a piece of scenery as opposed to the designer, the location can be recorded (if the fixture is only lighting the SR side of a drop, for example) as "SR @ DS Drop." Adding a photo of the focus can be helpful in these situations.

- **Photo**—A photo of a complicated focus or a drawing of the fixture on the groundplan, as discussed above.

- **Scenic needs**—Denotes which temporary scenic pieces are needed to focus the fixture, such as "DS Tree Drop," "UR Rolling Platform," or "Bedroom Set." This helps quickly identify those fixtures that must be focused on a specific scenic piece. If the scenic piece is used in multiple locations, also identify for which scene the fixture is being focused. If the set is a unit set with no flying, rolling, or tracking scenery or if no specific scenery is needed, then this field can be left blank. There is no need to denote scenery that is always stationary and present.

- **Beam**—Barrel or flood information. Fresnel: is the beam at spot or flood or somewhere along the continuum? Leko: barrel in, out, sharp, or anywhere in between? PAR: bottle running US/DS, SL/SR, or at an angle? Lightwright's focus charts use handy symbols that can be circled to represent this information.

  Running the barrel in or out has two very distinct looks—especially when using a gobo. Chances are your designer will have a preference so learn to identify the visual difference. An easy way to remember is: "forward-fuzzy, backward-blobby"—running the barrel *out* makes the edges of the image look slightly more blue and fuzzy ("forward-fuzzy") and running the barrel *in* makes the edges look more orange and blobby ("backward-blobby"). (See Figure 10.5.)

**Figure 10.5**  Focus options.

- **Cuts**—Pertains to either shutter cuts or barndoor "cuts"—SR, SL, US, and DS. Use abbreviations when possible. Some examples of shutter cut descriptions are: "to EOD" (Edge of Deck), "off prosc" (proscenium), or "to plat" (platform). Also, if needed, you can be more specific such as "< from 2L to 4R" (< meaning "angle"). In Lightwright, fields called "Bottom" and "Top" are also included. These can be used when it seems less confusing to identify the top and bottom of the beam instead of identifying a specific stage direction.

- **Notes**—This is a great place to write "no cuts" if there are no shutter cuts—to assure the information was left blank purposefully. Another common note used is "SAA" (Same As Above), which illustrates that the current fixture focuses identically to the previous fixture listed above it in the focus charts.

## FOCUS CHART COVER PAGE

The **Focus Chart Cover Page** is a separate document (usually one to two pages) that, as the title suggests, creates a cover page for the focus charts. (See Figure 10.6.) It includes the standard title information such as the show name/logo, theatre name and location, lighting designer's name, and assistant/associate names as well as the location of 0,0 and relevant information regarding how to read the focus charts.

## CHAPLIN

# FOCUS   CHARTS

Lighting Design:     Ken Billington
Associate:     John Demous

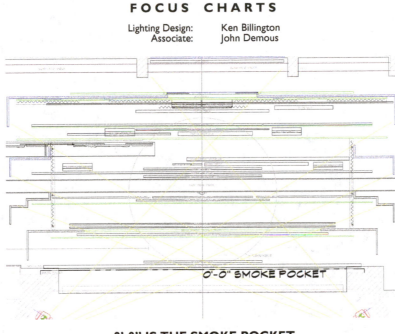

**0'-0" IS THE SMOKE POCKET**

**Basic explanation of the focus chart system and how to read it:**

6L @     +2     =     Hot spot of lamp standing
6' SL of Center and 2'-0" Up Stage of the Smoke Pocket

## COMMON ABBREVIATIONS:

HH+...................................Head High Plus #
L/A......................................Land At (Edge of Beam)
L/O......................................Land Off (Edge of Beam)
F/O......................................Fall Off (Edge of soft Beam)

## BEAM:

The "+" mark is focused sharp. To the right of that mark is barrel out, to the left is barrel in.

Shutter cuts "to" an item include that item in the light.  Shutter cuts "off" an item do not.

PAR fixtures include a notation for the filament orientation.  SL/SR or US/DS refer to the orientation of the filament IN THE FIXTURE - unless there is a specific note relating to either the deck or Scenery.

**Figure 10.6**  *Chaplin focus chart cover page.*
*Lighting by: Ken Billington*
*Assoc. LD: John Demous*

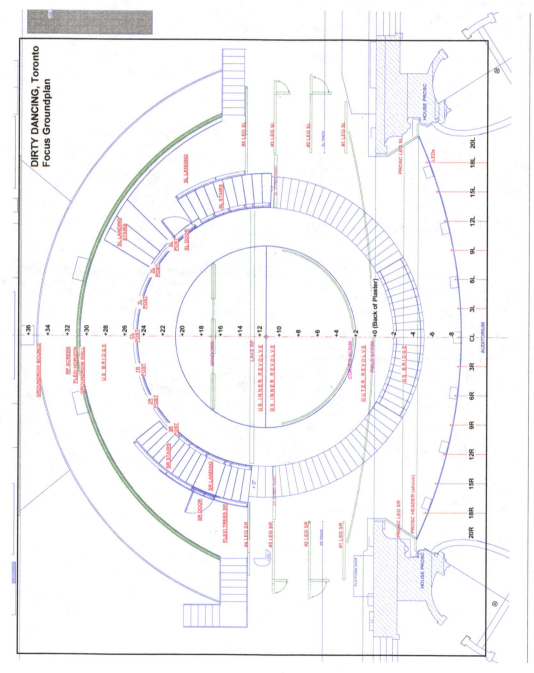

**Figure 10.7** *Dirty Dancing* focus groundplan.
*Lighting by: Tim Mitchell*
*Assoc. LD: Vivien Leone*

The focus chart cover page should specifically do the following:

- It should describe how the light is to be focused. Typically the light is focused by standing with the hotspot of the fixture on the designer's face (or back of head). However, some designers prefer to focus by looking at where the beam of light lands onstage. The difference between these two styles of focusing is significant in terms of placement of the beam, so be specific.

- A groundplan, or "focus groundplan" should be included that pinpoints where 0,0 falls onstage. (See Figure 10.7.) Does 0,0 cross at the plaster line, smoke pocket line, or at the edge of the orchestra pit or deck? Determining this point of origin is vital to producing accurate focus charts and reproducing the focus of the show. It may also be helpful to label some of the items that you refer to in the focus charts, such as "#1 Legs" or "Portal #2."

- A brief explanation of how to read the focus charts and general abbreviations should also be included. (See Figures 10.8a-b.) Examples include the meaning of beam/barrel terms such as "out" or "sharp," accessory abbreviations such as "BD" for barndoor, or how to read a location such as "4L @ +12."

Basic explanation of the focus chart system and how to read it:

| | | | |
|---|---|---|---|
| SL | = | Stage Left | } |
| SR | = | Stage Right | } Direction of shutter cut on stage, |
| US | = | Upstage | } regardless of shutter or unit |
| DS | = | Downstage | } orientation. |
| CL | = | Center Line | |
| | | | |
| 6L @ | = | Hot spot of lamp standing 6' SL of Center | |
| 4R @ | = | Hot spot of lamp standing 4' SR of Center | |
| @ +12 | = | Hot spot of lamp standing 12' US of 0'-0" | |
| @ -2 | = | Hot spot of lamp standing 2' DS of 0'-0" | |

**Figure 10.8a**  How to read a focus chart example.
*Courtesy of: KB Associates, Inc.*

## CUE SYNOPSIS

The **cue synopsis**, also called the **cue list**, displays the cue number, what it does, and when it is called. (See Figures 10.9a-b.) During the tech and preview process, always keep the cue synopsis open to stay on top of the designer's changes.

The cue list can be created in many different programs such as Microsoft Excel and FileMaker Pro. It can also be exported directly from the console when using programs such as Moving Light Assistant and FocusTrack. (More on these in Chapter 2.)

# GENERAL ABREVIATIONS

@ ................................................At
o/ ................................................Off (Shutter Cut)
CL ................................................Center Line
DS ................................................Down Stage
US ................................................Up Stage
SL ................................................Stage Left
SR ................................................Stage Right
BT................................................Bottom
CTR or C ................................................Center
EOD ................................................Edge of Deck
HH ................................................Head High
HH+................................................Head High Plus #
Hand High ................................................Hand held over Head
L/A ................................................Land At (Edge of Beam)
L/O................................................Land Off (Edge of Beam)
F/O................................................Fall Off (Edge of soft Beam)
SQ OFF................................................Square Off (Shutter Cut to eliminate round edge)
PROSC................................................Theatre Proscenium
SMK PKT................................................Smoke Pocket
< ................................................Angled shutter cut
||................................................Parallel to
SAA................................................Same as Above
OOH................................................Out of House
OOP................................................Off of Portal
C/O................................................Cut Off
C/T................................................Cut To

## BEAM:

Out/Soft................................................Leko focused with barrel out
Out past Sharp................................................Leko focused barrel 1/4 way in ("Fuzzy")
Off Sharp ................................................Leko focused barrel just out from sharp
Sharp................................................Leko sharp focus (best contrast)
Sharp w/Frost................................................Leko focused sharp, with frost
In past Sharp................................................Leko focused with barrel 3/4 way in ("Blobby")
Spot................................................Fresnel lamp all the way back
1/2 Flood................................................Fresnel lamp half way between spot & flood
FL Flood................................................Fresnel lamp all the way forward

BD................................................Barn Door

N/U................................................Not Used

Source Fours focused with a hard edge that also have R-132 or other frost should have a Sharp edge without the color.

Shutter cuts "to" an item include that item in the light. Shutter cuts "off" an item do not.

**Figure 10.8b**  General focus chart abbreviations.
*Courtesy of: KB Associates, Inc.*

PASADENA PLAYHOUSE
Lighting Design by: Jared A. Sayeg

# UNDER MY SKIN
### CUE SYNOPSIS

PAGE **1** of 7
8/18/2013  12:34 PM
***REVISION #8 PREVIEW***

| CUE | TIME | Wait | Link | Foll | PURPOSE | CALLED ON | PG |
|---|---|---|---|---|---|---|---|
| 1 | 5 | | | | PRESET w/ HOUSE TO FULL US WORKS ON | BEFORE HOUSE OPENS | 1 |
| 2 | 5 | | | | HOUSE TO HALF & US WORKS OUT | AT HOUSE READY w/ WAITING MUSIC & VO | 1 |
| 3 | 5 | | | 5 | HOUSE OUT | AT SHOW READY VO STILL GOING | 1 |
| 3.1 | 4 | | | | FADE TO BLACK | AUTO-FOLLOW | |
| **SCENE 1** | | | | | MELODY'S KITCHEN (STATEN ISLAND) | 7AM MORNING | 1 |
| 4 | 0 | | | | BUILD KITCHEN INTERIOR MORNING (R-CS) WORKING CLASS WINDOW COOL BRIGHT FRIDGE LIGHT ON | SHOW WALL OUT BUMP TOP OF SCENE w/ VOICE "YOUR CALL IS VERY IMPORTANT" | 1 |
| 5 | 6/15 | | | | BOOST TABLE  LC SLIGHTLY | PAPA SAM & MELODY SIT AT KITCHEN TABLE L | |
| 6 | 1/2 | | | | X TO TRANSITION FADEOUT KITCHEN **BLOCK** PAPA SAM L201 PATHWAY DS L-R | SR PALETTE OFF PAPA SAM WALK SOFF SL | |
| **SCENE 2** | | | | | AMALGAMATED HEATHCARE LOBBY | 9AM MORNING | 7 |
| 7 | 5 | | | | BUILD BADISH USC & NYC SKYLINE | UTILITY WALL OUT | |
| 8 | 4 | | | | BUILD X TO  HEALTHCARE LOBBY USC LIVE OPEN SHUTTER TO FULL LOBBY **BLOCK** | HARRISON BADDISH ON PHONE | |
| 9 | 3 | | | | TRANSITION LIVE MOVE COFFEE L-C | UTILITY WALL IN | |
| **SCENE 3** | | | | | AMALGAMATED COFFEE ROOM | 9:30 MORNING | 9 |
| 10 | 1/3 | | | | BUILD UTILTIY WALL SCROLLERS L179 (DEL 2, UP 2) FIXTURE 15 TIME 0 (BLACKOUT US) | UTILITY WALL ALMOST COMPLETE | |
| 11 | 3 | | | | BUILD COFFEE ROOM SL @ SL **BLOCK** ON LADDER - WARM BRIGHT | COFFEE ROOM IN PLACE | |
| **SCENE 4** | | | | | ELEVATOR | C IN PIT ON LIFT | 13 |
| 12 | 3 | | | | X TO ELEVATOR AREA (C PIT LIFT) TRANSITION - FADEOUT COFFEE ROOM | X DOWN TO ELEVATOR | |
| 13 | 0 | | Q3/1 | | ELEVATOR BUTTONS GOING DOWN TO FLOOR 1 & DOWN ARROW | ELEVATOR RISING (APPEARS) | |
| 14 | 0 | | | | X TO ELEVATOR INTERIOR | ONCE INSIDE ELEVATOR w/ SFX DING ELEVATOR DOORS CLOSE | |
| 15 | 0 | | | 0.5 | TO FLOOR 8 | PUSHES BUTTON | |
| 15.1 | 0 | | Q5/1 | | | AUTO-FOLLOW | |
| 16 | 0 | E1 | Q11/1 | | FLICKER ELEVATOR SUBTLE POWER OUTAGE TOGETHER | ELEVATOR JERKS POWER SURGE | |
| 17 | 0 | | Q11/2 | | STOP & RESTORE | RESTORE | |
| 18 | 0 | E2 | Q11/3 | | FLICKER ELEVATOR SUBTLE MORE | ELEVATOR SUDDEN JOLT DOWN -12" | |
| 19 | 0 | | Q11/4 | | STOP & RESTORE | RESTORE | |
| 20 | 0 | E3 | Q11/5 | | FLICKER ELEVATOR BIG | ELEVATOR MOVING UP TO 0 | |
| 21 | 0 | | Q11/6 | | STOP & RESTORE | ELEVATOR LANDS | |
| 22 | 0 | E5 | Q5/0 | | BUMP ALL BRIGHT | FREE FALL | |
| 23 | 0 | E55 | | | BLACKOUT | PLUNGE HALF WAY DOWN | |
| 24 | 0 | FX | | 1.2 | STROBE / FLICKER | w/ SFX CRASH  (S16) | |

**Figure 10.9a**  *Under My Skin* cue synopsis.
Lighting by: Jared A. Sayeg

# 33 VARIATIONS — CUE SYNOPSIS

| Cue # | Time | Part | Placement | Description | Moving Light Information 1 (5CH) | 2 (5dt) | 3 (42t) | 4 (43t) | 5 (44t) | 6 (45t) | 11 (6CH) | 12 (6d1) | Scroller Information Sliders (Scrolls) | Wash (Scrolls) | Shelves (Scrolls) |
|---|---|---|---|---|---|---|---|---|---|---|---|---|---|---|---|
| 219 | 10 w1 | 2 | Transition Physical Therapy | Path for Diabelli's Exit UL (259-260) | | | | | | | | | | | |
| 8 | 1 | | | Fixture 2, 5, & 12 Out; Fix 6 Dim / Dim to one down light | | OUT | | | | Dim | | OUT | | | |
| 219.3 | 15 w11 | 1 | AF | 259 & 260 Out (UL Path for Diabelli's exit) / Single pendant (380) ON, | | | | | | | | | | | |
| | 4 | 2 | | Fixture 6 intensity Build | | | | | | Build | | | | | |
| 7 | 3 | | | Fixture 1,4,5,6 Mark to FG763 | | | | Mark 763 Kath. | Mari 763 Mike | Live Mark 763 | | Mark 763 Chair ON | 112-114 Frame 2 (R83) | | |
| 8 | 3 | | | Build DL & Ctr/L Fixture 6 OUT | ON | | | | | | | | | | |
| 220 | 30/60 | | Clara Cross w/ Chair closer to Kath | Iso to chair, Dim Ctr, Build Slider grazer SL (102-104), Build down (Ch. 204) Fixture 5 & 6 ON | Build | | | ON Kath. | ON Kath. | | | Build | 102-104 ON | | |
| 221 | 20 | | w. Piano | Dim Froms, ISO to Ctr chars, Slider grazer Build Fixture 4 ON; Fixture 5 & 6 FULL Haze Build | | | | | | | | | | | |
| 222.1 | 1.1 | | Projection | Projection | | | | | | | | | | | |
| 225 | 5 Prof 4 | 1 | JOYFULL SILENCE Transition to Beer way way US | Preheat Path Front (198) | OUT | Mark 765 Shh. DR | | | | Mark 770 Table | | | | | |
| 7 | 2 w2 | | | Fixture 2 Mark @ FG 765 / Fixture 6 Mark @ FG770 | | | | | | | | | | | |
| 8 | 3/0 | | | Fixtuer 164~6 & 12 OUT; Fixture 4 LIVE IRIS to 50% Fade ALL Beethoven Way up CTR Through sliders (ch. 197), 102-104 OUT | OUT | | | OUT/ Iris @ 50% | OUT | OUT | | OUT | 102-104 OUT | R08/R32 3/R343/ R79 DS | |
| 226 | 4/40 | | Beeth. Cross DS | Build Path (Ch. 190-297-298) Haze Restore | | Preheat | | | | | | | | | |

Tab/Video

**Figure 10.9b** *33 Variations* cue synopsis.
Lighting by: David Lander
Assoc. LD: Justin A. Partier

A good cue synopsis includes:

- Act/scene and/or song title (shown as headings)
- Cue number
- Time (overall cue time, split time, or discreet timing)
- Follow, wait, or delay time
- Note (such as Block Cue, Mark Cue, Linked to Cue, etc.)
- Placement (where the cue is called in the script, such as on a line or actor's movement—indicate the specific word or syllable the cue is called upon by using a different font color, underline, CAPitalization, or *asterisks*)
- Page number in the script
- Description (what the cue looks like or does, such as "Pull down," or "Add in Blue Backlight," "Transition Look," etc.)
- Any relevant tracking information—such as basic scroller color information or moving light focuses

Incorporate your designer's language style into your cue synopsis. For example, some designers generically use the word "blackout" (when the lighting change results in complete blackness) no matter how fast it happens. However, some specifically distinguish between "blackout" (abbreviated BO) and "Fade to Black" (FTB). BO happens in a zero count (or bump), and FTB in a timed fade in anything other than a zero.

Another common term used in place of blackout (in a zero count) is DBO, which stands for "Dead Blackout." This term is used most frequently by British designers.

In addition to the cues created by the designer, the programmer may need to write additional cues to finesse the moving lights. Discuss ahead of time with your programmer if he prefers these to be included in your cue synopsis or not.

Before opening night, hand a copy of the cue synopsis to the PSM to be placed in her prompt script as an archive. If there are any questions or emergencies it becomes a fast reference to ease trouble-shooting.

## FOLLOWSPOT CUE SHEETS

The **followspot cue sheets**, or "**spot sheets**," are documents created by the followspot assistant that outline every move or change made by each followspot throughout the show.

The software program, SpotTrack, (more in Chapter 2) provides a layout for you (see Figures 10.10a-c), or you can make your own in programs such as Microsoft Excel or FileMaker Pro (see Figures 10.11a-c). No matter what software program you use, structure the paperwork to allow for printing both a master copy (showing all followspots at once) and individual sheets (displaying only one spot at a time). Use fonts that are large enough for the spot ops to read easily while running a spot, but not so big that they need to turn copious pages while doing so.

Begin with a header on the first page displaying show title and logo, designer's name, associate and assistants' names, and the list of followspot colors. The body of the spot sheets should contain the information below. Be as concise, but as complete, as possible when filling in the information.

- **Followspot Number**—Spot 1, Spot 2, or Spot 3, etc.
- **Followspot Operators' Names** (in relation to their spot number)—not recommended for a tour because the names change frequently.
- **Act/Scene and/or Song Name**—use these as headers when printing to break up the page.
- **Placement or Call of Spot Action** (usually on light cue or stage action)—such as "w/ LQ3" or "as x DS."
- **Reference Lighting Cue**—references the lighting console if the spot ops get lost during the show. If the followspot action happens at the same time as a specific lighting cue,

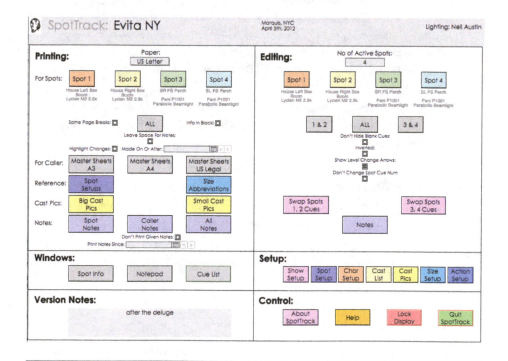

**Figure 10.10a**    SpotTrack initial set-up.
*Courtesy of: Rob Halliday*

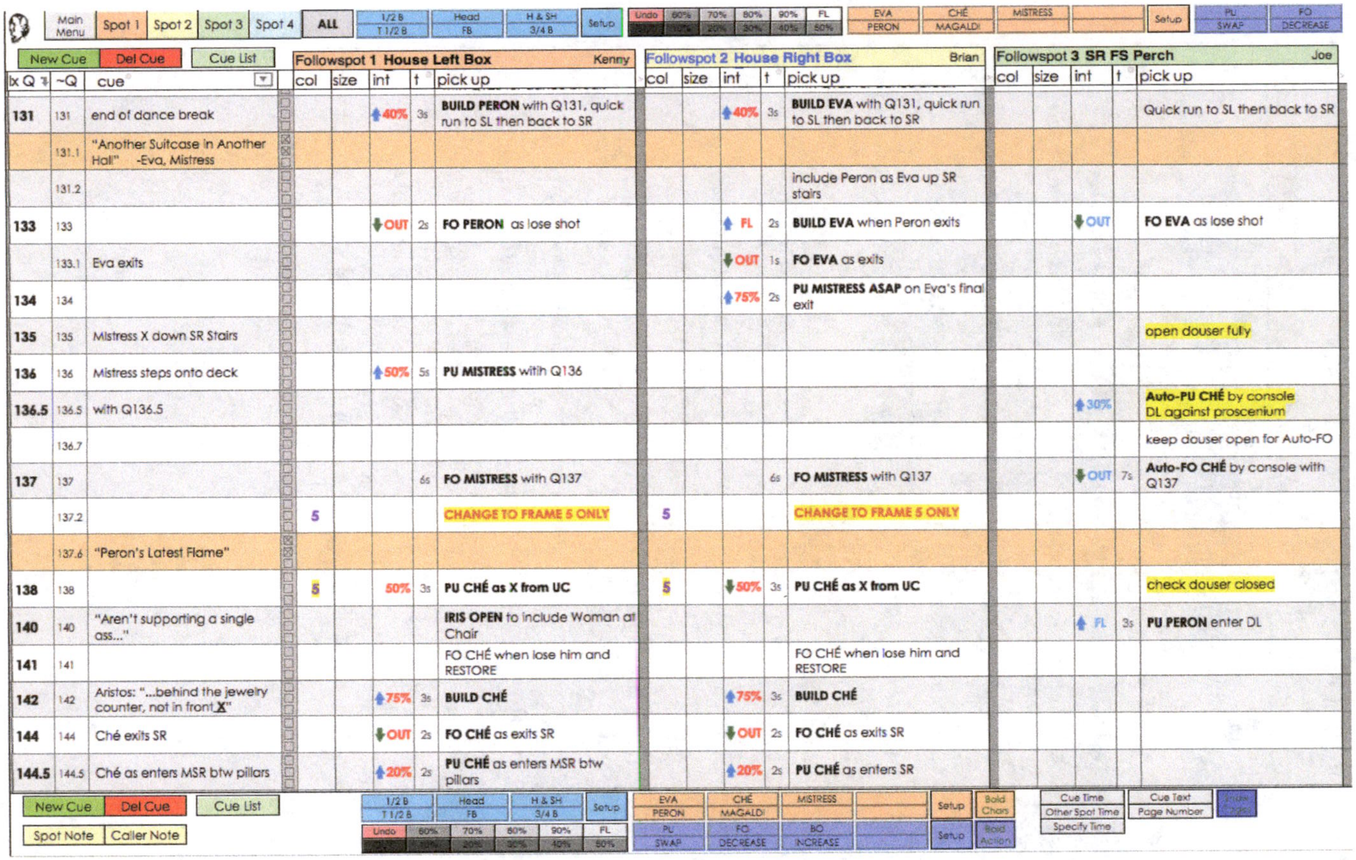

| lx Q | ~Q | cue | FS1 col | FS1 size | FS1 int | FS1 t | Followspot 1 House Left Box (Kenny) pick up | FS2 col | FS2 size | FS2 int | FS2 t | Followspot 2 House Right Box (Brian) pick up | FS3 col | FS3 size | FS3 int | FS3 t | Followspot 3 SR FS Perch (Joe) pick up |
|---|---|---|---|---|---|---|---|---|---|---|---|---|---|---|---|---|---|
| 131 | 131 | end of dance break | | | 40% | 3s | **BUILD PERON** with Q131, quick run to SL then back to SR | | | 40% | 3s | **BUILD EVA** with Q131, quick run to SL then back to SR | | | | | Quick run to SL then back to SR |
| | 131.1 | "Another Suitcase in Another Hall" -Eva, Mistress | | | | | | | | | | | | | | | |
| | 131.2 | | | | | | | | | | | include Peron as Eva up SR stairs | | | | | |
| 133 | 133 | | | | OUT | 2s | **FO PERON** as lose shot | | | FL | 2s | **BUILD EVA** when Peron exits | | | OUT | | **FO EVA** as lose shot |
| | 133.1 | Eva exits | | | | | | | | OUT | 1s | **FO EVA** as exits | | | | | |
| 134 | 134 | | | | | | | | | 75% | 2s | **PU MISTRESS ASAP** on Eva's final exit | | | | | |
| 135 | 135 | Mistress X down SR Stairs | | | | | | | | | | | | | | | open douser fully |
| 136 | 136 | Mistress steps onto deck | | | 50% | 5s | **PU MISTRESS** with Q136 | | | | | | | | | | |
| 136.5 | 136.5 | with Q136.5 | | | | | | | | | | | | | 30% | | **Auto-PU CHÉ** by console DL against proscenium |
| | 136.7 | | | | | | | | | | | | | | | | keep douser open for Auto-FO |
| 137 | 137 | | | | | 6s | **FO MISTRESS** with Q137 | | | | 6s | **FO MISTRESS** with Q137 | | | OUT | 7s | **Auto-FO CHÉ** by console with Q137 |
| | 137.2 | | 5 | | | | CHANGE TO FRAME 5 ONLY | 5 | | | | CHANGE TO FRAME 5 ONLY | | | | | |
| | 137.6 | "Peron's Latest Flame" | | | | | | | | | | | | | | | |
| 138 | 138 | | 5 | | 50% | 3s | **PU CHÉ as X from UC** | 5 | | 50% | 3s | **PU CHÉ as X from UC** | | | | | check douser closed |
| 140 | 140 | "Aren't supporting a single ass..." | | | | | **IRIS OPEN** to include Woman at Chair | | | | | | | | FL | 3s | **PU PERON** enter DL |
| 141 | 141 | | | | | | FO CHÉ when lose him and RESTORE | | | | | FO CHÉ when lose him and RESTORE | | | | | |
| 142 | 142 | Aristos: "...behind the jewelry counter, not in front X" | | | 75% | 3s | **BUILD CHÉ** | | | 75% | 3s | **BUILD CHÉ** | | | | | |
| 144 | 144 | Ché exits SR | | | OUT | 2s | **FO CHÉ** as exits SR | | | OUT | 2s | **FO CHÉ** as exits SR | | | | | |
| 144.5 | 144.5 | Ché as enters MSR btw pillars | | | 20% | 2s | **PU CHÉ** as enters MSR btw pillars | | | 20% | 2s | **PU CHÉ** as enters SR | | | | | |

**Figure 10.10b** *Evita* master followspot cue sheet made in SpotTrack.
*Courtesy of: Rob Halliday*
*Lighting by: Neil Austin*

# Evita NY
Marquis, NYC
April 5th, 2012

Lighting: Neil Austin

| | | | Followspot 1 | | | | Kenny |
|---|---|---|---|---|---|---|---|
| lx Q | ~Q | cue | col | size | int | t | pick up |
| **179** | 179 | **ACT TWO** | | | | | |
| **180** | 180 | "Don't Cry for Me Argentina" | | | | | |
| **181** | 181 | with Q181 | 2+5 | 1/2 B | ↑75% | 3s | **PU CHÉ** with Q181 |
| **182** | 182 | Ché finishes speaking and turns back to DS | | | | 4s | **FO CHÉ** as finishes speaking and turns US |
| **184** | 184 | for Ché's speech: "As a mere observer of this | | | 75% | 3s | **PU CHÉ** DR with Q184 in 3 count |
| **185** | 185 | End of Ché speech | | | ↓OUT | 9s | **FO CHÉ** slowly |
| **196** | 196 | end Eva's second: "All of us!",CHE sings | | | ↑ FL | 3s | **PU CHÉ** under balcony in **3 ct** |
| | 196.9 | "High Flying, Adored" -Ché | | | | | |
| **198** | 198 | | | | | | FO and RESTORE as necessary off Pros. |
| **198.6** | 198.6 | Eva sings | | | ↓40% | 4s | **DIM DOWN CHÉ** |
| | 198.9 | "Rainbow High" -Eva & 2 Valets | | | | | |
| **199** | 199 | before Eva sings: "X̲ I don't really think I need the | 2+5 | | ↓OUT | 3s | **FO CHÉ** with new music of: "X̲ I don't really think I need the |
| | 199.1 | | | | ↑60% | 3s | **ASAP PU EVA** CS |
| **206** | 206 | with Q206, for Eva: "I'm their saviour" | | | ↑ FL | 3s | **BUILD EVA** with Q206 |
| | 213.8 | "Rainbow Tour" | | | | | |
| **214** | 214 | Peron: "X̲ People of Europe..." | | | ↓OUT | 3s | **FO EVA** wtih Q214 |
| | 214.1 | **ASAP** | | | ↑ FL | 2s | **PU CHÉ ASAP** DL |

SpotTrack   Printed: Sat, Jul 27, 2013   6:43pm   Track Version: Marquis final        Track Date: Mon, Apr 2, 2012        Page **8**

**Figure 10.10c**   *Evita* individual followspot cue sheet made in SpotTrack.
*Courtesy of: Rob Halliday*
*Lighting by: Neil Austin*

list that cue number. If it happens after a cue is called, list it as "A32," for example, meaning "after Cue 32," or "IN 32" indicating that it happens while cue 32 is onstage.

- **Standby** (optional)—gives the operator something to watch for in the show that happens just prior to his next pick up.

- **Followspot Action**—such as "pick up," "fade out," or "change color to."

- **Target**—the character or object that the followspot will be illuminating. (Always use character names—not actors' names—to account for understudies.) With unnamed chorus members that are picked up multiple times, distinguish them in some way by describing their part or costume, such as "man with dog" or "bikini girl." Do not use names such as "blond woman." If that character does not wear a wig, her hair color may change when the understudy or swing steps in.

- **Location**—where the target is located or entering from—i.e., DR, UL, UC, etc.

- **Iris size**—such as "Fullbody" or "Waist" shot.

- **Timing**—time it should take for spot op to complete the action described—i.e., 3 secs, 10 secs, etc.

**9 to 5 National Tour — FOLLOWSPOT CUES**
September 24, 2010 — LIGHTING BY KEN BILLINGTON

KEY:
- ● Iris Change / ◎ Color Change
- ▲ Pick Up / ▼ Out / ▸ Slide (No Fade/Restore)

SIZES: 1/2 Half Body | 3/4 Three Quarter Body | FB Full Body | HS Head Shot | H&S Head & Shoulders

FRAMES: 1. R-132 1/4 Hamburg Frost | 2. G-155 Light Pink | 3. L-110 Middle Rose | 4. L-111 Dark Pink | 5. L-194 Surprise Pink | 6. R-04+L-223 B-Roll

| LT Cue | FR | SIZE | INT | TIME | ACTION (SPOT 3 / SR) | | FR | SIZE | INT | TIME | ACTION (SPOT 2 / CTR) | | FR | SIZE | INT | TIME | ACTION (SPOT 1 / SL) | | PG |
|---|---|---|---|---|---|---|---|---|---|---|---|---|---|---|---|---|---|---|---|---|
| | | | | | ACT I | | | | | | ACT I | | | | | | ACT I | | 4 |
| | | | | | SCENE I (Opening) | | | | | | SCENE I (Opening) | | | | | | SCENE I (Opening) | | 4 |
| | | | | | 9 TO 5 | | | | | | 9 TO 5 | | | | | | 9 TO 5 | | 4 |
| LQ 9 | | | | | | | 1 | 3/4 | 75% | 1ct | ROZ / DSC w/LQ 9 | ▲ | | | | | | | 5 |
| LQ 11 | | | | | | | | | | 3ct | FADE OUT / X's USC | ▼ | | | | | | | 5 |
| LQ 12 | | | | | | | | | | | | | 1+2 | 1/2 | FL | 2ct | VIOLET / Enters DSR | ▲ | 5 |
| IN LQ 12 | | | | | | | 1+2 | 1/2 | FL | 2ct | JOSH / Enters DSL on Skateboard | ▲ | | | | | | | 5 |
| LQ 13 | | | | | | | | | 60% | 5ct | INT DOWN TO 60% / VIOLET Sings | INT | | | | | | | 5 |
| LQ 14 | | | | | | | | | | 3ct | FADE OUT / Leaves DSL to Exit | ▼ | | | | | | | 5 |
| LQ 15 | | | | | | | | | | | | | | | | 3ct | FADE OUT / X's USL to Exit | ▼ | 6 |
| LQ 16 | 1+2 | 1/2 | FL | 2ct | DWAYNE / X's from DSR to DSL | ▲ | 1+2 | 1/2 | FL | 2ct | DORALEE / Enters DSL | ▲ | | | | | | | 6 |
| LQ 19 | | | | 2ct | FADE OUT / Exits DSL | ▼ | | | | 2ct | FADE OUT / Exits DSL | ▼ | | | | | | | 7 |
| LQ 25 | | | | | | | | | | | | | 1+2 | 1/2 | FL | 3ct | JUDY / Emerges MSL w/X DS | ▲ | 8 |
| LQ 31 | 1+2 | 1/2 | FL | 0ct | VIOLET / w/LQ 31 (Enters DSR) | ▲ | 1+2 | 1/2 | FL | 0ct | DORALEE / w/LQ 31 (Enters USL) | ▲ | | | | | | | 8 |
| LQ 32 | | | FL | 2ct | FADE & RESTORE VIOLET / X's US Behind Scenic Cubes | ▼▲ | | | FL | 2ct | FADE & RESTORE DORALEE / X's US Behind Scenic Cubes | ▼▲ | | | FL | 2ct | FADE & RESTORE JUDY / X's US Behind Scenic Cubes | ▼▲ | 8 |
| LQ 33 | | | | 2ct | FADE OUT / Exits DSL | ▼ | | | | 2ct | FADE OUT / Exits DSR | ▼ | | | | | | | 9 |
| IN LQ 33 | 1+2 | 1/2 | FL | 2ct | VIOLET / Enters MSL | ▲ | 1+2 | 1/2 | FL | 2ct | DORALEE / Enters MSR | ▲ | | | | | | | 9 |
| LQ 39 | | | 75% | 5ct | INT DOWN TO 75% / w/Applause | INT | | | | 5ct | FADE OUT / w/Applause | ▼ | | | 75% | 5ct | INT DOWN TO 75% / w/Applause | INT | 9 |
| | | | | | SCENE 2 (Office Bullpen) | | | | | | SCENE 2 (Office Bullpen) | | | | | | SCENE 2 (Office Bullpen) | | 10 |
| | | | | | BOOK SCENE | | | | | | BOOK SCENE | | | | | | BOOK SCENE | | 10 |
| IN LQ 39 | | | | | | | 1+2 | 1/2 | 75% | 3ct | KATHY & MARIA / ASAP at DSR Desk | ▲ | | | | | | | 10 |

**Figure 10.11a** *9 to 5 master followspot cue sheet.*
*Lighting by: Ken Billington*
*Assoc. LD: Anthony Pearson*

**BRING IT ON: The Musical**
# FollowSpot Cue Sheet - Spot Master

**COLOR FRAMES:**
1 - R132
2 - R05
3 - L203
4 - R33
5 - R4615
6 - R336 x2

**IRIS:**
FULL BODY: INCLUDE FEET
3/4 BODY: INCLUDE KNEES
SKIRT: NO KNEES @ SKIRT
KNEE: @ KNEE
HALF BODY: INCLUDE WAIST

BUST: HEAD AND CHEST
HEAD: HEAD ONLY

### SPOT TWO / Spot Q# / SPOT ONE

| ACTION | TARGET LOCATION NOTE | FRAME IRIS INT. TIME | Q Proximity / LX CUE | ACTION | TARGET LOCATION NOTE | FRAME IRIS INT. TIME |
|---|---|---|---|---|---|---|

**Scene: 1.1 - Arena: "What I Was Born"**

| ACTION | TARGET LOCATION NOTE | FRAME/IRIS/INT/TIME | Spot Q# / LX CUE | ACTION | TARGET LOCATION NOTE | FRAME/IRIS/INT/TIME |
|---|---|---|---|---|---|---|
| OFF / OFF | | 1+2 | FSQ: 1 With 8 | Pick Up ↑ | Campbell / MSC / SLOW START | 1+2 SKIRT 25% 6 CT |
| OFF / OFF | | 1+2 | FSQ: 3 With 12 | Fade Up Int. % ↑ | Campbell / MSC | 1+2 SKIRT 50% 4 CT |
| Pick Up ↑ | Campbell / w/ Full Lights | 1+2 SKIRT 100% 3 CT | FSQ: 5 With 16 | Fade Up Int. % ↑ | Campbell / w/ Full Lights | 1+2 SKIRT 100% 3 CT |
| Include Both ◇ | +Steven / SL Side | 1+2 TIGHT, 100% 1 CT | FSQ: 7 With 22 | Slide US to ↑ | Skylar / SR Side | 1+2 SKIRT 100% 1 CT |
| Iris In To ○ | Campbell / DSC / GROUP SPLITS | 1+2 SKIRT 100% 1 CT | FSQ: 9 Near 24 | Iris In To ○ | Campbell / DSC / GROUP SPLITS | 1+2 SKIRT 100% 1 CT |
| Dump & Restore ⇩ | Brooklyn / DSL / BIG HIGH RED BOW | 1+2 SKIRT 100% 1 CT | FSQ: 11 With 26 | Fade in Place ↓ | Campbell / CS / Turn to Exit | 1+2 SKIRT OUT 2 CT |
| Fade w/ Exit ↓ | Brooklyn / EXIT SR / FASHION TURN B4 EXIT | 1+2 SKIRT OUT 1 CT | FSQ: 13 In 26 | OFF / OFF | | 1+2 |
| OFF / OFF | | 1+2 | FSQ: 15 Near 30 | Pick Up ↑ | Lauren / DSL Lift / Quick Move Towards CS | 1+2 FULL BODY 100% 1 CT |
| OFF / OFF | | 1+2 | FSQ: 17 In 30 | Fade Out ↓ | Lauren / SR / After 2nd Lift USR | 1+2 FULL BODY OUT 2 CT |

**Figure 10.11b** *Bring It On* master followspot cue sheet.
*Lighting by: Jason Lyons*
*Assoc. LD: Peter Hoerburger*

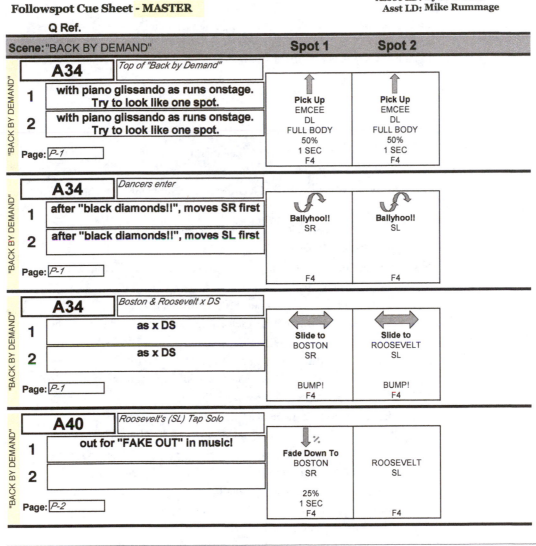

**Figure 10.11c** *Twist* master followspot cue sheet.
*Lighting by: Howell Binkley*
*ALD: Anne E. McMills*
*Database Created By: Charles Pennebaker*

- **Intensity**

- **Color Frame(s)**

- **Notes**—such as "include broomstick handle" or "keep off bookcase SR" or specific details about the character being picked up if there are a lot of others onstage, such as "in red dress" or "4th in line from SR."

## FOLLOWSPOT ACTIONS

Followspot operators use a common language to communicate typical actions and changes. The following are some examples. (These terms may vary—explain any unfamiliar vocabulary at the beginning of the process if your operators ask.)

# ACTIONS

- Intensity-related actions:
  - **"Pick Up" (PU)**—to fade up the intensity (from total blackness) to illuminate the target.
  - **"Bump Up"**—to pick up the target at the desired intensity instantly in a zero count, or "bump."
  - **"Fade Out,"** also called "FTB" ("Fade to Black")—to fade out the intensity of the followspot.
  - **"Bump Out"**—to instantly black out the intensity of the followspot in a zero count, or "bump."
  - **"Fade in Place"**—to fade out the intensity while not moving the followspot from where it is onstage, even if the actor walks out of the light.
  - **"Fade Out & PU,"** also called "Out & PU" or "Out & Up"—to fade out intensity and immediately pick up a different target as soon as possible.
  - **"Bump Out/Up"**—same as a "fade out & PU" except that the intensity is dowsed and reinstituted in a zero count, or "bump."
  - **"Fade Up & Out,"** also called "Up & Out"—a quick pick up usually used to illuminate an actor for a single line or quick action and immediately fading out after the moment.
  - **"Bump Up/Out"**—same as the "fade up & out" but performed in a zero count, or "bump."
  - **"Tag"**—when "tag" is called, the followspot that is currently up will bump out, and the followspot waiting for his next pick up will bump up simultaneously. Used typically in a musical when several one-liners from different characters happen in a fast sequence.
  - **"Fade Down to" or "Intensity Down to"**—to fade the intensity to a lower level, but not "out."
  - **"Fade Up to" or "Intensity Up to"**—to fade the intensity to a brighter level.

- **"Bump Intensity to," "Bump Up to," or "Bump Down to"**—to change to a different intensity level in a zero count, or "bump."
- **"Off"**—the followspot is completely doused, or blacked out, and the operator is standing by for his next pick up.

- Iris-related actions:
  - **"Open & Include"**—to open iris larger to include other items and/or characters in a group shot.
  - **"Include Both,"** also called "Share With,"– similar to "open & include;" does not necessarily require opening of the iris but involves sharing the existing followspot shot with two characters by either letting the other character walk into the light or by shifting the followspot slightly so that it includes the two characters.
  - **"Open Iris to"**—to open the iris to a larger aperture on the target (such as changing from a head shot to fullbody).
  - **"Iris Down to"**—to close the iris to a smaller aperture on the target (the opposite of "open iris to").

- Movement-related actions:
  - **"Swap to"**—to change seamlessly to a different target while spot is still illuminated. This is done by following target A (that is already illuminated) towards new target B and then changing to follow target B when target A crosses in front of or behind target B (and allowing target A to walk out of light). This method is also used extensively during "zoning" (see below).
  - **"Slide to"**—to change from following one target to following another target by moving, or "sliding," the followspot from one character to another onstage without fading out. This is least obvious when performed in bright scenes when targets stand near each other—otherwise it may draw too much attention. This technique may also be used as a choice when there is not enough time to perform an "out & up."
  - **"Stay With"**—choosing a target to "stay with" after multiple targets that are lit in a group iris split apart. "Stay with" may also be similar to a "swap." For example, a spot op might follow the male lead target towards center to where he stands next to the female lead. The spot op would then need to "open & include" the iris so that both leads are in the spot. But when the female lead crosses away from the man, the spot op would "stay with" the female lead target as she walks away from him and iris only to her.

– **"Begin to Zone"**—"zoning," (also known as "zone defense") is a reference derived from team sports describing when players guard an area of the playing field rather than a specific person. This term has been adapted to followspot operation to mean covering a side of the stage (SL or SR). It *does not* mean to open the iris wide and cover the full side of the stage, but instead instructs the spot op to cover whichever actor is on SL or SR when a series of "swaps" are being performed. This technique is especially useful when **"side spots"** are being used (as opposed to **"straight-on spots"**)—a technique where the followspots are placed at angles from centerline and not straight-on from the stage. Due to the nature of side spots, more swapping and zoning is required to illuminate the actors' faces (instead of the backs of their heads) when the actors face in towards each other. (See Figure 10.12—note: the color is simply for reference and does not pertain to the color of the beam.)

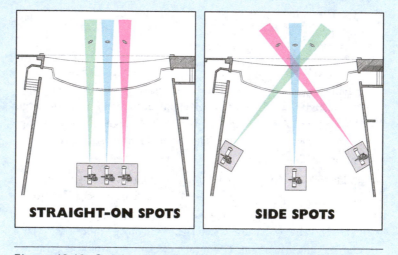

**STRAIGHT-ON SPOTS**          **SIDE SPOTS**

**Figure 10.12**   Straight-on spots vs. side spots.

– **"Hold at"**—to hold the followspot on one area of the stage and let the actors walk into the light. This is a common method used during curtain call to "hold at center" while actors run into the light for bows.

– **"Sweep"**—to slide and catch an actor running onstage and then follow him. This is another common method used during curtain call. Typically the followspots sweep US from center to catch actors running into the light, follow them DS to bow, and then sweep up for the next actor running in to bow, and so on.

– **"Ballyhoo"**—a fun and showy technique often used for effect during a heightened moment in a musical number or as a convention to create a "stage," "cabaret," or "theatrical" look. A ballyhoo is performed by two followspot operators working in tandem to create a sideways figure-8 pattern (or infinity sign) onstage by moving their followspots around the stage in opposition to each other within that pattern. It is usually performed with hard-edge spots starting on opposite sides of the stage and moving up, then towards center where they cross, continuing down and out to the opposite sides of the stage and reversing the pattern continuously at the same rate in the sideways figure-8 pattern until the end of the cue. (See Figure 10.13.)

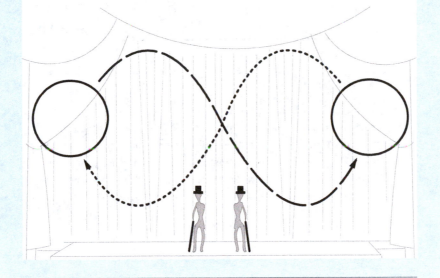

**Figure 10.13** Ballyhoo.

– **"Hollywood"**—the Hollywood is often used during large SL–SR lineups of performers during a heightened section of a musical number, such as a kick line, or during curtain call. Like a ballyhoo, this technique is also performed in tandem between two followspots in hard-edge and begins at either side of the stage. However, instead of creating a figure-8 pattern, the followspots slide directly left and right at the same rate so that they cross at center, continue offstage to the edge of the lineup, and then reverse to repeat the pattern continuously until the end of the cue. (See Figure 10.14.)

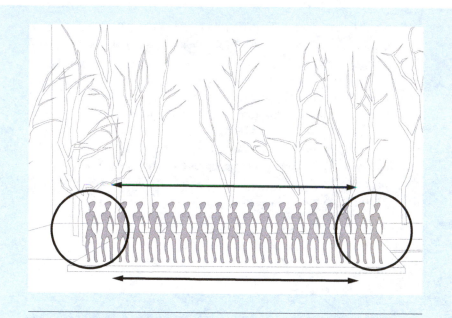

**Figure 10.14**  Hollywood.

– **"Rockette"**—a technique used during a large lineup of performers usually in a SL–SR kick-line formation. When one actor/dancer performs a specific move that each following dancer quickly repeats to create a ripple-down effect through the lineup and back again, one followspot, in hard-edge, begins with picking up the first dancer (who performs the move) and follows the move (precisely at the same rate as

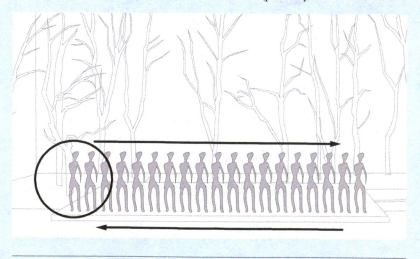

**Figure 10.15**  Rockette.

the other dancers perform the move) down the line and back again as they reverse. (See Figure 10.15.) This technique is named after the famous Radio City Rockettes, a world-renowned precision dance company known for its famous kick lines.

- Color-related actions:
  - **"Change Color to"**—to change color frames selected in the follow-spot. Usually performed after the spot has been doused.
  - **"Roll Color to"**—to change the color "live" while the followspot is illuminated during the performance. Rolling color should be performed as smoothly as possible.
  - **"Bump Color"**—similar to a "roll color," bumping color is performed live, but in a zero count, or "bump."

- Combined actions:
  - **"Out, Chg Color"**—to fade out the followspot, then change the color.
  - **"Bump Out, Chg Clr"**—same as "Out, Chg Color," but performed in a zero count.
  - **"Out, Color, Up"**—to fade out the followspot, change color as quickly as possible, then pick up the next target as soon as possible.
  - **"Bump Out, Clr, Up"**—same as "Out, Color, Up," but performed in a zero count.

- Miscellaneous actions:
  - **"Note!"**—an important note that the followspot operators need to remember. This may be a note such as "False exit!," "Leaps off couch!," or "Include letter in hand." Create a reminder for any unconventional forthcoming actions or concepts that may be easily forgotten while running a complicated show.

In the followspot cue sheets, simple visual symbols may also be used to represent each action, which may help provide a quick reference for the operators. (See Figure 10.16 for some examples.) This shorthand method may also be useful when sketching out rough followspot ideas in your script during a designer run.

When first beginning your spot sheets and during the first few days of tech, use a "default" set of parameters. For example, one set of defaults might be: Iris = HB, Intensity = Full, Color = F1+2, and Time = 3. (More on these terms to follow.) Having a default always gives the operators something to fall back on if they get lost or confused during tech.

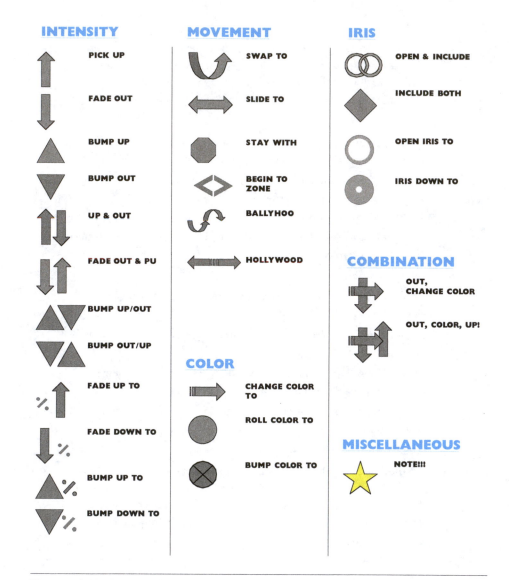

**Figure 10.16**  Example followspot action symbols.
*Symbols Courtesy of: Charles Pennebaker*

## IRIS SIZES

Several common iris size sizes exist that help the spot op to gauge generally how big to keep the beam of their spot. A good operator will use the desired iris size as a guide but make sure to keep the hotspot on the actor's face. (You may have heard the adage, "it's the face that sings.") When setting up spots during tech, the ops may prefer to use a lightwalker to set iris sizes relative to each other as well as have the assistant on headset during this process to corroborate their decisions.

## IRIS SIZES

- **"Head"**—includes just the actor's head
- **"H&S"**—"Head & Shoulders"—illuminates only the actor's head and shoulders
- **"Waist"**—from the waist up. Used when you want HB, but need a bit of a tighter spot to stay off of scenery or other distracting items.
- **"HB"**—"Half Body"—from the actor's groin area up, including the actor's arms and hands. This is the most standard iris size to use as a default particularly for plays and book scenes (scenes not containing songs) in musicals. It is large enough to illuminate the actor properly and yet not too large to spill over too much of the stage.
- **"3/4 Body,"** also called "Knees shot"—includes from the knees up. Often used when you want to include a full hem of a knee-length dress so it does not look cut off halfway down, or if a character has an important prop in their hands that gets cut off in HB.
- **"FB"**—stands for "Full Body," which includes the actor's entire body from the toes up. This iris size is the second most common and is often used during dance numbers. During especially acrobatic dance sequences keep the iris slightly larger than full body to account for sprawling arms and legs. (Called **"FB+."**)
- **"Group"**—used when covering more than one individual. This iris should be large enough to cover the group required rather than worrying about where it falls on the actors' bodies.
- **"Dress"**—a common moment in traditional musicals is the reveal of a woman wearing a beautiful dress. To make the dress look extra lovely, give the dress its own followspot in a saturate color that matches the dress. A saturate color would not look lovely on the actress's face, therefore a "dress" iris should be full body but from the neck down. No head and neck should be included. In conjunction, use an additional followspot in H&S (and a standard color) to capture the actress's face.
- **"Custom"**—used for lighting an object such as a prop or something unusual like just an actor's feet.

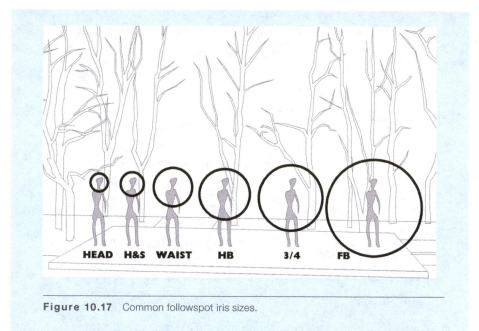

**Figure 10.17**  Common followspot iris sizes.

## INTENSITIES

Intensities when dealing with followspots, as opposed to a lighting console, are a relative measure. Unless you are using conventional fixtures being controlled by the lighting console, there is no way to dial in a concrete intensity such as 65 percent. The best way to handle this is to create some baseline intensities (usually in increments of approximately 25 percent) that become the guidelines for the show, and encourage the followspot operators to balance their levels by eye if needed.

During set-up in tech, the operators will form a consensus with the assistant regarding what should be called "75 percent," "50 percent," "25 percent," and "glow" to assure that each intensity looks the same on all of the spots. (See Figure 10.18.) They may prefer to use light-walkers or just a white wall to determine these markings. A light meter can also be useful when determining relative intensities—especially if any part of the show is filmed and/or broadcast.

## INTENSITIES

- **"Out"**—the followspot is completely doused.
- **"Glow"**—the followspot douser is just barely cracked open to allow a small glow of light to hit the target. Roughly equivalent to 10 percent in a conventional setting.

- **"25%"**—roughly 25 percent output

- **"50%"**—roughly 50 percent output

- **"75%"**—roughly 75 percent output

- **"Full"**—the followspot douser is completely open allowing as much light as possible to illuminate the target.

- **"25 plus," etc.**—because followspot intensity is not an exact science, sometimes "plus" or "minus" is used to indicate a level ever so slightly higher or lower than the baseline intensity. Therefore if a level is listed as "25 plus," the operator should illuminate the followspot to the agreed upon 25 percent mark and then open the douser ever so slightly more so that the intensity is barely brighter.

- **"50 minus," etc.**—see "25 plus." Although "25 plus" and "50 minus" fall into the same range of intensities, "25 plus" would be closer to 25 percent and "50 minus" would fall closer to 50 percent.

**Figure 10.18** Intensities marked on a followspot with gaff tape and a Sharpie.
*Photo by: Jonathan Mulvaney*

## TIMINGS

Timings, when dealing with followspots, are also a guideline-based system. Unless you are using conventional units being controlled through the lighting console, exact timings are not possible. Spot ops often count to themselves in seconds ("one-one-thousand, two-one-thousand, three-one-thousand," and so forth). As they begin to know the show, they will *feel* the moment. Start by using benchmark timings to create a framework for your spot ops, such as BUMP! (0), 1, 3, 5, and 10 seconds.

## COLOR FRAMES

When discussing color for followspots, the word "**frame**" is used to indicate which colors are desired. Most followspots house their color in "**boomerangs**" that hold typically six individual gel frames within one mechanism. (See Figure 10.19.)

Each frame ordinarily holds a different color—perhaps (1) a frost/diffusion frame, (2) a light pink, (3) light amber CTO, (4) light blue CTB, (5) light lavender, and maybe (6) a saturate color depending on the needs of the show. Perhaps, based on this example, the first pick up on the cue sheets calls for frost and amber—Frames 1 & 3. This is written on the spot sheets as "F1+3." If preferred, several colors can be combined together. For example the amber, the pink, and the frost may be written as "F1+2+3." If no color or frost is desired, it is written as "open."

**Figure 10.19**  Followspot boomerang with labels.
*Photo by: Jonathan Mulvaney*

## CALLING PATTERNS

When designing followspots, some assistants find it helpful to work with a calling pattern. Due to the complicated nature of followspot design, a pattern cannot always be consistent but it is a good place to start.

One possible calling pattern example is: have Spot #1 pick up all female leads, Spot #2 pick up all male leads, and Spot #3 pick up all others. This way if you are confused during tech and a female lead walks onstage you can be fairly certain that Spot #1 should be picking her up.

Some assistants, especially when dealing with a tour, will have Spot #1—usually the lead spot that travels with the show—pick up all of the miscellaneous characters and tricky or important pickups. After memorizing the show, Spot #1 will be able to more easily call the rest of the show to new spot ops in each city that will mostly have lead pickups.

When designing for side spots, one good method is that the HR spot always picks up the SR entrances, the HL spot always picks up the SL entrances, and the center spot picks up all others. This keeps light on the actors' faces (as opposed to the back of their heads) as they look and walk center. The side spots can then swap when the actors cross center and zone to keep their faces lit.

## CALLING TECHNIQUES

Keep in mind that the spot ops have not seen the show before tech. Do not assume they know who characters are if you simply say their character names. Reinforce the characters' names by also describing from where they will enter and any other characteristics or actions that might be helpful. During the start of tech, the characters will not be in costume, so do not describe their clothes.

Do not give the spot ops a copy of your cue sheets on the first day of tech. Chances are things will change so rapidly that the sheets will quickly become useless. Give them a set of cue sheets after you have teched through the entire show once, and make revisions from there.

Give clear standbys as best you can so the ops are prepared for what is coming up. Here is an example of a followspot standby as called by the followspot assistant during the beginning of the Brian MacDevitt's Broadway production of *The Wedding Singer*: (Refer to Figure 10.20.)

- "Standby for the top of the show and for the song, 'It's Your Wedding Day.' Spots 1 & 3 you are going to begin in Frames 1 and 2. Spot 2 you're going to begin in open.

- Standby Spot 2. Your first pick up will be on Robbie as he enters UC with LQ11. Fullbody, full intensity, open frames, comin' up in a 3 count.

- After that, standby Spots 1 and 3. Spots 1 and 3, you are going to bump up on Robbie at CL in half body, full intensity, in frames 1 & 2 with LQ12. Also, with LQ12 Spot 2, you will bump out and change your color to Frame 2."

That is a lot of words to say and the show has not even begun yet! As a followspot assistant you need to talk as quickly and clearly as possible. (Drink a lot of water. Laryngitis is common when working as a followspot assistant during the heavy weeks of tech.)

After giving the standby and just before the "go," repeat all or most of the information again, if possible. When the time comes, say "GO!" in a staccato manner so there is no mistaking when to take the cue. If a followspot cue happens with a light cue, at the beginning of

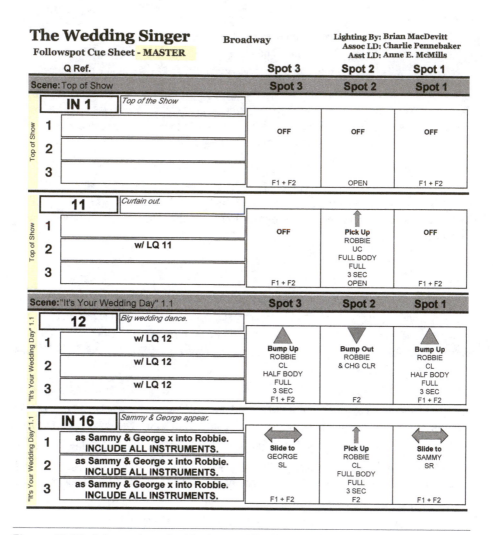

**Figure 10.20** Followspot cue sheet for the top of *The Wedding Singer*.
*Lighting by: Brian MacDevitt*
*ALD: Anne E. McMills*
*Database Created By: Charles Pennebaker*

the process you should listen to the SM channel and call the "go's" yourself. As the tech and preview process move on, you can ask the spots to listen to the PSM's "go's" once the show becomes more settled.

Call the information for the next move as soon as each followspot completes the previous move. Do not keep them in the dark waiting for direction, wondering what may happen next.

Some cues, such as entrances and exits, are better taken visually by the spot ops instead of on a "go." In these cases, call the standby and finish it by saying something like, "take it on your own" or "take it when you see her." This prompts the spot not to wait for a "go" from you. Treat these cases exactly the same as a standard "go" situation, without giving the actual call. Instead, warn the op with a statement such as "Spot 2, that exit is coming up. Remember to fade out on your own."

Large group scenes or songs can be extremely difficult. The designer may ask you to cover more characters than you have spots. If the characters spread themselves out too far on stage, it becomes difficult to cover them all. These situations become a followspot ballet—full of swaps, zoning, and open-and-includes. Discuss difficult sequences with your spot ops. They may provide helpful insights on how to cover the characters in ways you had not realized. Really talented spot ops will work out a system among themselves and ask that you simply write "begin to zone" in their spot sheets for hairy sequences. If you continue to struggle, video the sequence and watch it later with your spot ops to work out a plan for coverage.

## WORKING WITH SPOT OPS

Do not be offended if the spot ops make their own cue sheets or record the information in a different way. Give them your spot sheets at the beginning and as a reference for changes, but let them do whatever they need to make the show run smoothly. Go over any changes with them ahead of time before every rehearsal and/or preview. Do not assume they will catch anything new in your spot sheets. Go through changes carefully and make sure that all parties have a clear understanding. When calling spots, give them a long warning of upcoming changes that were previously discussed.

Treat your ops well and with respect. Ask that they are comfortable if you call them by "Spot 1," "Spot 2," and "Spot 3" instead of by their proper names. Assure them this is not out of disrespect, but rather for efficiency.

Try your best not to pass on any stress or tension being directed towards you at the tech table. Try to talk to them calmly and patiently during these times, if possible. If you do not, apologize immediately.

Be supportive—and not critical—if anything is missed, even if the designer is unhappy. The amount of skill it takes to be a good followspot operator is considerable. From the tech table it looks deceptively easy. There are many difficult maneuvers needed for large shows— octopus-like dexterity is required! Give them the patience they deserve. Always remember that you are dealing with human beings and not a computer. Human error will occur, but so will human brilliance.

## TECHNIQUES AND FINESSE

Without your prompting, good spot ops will take care of finessing the followspot design for you. As professionals, they know what looks good. For example, they will always have one hand on the iris. In order to keep the iris size the same no matter where the actor is onstage, they will iris in gently as an actor crosses US and out when they return back DS, which will end up looking uniform to the untrained eye. They will also iris off of furniture and walls, which may look ugly if hit with the spot, and fade before an actor exits so as not to hit the proscenium or other scenery.

Good spot ops will also keep an eye on their partners' intensities and balance their own intensity as needed—a little brighter or a little dimmer to match the others, if intended. Depending on the angle, it may be hard for the operators to see the other spots' intensities. If you find the intensity balance off and one actor appears brighter than the other, politely ask the ops to balance their intensities. They will do it on their own as best as possible.

## COLOR BALANCING

A note on color balancing: Sometimes the color temperature of an HMI followspot may be too harsh compared to the tungsten-halogen conventionals on stage. Or maybe the color temperature needs to shift according to how it is viewed on camera. This can be fixed by color balancing your spot to "permanently" change its innate color.

**Color balancing** involves choosing a selection of color correction gel to tape semi-permanently to the front of the spots to make their default color temperature emulate the color temperatures of the other lamp sources in the show. Equalizing the varying lamp sources gives the designer a baseline from which to work—colors may not match perfectly between the different sources, but the correction will help get them close.

Many followspots use HMI lamps (~ 6000°K) instead of the tungsten-halogen lamps (3250°K) used in standard conventional fixtures. Because the color temperature of these two sources differs so greatly, your designer may wish to color balance the followspots toward tungsten-halogen. (Many moving lights also use HMI sources. These fixtures usually have a built-in CTO color correction filter that can be added during cueing.)

Color correction gel is available from most of the major color manufacturers. Color correction gel is specially calibrated "to block out the specific wavelengths of the color spectrum to change the color temperature of one light source to another one"[1]—as opposed to standard theatrical gels that absorb certain wavelengths in order to produce a certain color, not match a specific source. These gels are "fairly pale filters that allow as much light as possible through—with the desired color temperature."[1] They also come in different strengths—$\frac{1}{8}$, $\frac{1}{4}$, $\frac{1}{2}$, $\frac{3}{4}$, full, and double.

Color correction was originally intended for use by photographers but has been adopted by theatre, film, and television. Several helpful types of correction are "**CTB**" ("correct to blue" or "color temperature blue"), "**CTO**" ("correct to orange" or "color temperature orange"), "plus green," and "minus green." Standard pink theatrical gel can also be useful. In addition, some gel books (swatch books) declare what color shift its gels intend, such as L204: "converts daylight to tungsten 3200K."[2]

There is no correct and absolute answer for color balancing spots. It is a trial and error process and depends on the model of followspot and your designer's preferences. Be sure to set aside no less than half an hour to an hour to find the right balance with your designer. You will need dark time and a specific cue where the designer noticed the need for balancing. Ask an additional assistant or other volunteer to lightwalk so you and your designer can see the effect of the color on skin.

The following are a few useful color correction filters to try from Rosco Laboratories and LEE Filters when balancing HMI followspots towards tungsten-halogen:

- R3314 or L249—¼ minus green

- R3409 or L206—¼ CTO

- R3408 or L205—½ CTO

- R333 or R33—pink

When attempting to transform HMI sources towards tungsten-halogen color temperatures, CTB will not be needed based on the amount of blue-end innate in HMI sources.

Make sure you add several corrections to your shop order to have on hand in the theatre.

Send several sheets of color correction up to the followspot booth with your followspot operators. They will need to turn on a followspot, point it at the lightwalker, and hold various combinations of sheets of gel in front of the spot when you request it over headset.

After choosing the preferred combination of colors with your designer, ask the spot ops to tape those sheets of gel directly to the front of all of the spots. This color that you have created now becomes your default color temperature over which you add the additional color in your boomerang. (There is no need to take up boomerang slots with this color because you will never want to take it off.) And because this color is now default, there is no need to notate it in your spot sheets; however, you should record the combination (of followspot and quantity and types of gel) in your designer profile sheet for future use. (More on this in Chapter 3.)

After looking at the spots in tech, your designer may want to further adjust your color correction. If there was a cue, or cues, where the designer was particularly unhappy with the spot color, write the cue number down so that you can recall it onstage when balancing the spots again.

## WORK NOTES

*"Remember that almost everything the designer says or does is a change or a note.... Stay with the designer so you don't miss anything."*

—*Craig Miller*[3]

**"Work notes"** refers generally to all types of lighting notes gathered for a production, which are split up into several categories: work notes, focus notes, cue notes, SM notes, ALD notes, PW notes, LD notes, FS notes, ML work notes, ML cue notes, set notes, and other or miscellaneous notes. Once compiled, these notes are used to communicate alterations requested from the lighting designer to all applicable parties—whether it is a non-working instrument or changing a gel (production electrician), fixing a live move (programmer), or calling a cue earlier (production stage manager). The notes are gathered each day by the assistant and distributed at the end of each night. Any notes not completed the following day stay on the list until the request is complete.

> **NFG** is a popular acronym used professionally for equipment that is not working properly. It stands for "No (F*—*insert inappropriate curse word here*) Good." Simply writing something like "(32) NFG" in your work notes is shorthand to the electrician that the equipment is not working. ("Not Functioning Good" can be said in G-rated situations.)
>
> Note: Channel numbers are typically written using parentheses, such as (32).

Lightwright has a work notes feature (see Figure 10.21a) but you can also make your own layout in FileMaker Pro, Microsoft Excel (Figure 10.21b), or—for less complicated shows—simply taking notes by hand (Figure 10.21c). When handwriting, use category abbreviations for each note and group them accordingly, such as "W" for work notes, "F" for focus notes, etc. Another method is dividing up your page into categories of notes—work, focus, cue, etc. Some notes belong in more than one category and should be written in all that apply.

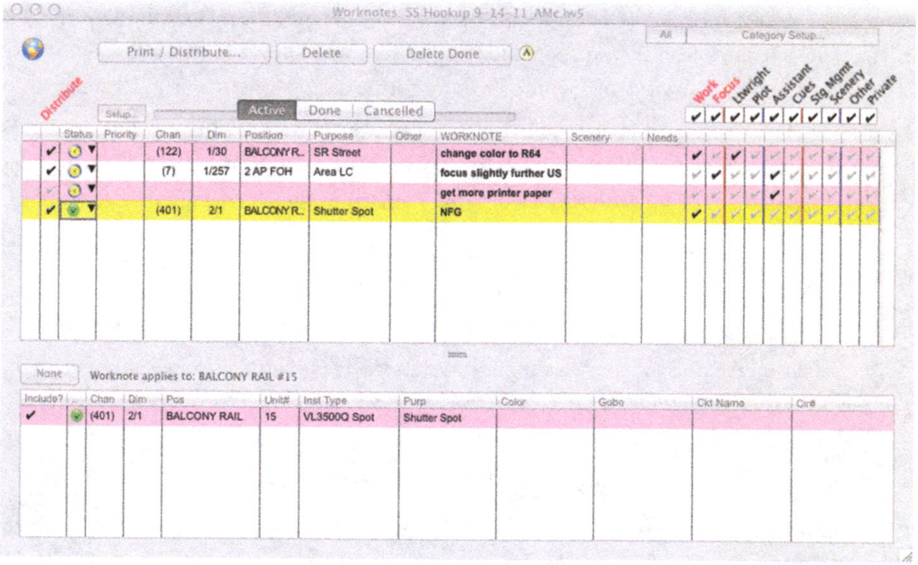

**Figure 10.21a** Work notes screenshot from Lightwright.

REPRISE THEATRE COMPANY
Lighting Design by: Jared Sayeg

CABARET
WORKNOTES

8/18/2013
11:47 AM

| DATE | SORT | CATEGORY | PRIORITY | CHAN | DIM | POSITION | UNIT | WORKNOTES 9/14/11 | DONE |
|---|---|---|---|---|---|---|---|---|---|
| 9/7/2011 | 1 | WK | | | | | | ADD RUNNING LIGHTS | X |
| 9/7/2011 | 1 | WK | | 602 | | SR PINRAIL | | RE-FOCUS USR RUNNING LIGHT INTO XOVER | X |
| 9/7/2011 | 1 | WK | | | | BOX BOOMS | | BLACKWRAP BB SCROLLERS | X |
| 9/7/2011 | 1 | WK | | 19 | | | | FIXTURE DIED - CHECK LAMP | X |
| 9/7/2011 | 1 | WK | | 361 | | BEAM 1 | | IF POSS: SET UP 4-INST SPECS ON DRAPE. SEE B | X |
| 9/8/2011 | 1 | WK | | | | | | STRIKE LAMP CABLES | X |
| 9/8/2011 | 1 | WK | | | | | | BUILD ADAPTERS FOR CONDUCTOR Q LITE | X |
| 9/8/2011 | 1 | WK | | | | | | LOCATE 4X SOURCE 4 IRIS | X |
| 9/9/2011 | 1 | WK | | 431 | 3/458 | BAR SL | | CIRCUIT LAMP PRAC ON BAR (RUN CABLE FROM US) | X |
| 9/8/2011 | 1 | WK | | 434 | | SET: PYLON | | POSSIBLE RE-APPEARANCE OF BARE BULB AS PRAC ON DR PYLON | x |
| 9/9/2011 | 1 | WK | | 3 | | 4 ELEC | | CHECK LAMP | X |
| 9/9/2011 | 1 | WK | | | | | | MOVE HAZE TO SL | X |
| 9/9/2011 | 1 | WK | | 445 | 266,148 | BOOMS 1 L/R | | MOVE MIRROR BALL SPECIALS | X |
| 9/8/2011 | 1 | WK | | | | DS FOOTLIGHTS | | NOTATE DIMS AND RE-PATCH IN ORDER | X |
| 9/8/2011 | 1 | WK | | 19 | | 1 ELEC | | CHECK MAGENTA FLAG CAL | x |
| 9/8/2011 | 1 | WK | | | | BOOM 2 R | | GEL FALLING OUT OF INST HUNG UPSIDE DOWN | X |
| 9/8/2011 | 1 | WK | | 411-415 | | FOOTS DS | | CHECK PATCH ORDER | X |
| 9/8/2011 | 1 | WK | | 444 | 259 | LS 28 | | INSTALL MIRROR BALL CHAIN EXT + TRIM | X |
| 9/7/2011 | 1 | WK | | 361 | | BEAM 1 | | RESEARCH: IS AVAILABLE(4X DROP-IN IRIS) USE | X |
| | 2 | F | | 0 FOCUS | | | | | |
| 9/8/2011 | 2 | F | | 361 | | BEAM 1 | | FOCUS FINALE SPECS TO SCENIC | X |
| 9/9/2011 | 2 | F | | 49 | | BOOM 4R | | FOCUS NOTE - KNOCKED BY SCENIC | X |
| 9/10/2011 | 2 | F | | 411-413, 421-423 | | FOOTLIGHTS | | FOCUS WHEN COVERS INSTALLED | X |
| 9/10/2011 | 2 | F | | | | BOOM 3L | | CHECK SIDE LT FOCUS W/ SCREEN INTERACTION | |
| 9/12/2011 | 2 | F | | 391-396 | | 2 ELEC | | TOUCH UP PORTAL SYSTEM | X |
| 9/10/2011 | 2 | F | | 215+16/30/40 | | ELEC 8 + 10 | | BAND B/L SYSTEMS check >> beams off plexi | X |

**Figure 10.21b** Work notes created with Microsoft Excel.
Courtesy of: Jared A. Sayeg.

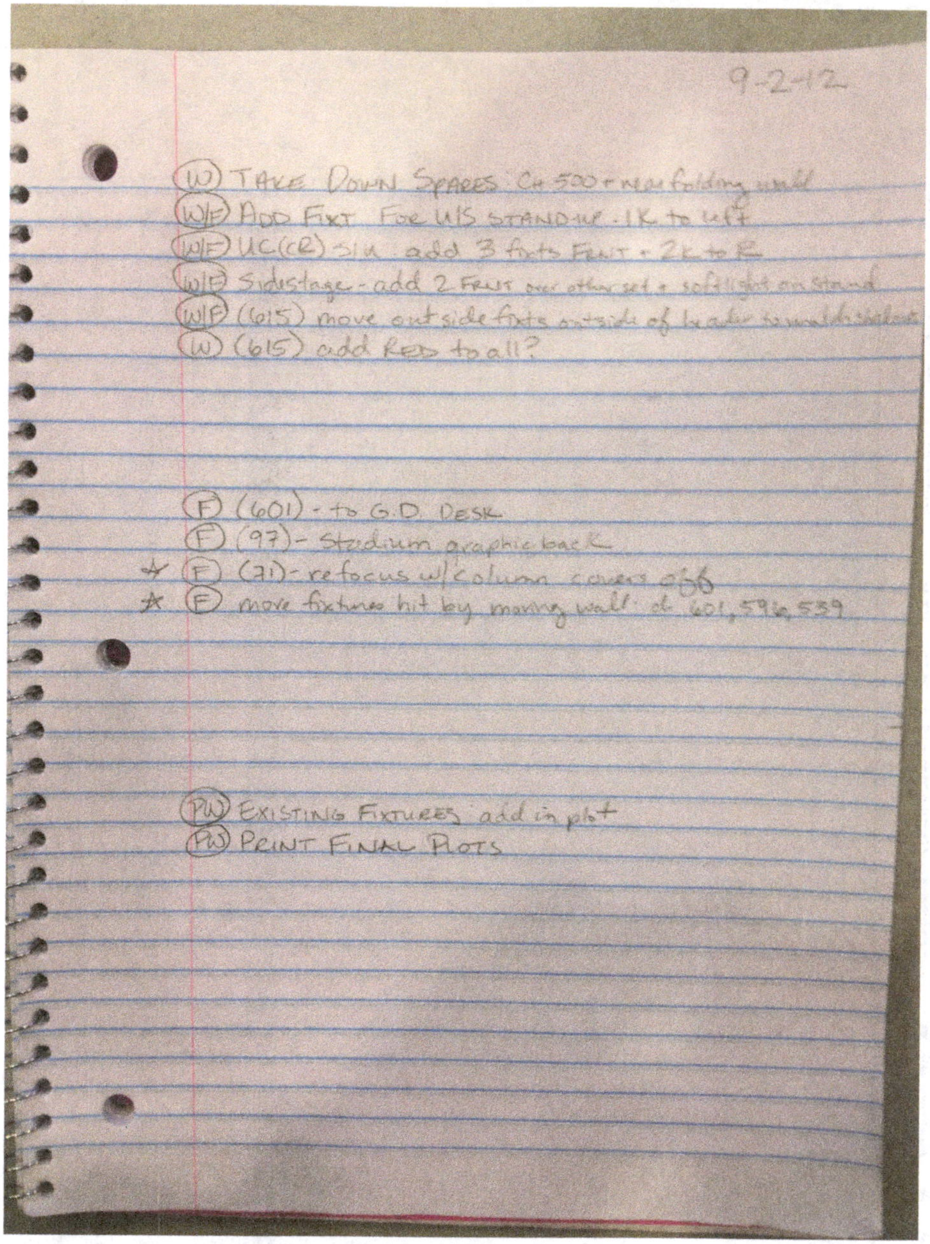

**Figure 10.21c** Handwritten work notes with abbreviations.

The categories most often used for work notes are defined as follows:

- **Work notes**—(both an overall term and a category)—equipment-related notes that can be completed by the electricians without the presence of the design team. This includes tasks such as gel changes, moving of instruments, repatching, fixing or replacing non-working fixtures, lamp changes, and so on. Sometimes work notes are also "work/focus notes." For example, moving a fixture would also require its refocusing once the design team arrives. (Shorthand abbreviations = "W" or "W/F" for work/focus)

- **Focus notes**—pertaining to the focus of a fixture or fixtures. Typically these notes will not be completed without the presence of the designer and/or associate to execute them—although occasionally straightforward focus changes can be completed such as "cut off of the scrim." Along with the work notes, give the focus notes to the production electrician at the end of every night so he can plan effectively for the morning work call. (Shorthand abbreviation = "F")

- **Cue notes**—these notes are for internal use by the designer. They pertain to the cueing of the show and will be completed by the designer when time is made available. (Occasionally straightforward cueing notes will be completed by the associate, if the designer requests.) Some designers prefer to write down their own cue notes during tech, and others prefer their assistants to take the notes for them. Ask your designer's preference before tech begins. (Shorthand abbreviation = "Q")

- **SM notes**—(Stage Manager notes)—applies to the calling of cues. If during a run of the show a cue is called early or late or a change is requested, a SM note will be taken. Give these notes to the PSM at the end of every night so adjustments can be made within the calling script before the next rehearsal. (Shorthand abbreviation = "SM")

- **ALD notes**—(Assistant Lighting Designer notes)—internal notes that pertain to items that can be completed by the assistant. These can be general notes such as "finish focus charts," "ask to have the trash taken out," or "buy more pencils." (Shorthand abbreviation = "ALD")

- **PW notes**—(Paperwork notes)—items that need to be updated within the paperwork such as channel, purpose, fixture type, color changes and fixture moves. These notes are also ALD notes, but it is helpful to separate them out into their own category so they are easily located when updating paperwork. (Shorthand abbreviation = "PW")

- **LD notes**—(Lighting Designer notes)—internal notes regarding design ideas that the designer has mentioned as possibilities but may not be sure of yet. (Sometimes playfully called "wait notes," a play on words from "work notes.") Some examples might be: "Think about changing all back-light to a warmer amber;" or "Think about moving two US moving lights DS to next electric." Once the designer decides to execute the ideas, the notes would shift into other categories, such as work, focus, or cue notes. (Shorthand abbreviation = "LD")

- **FS notes**—(Followspot notes)—notes for the followspot operators of changes to existing cues or mistakes made during the previous rehearsal. Give these notes to the followspot operators at the end of every night or first thing in the morning so questions can be asked in a timely manner before the next rehearsal. (Shorthand abbreviation = "FS")

- **ML work notes**—(Moving Light work notes)—same as standard work notes but pertain only to the moving lights, not conventional fixtures. There may be a moving light that is not working or perhaps has a stuck color flag or other malfunction. Separating these from standard work notes is beneficial on shows that have a moving light tech because the tech can work on these notes separately from the rest of the crew. (Shorthand abbreviation = "MLW")

- **ML cue notes**—(Moving Light cue notes)—like standard cue notes, but notes that pertain specifically to moving lights and may be able to be completed by the programmer without the designer's help. This may include **"live moves"** (a fixture seen moving by accident while still illuminated) or changes in color, etc. Give these notes to the programmer at the end of the night so the programmer can gauge her call time the next morning. (Abbreviated "MLQ")

- **Set notes**—cover discussion topics that the lighting designer desires to have with the set designer regarding possible set changes. This may be something like, "Can the bed sheets be dyed down so that they are not so white?," or "Can the door handles be less shiny?," or, more drastically, "Can we discuss changing the color of the walls?" These notes should be considered internal. An assistant should never give notes like these to a set designer (unless directed) because they could be perceived as demands rather than a collegial discussion. Instead, remind the designer about these set requests so that he can broach the subject in a respectful and timely manner. (There is no real shorthand for this category besides the word "set.")

- **Other or Misc. notes**—notes that pertain to any other department. Just as with set notes, discuss these items with your designer before assuming that they should be distributed. (Abbreviated Misc.)

If possible in your software program, include the creation date on each note. In addition, within cue notes, indicate which items the director requested by adding a large "DIR" in front of each applicable note. Politically, the designer will often complete the director's notes first before fixing his own notes. The "DIR" demarcation helps to easily locate the priorities.

Some designers also like using an icon that indicates they need to *look* at the cue in their cue notes—meaning that they need dark time to see the cue intensities in the actual production setting as opposed to changing the cue in worklight. If the software allows, import an icon of eyes or eye glasses next to each of these cues. If you cannot add an icon, the word "LOOK" in capital letters also works. This makes it easy to locate these cues all at once when rare dark time is presented.

Work and focus notes should include all instrument details (channel number, position, unit number, instrument type, color, dimmer/address number, etc.) so that the production electrician does not have to hunt for any information. (Using the Lightwright work notes feature can help streamline this process.) Also, do not submit vague requests like "change color" or "repatch groundrow." You need to be specific regarding which color you want to change it to, or what specifically the patch change is.

Sort work and focus notes by position before printing. Sorting by position allows your electrician to easily go "down the pipe" and complete all notes on each position at once instead of bouncing between multiple locations.

Include a "done" checkbox with each note to easily indicate which items have been completed. Many notes cross over a few of the categories. For example, moving an instrument to a different electric would be considered a work note, a focus note, and a PW note—both paperwork and plot. Including a bank of "done" checkboxes for each category will help you keep track of the process.

## RIPPLE SHEET

A **ripple sheet** is the same idea as the "done" checkboxes on the work notes, only expanded. Instead of a daily report, the ripple sheet provides a running list of every change made throughout the production and when it was updated. (See Figure 10.22.) For example, if the designer wants to change a channel, then it must be changed in the patch, the Lightwright file, the Vectorworks file, the magic sheet, possibly the groups list, and any other relevant piece of paperwork. Having a ripple sheet allows the assistant to be assured they did not miss any of these steps.

Create the ripple sheet by listing the notes down the left-hand column of the page and the paperwork elements in columns along the top. Indicate when items are complete by checking them off and dating the box where the two items meet or in another logical location. Ripple sheets can be created using Microsoft Excel, FileMaker Pro, or Lightwright. (Lightwright's work note feature has a built-in ripple sheet—when indicating notes as "done" they are automatically archived and dated.)

Marquis Theater, NY
Lighting Design: Paul Pyant

# The WOMAN in WHITE

## Ripple Sheet

| DATE | SORT | CATEGORY | PRIORITY | CHAN | DIM | POSITION | UNIT | WORKNOTES | DONE | LW | FOCUS CHART | LIGHT PLOT | CHEAT | MAGIC | GROUPS | AUTOMATED | LTNG BOARD | FOCUS TRACK |
|---|---|---|---|---|---|---|---|---|---|---|---|---|---|---|---|---|---|---|
| | 1 | WK | | | | WORKNOTES | | | | | | | | | | | | |
| | 2 | F | | | | FOCUS | | | | | | | | | | | | |
| | 3 | ML | | | | ML PENDING | | | | | | | | | | | | |
| | 4 | ? | | | | DESIGN PENDING | | | | | | | | | | | | |
| | 5 | R | | | | TO RIPPLE | | | | | | | | | | | | |
| 10/27/05 | 5 | R | 1 | (212) | | COVE #2 | 9 | ADD DROP-IN IRIS & FOCUS INTO "EVENING THAT GOES WRONG" | X | X | | | | | | | | X |
| 10/24/05 | 5 | R | 1 | (47+48+62+63) | | | | WAITING ON (4) THIN LINE GOBO'S TO INSTALL ON VL3K'S (TRAIN) | X | | | X | | | | | | |
| 10/24/05 | 5 | R | 1 | (325) | | APRON PIPE L | 7 | IRIS IN & MOVE FURTHER DS | X | | | | | | | | | |
| 10/21/05 | 5 | R | 1 | | | SET ELECTRICS | | ADD 2 WIRELESS SET PRACTICALS AS DISCUSSED WITH JOHN LAWSON | X | X | X | | | | X | X | X | X |
| 10/20/05 | 5 | R | 1 | (140) | | SL PIPE 2 | | REGOBO R77337 Eastern. REFOCUS | X | | X | | | | X | X | X | X |
| 10/20/05 | 5 | R | 1 | (325) | | APRON PIPE L | 7 | | X | | X | | X | X | X | X | X | X |
| 10/19/05 | 5 | R | 1 | (324) | 184 | US BRIDGE | | CHECK FOCUS / HANG (2) 50° FROM SR IN L200 TO X FOCUS CENTER ON US BRIDGE | X | X | X | X | X | X | X | X | X | X |
| 10/18/04 | 5 | R | 1 | (427) | | BOX BOOM L | 3 | OPEN DS CUT TO EDGE OF DECK | X | X | X | X | X | X | X | X | X | X |
| 10/17/05 | 5 | R | 1 | 427+428 | | | | US CUT OFF WALL (Top Unit) | X | X | X | X | X | X | X | X | X | X |
| 10/17/05 | 5 | R | 1 | (196) | | LADDER L | 13 | FOCUS INTO ATTIC. LIFT & STRAIGHT ACROSS (TRACK WALL POSITION #2) | X | X | X | X | X | X | X | X | X | X |
| 10/17/05 | 5 | R | 1 | (195) | | LADDER R | 16 | BOTTOM CUT, DROPPED OPEN | X | X | X | X | X | X | X | X | X | X |
| 10/19/05 | 5 | R | 1 | (209) | | COVE #2 | 17 | LOSE GOBO, CHANGED FOCUS/PURPOSE TO ALLEYWAY. REDO FOCUS CHART | | X | X | X | X | X | X | X | X | X |
| 10/14/05 | 5 | R | 1 | | | HOUSELIGHTS | | SET HOUSELIGHT LEVELS 80%, LOSE LTS OVER APRON? | X | X | X | X | X | X | X | X | X | X |
| 10/24/05 | 5 | R | 2 | (500) | | CATWALK | | SWAP OUT S4'S TO INKIE'S FOR USC DOORWAY X (400w | X | | | | | | | | | X |
| 10/20/05 | 5 | R | 2 | (336)(339)(341) | | COVE #1 | 13 8 4 | SOFTER EDGE | X | | | | | X | X | X | X | X |

F=Focus WK=Work ML=Moving Lt ?=Pending R=Ripple

**Figure 10.22** The Woman in White ripple sheet.
Courtesy of: Vivien Leone

3D THEATRICALS
Lighting Design by: Jared A. Sayeg

**SHREK - TOUR**
**DISTRIBUTION CHART**

8/17/2013  1:24 PM
PAGE 1 of 1
*REVISION #3*

| ITEM | REV. | JARED | Asc LD | ALD | Prog. | Prd LX | SPOTS | Audio | SM | TD | SHOP | TOTAL |
|---|---|---|---|---|---|---|---|---|---|---|---|---|
| **LIGHTING BIBLE** | | | | | | | | | | | | |
| *1 1/2" Binder* | | | | | | | | | | | | 0 |
| **Contact Sheet** | 6/15/2013 | 1 | 1 | 1 | 1 | | | | 1 | | | 5 |
| **Production Schedule** | 6/15/2013 | 1 | 1 | 1 | 1 | | | | 1 | | | 5 |
| **Ripple Sheet Worknotes** | 7/3/2013 | 1 | 1 | 1 | 1 | 1 | | | | 1 | | 6 |
| Channel Hookup | 7/8/2013 | 1 | 1 | 1 | 1 | 1 | | | | | | 5 |
| Instrument Schedule | 7/8/2013 | 1 | 1 | 1 | 1 | 1 | | | | | | 5 |
| Dimmer Hookup | 7/12/2013 | | 1 | 1 | | 1 | | | | | | 3 |
| Circuit Hookup | 7/12/2013 | | 1 | 1 | | 1 | | | | | | 3 |
| DMX Assignment Sheet | 7/1/2013 | 1 | 1 | 1 | 1 | 1 | | | | | 1 | |
| Focus Chart Guide | 7/2/2013 | 1 | 1 | 1 | | | | | | | | 3 |
| Focus Charts | 7/13/2013 | 1 | 1 | 1 | | | | | | | | 3 |
| Line-Set Schedule | 7/11/2013 | 1 | 1 | | | 1 | 1 | | 1 | 1 | | 6 |
| Set Electrics Breakdown | 7/7/2013 | 1 | 1 | | | 1 | | | | 1 | 1 | 5 |
| Shop Order | 6/17/2013 | 1 | 1 | | | 1 | | | | | 1 | 4 |
| Color Order | 7/5/2013 | 1 | 1 | | | 1 | | | | | 1 | 4 |
| Shop Labels (Automation) | 7/1/2013 | 1 | | | | | | | | | 1 | |
| Conventional Gobo Order | 7/8/2013 | 1 | 1 | | | 1 | | | | | 1 | 4 |
| ML Gobo+Color Load | 7/1/2013 | 1 | 1 | 1 | 1 | | | | | | 1 | 5 |
| **MAGIC SHEETS** | | | | | | | | | | | | |
| Conv. Magic Sheet | 7/7/2013 | 1 | 1 | | 1 | | | | | | | 3 |
| ML Magic Sheet | 6/30/2013 | 1 | 1 | 1 | 1 | 1 | | | | | 1 | 6 |
| ML Gobo Magic Sheet | 6/30/2013 | 1 | 1 | | 1 | | | | | | | 3 |
| Color Library | 7/2/2013 | 1 | 1 | | 1 | | | | | | | |
| Group Palettes | 7/7/13 | 1 | | | 1 | | | | | | | 2 |
| Focus Palettes | 7/7/13 | 1 | 1 | | 1 | | | | | | | 3 |
| Color Palettes | 7/7/13 | 1 | 1 | | 1 | | | | | | | 3 |
| Beam Palettes | 7/7/13 | 1 | 1 | | 1 | | | | | | | 3 |
| Effects List | 7/15/2013 | 1 | 1 | | 1 | | | | | | | 3 |
| Macro's List | 7/15/2013 | | | | 1 | | | | | | | 1 |
| Scroller Track Sheet | 7/15//13 | 1 | 1 | | 1 | | | | | | | 3 |
| Channels NOT In Use | 7/15/2013 | 1 | 1 | | 1 | | | | | | | 3 |
| **CUE STRUCTURE** | | | | | | | | | | | | |
| Cue Scene/Songs List | 6/17/2013 | 1 | | | 1 | | | | 1 | | | 3 |
| Cue Synopsis | | 1 | | | 1 | | | | 1 | | | 3 |
| LX Script (Q's & Spots) | 7/11/2013 | 1 | 1 | 1 | 1 | | | | 1 | | | 5 |
| SPFX Cue List | | 1 | | | 1 | | | | | | | 2 |
| ML Scene State | 6/21/2013 | 1 | 1 | 1 | 1 | | | | | | | 4 |
| ML Focus Track | | 1 | | | 1 | | | | | | | 2 |
| Turntable Revolution Tracks | | 1 | 1 | 1 | | | | | 1 | | | 4 |
| *1" Binder* | | 1 | 1 | 1 | | | 3 | | | | | 6 |
| Followspot Master | | 1 | 1 | 1 | | 1 | 3 | | 1 | | | 8 |
| Followspot Cue Sheets | 7/15/2013 | 1 | 1 | 1 | | | 3 | | | | | 6 |
| Followspot Script | | 1 | 1 | 1 | | | 3 | | 1 | | | 7 |
| **DRAWINGS** | | | | | | | | | | | | |
| #1 Light Plot | 7/7/2013 | 1 | 1 | 1 | 1 | 1 | | | | 1 | 1 | 7 |
| #1A Hanging Plot | 7/7/2013 | 1 | 1 | 1 | 1 | 1 | | | | 1 | 1 | 7 |
| #1B Light Plot w/ SET | 7/7/2013 | 1 | 1 | 1 | 1 | 1 | | | | 1 | 1 | 7 |
| #2 Sidelight | 7/7/2013 | 1 | 1 | 1 | 1 | 1 | | | | 1 | 1 | 7 |
| #3 Set LX | 7/7/2013 | 1 | 1 | 1 | 1 | 1 | | | | 1 | 1 | 7 |
| #4 Deck LX | 7/7/2013 | 1 | 1 | 1 | 1 | 1 | | | 1 | 1 | 1 | 8 |
| #5 Section | 7/7/2013 | 1 | 1 | 1 | 1 | 1 | | | | 1 | 1 | 7 |
| #6 Focus Grid | 7/7/2013 | 1 | | | | | | | | | | 1 |
| #7 Set-Plan | 7/7/2013 | 1 | | | | | | | 1 | 1 | | 3 |
| Tech Table & Com Layout | 6/30/2013 | 1 | 1 | 1 | 1 | 1 | | 1 | 1 | 1 | | 8 |
| Deck Mini's | | 1 | | | | | | | 1 | 1 | | 3 |
| **DISKS** | | | | | | | | | | | | |
| SHOWFILE EOS | 7/22/2013 | 1 | | | 1 | 1 | | | | | | 3 |
| MEDIA SERVER | 7/22/2013 | 1 | | | 1 | 1 | | | | | | 3 |
| **TOTALS** | | 50 | 41 | 27 | 35 | 23 | 12 | 2 | 13 | 13 | 15 | 231 |

*Shrek Distro Sheet*

**Figure 10.23**  Distribution chart.
*Courtesy of: Jared A. Sayeg*

# DISTRIBUTION CHART

Similar to the ripple sheet, a **Distribution Chart** allows you to check off which individuals received distributed paperwork. (See Figure 10.23.) For example, did the production electrician receive the plot, the paperwork, and the shop order? Did the production stage manager receive the archival cue list? Did you get a copy of the script for the designer, the programmer, the bible, and the followspot assistant?

List the types of paperwork running down one column on the left-hand side of the page and titles of the people needing to receive the paperwork in columns across the top of the page. The assistant can track which individual got each piece of paperwork (and when) by writing a date in its corresponding box.

# ML FOCUS CHARTS AND ML TRACKING

With the use of software programs such as FocusTrack, Moving Light Assistant, and FastFocus Pro (discussed in Chapter 2), standards are beginning to emerge for moving light focus charts (ML focus charts) and moving light tracking (ML tracking). Both of these documents act as an archival record of moving light information that allows the show to be easily restored if a fixture needs replacing or if the show is toured or remounted.

## ML FOCUS CHARTS

The **Moving Light Focus Charts** are photos of each moving light focus (palette) used as a visual reference to assure each focus and all its attributes look the same as they did when originally created. (See Figures 10.24a-d.) Detailed ML focus charts also ease the process when remounting or touring a production—which may choose to use a different brand of moving light.

When a malfunctioning moving light is replaced, if the new unit is hung in the same orientation and level the focus will be fairly accurate but should be compared to the moving light focus charts to be sure. For example, the edge (sharpness or fuzziness) may need to be adjusted and/or the proper orientation of a gobo may need to be touched up (especially if the fixture has no indexing properties, which orients the gobo according to a start position).

Moving light information in the console is usually stored in a function called a **palette** (also called a preset or a focus group)—a user-programmable feature that stores desired fixture parameters such as position, color, gobo, etc. For example, the designer asks the programmer to focus several fixtures to the DR bedroom scenic piece. The programmer focuses the fixtures on the scenery and saves the information in a palette that can then be referenced into the cue. Once stored in a palette, the focus can be easily recalled each time the DR bedroom reappears on stage and used in any cue. Therefore if the DR bedroom focus is referenced in cues 2, 4, 6, 9, 110, and 206—and the director suddenly decides to move the bed three feet to SR—the

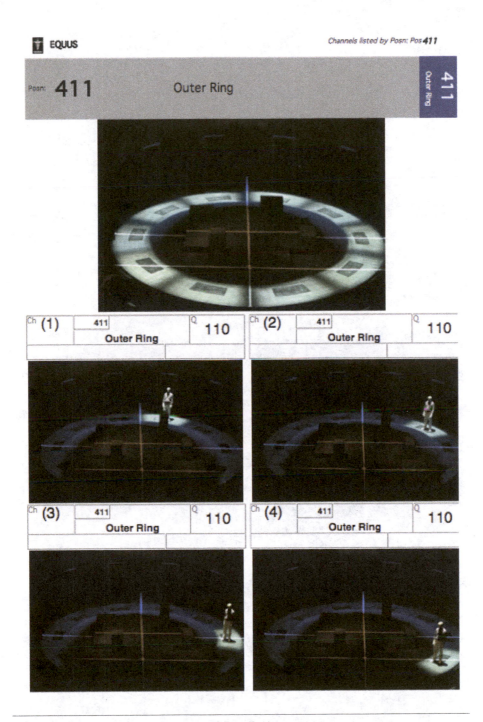

**Figure 10.24a**  ML focus charts created in FocusTrack.
*Courtesy of: Rob Halliday*

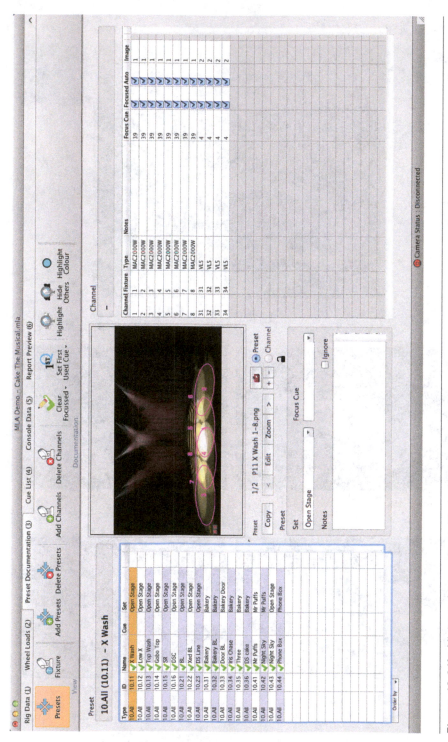

**Figure 10.24b** ML focus charts created in Moving Light Assistant.
*Courtesy of: Andrew Voller*

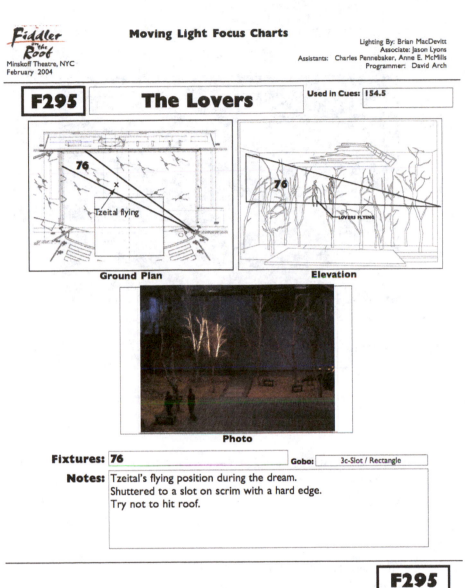

**Figure 10.24c** *Fiddler on the Roof* ML focus charts.
*Lighting by: Brian MacDevitt*
*ALD: Anne E. McMills*

| The PHANTOM of the OPERA<br>VENETIAN HOTEL | PRESET FOCUS VISUAL REFERANCE<br>LIGHTING BY ANDREW BRIDGE<br>ML PROGRAMMING BY PATRICK SCHULZE | units:<br>18,45,63,66, 68,145, 146, 95, 96,<br>101,102,104>106,109,119, 120 | PRESET FOCUS<br>**81** |

**Figure 10.24d**  *The Phantom of the Opera* ML focus charts.
*Lighting by: Andrew Bridge*
*Assoc. LD: Vivien Leone*

programmer only needs to update the palette. Once updated, it automatically updates all the cues that recall that palette.

This explanation of palettes is extremely basic, but helps to explain why moving light focus charts vary slightly from their cousins, the conventional focus charts. While conventional focus

The ML focus charts should begin with the relevant title information such as the show title/logo, name of theatre and city, date, and the names of the designer, assistants, and programmer. After that, whether creating the focus charts with specialized software, such as FocusTrack, Moving Light Assistant, and FastFocus Pro or a database program like FileMaker Pro, the following are some items that are useful to include:

- Palette name and number
- Which fixtures are used in the palette
- Gobos and/or colors that are recorded as part of the palette (if applicable)

- Scenery required—specific flown, rolled, or tracked scenery that is necessary for the focus
- Ground plan and/or elevation—indicate the separate fixtures by drawing the beam and adding fixture numbers on top of the sketch
- Photo—photo of the overall focus palette on stage and/or individual fixture focuses within the palette
- Notes—details such as a hard or soft edges, gobo orientation, or items to avoid lighting, such as the proscenium. Also useful for intentional choices that may look out of place such as one gobo orientated a different direction than the others.

charts detail the absolute focus of each conventional fixture separately, the ML focus charts may display the focus for multiple fixtures focused within one focus group, or palette.

Arrange a time with your programmer to take the photos towards the end of the process as the show begins to settle—ideally within the last week before opening. (This helps to weed out which palettes are not being used.) The photos can either be taken manually or through the use of your moving light tracking software.

Producers frown over taking photos later in the process because it often requires paying for an extra work call. In reality, taking photos towards the end of the process actually promotes efficiency and does not waste time by taking photos of dozens to even hundreds of palettes that end up unused in the show.

The ML focus charts do not need to include unused focuses. However, some positions are used for movement purposes, but the fixture may not be illuminated when in that focus. For example, if a light is off in position 1, fades up as it is moving to position 2, fades out as it is moving to position 3, be aware that position 1 and position 3 need to be documented as they help define the movement of the light even though the light never sits "on" in those positions.

Set aside several hours to complete the photo session. Estimate roughly four to five photos a minute to allow for the additional time it takes to change scenery on multi-set shows, the fixtures themselves to move, and the lightwalker to get into place, if applicable.

When working on multi-set productions, determine ahead of time which pieces of scenery you need onstage for each photo. After taking all of the photos required on the base set, group your other photo needs by scenic piece so that you can fly a piece in once and take all the photos needed at the same time. Do not waste the stagehands' time by asking for a piece to be flown in, then out, and in again.

Sometimes it can be helpful to take photos of the palettes with scenery as well as on a bare stage (with a few reference marks added in spike tape for major scenic pieces). This allows the lights to be focused without scenery, which may happen during accelerated touring load-in schedules or fixtures swapped out just before a show when it is not possible to access the scenic piece in time.

Take each photo in isolation, not within a cue, so that only the lights within the palette you are documenting are displayed. Ask the programmer to take the color out of the fixtures so that the beam is more easily seen in the photos. If preferred, you can also ask for all fixtures to be shown in the UV color and isolate each fixture in white ("highlight")—one by one—for more thorough documentation. If the palette includes gobos, leave them in place so that the photo accurately depicts the overall look. Keep the worklights and houselights on at half or a glow so that the photos show the context of the scenery and theatre architecture. Mini traffic cones can also used in standard measured intervals or set on the designer's focus areas for further reference.

Focus chart photos do not necessarily need to be high-resolution to display the information adequately. In fact, an abundance of high-resolution photos in ML focus charts will create a file size that is very large. Experiment with lower-resolution settings on your camera beforehand so that you know what will work best. If the photos are still too large after using the lowest setting on your camera, use a program such as Photoshop or GraphicConverter to downsize the images to a more manageable size.

### ML TRACKING

**Moving Light Tracking** is a vague term that can encompass a veritable cornucopia of information. Essentially it means recording every single move and change that each moving light does throughout the entire production—a daunting task. Thankfully, software such as FocusTrack, Moving Light Assistant, and FastFocus Pro simplify this chore by integrating with the lighting console and enabling you to extract the information that you need to archive the show.

Discuss with your designer, programmer, and electricians what needs to be archived. One of the most useful documents to create, or extract, is called the **"Fixture Callout."** A fixture callout lists each fixture and in what palettes it is focused. (See Figures 10.25a-d.) That way, when a fixture needs to be replaced, the fixture callouts allow the electrician to go down the list and touch up each focus that uses the replaced fixture.

## ARCHIVAL BIBLE

During the final push in the week before opening (and usually after the freeze date), the assistant must prepare **Archival Bibles:** typically one for the designer and one to stay with the show. Depending on the desires of the designer, the design office, the production electrician, and head electrician, the archival bible may be physical, digital, or both. Ask early on in the process to see who would like which version so you know what to plan for. Ideally a printed

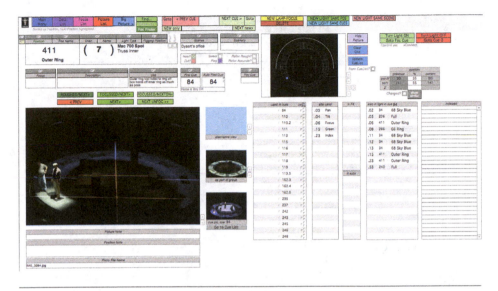

**Figure 10.25a** Fixture callout created in FocusTrack.
*Courtesy of: Rob Halliday*

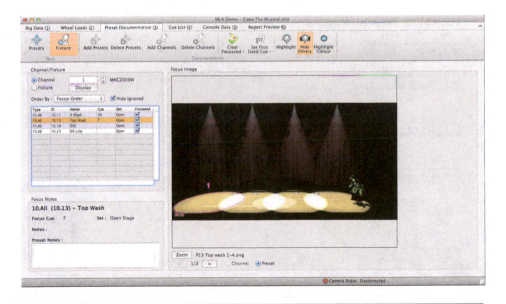

**Figure 10.25b** Fixture callout created in Moving Light Assistant.
*Courtesy of: Andrew Voller*

# FIXTURE #1 CALLOUT

Alfred Molina
*Fiddler*
*on the*
*Roof*

Lighting By: Brian MacDevitt
Programmer: David Arch

**F142-Trees surround**

| Cue #: | 2 | On |

**F199-Trees**

| Cue #: | 59.7 | On |

**F265-Fullstage Shadows**

| Cue #: | 106 | On |

**F277-Move to Stage**

| Cue #: | 118 | LiveMove |
| Cue #: | 207 | On |

**F344-Deck**

| Cue #: | 241 | On |

**F353-Shop Area**

| Cue #: | 238 | On |

**F365-Golde US**

| Cue #: | 248 | On |

**F383-Tevye Cart**

| Cue #: | 63 | On |

**F427-USL Area**

| Cue #: | 34 | On |

**F429-Path to DSL**

| Cue #: | 46.5 | On |

**F469-Golde Sits**

| Cue #: | 258 | On |
| Cue #: | 260.5 | On |

**F484-Stage Area**

| Cue #: | 20 | On |
| Cue #: | 24 | On |

**F505-Snow**

| Cue #: | 204 | On |

Thursday, February 19, 2004

1

**Figure 10.25c** *Fiddler on the Roof* fixture callout.
*Lighting by: Brian MacDevitt*
*ALD: Anne E. McMills*

**Chaplin**

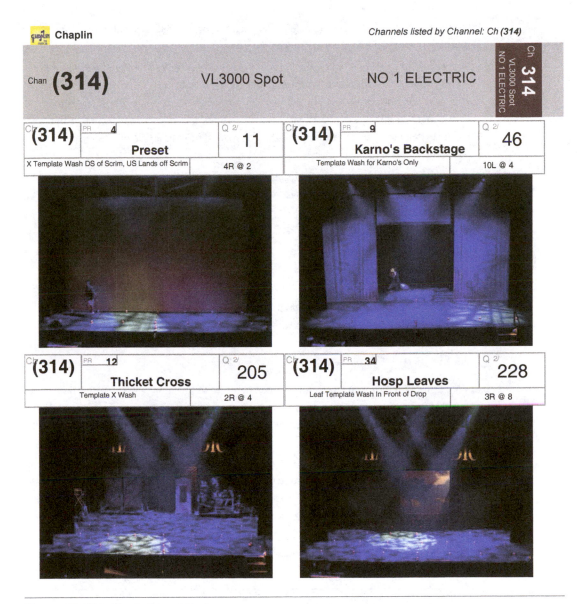

| | |
|---|---|
| Chan **(314)** | VL3000 Spot |

NO 1 ELECTRIC

Ch **314** VL3000 Spot NO 1 ELECTRIC

| **(314)** | PR **4** | Q 2/ **11** |
|---|---|---|
| **Preset** | | |
| X Template Wash DS of Scrim, US Lands off Scrim | | 4R @ 2 |

| **(314)** | PR **9** | Q 2/ **46** |
|---|---|---|
| **Karno's Backstage** | | |
| Template Wash for Karno's Only | | 10L @ 4 |

| **(314)** | PR **12** | Q 2/ **205** |
|---|---|---|
| **Thicket Cross** | | |
| Template X Wash | | 2R @ 4 |

| **(314)** | PR **34** | Q 2/ **228** |
|---|---|---|
| **Hosp Leaves** | | |
| Leaf Template Wash In Front of Drop | | 3R @ 8 |

**Figure 10.25d**  *Chaplin* fixture callout.
*Lighting by: Ken Billington*
*Assoc. LD: John Demous*

bible should stay with the show to help protect against technical issues that may not allow the electricians to view the files when needed.

Physically, the archival bible is the completed lighting bible with all items printed out and inserted. Digitally, it is the same as the lighting bible only made into one large PDF file. Include a title page and bookmarks in your PDF bible so it is easy to navigate. For the design office and designer's archives, additionally include all original documents in their native file type. Transfer the materials on to the designer's hard drive and provide a labeled flash drive or other media device to store at the office.

In addition to the full archival bibles, a printed and/or PDF copy of the cue list should be given to the PSM, and the final followspot cue sheets should be printed for the spot ops. All archival items should be complete before opening night.

Occasionally assistants will build in an **"archival week"** into their contract that extends one week past opening. Although difficult to negotiate, sometimes this extra week can be a trade-off to the producers in exchange for not hiring an ML assistant.

An extra week can be helpful if the show is planning a move to another city soon thereafter—especially if there are a lot of moving lights to document. The extra time provides the opportunity to record the information with additional accuracy without contending with the rush of tech.

## NEXT TIME SHEET

Keep a running list of items to do for the next iteration of the show—whether the show tours or mounts in another city. Keep this list even if you think the show may never move. In the event that it does, this list can assure a successful remount when you have had weeks, months, or even years between productions.

This document is internal just to you, so jot down anything that seems pertinent. For example, you may catch your designer saying something like, "I really wish I had lit the portal better," or, "A deeper blue backlight probably would have helped." Add it to the list! Also include any information that you wish you had known before beginning the production that might have saved you some hassle.

You can also keep a next time list specific to the venue for when you return to do another show in that same space.

Some sample *show* "next time" notes are:
- Double-up PARs behind window for stronger look
- Change warm backlight to slightly less saturated amber

Some sample *venue* "next time" notes are:
- House electrician's name is: xxxx
- Limited circuits on the 3E
- Box boom positions are permanent and cannot be moved

## RUNNING GIFTS LIST

Some designers prefer the assistant to keep a running list of people involved in the show. This allows the designer to have a gifts list on hand for opening night cards and gift purchases. You can begin by working off the contact sheet. Start by including those individuals who influence hiring—producers, directors, management, etc. Continue by adding other colleagues and collaborators such as the other designers, their associates, the playwright and composer, the conductor/maestro, and the stage management team. Next include the entire lighting team from the production electrician and her team to the programmer to the assistants and any interns—be sure to include yourself. After that, keep a running list for the designer of anyone else that he may find significant. (Perhaps add the designer's spouse or partner—it never hurts to send a "thank you for putting up with me during tech" card.) Opening night gifts are often a forgotten item for busy designers, so having a quick list on hand will be appreciated. As opening approaches, ask the designer if he would like a copy of the list.  He may or may not choose to use it.


The amount of paperwork for an assistant lighting designer to create, update, and keep track of on a daily basis is astounding. This is part of the excitement and challenge of the career—to stay one step ahead of every change or new idea that gets thrown your way. Those who love assisting love the rush!

# PART 4

# The Industry

Working in the theatrical industry as an assistant lighting designer can mean working in many different situations and with many different types of organizations. You can work on high-end theatrical productions, such as Broadway and West End, or high-budget mega-productions, such as the Super Bowl, the Grammy Awards, and the Olympics. Or you can work in lower-budget situations, such as summer stock, regional theatre, or Off-Broadway. It may mean a steady job such as a lighting director or associate at a rotating repertory company like an opera or a lighting supervisor at a roadhouse. It can also mean stretching into other professions such as television and film, architectural lighting, industrials, and themed entertainment.

Many professional assistants bounce between these various situations on a weekly or monthly basis; one week he may be drafting the lighting for a new ride at a theme park while the next week begins a new Broadway sit-down in a foreign city. When working as a professional assistant, the possibilities are wide open.

## CHAPTER 11

# U.S.-based Employment Opportunities

## BROADWAY

> *"There isn't a school in this country that teaches the system that we use in New York. I'm sure it has faults, but it's one of the best I've ever run into."*
>
> —*Tharon Musser*[1]

The largest and most well known of the American theatrical organizations is Broadway (often abbreviated "Bway" or "B'way"). **Broadway** is a high-budget theatrical machine located in the theatre district of New York City that produces many new works each year. It is widely considered, along with the West End in London, to be the top level of commercial theatre in the English-speaking world. Productions within Broadway theatres are eligible for Tony Awards—considered to be one of the most prestigious awards in the American theatrical profession. At the time of publication, there are 39 Broadway theatres in existence.

New York City and the Broadway system are considered the hub of the assisting profession. Assisting jobs are plentiful, but also demanding and competitive. A good assistant can be gainfully employed and make a good living while based in New York.

Broadway theatres are also called "**union houses**" because everyone who works in a Broadway house must belong to their respective unions. "**The Broadway League**," a national trade association, works as a bargaining representative with the producers and theatre owners to negotiate collective bargaining agreements (CBAs) for the many theatrical unions that work within a Broadway theatre.

To be considered a Broadway theatre, the theatre must have the following criteria:

1.  499 seats minimum in the audience
2.  Located within the Theatre District in Manhattan (New York City). This district is also referred to as the "Broadway Box" or the "Broadway District": between 5th to 9th Avenue and from 34th to 56th Street.[2] (Although a few exceptions exist.)

Most of these theatres are owned or managed by three organizations: the Shubert Organization owns 17 theatres, the Nederlander Organization controls 9, and Jujamcyn owns 5. There are also three non-profit LORT (League of Resident Theatres) theatre companies that work within Broadway theatres—Lincoln Center Theatre, Manhattan Theatre Club, and Roundabout Theatre Company. These companies, as well as Disney, negotiate individualized CBAs.

The smallest of the Broadway theatres is the Helen Hayes Theatre at 597 seats and the largest is the Gershwin Theatre at 1933. The average size ranges from around 1100 to 1200 seats. Mostly built almost one hundred years ago, they are smaller than most regional and touring venues—especially in wing space.

Most Broadway performances take place Tuesday through Sunday at 8pm with matinees on Wednesdays, Saturdays, and Sundays at 2pm. Sunday evenings and Mondays are usually "dark." Some productions choose to offer performances on non-traditional days and times, including an earlier 7pm showing for family audiences.

### FOUR-WALL CONTRACT

Unlike regional theatres that come fully equipped, a Broadway theatre is essentially an empty room. When a producing company rents a Broadway theatre they sign what is called a "**Four-Wall Contract**." This means that they are renting a space with four walls, a floor, a grid, power coming into the building, audience seating, and a main curtain. That's it. The technicians will have to install nearly everything else needed for the show including the electrics and even a fly system (if required).

Broadway shows, which like to stretch all boundaries, can make good use of a four-wall contract by creating incredibly technical shows that think outside the confines of a typical show set-up. Also, because all equipment is rented, the lighting designer and assistants can work with state-of-the-art equipment with every new show.

## OFF-BROADWAY

**Off-Broadway** theatres, also located in Manhattan, seat 100 to 499 audience members and are not always fully union-affiliated. The commercial productions produced in these spaces are eligible for the Lucille Lortel Award, which recognizes achievement for excellence in Off-Broadway productions. Historically, many productions start Off-Broadway, find success, then move on to become Broadway shows. More recently, the reverse is also true. Some shows move from Broadway to Off-Broadway to extend their run (due to lower costs).

---

To be considered an Off-Broadway theatre, the theatre must have the following criteria:

1. 100 to 499 seats in the audience
2. Located anywhere within Manhattan (New York City)

---

As an assistant, working Off-Broadway is similar to working on a Broadway show except for lower budgets, smaller venues, and possibly shorter production periods. Typically these shows will have no more than one assistant paid at a minimum. Depending on the venue, some house equipment may be included when renting the space, which can be augmented with additional rentals.

## OFF-OFF-BROADWAY AND STOREFRONT THEATRE

**Off-Off-Broadway** theatres must also be located in Manhattan and must have 99 seats or less. Typically these houses are non-union and often spring from non-traditional spaces, such as old churches, gymnasiums, storefronts, and other found spaces. Many non-commercial, smaller, and/or experimental shows find their footing in "Off-Off." These venues can also be a valuable environment for workshops that want to work their way through the ranks of "Off-Off" to "Off" and, finally, to Broadway.

Usually Off-Off cannot afford to pay assistants. However, volunteering to work Off-Off can be an excellent learning experience and a place to hone your skills. Many of the designers who work there also work in larger venues, therefore networking opportunities can be at a premium.

---

*"Don't be [too] proud to take on any job no matter how modest. You never know when you [will] make a new contact in the most unlikely circumstances. And making contacts is always what will one day bring success."*

—Richard Pilbrow

---

Typically, Off-Off-Broadway productions use the house equipment provided with the venue. Be prepared for a myriad of possibilities. The equipment can be very old, minimal, or need repair before use. Sometimes the show's producers will provide the lighting team a minimal budget (usually enough for a few sheets of gel, an important gobo, or rental of a few extra cables).

A **Storefront** Theatre is the same as an Off-Off-Broadway theatre except it is located in any area *other* than Manhattan. This style of theatre is prevalent in Chicago and Los Angeles, but can also be found in most metropolitan areas across the United States.

## REGIONAL THEATRE

A **Regional** theatre is any professional theatre company outside of New York City that produces its own season. It can be commercial or not-for-profit, union or non-union. Often new works are created along with a mix of tried-and-true classics and popular musicals. The audiences for regionals are typically subscription-based. Some well-respected regionals gain acclaim by regularly sending their shows to Broadway.

Regional theatres often belong to a network or association. **LORT**, League of Resident Theatres, is a professional theatre association across the United States that includes 74 member theatres. Other networks are geographically determined, such as CAT (Chicago Area Theatres) and TBA (Theatre Bay Area—San Francisco). These networks often have their own collective bargaining agreements with the theatrical unions.

LORT houses are divided into categories: LORT "A" through "D." LORT A+ facilities are eligible for a special non-competitive Tony Award given each year to a regional theatre company in the United States.

Regional theatres are not four-wall contracts—everything is installed from the fly system and electric raceways to even a breakroom with a microwave and a copy machine. Other than that, working in a regional theatre is a lot like working in a Broadway house. They may have slightly lower budgets and encourage the designer to use house equipment, but the professional sentiment is usually very similar.

Regionals often pull their designers from New York. Often these designers will bring an associate or assistant with them and hire an additional local assistant to save money. If you are living outside of New York, working as a local assistant is a great way to get your foot in the door and network with some wonderful designers and associates.

## SUMMER STOCK

**Summer Stock** theatre is any theatre that produces shows primarily in the summer, often using stock scenery, costumes, and house lighting and sound equipment. Summer stock seasons are usually anywhere from June through September, and often consist of classics, musicals, or operas.

Often viewed as a starting-off point for young actors and technicians, it can also be a good place to get your feet wet in assisting. Some summer stock shows run in rotating rep or mount quickly, so an assistant (sometimes called lighting supervisor) is needed to restore each show. Working in these environments can expose you to some wonderful designers and a new level of professional work that you may not have experienced yet, depending on your level.

While still in school, work each summer in the best summer stock companies that will hire you; it will transform you into a professional. Succeed there, and you will be remembered. Many of your summer stock contacts will end up hiring you for big-profile jobs later in your career.

## ROADHOUSE

A **Roadhouse** is a professional theatre that typically does not produce its own work, but houses short-term touring productions instead (referred to as a receiving house as opposed to a production house). In this case, an assistant can work full time as a lighting supervisor or other title; a position somewhat similar to a house electrician on Broadway. She would help each company adapt to the space and integrate their light plot into the house hang. (Although some situations may allow time to change over to the company's light plot completely.)

A **"House Hang"** or **"Rep Plot"** is a light plot hung semi-permanently in the theatre. Its flexible lighting systems allow for easy changeover between frequently changing shows. This is often used in any situation that houses rotating productions, such as an opera house, dance company, or roadhouse. Designers who work within these situations usually incorporate their light plot into the existing rep plot so that the crew does not need to constantly change over to a new light plot with each new show.

Rep plots usually consist of several standard systems and a few refocusable specials. Color and gobo changes are usually allowed.

## OPERA HOUSE

An **Opera House** is any professional theatre that produces an opera season. Some of the most reputable in the United States are: The Metropolitan Opera ("The Met"), the New York City Opera (NYCO), the Lyric Opera of Chicago, the Los Angeles Opera, the Houston Grand Opera, and the San Francisco Opera.

Professional large-scale operas typically run in **"rotating rep"** (repertory), which means that several operas will perform within a single week. This requires the lights and scenery to be changed out and refocused several times a week and, often, several times a day.

Similar to a roadhouse, an opera house often hires assistant-types full time as lighting directors or house lighting assistants. The lighting director works closely with the designers to incorporate their light plots into the rep plot, and the assistants take care of the nitty-gritty of each production, such as focusing each upcoming show or rehearsal and notating focus and color changes.

In addition to the lighting director and house lighting assistants, other assistant lighting designers may be hired to work with the designer just as they would in any standard show depending on the structure of the individual opera house.

## WORKING ON THE ROAD

When working as an assistant lighting designer, you will probably find yourself "on the road" at some point in your career. Traveling for work can be both exciting and exhausting. The assisting profession provides many travel opportunities. Always keep your passport and other identification current—you never know when that next call may come in.

> *"Travel can be grueling but the opportunity to learn more about the world, its people, and [its] cultures is the best perk of the work."*
>
> —Christopher Akerlind

As an assistant lighting designer, being on the road is not as you may traditionally picture it—visions of roadies loading in a different show every night and traveling on a bus come to mind. There *are* shows out there that employ assistant lighting designers in this fashion (usually in the world of dance), but more often the assistant's role is a little less long-term and usually a little more comfortable.

For each new production remounted from an original, a unique title is used internally to distinguish the company from the original Broadway show. Sit-downs are usually named for the city or country where they are located: "*Wicked* Los Angeles," "*Wicked* Germany," etc. Tours are often named thematically. For example, each new *Riverdance* company was named after a different river in Ireland—the "Boyne company" and "Lagan company," etc. *Wicked* focuses on production-specific items and named its first tours the "Shiz company" and the "Emerald City company." Some productions use creative names for all of their new companies: *Spamalot* created fun names such as "Touralot" (1st national tour), "Wynalot" (sit-down at the Wynn Las Vegas Resort), "Laughalot" (London), and "Ozalot" (Australia). Add the proper name to the title information on all of your paperwork so that each company is easily identifiable from the last.

### PRE-BROADWAY TRY-OUT

A **Pre-Broadway Try-Out**, sometimes called an **"Out-of-Town Try-Out,"** is a soon-to-be Broadway show mounted in another city to test audience reaction *before* taking the production to Broadway. It allows the writers and director to work out ideas (and any kinks) before opening the show in New York.

> *"Remember with local crew that you are a guest in their house and, as such, you should treat the crew (and the building) with respect."*
>
> *—Anthony Pearson*

When working on a try-out, the assistants and the rest of the team live in the try-out city for several weeks while fully teching and opening the production the first time—returning home after opening. Once the show finishes its limited run in the try-out city, it will transfer to Broadway to be completely re-teched and reopened a second time—usually with some new script changes based on initial reviews.

---

Any city with a LORT A+ theatre can become a **Try-Out City**. Occasionally even cities outside the United States are used for try-outs: Toronto and (in some ways) London to name a few.

Some American favorites include:

| | | |
|---|---|---|
| • Atlanta | • Denver | • San Diego |
| • Atlantic City | • Houston | • San Francisco |
| • Baltimore | • Los Angeles | • Seattle |
| • Boston | • Minneapolis | • Washington D.C. |
| • Chicago | • New Haven | |
| | • Philadelphia | |

---

## BROADWAY SIT-DOWN

A **Sit-Down** is a replica of an already-successful Broadway show mounted in a different city—usually with an **open-ended** run (no planned closing date). The sit-down may run concurrently with the Broadway production. There may be several sit-down productions of the same show running at the same time in various cities.

For each new sit-down, just as with a try-out, the assistants live in the new city for a few weeks while mounting the production. The designer may be present for all, part, or none of the process depending on the director's preferences. If the designer is not present, an associate will work in place of the designer. Other assistants, the production electrician, and the programmer may also be there.

Because the show is not teching from scratch, a sit-down's timeframe may be slightly shorter than the original production's tech process. However, occasionally directorial changes will be made on a sit-down, such as a new opening number or added scenic element, which will add additional tech time to the sit-down. If successful, these changes may be retrofit into previous versions of the show (including the Broadway production) at a later date. The associate is usually rehired—often on a daily rate—to retrofit these productions.

Occasionally, but very rarely, a production company may hire an associate at a small weekly rate to maintain their long-running companies throughout the world. **Maintaining** means that the associate would fly out for a day or two and give notes or touch up any focus that has become sloppy over the years. If a new lead actor is added into the show, the associate may also make small timing or color changes that work better with the new talent.

## BROADWAY NATIONAL TOUR

A **Broadway National Tour** is widely considered the crème de la crème of theatrical touring situations, and the closest possible replica of the Broadway show on tour. Each new touring production is denoted as the "1st National Broadway Tour," "2nd National Broadway Tour," and so on. These tours are multi-week tours and may stay in a city for a month or more at a time. Many successful productions choose to run a Broadway production, several sit-down productions, and multiple national tours concurrently.

Sometimes these tours are referred to as "**yellow-card tours**"—there must be IATSE stagehands both traveling with the show as well as yellow-card local stagehands at every stop. The cast and orchestra are also union, and the leads are usually well-known Equity veterans.

On a national tour, most of the scenery is recreated without alteration. Some front-of-house lighting may be pared down to enable easier touring, but the majority of the overstage plot is often the same as the original production.

The associate and the assistants do not tour with the production, but rather show up at the start of the first few cities to check the accuracy of each reproduction. The designer may or may not be present in the initial city and probably will not participate in the following city checks. For long-running tours, the assistant may be rehired to check on the tour annually.

The initial city requires roughly the same amount of tech time as a sit-down, but the subsequent cities have a much shorter turn-around time. On a 1st and 2nd national, a typical tour loads out of the first city on a Sunday after the matinee and opens a show in the next city on a Tuesday evening.

## BUS AND TRUCK

A **Bus and Truck** production is a cost-saving tour with reduced technical elements. The name is derived from the goal to fit everything and everyone on one bus and one truck. Often the production quality is diminished from the original Broadway show, and the production is often non-union. Main scenic elements may be reduced down to less elaborate versions or simple drops that take up less room in a truck. The light plot is usually very pared down and/or uses house equipment owned by each venue.

Sometimes these productions are also called "**One-Offs**" or "**One-Nighters**"—typically not staying in a city longer than a few days or a week. On "**split-weeks**" where the show is performed in one city half of the week and another city the other half of the week, "**jump-crews**" or "**split crews**" are used to leap-frog a city ahead to load in select technical elements that may prove difficult in a tight timeframe.

The associate and assistant or local assistant may be hired to simplify the production in the first city. The associate may or may not be hired to check on the subsequent cities.

## U.S.-BASED INTERNATIONAL PRODUCTION

A U.S.-based international production may be a sit-down, a tour, or a combination—one that sits-down for several months before beginning to tour. Just like any other sit-down or national Broadway tour, these productions are nearly exact replicas of the Broadway production with one major exception—the script is performed in the native language of the area. (See Figures 11.1a-c.)

When working in a foreign country, the American production team works from a "**reverse-translation**" of the script. This means that the translators adapt the original script into their native tongue, and, then, *retranslate* the script back into English for the American production team. Due to the nature of language and colloquial expressions, exact translations are not possible so some lines may be different in the reverse-script. Usually these changes are small, but some cues may shift if placed on actors' lines.

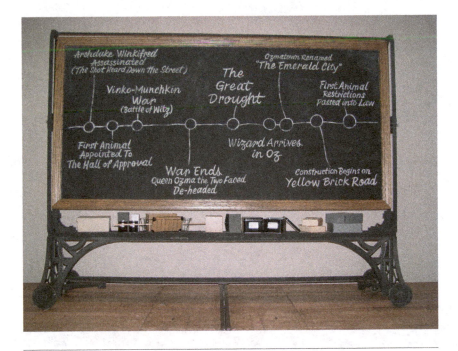

**Figure 11.1a**  Chalkboard prop in *Wicked* London.
*Designed by: Eugene Lee*
*Courtesy of: Edward Pierce*

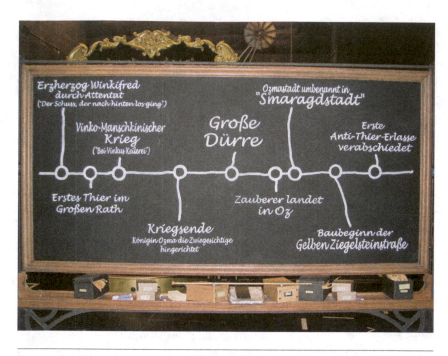

**Figure 11.1b**  Chalkboard prop in *Wicked* Germany.
*Designed by: Eugene Lee*
*Courtesy of: Edward Pierce*

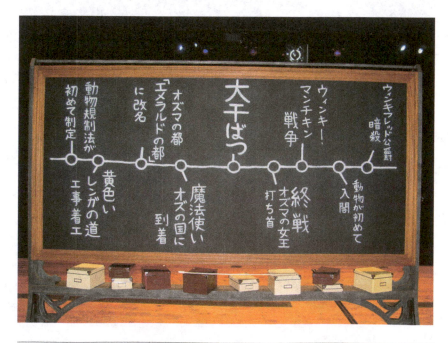

**Figure 11.1c**  Chalkboard prop in *Wicked* Japan.
*Designed by: Eugene Lee*
*Courtesy of: Edward Pierce*

> *"Hire a local assistant who understands how the local situation works, and learn what the expectations are there, so that you can adapt to them or adapt them to you."*
>
> *—Vivien Leone*

In addition to the reverse-translation script, each production department is usually provided with a translator, or interpreter, if English is not widely spoken in the area. The translator will help communicate with local crew.

Sometimes using a translator can be a challenge because often his knowledge of technical theatre terms is limited. The more terms you can teach yourself, the better. (See discussion on *Theatre Words* in the following chapter.)

> *"In general I enjoy working in foreign countries because you get a good sense of the people, the culture, work ethic, etc. of a particular place in a way that's much deeper than what you would typically experience as a tourist. You also gain an appreciation of how small the world really is, and that our similarities vastly outweigh our differences, both in and outside the workplace. The only major obstacle that I often encounter is the language barrier. Even with an interpreter at your side, there are certain procedures and directions in lighting that are difficult to communicate without a complete command of the language.*
>
> *—Donald Holder*

While mounting the production, the associate will live in the country for several weeks. The designer may or may not be present, and usually an additional local assistant is provided. The associate's contract usually ends after opening night, although some producers may try to end it earlier to save money. If so, adjust your archival activities accordingly.

Additionally, international productions may be "**licensed**"—signifying that an international company has purchased the rights to the entire production and its design elements. If this is the case, the associate must teach the local crew how to run the production (and mount it in other cities) without the assistance of the design team.

## OTHER TRAVEL SITUATIONS

Many other types of theatrical travel situations exist. For example, popular Off-Broadway shows, like *Blue Man Group*, may produce a U.S. tour, a U.K. tour, a world tour, and/or various sit-down productions. A regional show may tour to additional cities before making its way towards Broadway. And popular U.K.-based shows, such as *Stomp* or *Cats* or *Mary Poppins* (or productions from other countries like France or Germany), may tour in the United States or other countries abroad—not to mention large-scale blockbuster events, such as the Canadian-based Cirque Du Soleil, that simultaneously produces sit-downs and tours within every continent in the world except Antarctica.

CHAPTER 12

# Working Outside the United States

When working outside the United States on a U.S.-based production, many things will seem familiar. You may come across some language barriers and learn some idiosyncrasies of the area, but for the most part, the job of the assistant is the same in terms of dealing with the designer.

Before working outside of your native country, educate yourself on local customs and learn how to be sensitive to them. (Due to the widespread popularity of American television, most foreign cultures know vastly more about our culture than we know about theirs.) Research the culture thoroughly to avoid offense. Travel guides can be a great place to start. Always remember that *you* are the foreign one when working on others' turf so be as courteous as possible.

Know how to interact appropriately, how to show politeness, and what to do (or not to do) in social and professional situations. Be sensitive to local clothing norms—depending on the culture, simply wearing items such as a tank top and shorts can be considered offensive.

Respect local theatre folklore; theatre people in most countries (including the U.S.) are surrounded by superstitions and ghost stories. If you become aware of any, do not insult the locals by making light of these traditions.

When prepping a show in another country, ask your designer and production manager in what scale you should draft the plot. Some teams opt to keep the drawings in imperial scales (½" = 1'-0" or ¼" = 1'-0") or they may choose to convert them to metric dimensions and scales (1:25 or 1:50). Most often you will be asked to convert your drawings because the U.S. "is now the only country in the world not officially using the metric system."[1] Written English can still be used since it is spoken in most countries.

Depending on the length of your stay, you may choose to have two suitcases for personal use instead of reserving one spot for your assistant's kit. (More on this in Chapter 2.) You may opt to have your kit shipped by an international carrier. Check the country's customs policies and fill out the proper forms with the appropriate declared values. Ensure you are not shipping anything that will delay the delivery of your kit in the arriving country. Ask the production company if they are willing to provide an account number to cover the charges of the shipment.

If your designer prefers to archive a show with a printed bible, ask her what type of paper she would like it printed on—local-size or U.S.-size. Some designers prefer consistent binder sizes, and therefore prefer American binders and paper sizes. If so, ship a few reams of American paper and a binder in your kit so you have it available. However, purchase and print the archival bible for the local crew in local paper and binder sizes. If you use your own printer, ensure that it can print both desired paper sizes.

> *"I've done shows in Athens, Rome, Cape Town, Paris, London, Tokyo and Hong Kong among many others … each had their own challenges and rewards."*
>
> —*Brian Monahan*

It is not possible for this book to cover working in every country, but the following are some common destinations for theatrical shows.

# WORKING IN THE UNITED KINGDOM

> *"I'm not sure that design approaches differ on either side of the Atlantic…. The paperwork side, though, does definitely differ across the pond. In the U.K., the plan [light plot] is the only piece of paperwork; every piece of information is on it. Lightwright is used a little bit on larger shows, but it is the responsibility of the electrician, not the designers. When I sit down at the production desk, I have the plan alone—not even a magic sheet."*
>
> —*Neil Austin*[2]

The U.K. is known worldwide for its prestigious theatre culture. Full of rich history, London, especially, is brimming with theatrical opportunities.

The **West End** in London is the U.K.'s highest level of commercial theatre. There are approximately 40 West End theatres located mostly in "Theatreland" in the West End of central London. The West End is bordered by Oxford Street to the north, The Strand to the south, Kingsway to the east, and Regent Street to the west. (There is at least one exception—The Playhouse, which is located outside of Theatreland.) Performance schedules in West End theatres are similar to Broadway theatres except that the dark day is usually Sunday instead of Monday.

> Performances at West End theatres vary their start times between 7:15pm and 8pm. Some shows (that are not selling well) may choose to start later to try to catch audiences unable to get tickets to more popular shows earlier in the evening. Other shows choose to start later to gather audiences who prefer not to pay London's "congestion charge"—an extra expense aimed at those entering the city between 7am and 6pm to help reduce the flow of traffic into and around central London. (There is no congestion charge on the weekends.)

Aside from the West End, many prestigious non-commercial theatres are located in London; among them the Royal National Theatre, the Royal Court Theatre, the Barbican Centre, Shakespeare's Globe, the Young Vic, and the (somewhat commercial) Old Vic and Donmar Warehouse. Unlike the West End theatres, which mostly present musicals, these theatres largely produce important classics such as Shakespeare—although cutting-edge new work is also created. Similar to the U.S., regional theatres are also sprinkled across the United Kingdom's countryside and city centers.

Other notable London institutions are the Royal Opera House at Covent Garden—widely considered one of the greatest opera houses in the world and home to the Royal Opera and the Royal Ballet, as well as the London Coliseum—home to the English National Opera (ENO) and the English National Ballet. The Royal Opera House (often referred to as "Covent Garden" due to its location) is considered one of the most advanced automated lighting houses in the world.

Additionally a great amount of theatre can be found in London's "**fringe theatres.**" A fringe theatre is the equal to an Off-Off-Broadway theatre or a storefront theatre in the U.S.

Fringe theatre is popular all over the U.K. especially during Scotland's Edinburgh Fringe Festival—the largest arts festival in the world—which takes place for three weeks every August. Theatres all over the city light up with a cornucopia of fringe performances. Also in August, the famous Royal Edinburgh Military Tattoo entertains audiences with theatrical displays. Running alongside these great celebrations, the Edinburgh International Festival (a separate entity from the Fringe Festival) erupts with a celebration of music, theatre, opera, and dance including visual art exhibitions, talks, and workshops.

Similar to the U.S., Equity covers union actors and stage managers in the U.K. However, in contrast, Equity also represents the U.K.'s scenic and lighting designers, although membership for designers is not mandatory.

Most stagehands in the U.K. belong to **BECTU**—the Broadcasting, Entertainment, Cinematography, and Theatre Union. BECTU also covers a select number of organizations—such as The Royal Opera House, The Royal Shakespeare Company, The Royal Court, etc.

Another organization specific to the London area is **SOLT**—the Society of London Theatres. This organization "represents the producers, theatre owners and managers of the major commercial and grant-aided theatres in central London."[3] SOLT is connected with many of the West End theatres. And, finally, **TMA**—Theatrical Management Association—supports many theatres and other entertainment venues, such as producing houses outside the West End like the Lyric Theatre Hammersmith. Therefore, when working in the U.K. you may come across three different types of house contracts—BECTU, SOLT, or TMA (although TMA makes many of its agreements through BECTU.)

The U.K. is very strict when it comes to health and safety. Electricians of all types (not just theatrical) go through several levels of training, and all electrical equipment—including cable—must be tested, recorded, and tagged individually by using the Portable Appliance Test, or "PAT Test."

For further safety (and due to the frequency of theatre fires in London's past), the fire curtain (known in the U.K. as the "iron" or "safety curtain") must be flown in to the stage floor at least once during each performance to prove it is operational. This usually occurs during intermission ("interval").

In addition, fire alarms in theatre buildings are required by law to be checked once a week. However, unlike the U.S., during a fire emergency no visible or audible sounds of a fire alarm are allowed in the house during a performance (although alarms will sound backstage). The intent is to not cause panic in the audience, which may heighten the emergency. It is up to the stage manager to stop the show to make the appropriate safety announcements and provide further instructions.

Like the U.S., ETC equipment is primarily used in most U.K. commercial productions—with the Source Four overtaking Strand equipment in recent years as the industry standard. Also within the last few years, ETC and MA Lighting consoles have largely displaced older Strand Lighting boards. (However, regionally in rep houses and older theatres that own stock inventory, you may still find a lot of Strand Lighting equipment and a mix of equipment from Europe.) Additionally, Rosco gel is now as common as LEE Filters.

> *"In England there is never money for an assistant. If you have an assistant, you pay for it yourself, except in the very biggest spectaculars."*
>
> —David Hersey[4]

Working as an assistant lighting designer in the U.K. has become more prevalent in recent years. Previously the designer worked alone, but as shows have begun to grow in complexity and have had more influence from the U.S., the vocation of the U.K. assistant (and associate) lighting designer has grown in popularity. However, the paperwork is much more focused on the light plot—which acts like a giant magic sheet during the production.

Like the U.S., Vectorworks is the most prevalent drafting program to use for theatre. WYSIWYG is also popular, although used more prominently for concert production.

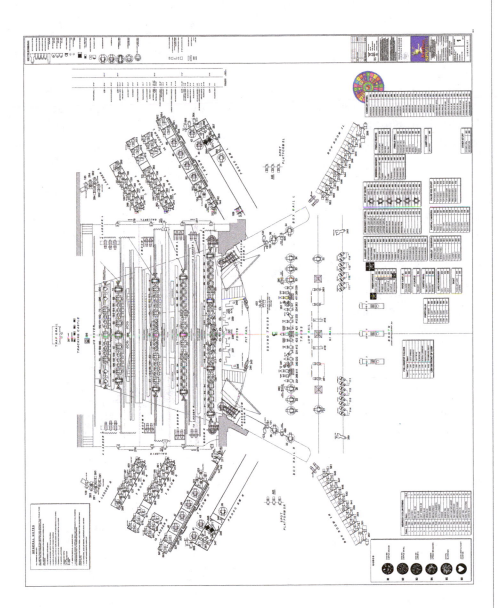

**Figure 12.1** *Spamalot* (British-style) light plot.
*Lighting by: Hugh Vanstone*
*Assoc. LD: Philip S. Rosenberg*

*"Since being in the States, that's one thing [the Americans] have taught me—have an assistant. 'Here's the plot, here's the ideas—go deal with it.' The ideas are done. I'm bored with the rest of it . ... I love that help—I'm willing to pay for that."*

—*Chris Parry*[5]

The people of the U.K. are wonderful, warm, and fun people. They are also a social people. Be sure to partake in tea break each day and a drink at the pub after the show (in moderation if they will let you). The team will appreciate getting to know you, and your working relationships will grow stronger for it.

## BRITISH THEATRICAL TERMINOLOGY

Most vocabulary you come across in the U.K. will be the same as the U.S., but some terms will be different. Terms may also vary by location.

| American English | British English |
|---|---|
| **Stage Directions** | |
| Stage Right | Opposite Prompt (OP) |
| Stage Left | Prompt Side (PS) |
| Prompt when placed SR | Bastard Prompt |

(Note: "Prompt" is from "Prompt Desk"—traditionally the place the "prompter" sat to feed lines to forgetful actors, now the position occupied by the deputy stage manager—i.e. the person calling cues.)

| American English | British English |
|---|---|
| **The Theatre Building** | |
| Orchestra | Stalls |
| Mezzanine | Dress Circle |
| Balcony | Upper Circle or Grand Circle |
| Upper Balcony (Nose Bleeds) | Gallery of the Gods |
| Booth | Control Room or Lighting Box |
| **Production Process** | |
| Intermission | Interval |
| Load-in | Get-in or Fit-up |
| Strike/Load-out | Get-out |

| American English | British English |
|---|---|
| Opening Night | First Night |
| Opening Night Party | First Night Party |
| Cueing | Plotting |
| Dimmer Check | Rig Check |

**Lighting and Electrical Terms**

| | |
|---|---|
| Instrument/Fixture | Lantern |
| Ellipsoidal/Leko | Profile |
| Lamp | Bubble |
| No Color (N/C) | Open White (O/W) |
| 2-fer | Grelco |
| 3-fer | Trelco |
| Adaptor | Jumper |
| Floor Stand | Bench Base |
| Electrical Tape or E-tape | PVC Tape or Plastic Tape |
| Lighting Board/Console | Lighting Desk |
| Tech Table | Production Desk |
| Followspots | Limes (from the days of limelight) |

**Personnel**

| | |
|---|---|
| Head Electrician | Chief Electrician |
| Intern | Work-Placement |

**Miscellaneous**

| | |
|---|---|
| Fire Curtain | Iron or Safety Curtain |
| Crescent Wrench | A.J. (Adjustable Wrench) or Adjustable Spanner |
| China Marker | China Graph |
| Fog | Smoke |

# WORKING IN CONTINENTAL EUROPE

Working in continental Europe is as varied as the cultures therein. Each culture has its own unique history, and its own working identity. There are a few generalities that perhaps blanket many of the cultures thriving within the Continent. The following will attempt to discuss those ideas and break out a few specifics.

Western Europe is best known for its world-renowned opera houses. The list is astounding: Italy has Teatro la Fenice in Venice and arguably the most famous opera house in the world, La Scala de Milán; France has the Opéra de Lyon (also called Opéra Nouvel) and is home of the Phantom of the Opera himself at the Palais Garnier (The Paris Opera House); Spain has Teatro Real de Madrid and The Liceo de Barcelona; Austria has the Wiener Staatsoper in Vienna; and Germany has the Bayreuth Festspielhaus, home to the annual Bayreuth Festival dedicated to the works of Wagner. This list is hardly exhaustive.

Germany and Austria are also known for the tradition of Stadttheater (City Theatre)— repertory houses in larger towns and cities—which perform a mix of drama, opera, dance, and musicals. European regional theatres are also abundant as well as a number of receiving houses that mount international tours and sit-downs—from Broadway, the West End, France, Germany, and beyond.

European designers tend to light scenes very specifically and often do not work as systematically as American designers do. Each scene is often constructed with specific key lights for each moment rather than systems of light covering every area of the stage. European lighting designers generally have a fondness for fewer, bigger instruments (such as the 5K tungsten or 4K HMI Fresnel)—lighting the stage with one big brush stroke of light rather than lots of little pools blended together. Strong directionality is also valued, often created by using fixtures like the beamlight (or beam projector) and the Svoboda.

Designer support is much more relaxed in Europe. For example, the tech table may be nothing more than that—a table—with usually a headset and desk light. The absence of console monitors on the tech table is common in a European house.

European crews are very proud of European equipment. If using house equipment, you will often find a mix of manufacturers—companies like Robert Juliat from France, ADB Lighting Technologies from Belgium, Strand Lighting and LEE Filters from the U.K., and MA Lighting from Germany. Occasionally you may come across a few ETC units, but American manufactured items are not as common. European designers also tend to design with adjustable-focus fixtures, or "zooms," (not fixed barrels like Americans tend to prefer). Other fixtures you may find include PCs and Svobodas, which are rarely seen in America.

---

**PC (Pebble Convex):** The modern PC is a fixture similar to a Fresnel with one important difference. It has a plano-convex lens, instead of a Fresnel lens, with a pebbled effect on the flat (plano) side. The result is a soft round beam, much like a Fresnel, only more controlled. Generally, PCs are used more frequently in Europe than Fresnels.

**Beamlight or Beam Projector:** similar to a searchlight; produces a very narrow and intense beam of light with a soft edge which provides a parallel-beamed, strongly directional look. Although not used as much anymore in the U.S., these fixtures are still popular in Germany and other European countries.

**Svoboda:** named for and designed by the legendary designer and visionary, Josef Svoboda. This fixture consists of a bank of multiple small, low-voltage lamps with intense, quasi-parallel beams. The result is a soft, yet dramatic, curtain-of-light effect known simply as the "Light Curtain." Svoboda created the fixture while looking for a unique way to create dramatic scenery using only light.

---

Most European countries utilize theatrical unions. For example, France has the **CGT— Confédération Générale du Travail**, a confederation of unions including those who represent stagehands and designers. Germany has **Ver.di**—Vereinte Dienstleistungsgewerkschaft—which roughly translates as "United Services Union." It is Germany's second largest theatrical union (following its orchestral union) and covers "non-artistic staff, administrators and non-artistically employed technicians."[6] Germany's third largest theatrical union is the **GBDA** (Genossenschaft der Deutschen Bühnenangehörigen) or "German Stage Workers Union," which covers "artistic technical employees."[7]

European unions help to protect the enchanting European way of life. The unions may stipulate maximum hours worked in a day or week, break and meal schedules, annual vacation weeks, which hours are considered working hours, and even crew availability. In France, workers usually take two-hour lunch breaks, workdays are limited to a maximum of 13 hours a day, and Sundays and evenings earn double-time.

The union stipulations may vary by country; however, the European Union (EU) has been making strides towards standardizing many of its labor laws. For example, as defined by European Law, EU employees are required to have an 11-hour overnight break; most rehearsals end at 10pm to allow crews to return again the next morning at 9am.

European theatre crews operate on a shift system defined by their working hours rather than by the needs of the show. Therefore, you may get different spot ops at different times of the day or on different days of the week. Make sure your followspot cue sheets are as accurate as possible. For further assurance, translate your spot sheets into the locals' native language with the help of your translator.

Concern for safety varies depending on the culture too. For example, many French theatres allow smoking inside the building, but, in contrast, in Germany the technical director can be found legally liable for accidents and fined or even jailed. One approach is not better than the other, but you will find a range of different attitudes on the subject when traveling between countries.

Assistants are not as widely used in Europe at this time as in the States, but with the influx of American and British sit-downs and growing lighting design programs in European universities the culture is slowly shifting.

## EUROPEAN THEATRICAL TERMINOLOGY[8]:

| American English | French | German | Italian |
|---|---|---|---|
| **Stage Directions** | | | |
| Stage Left | La Cour | Rechts | a Destra |
| Stage Right | Le Jardin | Links | Lato Giardino |
| Up Stage | Le Lointain | In Der Tiefe der Bühne | Fondo Palcoscenico |
| Down Stage | La Face | Nach Vorn | Davanti |
| **Stage Terms** | | | |
| Stage | La Scène | Bühne | Palcoscenico |
| Apron | L'Avant-Scène | Vorbühne | Proscenio |
| Backstage | La Coulisse | Bereich Ausserhalb der Szene | il Ridotto per gli Addetti allo Spettacolo |
| House | La Salle | Zuschauerraum | Sala |
| Main Curtain | Le Rideau | Vorhang | Sipario |
| Fire Curtain | Le Rideau de Fer | Sicherheitsvorhang | Sipario di Sicurezza |
| Leg | Le Pendrillon | Seitenschenkel | Quinta |
| Border | La Frise | Soffitte | Soffitto |
| Cyc | Le Cyclo | Rundhorizont | Panorama |
| Batten | Le Porteuse or La Perche | Prospektlatte | Stangone |
| Lighting Bridge | Le Pont Lumière | Beleuchtungsbrücke | Ponte Luci |
| **Lighting Design Terms** | | | |
| Front Light | La Face | Vorbühnenlicht | Luci di Proscenio e di Sala |
| Back Light | Le Contre | Rücklicht | Contro Luce |
| Down Light | La Douche | Spielflächenlicht | Illuminazione dall'alto |
| Side Light | La Latéral Aveuglant | Seitenlicht | Luce Laterale |
| Shins | La Latéral Rasante | Fußbeleuchtung | Serpente Luminoso |

| American English | French | German | Italian |
|---|---|---|---|
| **Instruments** | | | |
| Instrument | La Découpe | Beleuchtungsgerät | Lanterna |
| Gel Frame | La Porte-Filtre | Farbfilterrahmen | Telaio per Gelatina |
| Lens | Lentille | Linse | Lente |
| C-clamp | Le Crochet or Le Collier | Befestigungsklammer | Gancio |
| Scroller | La Changeur de Couleur | Farbwechsler | Cambio Colore |
| **The Production Process** | | | |
| Load-in | Montage | Erster Aufbau | Primo Montaggio |
| Rehearsal | Répétition | Beleuchtungsprobe | Prova Luci |
| Strike | Démontage | Abbauen | Smontare |
| **Electrics** | | | |
| Circuit | La Circuit | Stromkreis | Circuito |
| Dimmer | La Gradateur | Lichtregler | Regolatore Luce |
| Channel | Le Canal | Kanal | Canale |
| **Focusing** | | | |
| To Focus | Régler | Abrichten | Orientare |
| To Turn On | Allumer | Einschalten | Accendere |
| To Turn Off | Couper | Ausschalten | Spegnere |
| Sharp | Net | Scharf | Chiaro |
| Fuzzy | Flou | Unscharf | Non a fuoco |
| **Miscellaneous** | | | |
| Lighting Console | Le Pupitre | Lichtpult | Consolle a Comando |
| Go! | Top! | Los! | Via! |
| Followspot | La Poursuite | Verfolger | Seguipersona |
| WorkLights | Les Services | Arbeitslicht | Luce di Serviszio |
| To Fly In | Charger/ Descendre | Zug Nach Unten Bewegen | Abbassare |
| To Fly Out | Appuyer/ Monter | Zug Nach Oben Bewegen | Alzare |
| Please | S'il vous plaît | Bitte | Per favore |
| Thank you | Merci | Danke | Grazie |

# WORKING IN ASIA

Asia is another area with vastly different cultures that would be impossible to explore adequately in this text. Each culture's singular identity makes for a unique experience. This section will focus mainly on Japan.

Japan is considered the largest of the Asian markets for American and European productions, but many other Asian countries have begun to follow Japan's lead.

There are over 2000 major theatres in Japan. Most of them were built after World War II and are government owned. Many of the theatres are quite large by American standards (some with 100'-0" wide proscenium openings), but may seem shallow US to DS because often they are constructed to conform to the needs of traditional Kabuki theatre.

The average theatre in Japan has fewer than 3000 audience seats, but some larger houses hold 5000 to 7000. There are even a few large concert venues that hold over 10,000 audience members.

Theatre in Japan ranges broadly from traditional art forms such as Noh, Kabuki, and Bunraku all the way to international sit-down productions. With the influx of American, British, and European musicals, western work (performed by Japanese companies) has also become a popular pastime.

No standardized union exists for stagehands in Japan, but some privately owned venues have their own in-house labor unions. In government-owned theatres, one or two "house guys" may be employed full-time by the hall and local freelancers will be contracted separately for incoming productions.

Typically Japanese crews do not have set break schedules or hourly rates. They are often paid a flat fee for the day. However, overnight hours may result in additional pay.

Within Japanese culture, hierarchy is a very important construct. It is based in the strong cultural institution of respect for your elders and a sense of order. Therefore, when speaking directly to a member of the crew, you may not get the answers you desire. Make sure a superior is present. Japanese culture dictates that all decisions must be made by the highest-ranking person in a position of business.

In general, the people of Japan embrace all things American and enjoy a chance to speak English. Most Japanese workers will show up early and be ready to work as soon as the day begins. Theatrical crew members are often very friendly and eager. They may even take off in a run to complete a request. However, be cautious that the task you have requested is possible. Japanese upbringing is an eager-to-please culture that will often say, "yes" instead of first communicating the improbability of the charge.

Stage managers are non-existent for Japanese productions because the stagehands memorize the show in its entirety and all that they are tasked to perform. As a culture proudly rooted in the precise movements of exact art forms such as Noh theatre, Japanese-crewed shows are usually executed with absolute precision.

At the end of every rehearsal before everyone goes home the phrase *otsukare sama deshita* is exchanged between co-workers. This roughly translates into, "You're tired," which is considered a very good compliment. It acknowledges that you worked hard, gave it your best that day, and are therefore tired and deserve a drink. "Job well done," "nice work today," or "good rehearsal" might be a closer approximation in English. Return the compliment by learning to say it back.

The business world in Japan includes a fair amount of socializing. If you are asked out for a drink or dinner, it is considered rude to refuse. Enjoying a little nightlife with your co-workers is considered a normal part of a business day.

You may receive many small gifts when working in Japan—a large part of Japanese culture. Bring small gifts of your own for the crew and bring enough for everyone—usually the same gift for each of the crew members and something slightly different for the highest-ranking individual. Small items (presented humbly) are the norm. The receiver may or may not open the gift in your

## JAPANESE THEATRICAL TERMINOLOGY[9]

| American English | Japanese |
| --- | --- |
| **Stage Directions** | |
| Stage Left | Kamite |
| Stage Right | Shimote |
| Up Stage | Butai/Stagey Oku |
| Down Stage | Butai/Stagey Mye |
| Offstage | Sodenaka |
| **Stage Terms** | |
| Stage | Butai |
| Apron | Epuron Sutêji |
| Backstage | Butaiura |
| House | Kankyakuseki |
| Main Curtain | Maku |
| Fire Curtain | Bôka Shattâ |
| Leg | Sodemaku |
| Border | Ichimonji |
| Cyc | Horizonto |
| Batten | Paipubaton |
| Lighting Bridge | Furai Burijji |
| **Lighting Design Terms** | |
| Front Light | Maeakari |
| Back Light | Ushirokara No Shômei, Bakkuraito |

| American English | Japanese |
| --- | --- |
| Down Light | Zujôkara No Shômei |
| Side Light | Yokokara No Shômei, Saido |
| Shins | Korogashi |

**Instruments**

| | |
| --- | --- |
| Instrument | Shômeikigu |
| Gel Frame | Shîto, Irowaku |
| Lens | Renzu |
| C-clamp | Kurampu, Kêburu No Tomekanagu |
| Scroller | Karâ Chenjâ |

**The Production Process**

| | |
| --- | --- |
| Load-in | Hannyû |
| Rehearsal | Rihâsaru, Keiko |
| Strike | Barasu, Tekkyo Suru |

**Electrics**

| | |
| --- | --- |
| Circuit | Kairo |
| Dimmer | Dimâ Chôkôki |
| Channel | Channeru |

**Focusing**

| | |
| --- | --- |
| To Focus | Hikari O Ateru |
| To Turn On | Suitch O Ireru, Tsukeru |
| To Turn Off | Suitchi O Kiru, Kesu |
| Sharp | Senmeina |
| Fuzzy | Atari Ga Hazureteiru |

**Miscellaneous**

| | |
| --- | --- |
| Lighting Console | Chôkô Sôsataku |
| Go! | Hai! |
| Followspot | Forô Supotto |
| WorkLights | Sagyôtô, Jiakari |
| To Fly In | Orosu |
| To Fly Out | Tobasu |
| Please | Onegai Shimas |
| Thank you | Arigato |

presence. Ask politely before opening a gift that you have received. Research gift-giving rituals before purchasing. The customs are very specific, and certain items are considered inappropriate.

## TRAVEL CONTRACT

When signing any contract for business travel (international or otherwise), ask the questions below before signing. If you are unclear about any of these items, refuse to sign and get on a plane until the contract is solidified. Otherwise you may find yourself stranded in an unfamiliar location spending money out of your own pocket.

### PAYMENT: HOW AND WHEN DO I GET PAID?

When you travel out of town, even for business, unfortunately you still need to pay your bills at home. Make sure that your contract clearly states how and when you will be paid. If international, ensure that you have a way to get the money into your account so that you do not fall behind in bills at home. Also, make sure that the contract allows for the proper exchange rate so that you are not getting paid less than you were promised.

### HOUSING: WHERE AM I GOING TO STAY?

The producers should provide you with adequate housing within close proximity to the theatre during your stay. (You should be given a room of your own unless you choose otherwise.) Sometimes you will be given money to find your own housing, but usually the company manager will find it for you. Ask to have a kitchenette or small refrigerator in your room, if possible, which can help immensely with money and calorie-saving food options while living out-of-town.

### TRAVEL: HOW DO I GET THERE?

Travel should also be covered. At the professional level this usually means airfare (not bus or train) unless the destination is close. The company manager should ask your preferences in terms of airport and seat assignments and book the flight for you (although you may request to book your own travel if you prefer). When traveling overseas, it is common courtesy for the company to book business class for you.

The company manager will also arrange your travel to and from the airport (such as a car service), reimburse you for taking a taxi, or arrange a rental car. If you take a taxi, keep the receipts for reimbursement purposes and write the total amount (including tip), from/to information, and date on the back of the receipt.

### CAR: WILL I NEED A RENTAL CAR?

How close am I to the theatre? Is it safe to walk at night? Is there a grocery store and restaurants nearby? If international, is it legal for me to drive there?

The company manager will try to find you housing close enough to the theatre that you can walk. If not, you may get your own rental car or share one between two or three people on your team. Ask for a GPS in unfamiliar areas if you do not have access on your phone.

## PER DIEM: HOW ARE MY FOOD EXPENSES COVERED?

**"Per Diem"** is Latin for "per day" or "for each day" and acts as your allowance while living away from home. It is meant to cover food expenses and other necessities while living out of town. If any amount goes unused, you do not have to give it back. The USA 829 Broadway CBA stipulates the amount of per diem required in your contract.

The company manager will usually bring your per diem to you weekly at the beginning of the workweek. If you are traveling internationally it may be given in local cash for easy access without the need for currency exchange. Make sure that the proper exchange rate has been accounted for so that you are getting the amount of per diem agreed to in your contract. Be sure the contract stipulates exactly how and when you will get your per diem, especially when working abroad.

If working under a contract that does not stipulate per diem, the U.S. federal government regulates per diem rates depending on location. If the producer of your show refuses to pay per diem, you can deduct this amount accrued during your stay from your taxes in the following year.

## VISAS: IS IT LEGAL FOR ME TO WORK THERE?

When traveling internationally for business, most countries require you to have a work visa to enter and work legally in any country other than your own. This costs money, and the producers must pay to secure it. Research the laws yourself to ensure that the producers provide the proper legal documentation that you need *before* you go. If you get caught, it will be you—not them—that is thrown out of the country.

# LIFESTYLE

Take care of yourself when traveling away from home, especially internationally. Travel can cause additional stress—even if you are enjoying a change of scenery. If traveling for a lengthy period of time, start packing early so nothing is forgotten.

Before you leave home, stock up on necessary prescription medications. Bring enough to cover your entire trip. (When traveling abroad, your prescription may not be available. When traveling domestically, it may be difficult to get your prescription from a new pharmacy.) On the airplane bring your medication in your carry-on so you do not have to worry about imperative medications getting lost if your luggage gets lost. If your medication requires special circumstances for travel, check your airline's policies before leaving for the airport to ensure there will be no problem carrying it on board.

Pack familiar over-the-counter medications. You may be in a foreign country where you are unfamiliar with their medications and how to obtain them, or you may simply want your favorite headache medicine. It is easy to get sick when traveling, so be sure to plan for it.

Pack any voltage converters and/or power adaptors needed for each country. Double-check that your appliances (laptops, cell phones, tablets, hair dryer, etc.) account for universal voltage or you may destroy them when you plug them in. To be sure, look for electrical information usually printed in fine print on the back or underside of your appliance. It may also be written on the power supply or charger. (See Figure 12.2.) Check that the voltage shown on the item matches the voltage used in the country to which you are traveling. If it says something like "100–240v" (universal voltage) it will work in any country that uses voltages within that range. If the voltages do not match, you will need to purchase a voltage convertor to travel with you. (These are available at any travel store.)

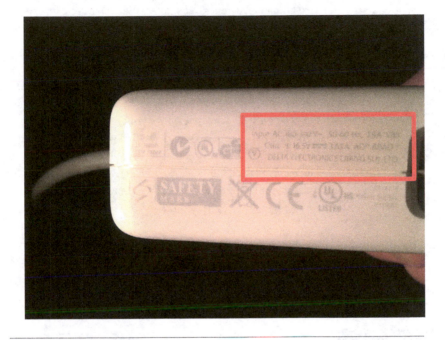

**Figure 12.2** Electrical information on a power supply.

Once you have determined that your appliance will work, you will still need to purchase power adaptors. (See Figure 12.3.) Some countries may have more than one type of standard outlet. Research which style of outlets the country uses and purchase all styles of power adaptors—both grounded and ungrounded, if applicable. Purchase enough for your appliances in the hotel room and at the tech table as well as extra in case your designer forgot to purchase some.

Check the details of your wireless plan. Depending on your cellular carrier, some phones may not work overseas. Even if they do, the cost of use may be astronomical. Some production companies provide local cell phones for inter-communication between production team members. If they do not, you may wish to get a local

Useful apps for determining voltage and outlet type:

- World Power Plug
- My Voltage
- Plugs World

**Figure 12.3**  World travel power adaptors.

pay-as-you-go cell phone simply to contact the design team when needed. Also check out apps such as Viber that allow free calls and texts from select countries. Skype also includes a feature called a "Skype In" number that allows others to use your regular phone number without accruing international roaming call charges. No matter what means of communication you decide to use, verify what extra costs may arise, if any, so that there are no surprises.

For personal calls home, investigate apps such as Skype or FaceTime. Working out-of-town can be tough on personal relationships. Use these apps to stay in touch. Also download a time zone app that displays the time where your loved ones are at all times. (See Figure 12.4.) That way if you find yourself with even a small break during the day (during a reasonable hour at home), you can make a quick call to say hi from the tech table. (Check with your designer to be sure he does not need anything before calling.)

Useful apps for easy time zone conversion:

- Synchronize
- World Clock—Time Zones

**Figure 12.4**  Synchronize screenshot.

Before leaving the country, call your bank to ask about overseas ATM fees. Also, call your bank's fraud department to inform them of your travels. If you forget, they may freeze your debit card the first time it is used in a foreign country, cutting you off from monetary access until they are assured of the absence of fraudulent activity. Just in case, bring your bank's international customer service phone number. Also before you leave, find a currency exchange in the States or in the airport and get a few hundred dollars of local cash to stow away in a safe place for emergencies.

Purchase a copy of OISTAT's *Theatre Words* (or download the app) covering the language of the country or countries you will be working in to carry with you at all times. (It may become your best friend!) *Theatre Words* provides translations for specialized technical theatre terms in 24 different languages. You can purchase an already established version or print-on-demand a customized version combining the languages that you need. (See Figure 12.5.)

In addition, consider purchasing a point-and-speak phrasebook. Your translator may only be with you in the theatre; you will be on your own for meals and days off. Using a point-and-speak guide can help bridge the gap with the locals.

Once you arrive in the new location, locate a grocery store within walking distance and stock up on simple meals. You can save a lot of money, calories, and find comfort in something as simple as a bowl of cereal or oatmeal in the morning. Even if you eat out for lunch and dinner, at least you will have one familiar meal "at home" each day. If your hotel room does not have a kitchenette, buy disposable utensils, plates, cups, and bowls or, for a more environmentally-friendly option, purchase one set that you can wash each day and donate before you leave town. When asked, most hotels will provide a small refrigerator at a small cost for storing juice, milk, and leftovers.

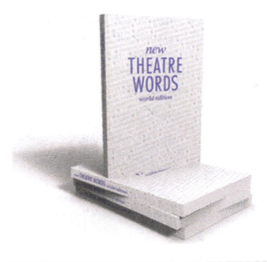

**Figure 12.5** *Theatre Words.*

If you have prescription medication that needs refrigeration, such as insulin for diabetes, most hotels will provide you with a small refrigerator at no cost. Bring a letter from your doctor as proof. Call the hotel ahead of time to reserve a unit (as supplies may be limited) and inquire further about their policies.

Utilize exercise amenities like the treadmills and swimming pools that most business hotels provide or find a nearby park for a quick jog. Always remember to pack a pair of sneakers and at least one workout outfit in your suitcase. A little bit of exercise can go a long way towards helping to maintain your overall health and stress level.

Also, locate laundry facilities close by. Your hotel may have machines you can use, or there may be a laundromat nearby. Sometimes even a drop-off service at a laundromat can be cheaper than using your hotel's laundry service, if there are no self-serve machines.

The hotel concierge can be a valuable resource for locating amenities within walking distance (or a short cab ride away) from your hotel. Many international business hotels cater to American and other foreign travelers so the concierge may know where to find many foreign comforts. (She may be able to tell you where to find a grocery store that has a small shelf of American items, such as peanut butter, or a place that serves a great American-style pizza for those desperate comfort-food cravings.)

Traveling for work may take a lot of planning, but it can also be a lot of fun! It gives you an excuse to see a part of the world that you may not have seen had work not sent you there. Get to know the others on the production team and crew and plan a fun outing on your day off. Maintaining some close relationships within the company can make your stay—and your daytrips—all the more fun.

> *"Try to find time to enjoy where you are, and not just be stuck at work. There's nothing worse than flying all the way across the world, only to sit in another dark room for the entire time."*
>
> —*Jason Lyons*

## CHAPTER 13

# Working in Industries Outside of Theatre

The lighting world is an exciting tinderbox of opportunities for assistant-types. As a freelance assistant lighting designer, chances are you may find yourself working in a variety of industries related to theatre, including: television, architectural lighting, museum design, dance, industrials, concerts, cruise ships, award shows, film, and themed entertainment just to name a few. Working outside of theatre in related industries is a great way to network, pay the bills, and grow as a lighting artisan. In this chapter a few of these industries are discussed, in brief.

> *"The reality of [New York] is that when you first arrive here, the shows that you are going to be able to qualify to design are going to be on small, not-for-profit productions. These theatres usually don't have very big budgets, so you will end up being the designer, electrician, and the programmer. You will probably be asked to hang the show, focus the show, and cue the show all for maybe one hundred dollars. That, however, will have to be your night job. You cannot survive on $100 a week. Your day job is what you use to pay the rest of your bills. As an assistant you [can] make between $18 and $40 per hour, depending on your skills. I know some design assistants who work on TV and films and make upwards of $65 per hour, which is certainly more than designing an entire show for one hundred dollars."*
>
> —David Lander[1]

## TELEVISION AND FILM

If theatre is your wheelhouse, working in television and film can, at first, seem like an alien world—the majority of the equipment may be new to you (or at least be called by different names). As Harry C. Box comically points out in the *Set Lighting Technician's Handbook,* you may think the gaffer is a great guy "until he starts giving orders: 'Hang a baby. Kill the midget and have two blondes standing by for the martini.'"[2]

Just like working in a foreign country, the equipment is similar; you just need to learn what it is called. For example, while theatre may delineate between only a few different types of Fresnels (6", 8", inky, etc.), television and film has names for over two dozen distinct types: each name is equally whimsical, such as the "pepper," the "baby-baby," and the clever "tweenie," "betweenie," and "inbetweenie."

Lighting for film and television differs from theatre because it involves lighting for the camera instead of the human eye. The human eye is much more forgiving than the camera, which sees variations in intensity and color dramatically. Because of this, dark spots must be carefully avoided. (A light meter is used to measure the consistency of light levels.) Color also appears in a different way on camera than to the naked eye—for example, a light blue may appear much darker blue in the camera's lens. Because of these idiosyncrasies, the lighting designer will cue while viewing the show through a video monitor so that he sees exactly what the camera sees.

> When working in television and film, you will run into both union and non-union situations. The technician's union is the same as it is in theatre—IATSE.

Television and film lighting situations vary depending on whether the shoot takes place inside a studio or on location. On location, you may use only a few large hot-patched fixtures, while studio work may more closely resemble theatre with dimmers, a lighting console, and, in some cases, moving lights and Source 4s.

Film sets on location commonly use individual lighting set-ups for each shot (as opposed to a stationary lighting rig like theatre or studio work). Dimmers are not usually used—partly because many fixtures are discharge sources (HMI) and partly because the red-shift that occurs when dimming tungsten-halogen is visible on camera. Therefore intensity is controlled by the use of "scrims"—screens made of wire mesh that fit into a fixture's gel frame holder to cut down light output. Color correction gel can also help reduce red-shift.

Assistant work varies in these two industries. Typically, lighting assistants are not as prevalent in the film profession. However, with the resurgence of movie musicals like *Chicago* (2002),

*Dream Girls* (2006), and *Nine* (2009), theatrical lighting designers and their assistants have made an appearance in the film world. In these situations, the theatrical lighting is considered a separate event from the film lighting; the theatrical lighting designer designs the theatrical lighting, and the film lighting is overseen by the director of photography (DP).

In television, more opportunities for assisting are available. In essence, it is not very different from assisting on a theatrical production. The equipment may vary, but you will still create a light plot, magic sheets, cue list, and run work notes.

> A good assistant must possess *"the ability to multitask and not get flustered. Often times you will end up managing multiple crews and taking in a lot of information at once. You need to be able to deal with being pulled in many directions, have your name yelled every five seconds, and not miss any of the data. And in all of this you need to stay cool and at least act like you're having fun."*
>
> —Matt Gordon

When creating a television light plot, one distinct difference stands out. Because most television studios are grid spaces, fixtures are identified by channel number alone—not by using position name and instrument number. In fact, fixtures in the air are often labeled with the channel number so that it can be easily read from the floor—either written on the fixture itself or on tape attached to the fixture. Refer to Figures 13.1a-b: the number shown in the middle of the instrument is the channel number, not the instrument number (as is standard in theatre).

Also, lighting angles for the camera are lower than theatre in order to fill more shadows and soften out an individual's face. In theatre, front light angles are usually at 45 degrees vertically from the subject, while television uses approximately a 30-degree angle or less. (See Figure 13.2a.) Additionally, instead of using sidelight (which *sculpts* faces) like theatre does, television lighting uses fill light to *round-out* faces. (See Figure 13.2b.) Television also tends to use heavier frost (such as L256, L257, and R114) than theatre (often R132) because the beams need to blend more seamlessly so as not to be seen by the camera.

Because television is lit more scene-by-scene than by system, the most popular form of magic sheet is the groundplan-style magic sheet with the addition of scenic magic sheets (discussed further in Chapter 9). These types of magic sheets allow the designer to pick out exactly which fixtures are lighting an individual or piece of scenery—as opposed to covering a large area (like the full stage) in theatre. (See Figures 13.3a-c.)

Besides your laptop and a small assistant's kit, two necessary items must always travel with you when assisting in television lighting—1) an extremely bright flashlight, and 2) an extremely bright laser pointer. Grid spaces can be very dark and saturated with a multitude of lighting fixtures. You may spend a lot of your day looking up and trying to point out fixtures, channels,

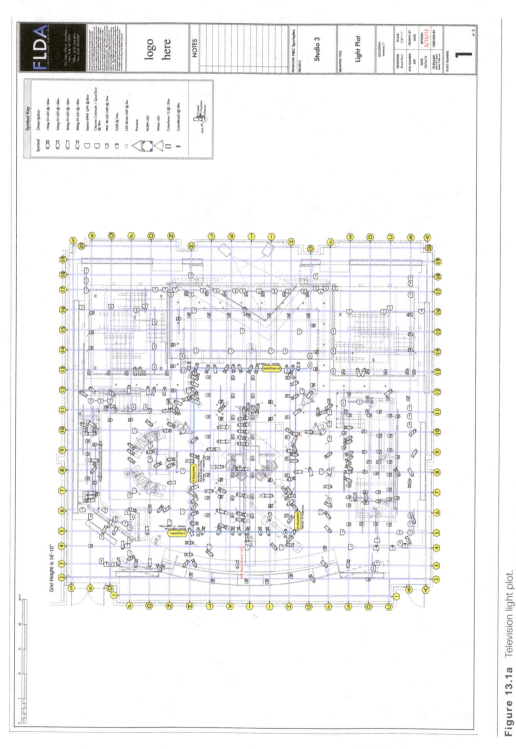

**Figure 13.1a** Television light plot.
*Lighting by: Ferri Lighting Design & Associates*

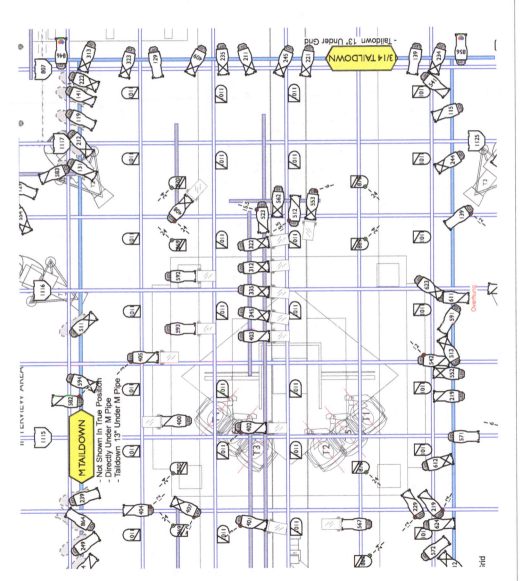

**Figure 13.1b** Close-up of television light plot.
*Lighting by: Ferri Lighting Design & Associates*

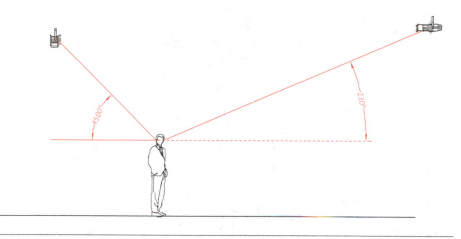

**Figure 13.2a**    FLDA talent angles (section).
*Courtesy of: Ferri Lighting Design & Associates*

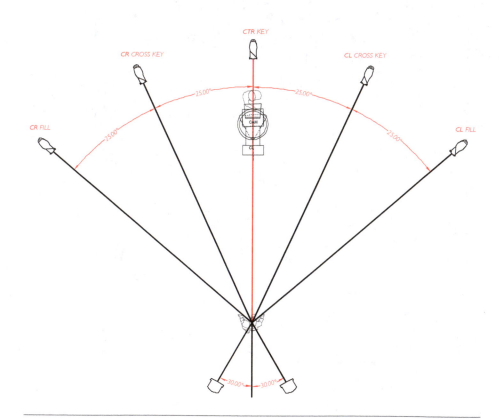

**Figure 13.2b**    FLDA talent angles (plan).
*Courtesy of: Ferri Lighting Design & Associates*

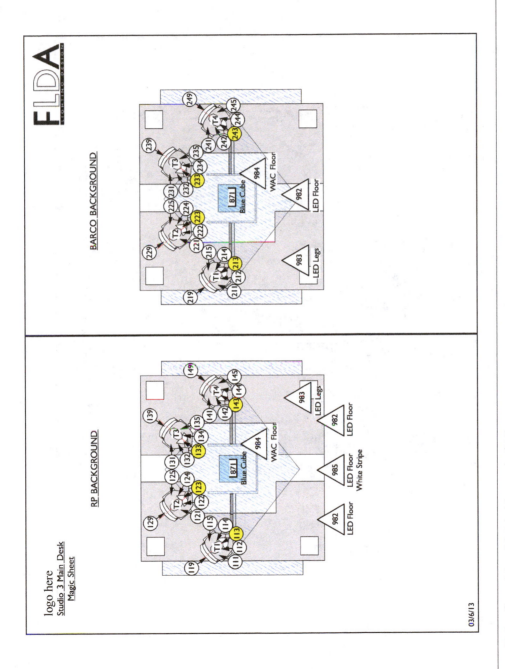

**Figure 13.3a** Groundplan-style television magic sheet.
*Lighting By: Ferri Lighting Design & Associates*

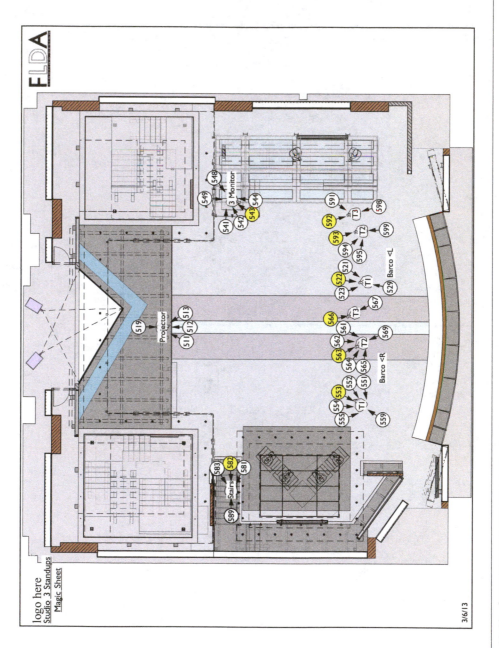

**Figure 13.3b** Groundplan-style television magic sheet.
*Lighting By: Femi Lighting Design & Associates*

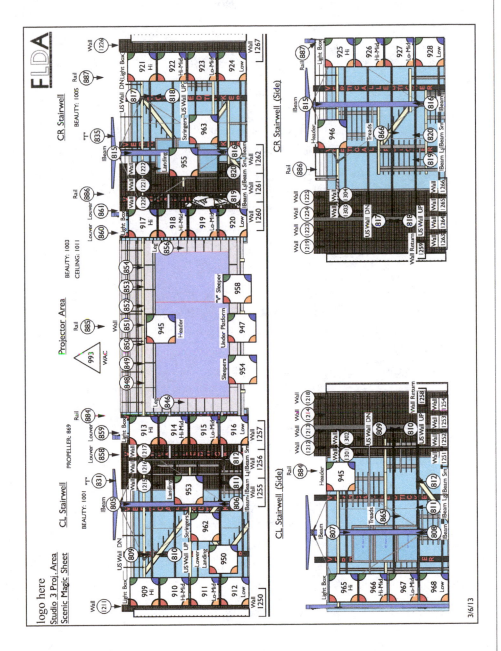

**Figure 13.3c** Television scenic magic sheet.
*Lighting by: Ferri Lighting Design & Associates*

and placements to the electricians. Flashlights and laser pointers short-cut this process and cut down vastly on the amount of frustration and misunderstandings that can occur from trying to point at the same dark spot on a black ceiling together.

# TELEVISION & FILM TERMINOLOGY[3]

## Fixtures/Electrical

| | |
|---|---|
| Baby | 1K Fresnel manufactured by Mole-Richardson |
| Midget | 200w Fresnel manufactured by Mole-Richardson |
| Blonde | 2K open-faced fixture made by Ianiro |
| Softlight | Floodlight used to produce extremely diffuse light |
| Eye Light | Fixture placed to light up the talent's eyes, often from below |
| Beauty Light | Fixtures facing the camera and cued in at a glow to create star-like patterns on the camera's lens as an accent |
| Globe | Lamp |
| Bail | Yoke |
| Stinger | Extension cord |

## Accessories

| | |
|---|---|
| Cucaloris | (1) "Cookie" for short, also spelled Kukaloris. Cut-out placed in front of a fixture to create a pattern—much like an external gobo. (2) Also: a term for a standard gobo |
| Branchaloris | Tree branch held in front of a fixture to create a moving or stationary foliage pattern |
| C-47 | Common, wooden spring-type clothespin often used to clip gel onto a barndoor |
| Flag | Black duvetyn cloth on a frame used to shape light |
| Scrim | (1) Screens made of wire mesh that fit into the gel frame holder on a fixture and cut down light output. (2) Also: a spun-glass material put in front of a light for increased diffusion |
| Trombone | Similar to an adjustable vertical sidearm that hooks over the top of a set wall |

## Personnel

| | |
|---|---|
| Director of Photography (DP) | Head of the electrics department, in charge of the lighting crew |
| Gaffer | Chief Lighting Technician |
| Best Boy Electric | Gaffer's chief assistant |
| Juicers or Sparks | Set lighting technicians / electricians |
| Grip | Crew member responsible for non-electrical aspects of lighting |

## Lighting Design

| | |
|---|---|
| Key Light | Main source of lighting on a subject |
| Fill Light | Secondary source of light on a subject used to fill shadows |
| Cross Key | Crossed key lights used for two people facing each other |

## Scenic

| | |
|---|---|
| Duratrans | (Durable Transparency) Originally a brandname of Kodak, now a generic term for backlit display prints used as background images on set |
| Gobo | (1) A decorative foreground object through which the camera can shoot. (2) Also: an opaque shield used in film to partially block light |
| Elvis | Gold lamé fabric stretched on a frame and used for bounce light |
| Priscilla | Silver lamé fabric stretched on a frame and used for bounce light |

## Miscellaneous

| | |
|---|---|
| Talent | On-camera people and/or animals |
| Camera Right | Stage Left (generally), orients to whichever direction the camera is shooting |
| Camera Left | Stage Right (generally), orients to whichever direction the camera is shooting |

| | |
|---|---|
| Beach | Sandbag used for stabilizing stands and other equipment |
| Applebox | A small crate or box used to raise shorter actors up in the camera shot |
| Visqueen | Plastic material used to protect equipment from moisture |
| Check the gate | Checking for hairs in the optical system of a camera (which would be visible on screen) before confirming a shot is complete |
| Bump in/Bump out | Shot moving to or from the main program and the commercial break |
| Martini | The last shot of the day |

## ARCHITECTURAL LIGHTING

Architectural lighting companies are an excellent source of additional employment for assistant lighting designer-types. Many skills from theatre easily cross over and the companies often appreciate having a theatrically trained designer as part of their team.

Research companies for which you would like to work and contact them to see if they employ freelancers or part-timers. (Some may not.) Find companies with projects that interest you.

Architectural lighting firms' personalities vary considerably. Some may be more engineering-focused companies that design lighting for things like hospitals and parking garages. Some firms may focus more on residential projects—lighting elaborate homes. Others may be retail-oriented—mostly upscale restaurants and shops. And others may have a flare for the theatrical—lighting art installations, creative building facades, and **Archi-tainment** (themed architectural elements); in fact, many theatrical lighting designers begin firms like this to complement their theatrical careers. You will find that most companies work on a mix of project types. Use the company's website to determine where the majority of their interests center.

Another architecturally based employment option is called "**Theatrical Consulting**." Theatrical consultants work as an intermediary between the theatrical and the architectural world—helping architects to design functional theatrical spaces. The architects rely on the consultant to advise on topics like lighting positions necessary for proper theatrical lighting angles, wing space, fly space, and house light control. Other services may include specifying the house equipment—dimming and control systems, lighting consoles, circuiting plans, and lighting equipment inventory.

In architectural lighting, your job as the assistant (called "junior designer") may be drafting, running calculations, specifying fixtures, and creating lighting renderings, among others. Therefore, before applying to an architectural lighting company or a theatrical consulting firm, have a basic working knowledge of the following software programs: Autodesk's AutoCAD and Revit; Lighting Analysts' AGi32; Adobe Photoshop, Illustrator, and InDesign; and Microsoft Word, Excel, and PowerPoint. Also, know the basics of using a PC (as opposed to a Mac) and have a good handle on basic computer functions, such as creating a PDF. Many software programs have free trial versions, helpful tutorials (both online and in print), and webinars that can help you learn the ropes.

> Most architectural lighting companies draft using the architecture world's mainstay software: Autodesk's AutoCAD or, more recently, Revit. Vectorworks is rarely used in the architectural profession.

Architectural lighting uses a variety of sources (types of lamps) in its fixtures, and each fixture may have many different features to choose from. For example, when specifying a downlight, you may be able to choose between several sources: halogen, compact fluorescent, metal halide, or LED; and you may be able to select from a variety of wattages, not to mention manufacturers. Therefore, a solid base knowledge of lamp source characteristics, such as color temperature (CCT), color rendering index (CRI), and lumen output (brightness), must also be added to your skill arsenal.

**Figure 13.4a**  Lamp source door test.
*Courtesy of: EarthLED*

**Figure 13.4b**  Source comparison.
*Courtesy of: Sewell Direct*

**Color Temperature** (also known as Correlated Color Temperature, or CCT) describes the color of white inherent to a source—warmer or cooler—and is described in degrees Kelvin. In fact, a lamp source, such as an LED or fluorescent, may be available in several different color temperatures ranging from 2700°K (warmer) to 6500°K (cooler)—which may look more amber or more blue (respectively) to the naked eye. (See Figure 13.5.)

**Figure 13.5**  Color temperature.

The **Color Rendering Index** (CRI) describes how well the source will render the colors in an object that it is illuminating. For example, depending on the source lighting an apple, the apple may appear bright red (under a high CRI source) or dull red to even brown (under a low CRI source). The higher the CRI of the source, the better colors appear—100 being the highest on the scale.

Architectural lighting drawings (Figures 13.6a-b) may look a little foreign at first, but the concepts are similar to theatrical drawings. Essentially, each type of fixture (downlight, wall washer, burial uplight, etc.) uses a different lighting symbol (called "blocks" in AutoCAD—Figure 13.7) and is labeled with a fixture type and control zone. This fixture type corresponds to a **fixture schedule** and **cut sheet** that details out the exact specifications (specs) of each fixture type. (This is very similar to the way that a Lightwright file details fixtures on a theatrical plot except that architectural lighting paperwork describes *groups* of fixtures instead of individual ones.) Schedules and cutsheets may be created in a variety of different software programs, such as: Microsoft Excel, PowerPoint, Adobe InDesign, and FileMaker Pro. (See Figures 13.8a-b.)

Depending on the firm, fixture types may be labeled by using different organizational methods. Some firms prefer all of their lighting fixtures to be labeled with the letter "L" (for "lighting"), such as L1, L2, L3, or "F" (for "fixture,") while others prefer to name them according to source and mounting. For example, LR1 may refer to the first **L**ED **R**ecessed fixtures, whereas FP1 may refer to the first **F**luorescent **P**endant fixtures. Every firm is different. Be prepared to learn each specific firm's nomenclature.

In addition to the lighting layout, fixture schedule, and cutsheets, a **circuiting layout** may also be included in the lighting package. (See Figure 13.9.) In a circuiting layout, the lights are circuited together in large groups, called "**zones**"—the equivalent of channels in the theatrical world. These zones may be controlled by button stations on the wall and/or other zone control placed throughout the building. An additional **control zone schedule** may be necessary for complex systems—a spreadsheet that lists the individual fixtures controlled by each zone, much like a channel or dimmer hookup in theatre.

When working on architectural lighting drawings, be aware of the scope of your project. Unlike theatre, a large project may have several different lighting firms involved, each with a different scope. For example, in a large hotel one firm may be designing the lighting for the guest rooms, another firm may be designing the public spaces, ballrooms, and meeting rooms, and yet another the landscape exterior. Another scenario may involve an interior designer designing the decorative fixtures, while the lighting designer designs the architecturally integrated fixtures. Also, certain areas may be designed by the engineers, such as the "back of house" (BOH), or utilitarian-type spaces. The principal designer works out the scope of the project in the original proposal and contract. Being aware of the scope prevents you from performing unnecessary work.

Occasionally, you may be sent "on site"—either by yourself, with a colleague, or with the principal designer. This may be local or out-of-town, depending on the project.

Site visits may occur for any of the following:

- **Meeting**—most meetings take place at the architect's office but occasionally on site is necessary.
- **Mock-up**—experimenting with equipment in real space and scale to get client approval prior to the procurement of fixtures.
- **Walk-through / Site Visit**—to check in on the progress of the work and/or to mark fixture placements physically that need to be determined on site.
- **Record existing light levels and fixture placements**—if retrofitting existing fixtures or comparing existing light levels to proposed light levels.
- **Aiming**—the architectural lighting world's name for focusing.
- **Commissioning**—the architectural lighting world's name for cueing: setting levels and looks for each room.

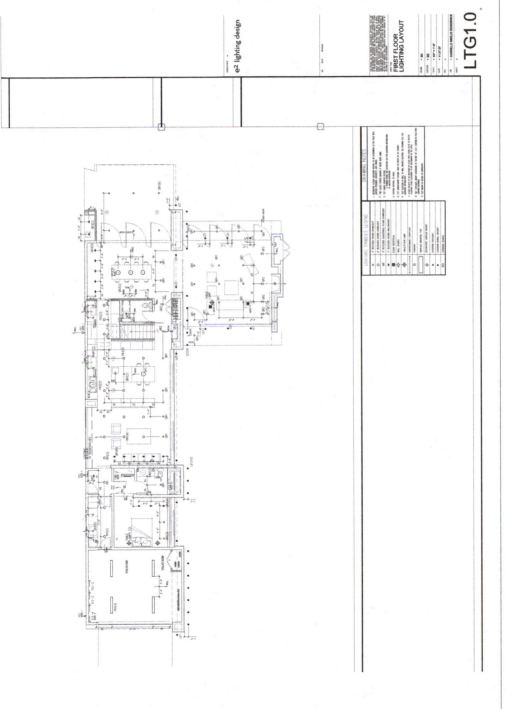

**Figure 13.6a** Architectural lighting layout.
*Lighting By: eSquared Lighting Design*

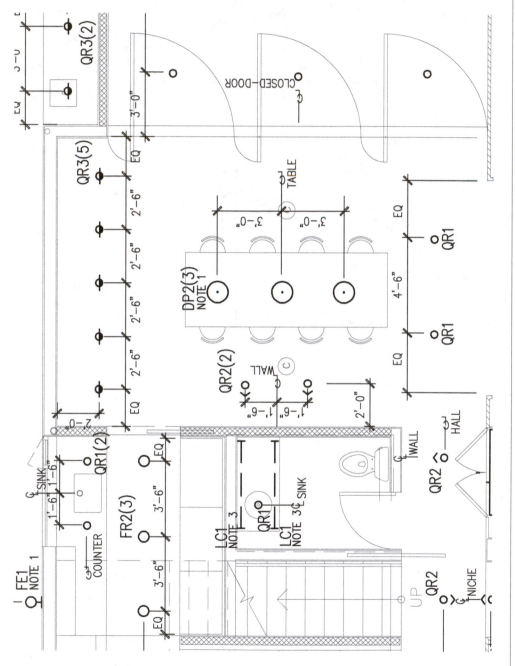

**Figure 13.6b** Architectural lighting layout (close-up).
*Lighting By: eSquared Lighting Design*

- Flags and/or fluorescent spray paint (to mark site-determined fixture placements)
- Tape measure
- Extra spread and soft focus lenses, if available and applicable
- A selection of CTB and CTO sheets of gel (to test various color temperatures)
- iPad or other tablet device (the Photo Measures app and 360 Panorama can be useful in these situations)
- Small first-aid kit—Band-aids, antibiotic ointment, and alcohol wipes
- Hand sanitizer
- Wet wipes / hand sanitizing wipes
- Another person (for safety concerns and assistance)

Although visiting a construction site, dress nicely for the visit. While you are there you are representing the firm, and, especially, the principal designer. However, much like working in the theatre, wear long pants and sturdy-soled shoes. Construction sites are dangerous; therefore the proper safety precautions should be taken.

Finally, in architectural lighting, be aware that all lighting levels must meet federal, state, and city codes for safety and energy efficiency. You may need to run calculations to ensure you have the consistent lighting levels required. (See Figure 13.10.)

## ARCHITECTURAL LIGHTING TERMINOLOGY

| Architectural | Theatrical |
|---|---|
| Snoot | Top hat |
| Filter | Gel |
| Bulb | Lamp (although some firms use the term lamp). In theatre we say, "bulbs grow, lamps glow." |
| Image projector | An architectural fixture that can project a gobo |
| Soft focus lens | Lens that acts like frost/diffusion |
| Aiming | Focusing |
| Commissioning | Cueing |

| LIGHTING SYMBOLS LEGEND | |
|---|---|
| O | 4" RECESSED ROUND DOWNLIGHT |
| O | 6" RECESSED ROUND DOWNLIGHT |
| O⟩ | 4" RECESSED ADJUSTABLE ROUND DOWNLIGHT |
| -⊕- | 4" RECESSED ROUND WALLWASHER |
| ⊞ | FLOOR RECEPTICAL |
| ⊢⊕- | WALL SCONCE |
| ⊕ | TABLE/FLOOR LAMP |
| ⊢———⊣ | UNDERCABINET STRIPLIGHT |
| ⊙ | PENDANT |
| ▭ | SURFACE MOUNTED 1'X4' |
| -⊕- | DECORATIVE SURFACE MOUNT |
| ▯I | EXTERIOR STEPLIGHT |
| ● | EXTERIOR BURIAL UPLIGHT |
| ⊢O | EXTERIOR SCONCE |

**Figure 13.7** Sample architectural lighting fixture blocks.
*Courtesy of: eSquared Lighting Design*

When visiting a construction site, bring a small, easy-to-carry kit containing the following items:

- Flashlight and extra batteries
- Notebook and pencil or pen
- Highlighters
- Laser pointer
- Copy of the drawings and specifications
- Camera
- Light meter

# CARRILLO MIELLE Lighting Fixture Schedule

| type | description | dimensions | color | access | electrical | locations | manufacturer | catalog number | lamp specification | watts |
|---|---|---|---|---|---|---|---|---|---|---|
| LE1 | Direct Burial exterior uplight with warm white LED. | OD: 3.5" | Stainless | | Integral driver | Uplighting | LUMASCAPE | LS563LED 1 1 H | Supplied with fixture | 1 |
| LE2 09.03.07 | Incandescent recessed wall steplight. | SQ: 4.88" | To be determined | Diffusing Lens | Integral electronic transform | Kid's Deck | HEVILITE | HL-240 (finish) 35 120 92 | (1) 35w bi-pin halogen | 35 |
| QR1 | Low voltage recessed downlight | ID: 3-1/2" | Matte White | Soft focus lens | Integral magnetic transform | Task Lighting | IRIS LIGHTING | P3MR E3MR MW | (1) GE Q50MR16/C/ FL55 | 55 |
| QR1a | Low voltage recessed downlight for wood ceilings. | ID: 3-1/2" | TBD | Soft focus lens | Integral magnetic transform | Living Room | IRIS LIGHTING | P3MR E3MR (color) | (1) GE Q50MR16/C/ FL55 | 55 |
| QR2 | Low voltage recessed adjustable accent light | ID: 3-1/2" | Matte White | Soft focus lens | Integral magnetic transform | Accent lighting | IRIS LIGHTING | P3MR E3AA MW | (1) GE Q50MR16/C/ FL40 | 55 |
| QR2a | Low voltage recessed adjustable accent light for wood ceilings | ID: 3-1/2" | TBD | Soft focus lens | Integral magnetic transform | Living Room | IRIS LIGHTING | P3MR E3AA (color) | (1) GE Q50MR16/C/ FL40 | 55 |
| QR3 | Low voltage recessed lensed wall washer | ID: 3-1/2" | Matte White | n/a | Integral magnetic transform | Art lighting | IRIS LIGHTING | P3MR E3LWW MW | (1) GE Q50MR16/C/ FL40 | 55 |
| QR4 | Low voltage recessed lensed adjustable shower light | ID: 3-1/2" | Haze reflector, self flanged | n/a | Integral magnetic transform | Showers | IRIS LIGHTING | P3MR E3AASR H SF | (1) GE Q50MR16/C/ FL55 | 55 |
| QR5 | MR16 recessed linear wall grazer. | W: 4.7" | Matte White | n/a | Integral magnetic transform | Living Room, Family Room | CV LIGHTING | | (1) GE Q35MR16/C/ WFL55 | 105 w/ft. |
| TR1 | Incandescent PAR lamp reflector downlight | ID: 5-1/4" | Matte White | n/a | 120v | Downlighting | IRIS LIGHTING | P5 M120 E5P30 MW | (1) GE 75PAR30L/H/F L25 | 75 |
| TR2 | Incandescent A-lamp recessed shower downlight with regressed white lens | ID: 5-1/4" | Haze | n/a | 120v | Showers | IRIS LIGHTING | 5/A19 SR (color) | (1) 75w soft white A19 | 75 |

**Figure 13.8a** Fixture schedule.
*Lighting By: eSquared Lighting Design*

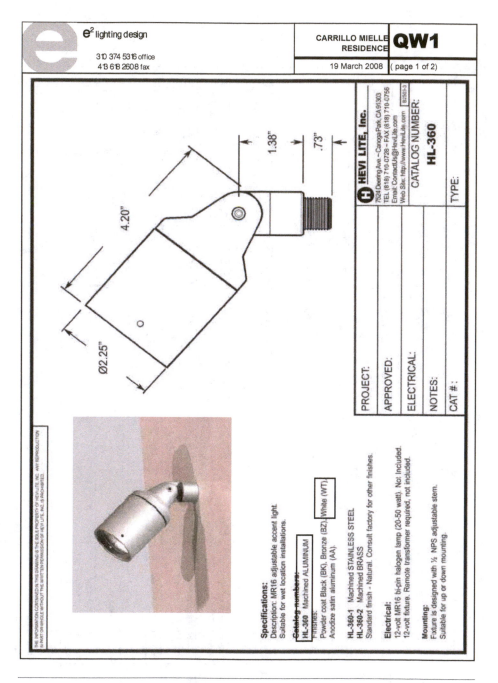

e² lighting design

310 374 5316 office
413 613 2608 fax

CARRILLO MIELLE
RESIDENCE **QW1**

19 March 2008    ( page 1 of 2)

**HEVI LITE, Inc.**
7524 Deering Ave. – Canoga Park, CA 91303
TEL (818) 710-0726 – FAX (818) 710-0756
Email: ContactUs@HeviLite.com
Web Site: http://www.HeviLite.com

B2563-3

CATALOG NUMBER:

**HL-360**

TYPE:

1.38"

.73"

4.20"

Ø2.25"

PROJECT:

APPROVED:

ELECTRICAL:

NOTES:

CAT # :

**Specifications:**
Description: MR16 adjustable accent light.
Suitable for wet location installations.

**Catalog numbers:**
**HL-360**   Machined ALUMINUM

Finishes:
Powder coat Black (BK), Bronze (BZ), White (WT),
Anodize satin aluminum (AA).

**HL-360-1**   Machined STAINLESS STEEL
**HL-360-2**   Machined BRASS
Standard finish - Natural. Consult factory for other finishes.

**Electrical:**
12-volt MR16 bi-pin halogen lamp (20-50 watt). Not Included.
12-volt fixture. Remote transformer required, not included.

**Mounting:**
Fixture is designed with ½ NPS adjustable stem.
Suitable for up or down mounting.

**Figure 13.8b**   Fixture cutsheet.
*Lighting By: eSquared Lighting Design*
*Image Courtesy of: Hevi Lite, Inc.*

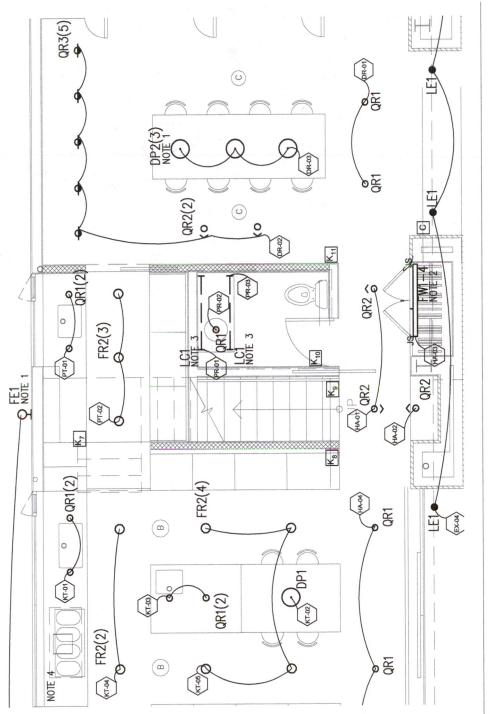

**Figure 13.9** Architectural circuiting layout (close-up).
*Lighting By: eSquared Lighting Design*

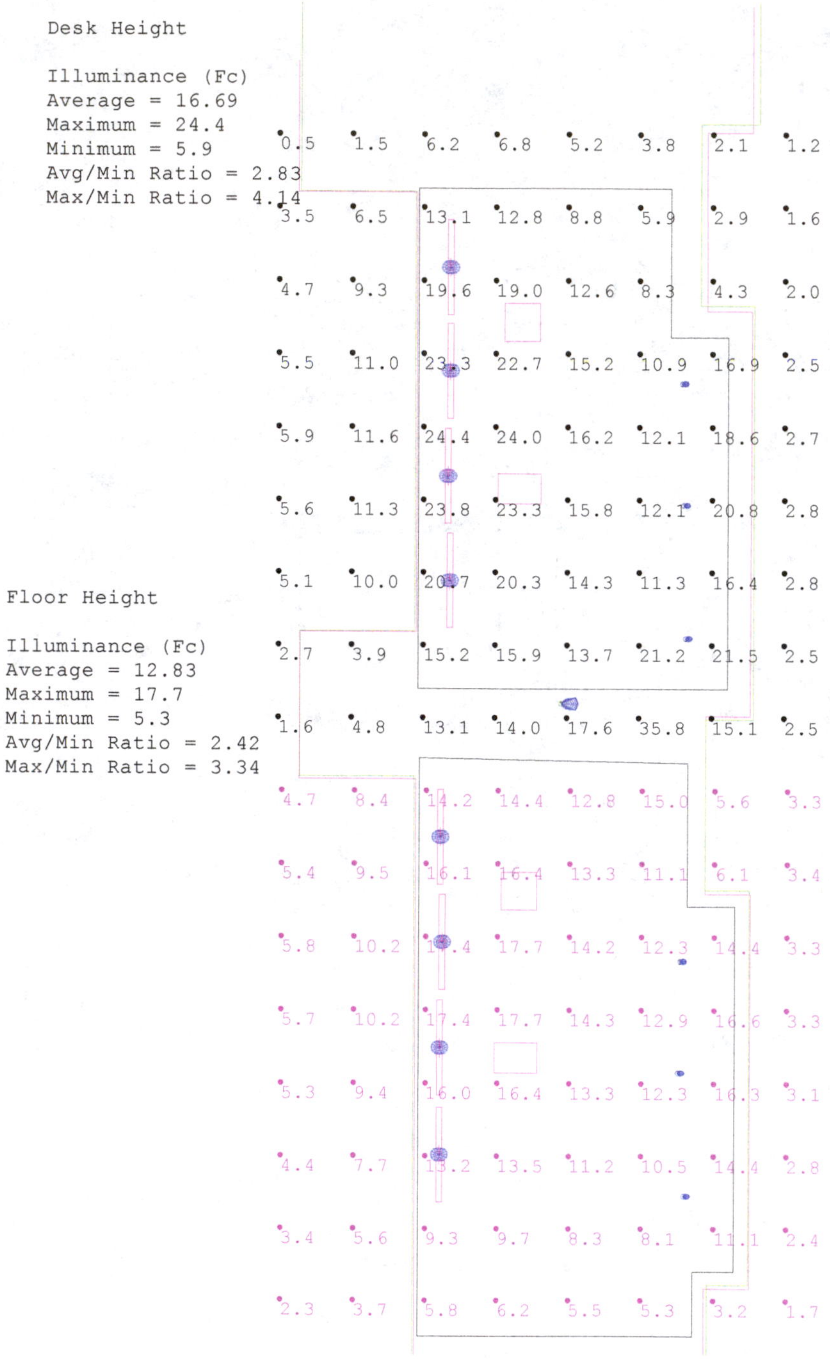

Desk Height

Illuminance (Fc)
Average = 16.69
Maximum = 24.4
Minimum = 5.9
Avg/Min Ratio = 2.83
Max/Min Ratio = 4.14

| 0.5 | 1.5 | 6.2 | 6.8 | 5.2 | 3.8 | 2.1 | 1.2 |
| 3.5 | 6.5 | 13.1 | 12.8 | 8.8 | 5.9 | 2.9 | 1.6 |
| 4.7 | 9.3 | 19.6 | 19.0 | 12.6 | 8.3 | 4.3 | 2.0 |
| 5.5 | 11.0 | 23.3 | 22.7 | 15.2 | 10.9 | 16.9 | 2.5 |
| 5.9 | 11.6 | 24.4 | 24.0 | 16.2 | 12.1 | 18.6 | 2.7 |
| 5.6 | 11.3 | 23.8 | 23.3 | 15.8 | 12.1 | 20.8 | 2.8 |
| 5.1 | 10.0 | 20.7 | 20.3 | 14.3 | 11.3 | 16.4 | 2.8 |

Floor Height

Illuminance (Fc)
Average = 12.83
Maximum = 17.7
Minimum = 5.3
Avg/Min Ratio = 2.42
Max/Min Ratio = 3.34

| 2.7 | 3.9 | 15.2 | 15.9 | 13.7 | 21.2 | 21.5 | 2.5 |
| 1.6 | 4.8 | 13.1 | 14.0 | 17.6 | 35.8 | 15.1 | 2.5 |
| 4.7 | 8.4 | 14.2 | 14.4 | 12.8 | 15.0 | 5.6 | 3.3 |
| 5.4 | 9.5 | 16.1 | 16.4 | 13.3 | 11.1 | 6.1 | 3.4 |
| 5.8 | 10.2 | 17.4 | 17.7 | 14.2 | 12.3 | 14.4 | 3.3 |
| 5.7 | 10.2 | 17.4 | 17.7 | 14.3 | 12.9 | 16.6 | 3.3 |
| 5.3 | 9.4 | 16.0 | 16.4 | 13.3 | 12.3 | 16.3 | 3.1 |
| 4.4 | 7.7 | 13.2 | 13.5 | 11.2 | 10.5 | 14.4 | 2.8 |
| 3.4 | 5.6 | 9.3 | 9.7 | 8.3 | 8.1 | 11.1 | 2.4 |
| 2.3 | 3.7 | 5.8 | 6.2 | 5.5 | 5.3 | 3.2 | 1.7 |

**Figure 13.10**  Architectural lighting calculation.
*Courtesy of: eSquared Lighting Design*

# INDUSTRIALS

"**Industrials**" is a term that describes a broad spectrum of business theatre, also called corporate theatre. Annually thousands of events are produced by industries and independent companies ranging from "small, single-speaker, audio-visually enhanced events, to large-scale, multi-million-dollar productions."[4] Some examples of industrials are car shows, developers' conferences, new product launches, corporate-sponsored fund-raisers, political conventions, corporate cruise-ship events, and corporate business or sales meetings.

The goal for these companies is to use the power of theatre to inform, excite, and motivate their employees and/or industry-insiders. These events typically strive to communicate a specific business message (i.e. information regarding a new product, marketing strategy, or ideology of the entity) using face-to-face communication enhanced through dramatic presentation. The keynote speaker is usually a high-level individual in the corporate hierarchy, such as the CEO of the company, or an important person in the industry.

Industrials are usually "**one-offs**," or shows that do not repeat. Although some may take place in theatres, most take place in atypical locations temporarily set-up for performances—most often hotels ballrooms—earning the insider term, "ballroom theatre." Sometimes these ballrooms are located within resorts in exotic locations. Therefore, working industrials may result in a fair amount of professional travel.

**Figure 13.11**  Industrial load-in in a ballroom.
*Designed and Produced by: Barkley Kalpak Agency*

The technical aspects of industrials are usually very high-tech, depending on the budget. Often a great amount of video is employed as well as moving lights, automation, video, atmospherics, and other cutting-edge equipment used to support a significant event and create an exciting atmosphere. For example, a moment like a dramatic new car reveal may use moving lights displaying a lot of movement, color, texture, and effects much like a rock concert (a lighting technique affectionately referred to as "flash and trash").

In addition to dynamic stage lighting techniques, camera-centric lighting (much like TV studio lighting) is also required for live video broadcast (known as IMAG, or Image Magnification). **IMAG** is the technique used to display the keynote speaker and others on large-scale projection or LED screens to enable the audience to easily see the details of the performer's body language and facial expressions from great distances. (See Figure 13.12.)

Event production (or planning) companies work in a variety of ways. Often a lead designer will design the overall production concept—including lighting, scenic elements, multi-media, and room layout. He will then work with the design and production team to produce the end result. An assistant lighting designer (by title) does not usually exist, but working as part of the design and production team is a great option for employment—although you may end up working on all aspects of the production. Sometimes these teams are in-house and sometimes freelance.

**Figure 13.12**  Industrial event using IMAG.
*Designed and Produced by: Barkley Kalpak Agency*

The lighting equipment for industrials depends on the scope of the project and is difficult to describe in general terms. It ranges from renting the entire rig to using in-house equipment. The planning varies as well: sometimes a full light plot is produced including a full truss package (Figures 13.14 and 13.15), and other times it is improvised on site using the available resources. Control varies too: ranging from the use of a hired-in programmer and console to creating some interesting looks from dimmer switches on the wall. Every situation is a new challenge.

Also, unique to the industrial environment is the employment of a wide range of diverse lighting design techniques. The projects may vary from architectural lighting (like lighting a national historic location) to concert lighting (big-name stars hired in for entertainment) to complete theatrical presentations (like Broadway musical reviews or custom written theatrical presentations).

These types of events constitute a huge industry thriving with professional theatrical designers and technicians supporting the design, staging, and audiovisual aspects of these productions. Working in the world of industrials allows you to use tools that you may not be able to afford in an average theatre, as well as gain a lot of quick-thinking, on-your-feet, professional experience. The pace is fast. Productions frequently move into a space, build a theatre-like environment (rigging, dimming, truss, lighting, staging, video, and audio), tech a show, go "live" before an audience (simultaneously both opening and closing night), and strike all in the course of four or five days. It can be a very exciting environment in which to work.

**Figure 13.13**  Industrial load-in.
*Designed and Produced by: Barkley Kalpak Agency*

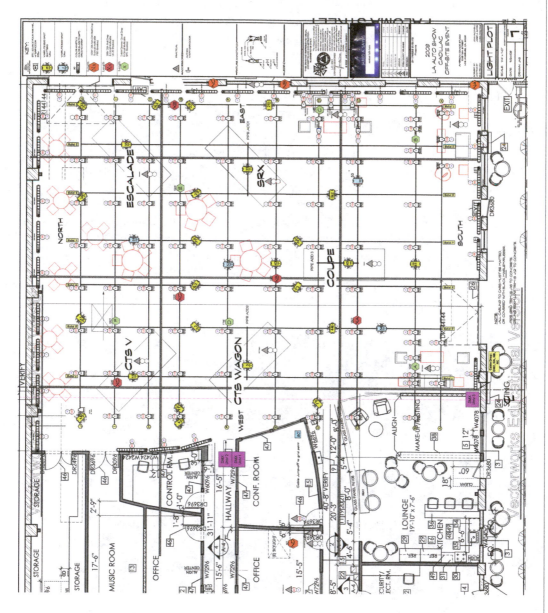

**Figure 13.14** Industrial light plot.
*Lighting By: Jared A. Sayeg*

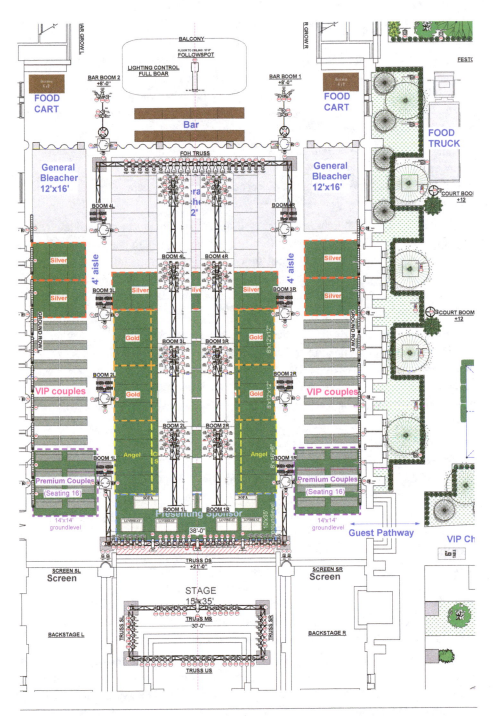

**Figure 13.15** Excerpt from an industrial light plot.
*Lighting By: Jared A. Sayeg*

# THEMED ENTERTAINMENT

Working in themed entertainment encompasses a wide-range of opportunities. For example, you may work for an architectural lighting firm that specializes in themed attractions (like Thinkwell Group or Lightswitch), work for a sector of a theme conglomerate (such as Walt Disney Imagineering—WDI), or work inside a park itself. (Depending on the park, it may have all in-house designers or pull freelancers from outside.)

Lighting design for themed entertainment can be extremely elaborate and creative. Ironically, it may also involve delving deeply into the technical side. Concepts such as wattage requirements, electrical code, fixture life, heat dissipation, and overall system design may fall under the list of concerns for the designer.

Themed entertainment lighting designers also may have input into the building design and often are not limited by an existing facility. They may be able to request changes to the physical design of the spaces, additional structure placements to hold fixtures, additional power requirements, location of the electrical equipment room (EER), and additional props or scenery placements for the concealment of fixtures. Most designs for themed attractions take years to design.

Theme park attractions often use the lighting fixtures for over 16 hours a day for many ongoing years. Therefore, lighting designers must be conscious of fixture choices for extended runs. In recent years, LED fixtures have become popular due to their low-maintenance requirements and color-changing properties. When using fixtures other than LED, dichroic glass filters, which can last for many years without replacement, are often used in place of standard gel.

Lighting design is literally everywhere in a theme park ("park-wide") but having the opportunity to design a dark ride is often a true joy for a lighting designer. A dark ride is just that—a ride that is mostly dark with specifically lit moments, such as Disney's *Pirates of the Caribbean* and *Haunted Mansion*. A dark ride can be in the form of a standard ride, walk-through ride, boat ride, or flume ride.

Dark rides, which use strong, contrasting, specific lighting effects, can be breathtaking and fun to design. Theme park lighting designers further enhance the experience by hiding all of the lighting fixtures behind the audience ("guests") or behind scenery and props. This is called **"look-back lighting"**—the guests never see the fixtures unless they turn fully around and look behind themselves. This effect keeps them engaged in the storyline instead of breaking the reality by having fixtures in view. Another popular technique for hiding the sources is specifying custom themed lighting fixtures. These fixtures both provide light as well as incorporate seamlessly into the theming of the surrounding scenery.

An assistant lighting designer working in themed entertainment goes by many names depending on the company. Nevertheless, the responsibilities are similar to the architectural world: drafting the plot, completing paperwork, detailing the control system, and specifying fixtures and lamping.

**Figure 13.16**   *The Haunted Mansion* at Disneyland.
© Disney. Used with permission.

The career of an assistant lighting designer can be varied and exciting. Opportunities are available all over the world and in many different industries. The more you experience all aspects of lighting, the more flexible and knowledgeable a professional you will be.

*"Be good at more than one thing.... Related skills in your arsenal will help make you more employable."*

—*K. C. Wilkerson*

# PART 5

# The Life

Assisting is a complex career. You are your own boss *and* your own company. You must spend as much time job seeking and money tracking as you do actually working. This section will explore some of the techniques you can use to ease these processes.

## CHAPTER 14

# Working as an Independent Contractor

> *"You have to get used to … the fact that one day you may have nothing going on, but the next day you'll have three productions at once…. If you need to know what you're doing each and every coming week, you're in the wrong business."*
>
> —*Vivien Leone[1]*

Most assistant lighting design jobs are freelance positions. A **freelancer** is someone who is self-employed and considered an independent contractor by the IRS. A freelancer is not a full-time employee of any particular entity, but instead is self-employed and moves from job to job without a steady paycheck.

It can be nerve-wracking at first as you struggle to become established. Work hard, remember that you are only as good as your last job, and continually network/send out resumes. Eventually when it begins to rain, it will pour.

> *"Network. This does not mean spouting off your resume to anyone who will listen. It means cultivating a group of people around you that share your same interests and passion; and that connect you to even more people with whom you share common ground."*
>
> —*K. C. Wilkerson*

> *"I get calls from other designers for recommendations of assistants…. Word of mouth is still the biggest plus; it's the biggest advantage that a young person has. If somebody screws up badly as an assistant to one person, it just doesn't take long; it's very hard for that person to overcome that.*
>
> —*Tom Munn*[2]

As the calls roll in, balance your schedule carefully so that no productions overlap. If they do, discuss any conflicts with your designers with plenty of lead-time. Conflicting schedules are a normal thing in the freelancing world, just be clear and upfront early so that any conflicts can be resolved immediately.

Keep an up-to-date resume and portfolio—whether printed or digital—with examples of your design work (to demonstrate your artful eye) and your best drafting. Create a professional website for yourself with an easy-to-remember and professional name, such as www.firstnamelastnamelighting.com. Also, obtain a professional sounding email address—*not* something like lighting_goddess@domainname.com. Try one that simply uses your full name. Record a professional-sounding outgoing message on your voicemail. And, finally, Google yourself and clean up any inappropriate items that may appear in poor taste to a would-be employer.

## MARKETING YOURSELF

### RESUMES

Never underestimate the power of a good resume and cover letter. Contrary to popular belief, it is not *only* "who you know" that gets you a job. It is often a clean, professional, well-constructed resume. (While reading this section, refer to the example theatrical resume and cover letter found in the Appendices of this text.)

A theatrical resume is usually displayed in list form, as opposed to descriptive form, which looks very different from other industries' resumes. It simply lists each production on which you worked in reverse chronological order. Unlike a business resume, no career objective is listed or street addresses for each company, and unlike an actor's resume, no photo or personal stats are included like height, weight, and eye color.

Overall your resume should be clean, organized, and professional looking. Stick to one page only, especially at the beginning of your career. Line up all columns neatly down the entire page. Keep all fonts the same, and use no more than two or three font sizes (no smaller than size 10). Your name should be the largest, followed by headings, and then details. Headings may also be distinguished by using underlined or bold text.

## Personal Information

At the top include your name, cell phone number, email address, union affiliation, website address, and your title (assistant lighting designer, lighting designer, etc.).

Many freelancers bounce between several job types—lighting designer, assistant lighting designer, electrician, programmer, etc. The secret is to create different resumes for each job type with identical information, but rearranged to emphasize the job for which you are applying. You may end up with four or five different resumes. At the top of each, include the title for the appropriate job and begin by listing that relevant experience first. (For example, do not send a resume titled "electrician" to a designer looking for a new assistant.)

## Experience

List your relevant theatrical jobs under the experience category. In columns running across the page, include the following information:

- **Production** (show name)—scripted show titles should be listed in italics
- **Supervisor's name**—designer's name if you are assisting, director's or occasionally production company's name if you are designing, and production electrician's name if you are an electrician
- **Venue and Location**—such as Pasadena Playhouse, Pasadena, CA
- **Date**—year only (even if you only worked one day on the show); listed in reverse chronological order (most current item is listed first)

The production and supervisor columns can be switched—whichever you feel should be highlighted for the resume. When creating an assistant resume, list the designer's name in the first column. Dates should run down the final right-hand column of the page and should be the only right-justified column.

Depending on where you are in your career, you may have enough experience to fill an entire page with relevant experience. If you do not, list the experience that matches the title at the top of the page under the "experience" heading, and add a "related experience" heading for the other categories. For example, when building an assistant lighting designer resume, list all of your assisting positions under "experience," then under "related experience" break job positions into categories such as design experience, electrician experience, etc. List each category in reverse chronological order. Also, only list theatrical and/or lighting experience. Do not list items such as your part-time job at Target or Starbucks.

On the flipside, if you find that you have too much experience and need to cut down to one page, you can further organize your information into categories such as theatre, industrials, television, architectural lighting, etc. Also, the terms "representative" or "selected work" can be used next to the experience heading to indicate that the work listed is not an exhaustive representation of your experience.

### Additional Information

At the end of the resume list the following information: education, additional skills, and references.

List your education in reverse chronological order. Include the degree title and emphasis, name of university, location, and year. If you have already obtained the degree, list the year as "achieved 2013." If you are still in school and working towards a degree, indicate your expected graduation year by stating "candidate 2018." Certificate programs can also be listed here, but do not include individual classes, such as "Tech Theatre 101."

The additional skills section should include skills relevant to the title listed at the top of the page. For an assistant lighting designer, include items such as software programs you know (Vectorworks, Lightwright, Photoshop, Excel, etc.), any languages you may speak besides English, and if you read music. If you have some skills in a subject but do not have a mastery of it, communicate this by using the word "basic," such as "basic Photoshop." Do not list talents such as guitar, juggling, and dialects—those are for actor resumes only.

References should be listed with current contact information—phone number and email address. List at least three references, and no more than four. Before including someone as a reference on your resume, it is polite protocol to ask permission. (Never assume a person will be your reference.) Also verify current contact information and ask which phone number and email is preferred for use. Always inform your references of all resumes being sent out so they are prepared. Never use a reference for more than a year without renewing permission.

Remember that a reference's reputation goes with you to the job. If you do a bad job, it reflects poorly on your reference. Therefore, do not be upset if an individual denies being a reference for you. Perhaps your level of skill is not ready for his endorsement, or he does not know your work ethic well enough to recommend you or not.

> *"Usually I will say to my first assistant, 'Who's going to be our second assistant?' And they will know someone that they've either gone to school with or have worked with in the past."*
>
> —*Kevin Adams*[3]

## BUSINESS CARDS

Make or purchase a large set of business cards for yourself. These can be ordered through online companies relatively inexpensively or printed at home using clean-edge business card paper. Keep your cards simple and professional looking. Include the same information shown at the top of your resume: name, cell phone number, email address, union affiliations, website address, and your title.

Keep a stack at all times in your wallet, purse, laptop bag, and assistant's kit. You never know when you might need to hand some out.

*"Don't be discouraged if you interview with someone and don't hear from them after a while. You never know when the call might come. I've done interviews for new assistants and not called them for gigs until literally a year later just because I didn't have anything for them."*

*—Matt Gordon*

## COVER LETTERS

*"A [cover] letter tells me who you are as a person."*

*—Kenneth Posner*

A cover letter is sent with each resume and serves as an introduction and summary of your skills. It also informs the employer of which position you are interested. It should not reiterate your resume, but instead tell a little more about yourself, why you are interested in that particular position, and why you think you are suited for the job. Also include the name of any individual that may have referred you to the position. Throughout the letter, show eagerness and confidence without appearing arrogant or over-assertive.

Research the designers, companies, and theatres to which you are sending your materials. The more informed you are about the employer, the easier it is to be specific about why you are a match for the job.

Write in a formal manner. Even if you are acquaintances with the employer, do not start out with things like, "Hey, Bob. How's it going?" Assume others, besides Bob, will also read your letter. Treat it like a formal interview.

Address the employer using the formal titles "Mr." or "Ms." (If not specified in the job advertisement, do not use "Mrs." unless you know for certain that the woman is married. "Miss" is also inappropriate because it refers to a young underage girl.) If the employer's name is something gender-neutral like Pat Smith, look online to find out if Pat is a man or woman. If you are unable to find the information, call the company. Tell the administrative assistant that you are applying for a position and do not know how to address Pat Smith. Chances are that it is a common question.

Your signature should be written in ink at the closing of the letter, not printed from a computer. Also include the word "enclosure" at the bottom of the page to indicate that your resume is included.

A cover letter should be short and sweet—one page maximum, and usually no more than three paragraphs. The standard format is specific and very formal. Refer to the example in the Appendices for more information.

When a job advertisement asks for emailed materials, the cover letter acts as the body of the email, and the resume should be attached (in PDF form). Do not cut and paste your resume into the body of the email—the formatting and spacing will look like a mess to the receiver. Include the name of the job position for which you are applying in the subject line of the email.

## COURTING DESIGNERS

*"It can be a total waste of everybody's time to assist a designer who wants to feel that the job is top-down and ideas from the bottom (i.e. the assistant) are not relevant. I recommend to my students that they be very careful [who] they assist. Find the designers who want you to be part of the team."*

—*F. Mitchell Dana*[4]

In the freelance world, job advertisements do not typically exist. Do not wait to find an ad. Instead, (if looking for an assistant position) send resumes and cover letters to all the major designers in your area.

*When looking for a new assistant, "I look for someone [that] can deal with me for 12 hours a day."*

—*Kenneth Posner*

Print both the cover letter and the resume on resume paper. You can find resume paper at local office supply chains. Choose a paper that is professional looking—perhaps off-white or cream—*not* something whimsical like one that looks like a blue sky covered in fluffy white clouds. (See Figure 14.1.)

Print the return and recipient's addresses on a business-size envelope using a printer. The cover letter should be placed on top of the resume and folded in thirds. Fold it neatly so that when the recipient unfolds the letter, the top of the cover letter including "Dear Mr. Smith:" is presented. (See Figure 14.2.)

Within the cover letter to each designer, ask if she needs help with anything—even on a volunteer basis. If you are new to the professional arena, ask the designer if you can meet simply to show her your resume and portfolio to gain her professional advice. Also ask if you can sit behind her in an upcoming tech simply to observe. (Use the *Theatrical Index* and Playbill Online to be informed on upcoming productions in your area.)

### Following Up

After sending your cover letter and resume, make a follow-up call a week or two later. Politely remind the designer that you had sent her a resume and asked if she would look at your materials or let you visit tech. If she accepts, great! If she asks you to call back in a few weeks instead, do exactly that. (Put a reminder in your calendar so that you do not forget.) If she

**Figure 14.1** Resume Paper Dos and Don'ts.

**Figure 14.2** Folding a Cover Letter and Resume.

declines, do not be upset. She is probably very busy. Ask politely if you could contact her again in the future. Do not call more than twice during the same time period.

> After sending a resume and cover letter, "follow-up two weeks later by phone. Do not make me find you. You want the job, you do the work."
>
> —F. Mitchell Dana

Repeat this process with each new designer and, then, every six months to a year, but do not be a pest. Stop after a year or 18 months so your resume does not become a bother.

If a designer invites you to sit behind her in tech, arrive promptly and bring your resume and (if previously discussed) your portfolio in case she offers to look at them. (If it turns out that she is too busy, do not feel hurt.) Dress nicely but wear sensible shoes in case you get a backstage tour. Be courteous and quiet. Only ask questions during breaks unless she turns to speak to you. Offer to get the team coffee, but do not overdo it if she declines.

It is an honor just to be allowed to watch a designer's tech. Make sure you treat it that way. Follow up in the next day or two with a thank you letter or email. Be sure to recognize what a generous donation of time you have been given. Once the designer gets to know you, you have a better chance of getting a job with her. Keep in touch occasionally to see if any openings have become available.

> "It's a great thing to contact designers and see if you can sit behind them in tech for a day or two and see how they work. It's also a great way for them to see you and chat in a more casual way than in an interview or just sending a [resume]."
>
> —Anthony Pearson

> When looking to hire a new assistant, "I'm most likely to consider/remember someone I've met in person. If you can organize a meet up on my coffee or dinner break … that is probably the best way to meet … Don't be afraid to be gently persistent."
>
> —Jen Schriever

## PAYING THE BILLS

As a freelancer, the work ebbs and flows. One month you will not have a minute to breathe, and the next month you will be sitting at home hoping the phone will ring. This is all just part of a freelancer's life. The upside is: you are your own boss, get to set your own schedule, take vacation whenever you want, do not have to take the jobs that you do not want or work with people you do not like.

Even when you are working steadily, continue sending resumes and cover letters and meeting designers to lay the groundwork. On the hard days, trust that you have done the work—the phone *will* ring.

---

In 1980, now Tony-award winning lighting designer, Brian MacDevitt, ran a fruit stand on 5th Avenue to help subsidize his budding lighting career.

---

## TEMPING

One method of filling slow weeks is temp work, or "temping," at a temporary job agency ("temp agency"). This type of employment allows you to work temporarily on a daily, weekly, monthly, or perma-temp basis with no long-term commitment. Temp jobs are available in nearly every field and location. Depending on your preferences, it may include office work, clerical work, manual work, retail work, or even drafting—just to name a few. You may be filling in for individuals on vacation or adding to a workforce with a temporary task at hand.

Sign up to work for several temp agencies at once. Signing up usually involves a basic interview and sometimes a computer competency test—such as the basics of Microsoft Word or Excel. You will also be asked to fill out a form regarding your preferences and availability. They may or may not have open positions at that time. Call each company at the beginning of each week you are available to see if any work has popped up.

## UNEMPLOYMENT BENEFITS

Later as your career begins to build and you begin to work more frequently, you may be eligible to claim unemployment benefits between jobs. Also called unemployment insurance or unemployment compensation, it is money you pay into with every taxed paycheck that is regulated by the state.

There are stipulations to being considered eligible, which vary by state. Generally to be approved, you must have worked a certain number of weeks in that state within the year under a W-2 (which pays into state unemployment benefits) and your employment must have ended through no fault of your own. (This text does not qualify as legal advice, so research your state's regulations carefully to assure that you qualify appropriately and understand all rules and regulations.)

Generally assisting jobs end because of the category "lack of work." Basically, when a show opens, there is no longer the need for an assistant lighting designer. Therefore a lack of work exists, and you are technically considered laid off, or redundant.

Register with the state online or over the phone and have your employment history on hand. They will verify employment and approve or deny your claim. If approved, you need to file a claim each week that you are unemployed and state any income that was made during that time (such as temp work). Continue filing claims until your next period of employment. You can begin claims again after your next production's position ends. Most states stipulate a total number of weeks that can be claimed throughout the year—typically around 26 weeks. Unemployment insurance may not provide a large amount of money, but every little bit helps to pay the bills during slow times.

## FINANCIALS

Keeping track of a freelancer's income can be a challenge. First things first, as soon as you start your career find yourself a tax professional and/or financial planner/advisor that understands freelance theatrical situations. Find a professional that specializes in the arts, not someone from a run-of-the-mill tax preparation center. A good financial planner can help you understand exactly what steps you need to take to protect yourself as an independent contractor. Getting your taxes done professionally each year does cost more than doing them on your own, but you will probably get more money back and avoid any costly mistakes.

In simplified terms, there are two other essential things that you must do when working as a freelancer: Number one—you must track how much money you earn, and number two—you must track how much money you spend on business-related items. This boils down to two spreadsheets (or databases if you prefer) that you must create for yourself and constantly monitor. Bring both of these documents with you when getting your taxes done. They will contain valuable information required to produce a proper return.

(The following is not legal advice. Consult a financial professional for further information.)

### TRACKING INCOME

Create a **financial workbook** showing what you have been paid on each job throughout the year. In this workbook, separate out your 1099 earnings (jobs that *don't* take out taxes) versus your W-2 earnings (jobs that *do* take out taxes). (See Figure 14.3.)

> In the United States, a W-2 employee is paid on a *salaried* basis—whether weekly, monthly, or annually. A 1099 employee is paid based on a *flat fee* contract. W-2 employees have taxes deducted from each paycheck, while a 1099 employee does not.

As a freelancer, you will probably be employed through both methods (W-2 and 1099) each year by various employers in various states. These two types of employment must be tracked separately. Track every job, no matter how small the paycheck—even if paid in cash.

The following information should be tracked in your financial workbook:

- Date (of employment)
- Name of production, project, or company
- Name of theatre and/or location

- Name of designer or supervisor

- Name of company or producer paying you

- Is it union or not?

- Gross income (money earned before taxes are deducted)

- Net income (what you take home after taxes are deducted)

- Did you get paid? (checkbox to assure you received the check)

- Your rate (flat fee, weekly fee, hourly rate, etc.)

- Subtotals for 1099 column and W-2 column

- Grand totals for money earned (both net and gross totals)

- Taxes owed—multiplies the 1099 earnings by 30 percent

- Notes (How many weeks does the paycheck cover? General information, etc.)

**(Name Here)**
**Financial Workbook 2014**

| DATE | PROJECT / COMPANY | THEATRE / LOCATION | DESIGNER / SUPERVISOR | PAID BY | USA | # Cks | FEE | Subtotal Independ (1099) | Subtotal Employee (W-2) | B/F Taxes (Gross) | SubT Gross | Taxes to save | PAID | P&W | Rate | Wks of Unemploy |
|---|---|---|---|---|---|---|---|---|---|---|---|---|---|---|---|---|
| Nov-14 | Show Name Bway Tour Check-in | Detroit | Joe Smith | Producer's Office | Y | 1.0 | 830.11 | | 830.11 | 1335 | 1335 | taken | yes | yes | 1335 /wk | |
| | Lincoln Center Special Event | Lincoln Center, NYC | Susie Miller | Susie Miller | N | 1 | 1500 | 1500 | | 1500 | 1500 | 450 | yes | no | 1500/ wk | |
| | Show Name Sit-down | St. Paul | Kevin George | 1201 Productions | Y | 2.0 | 762.66 | | 1525.32 | 1335 | 2670 | taken | 2 checks | yes | 1335 /wk | |
| | Show Name Concert | Mandalay Bay, Las Vegas | Don O'Hara | O'Hara Lighting, Inc. | N | 1.0 | 350 | 350 | | 350 | 350 | 105 | yes | no | 35/hr | |
| Dec-14 | Show Name Bway Retrofit | Bway Theare, NYC | Susie Miller | Grant Productions | Y | 1.0 | 476.54 | | 476.54 | 663 | 663 | taken | yes | yes | Day Rate = 221/day | |
| | UNEMPLOYMENT | n/a | n/a | New York State | N | 4.0 | 364.5 | | 1458 | 405 | 1620 | taken | 4 checks | no | $405/ wk | 4.0 |
| | Show Name TV Pilot | SONY Studios | Rick Nightly | Nightly Lights, Inc. | N | 1.0 | 116.81 | | 116.81 | 165 | 165 | taken | yes | no | 27.50/hr prep | |
| | | | | | | | SUBTOTALS: | 14050.3 | 30259.3 | | | | | | | |
| | | | | | | | NET TOTAL: | | 44310 | Total Gross: | 64051 | | | | | |
| | | | | | | | (30%) Taxes Owed: | 4215.1 | | | | | | | Total unempl | 12.0 |
| | | | | | | | | | | | | | | | Apr thru Apr | 26 total allowed |

**Figure 14.3** Financial Workbook.

The "taxes owed" cell is one of the most important pieces of information found in the financial workbook. Highlight it in a bright color because it tells you how much money to reserve in your savings account to be able to pay for taxes at the end of the year. (Easier said than done.) This is where the difference between a 1099 job and a W-2 job really matters.

Since 1099 jobs do not deduct taxes, you must save that amount of money yourself to give to the government later. 30 percent of each 1099 paycheck is a safe amount to keep in the bank. Keeping a "taxes owed" running tally will keep you from guessing if you have saved enough money come tax time.

One option that helps when freelancing is to pay taxes quarterly instead of annually. That way you do not have to keep quite as much money in your account for an entire year. Quarterly payments may also help avoid penalties that may accrue if you earn too much in 1099s annually. Your tax professional can help you determine if paying quarterly is the right path for you.

## TRACKING WRITE-OFFS

Saving 30 percent of each paycheck can be challenging—especially when your employment fluctuates. One way to help decrease the amount of money you owe each year in taxes is to track your write-offs.

Simply defined, a **"write-off"** is the amount of money spent on business-related expenses during an annual period, which can be balanced against your earnings. This means that every time you buy something for a production or for business-only use, it is considered a write-off.

---

Some examples of write-offs for assistant lighting designers are:

- Computer and printing equipment
- Camera, tablet, and other hardware expenses
- Software
- Office supplies
- Tools
- Website development, design, and hosting
- Resume supplies
- Portfolio supplies
- Business card supplies

- Assistant's kit supplies
- Home office expenses
- Cell phone bills (percentage)
- Internet access
- Trade books, scripts, and magazines
- Show tickets
- Conference fees
- Continuing education classes

- Travel (if not reimbursed)—does not include your daily commute
- Union dues
- Student loans
- Retirement accounts (most)
- Tax preparation
- Charitable donations

This list is not comprehensive. There are numerous write-offs for people working in the arts, and they can vary year-to-year. (Your tax professional will be up-to-date on yearly changes.) As a starting off point, purchase a reference book regarding tax information geared towards people in the arts.

---

Each time you spend money on business-related items, save the receipt. Write notes on the back of the receipt regarding the purpose of the expense, record it, and file it. These receipts must be kept for seven years for IRS purposes. Designate a shoebox or other container to act as your receipts archive. Inside the container, place seven large envelopes labeled with each year in which to keep the receipts. Rotate the envelopes annually to keep the most recent past seven years in your archive. (In place of a physical archive, you can also scan or take photos of your receipts and create an organized electronic filing system.)

If traveling, designate a large, manila envelope to keep in your suitcase. Keep your receipts in the envelope until you return home and can store them in your receipts archive.

Be aware that some receipts fade over time to the point that they are no longer legible. If using a paper system, rewrite the important information on the back of the receipt just in case: receipt total, date of receipt, items purchased, and vendor.

### Receipts Database

Create a **receipts database**, or spreadsheet, that tracks information regarding each receipt. (See Figures 14.4a-b.) Create a distinct receipt number for each receipt in your database and label each receipt with the number that matches its corresponding record. A good way to develop a distinct number is to begin with the year and add a sequential number at the end. For example, the 5th receipt being recorded in the year 2014 would have the receipt number of 201405. The next would be 201406, and so on. Begin with the new year number each January.

Devise categories in your database that subtotal similar items. For example, perhaps a receipt for resume paper and a receipt for pencil lead for the tech table both fall under the category of "supplies," and a purchase of Vectorworks and Lightwright are both in the category of "software." Other good categories are: hardware (for computers, phone, tablets, cameras, etc.), research (for show tickets, movies, etc.), home office (for utilities, etc.), and transportation (for non-reimbursed taxis, flights, train tickets, etc.). Ask your financial professional for further advice.

Note: Be very careful with the research category. It is often referred to as the "Arts Audit." Be scrupulous. Write specific notes on the back of each receipt detailing the direct tie to your business. "Research" items easily appear suspicious to the IRS and may result in an red flag.

The following information should be tracked in your receipts database:

- Year
- Receipt amount
- Receipt category
- Date of receipt
- Source (where the receipt originated—which store, restaurant, or vendor)

- Receipt number (as above—corresponding distinct number written on receipt)
- Subtotals per category
- Notes (such as the purpose for the receipt)

**Receipt Database**

| Year | 2013 | | Amount | 152.32 |
|------|------|--|--------|--------|

Category

- O Rent
- ◉ Computer-Hardware
- O Computer-Software
- O Supplies
- O Research

- O Transportation
- O Phone
- O Cable/Internet
- O Utilities
- O Renter's Insurance
- O Donations

- O Food/Meetings
- O Union Dues
- O Student Loans

Date    1-20-2013          Check #

Source   Apple Store

Receipt Number    201309

**Figure 14.4a**   Receipts Database (receipt entry).

## Receipt Totals 2013

| Category | Total |
|----------|-------|
| Cable/Internet | $1,183.26 |
| Computer-Hardware | $637.30 |
| Computer-Software | $225.55 |
| Donations | $135.00 |
| Food/Meetings | $253.01 |
| Phone | $1,373.97 |
| Research | $821.02 |
| Student Loans | $4,800.00 |
| Supplies | $406.99 |
| Transportation | $780.15 |
| Union Dues | $532.58 |

**Figure 14.4b**   Receipts Database (category totals).

At the end of every year, total each category and make notes of any large purchases, such as a new laptop. Bring this information with you to your tax professional. He will record each category in its proper place so that it balances against the taxes you owe. The more write-offs you are able to claim, the less in taxes you will need to repay the government.

Working as an independent contractor may seem daunting at first, but the required tasks will eventually become automatic. At the end of every day, make it a habit to input the day's receipts and any paychecks that you have received. When you begin to do it enough, it will become simple daily maintenance and start to feel like second nature.

# Conclusion

Now that you are armed with the insider secrets found within this text, you have the power to produce beautiful, professional, and well-organized paperwork. Furthermore, you can wow your designers from day one with your seemingly effortless people skills, proactive nature, and innate sense of the process.

Do not let others tell you that you are "just" an assistant. Always remember how much attention, precision, and care it takes to be successful in this profession. Work hard and have pride in what you do. Be proud to be an ALD!

> *"Be grateful. You work in an amazing industry. Embrace that."*
>
> —*K. C. Wilkerson*

# Step-by-Step Assistant's Checklist

The following are the responsibilities of the assistant lighting designer along each step of the production process. Use this checklist as a guide on your next show.

## DESIGN PREP

☐ Contract negotiation/signing

☐ Design meetings

☐ Production meetings

☐ Lighting meetings

☐ Site survey and drawing updates, if needed

☐ Prep plot/print plot for designer's rough

☐ Manufacturer demos

☐ Mock-ups

☐ Create and submit design package for bids

☐ Update design package if bid results require changes

☐ Designer run

☐ Print bible and/or desired documents for load-in

## SHOP PREP

☐ Shop visit to scenic studio to approve practical scenery

## PRE-HANG

☐ Check-in

## LOAD-IN/HANG

☐ Begin in theatre full-time

☐ Bring assistant's kit to theatre

☐ Tech table set-up

☐ Distribute magic sheets, etc., to designer's and programmer's tables

## FOCUS/MOVING LIGHT FOCUS

☐ Place focus tapes and indicate focus areas (if desired by designer)

☐ Ask for focus table

☐ Run focus

☐ Pre-cue—onstage or virtually (if possible and desired by designer)

☐ Followspot set-up and color balance (if applicable)

☐ Complete focus charts

## TECH

☐ Assist with tech

☐ Update paperwork as changes occur

☐ Organize/distribute end-of-night notes each evening

☐ Run morning work calls

## PREVIEWS

☐ Coordinate preview table with production electrician

☐ Check with management to verify seats blocked off for preview table

☐ Assure other assistants have locations in the booth during previews

☐ Continue to organize/distribute end-of-night notes

☐ Continue to run morning work calls

☐ Offer to print a copy of the running gifts list for the designer

☐ Complete and archive all paperwork by opening night

☐ Distribute final cue list to PSM and archival bible to head electrician by opening night

☐ Assure lighting team has tickets for the opening night performance and opening night party

## OPEN

- ☐ Bring and receive gifts
- ☐ Bring a "plus one" to enjoy the show
- ☐ Enjoy party!

## DAY AFTER OPENING

- ☐ Deliver opening night gifts to designer
- ☐ File archival materials at designer's office
- ☐ Bring home assistant's kit and other supplies from theatre
- ☐ Breathe!

# Design Package Checklist

When prepping a show, work off a checklist so that nothing is missed. The following is a sample checklist of items that should be completed and/or prepped when beginning a new show. After completion, remember to print, staple, hole-punch, protect, and/or laminate all preferred documents.

Requirements vary by designer and production. Customize as needed.

## DRAWING PACKAGE

☐ Light plot

☐ Section

☐ FOH

☐ Booms and ladders (if applicable)

---

Tasks to remember when creating the drawing package:

☐ Add spares

☐ Add dimensions

☐ Add trims to lineset callout

☐ Add boom footprints/locations (if applicable)

☐ Add focus/orientation arrows (if applicable)

☐ Check against inventory (if applicable)

☐ Customize title block, key, drawing schedule, and legend

☐ Customize general notes

☐ Clean up layers and classes

☐ Double-check before submission (by others)

☐ Floor plot (if applicable)

☐ Set practicals (if applicable)

## GENERAL PAPERWORK

☐ Lightwright file (instrument schedule and channel hookup)

☐ Shop order

☐ Tech table drawing

☐ Set electrics list (if applicable)

☐ Headset specification (if required)

☐ Custom gobo drawings (if applicable)

☐ Area layout

☐ Groups list

☐ Focus chart cover page

## MAGIC SHEETS

☐ Conventional magic sheets (pick one)

   ☐ System-style magic sheets

   ☐ Groundplan-style magic sheets

☐ Scenic magic sheets (if applicable)

☐ Cheat sheets (if preferred)

   ☐ Standard cheat sheet

   ☐ 20-across

☐ Equipment-specific magic sheets (if applicable)

   ☐ Moving light magic sheets

   ☐ Gobo wheel magic sheets

   ☐ LED magic sheets

   ☐ Scroller color cheat sheet

   ☐ Followspot color cheat sheet

## SKELETON FILES

☐ Focus charts

☐ Cue synopsis

☐ Work notes

☐ Followspot cue sheets (if applicable)

☐ ML focus charts and ML tracking (if applicable)

## MISCELLANEOUS

☐ Show bible and script with covers and spines

☐ Show bible and script tabs

☐ Printed script (for bible, script, and followspot assistant)

☐ Scene breakdown and scene-by-scenes (if applicable)

☐ Ripple sheet

☐ Distribution chart

☐ Instrument schedule and channel hookup printed in small booklet form, if desired

☐ Next time sheet

☐ Running gifts list

## ELECTRONIC

☐ Shared electronic show folder

☐ Literature (downloaded manuals)

    ☐ Moving lights (if applicable)

    ☐ LED fixtures (if applicable)

    ☐ Consoles

☐ Import site survey photos and other venue information

# Assistant's Kit Checklist

Although the assistant's kit varies according to the designer's preferences, the following checklist covers some basic recommended items to include:

## OFFICE SUPPLIES

☐ Pencils—you and your designer's favorites and a set of low-cost throwaways

☐ Pencil lead and eraser refills (for all applicable pencil types)

☐ Red pencils—both mechanical and wooden (if desired)

☐ Pencil sharpener—manual and electric

☐ Pens—black, blue, and red (felt-tip and ball-point)

☐ China marker/grease pencil (white)

☐ Erasers—pink erasers and extendables, such as Clic erasers by Pentel, with refills

☐ Highlighters—multiple colors (retractable styles eliminate the annoyance of lost caps)

☐ Sharpies—multiple thicknesses and colors, including silver for dark-colored items

☐ Paint pens—multiple colors, including white and silver

☐ Post-its—multiple sizes, colors, flags, and tabs. (Recommended sizes include 3" × 3", 1.5" × 2", and 4" × 6" (lined). A set of "super sticky" style also recommended.)

☐ Gel (swatch) books—all major manufacturers (wrapped with a rubber band to secure)

☐ Gobo catalogs—all major manufacturers

☐ Flashlight—incandescent and LED (100 lumens or better with good directionality). Use the incandescent to assess gel colors accurately for tungsten-halogen fixtures, and the LED for seeing into the flys when it is dark. (Purchase flashlights that use AA or AAA batteries. Styles that require charging or unique battery types may be inconvenient at inopportune times.)

☐ Extra lamps for the incandescent flashlight

☐ Extra batteries (for flashlights, wireless mice, etc.)

☐ Laser pointer—with high-lumen output (usually in green)

☐ Architectural scale rule (½" and ¼" scales required)

☐ Metric scale rule—for international productions (1:25 and 1:50 scale required)

☐ Stapler and extra staples

☐ Long-reach booklet stapler

☐ Staple-remover

☐ 3-hole punch (and a 2-hole punch if preferred); 4-hole punch (for international)

☐ Scotch tape

☐ Correction fluid or tape, such as BIC's Wite-out

☐ Pencil holders—preferably two (one for the assistants' table and one for the designer)

☐ Rubber bands, binder clips, and paperclips (in organized containers)

☐ Chalk

☐ Scissors

☐ Small plastic or wooden rulers (6" and 12")

☐ X-acto knife and extra #11 blades

☐ Small spiral-bound notepads

☐ Printer paper

☐ Heavy weight sheet protectors

☐ Page dividers and divider labels

☐ Matte black contact or shelf paper (for covering the tech table)

☐ Label maker with extra label cartridges

☐ Portable laminating machine and extra lamination sheets

☐ Small (hand-drafting) lighting template

## FOCUS ITEMS

☐ Focus tapes

☐ Gaff tape—black and white

☐ Blue painter's tape

☐ Drafting dots

## ELECTRONICS

☐ Extra mouse and mouse pad

☐ Extra laptop lock (combination lock is best; include extra keys if not)

- ☐ Extra power supplies and chargers for laptop, phone, and tablet, etc.
- ☐ Small dimmable tech table light, such as a LittLite
- ☐ Portable printer and extra ink
- ☐ Power strips (2)
- ☐ Small, grounded extension cord and cube tap
- ☐ International power adaptors—two minimum
- ☐ USB drive or rewritable CDs or DVDs with labels and holders (for archival materials)
- ☐ Spare USB flash drives of large storage capacity
- ☐ Extra cables, if needed (camera cable, USB cable, etc.)
- ☐ Digital camera (if not using your phone)
- ☐ Extra memory cards and batteries for digital camera
- ☐ Small, adjustable tripod
- ☐ Webcam
- ☐ Portable computer speakers
- ☐ Personal featherweight headset (note: not ideal for musicals due to high decibel levels)
- ☐ CD/DVD drive and a USB floppy disk drive with extra disks, if needed
- ☐ X-keys, or other programmable keyboard (used for cueing offline)
- ☐ Small, two-way radios (for venues without radios)

## TOOLS

- ☐ C-wrench (with tie-off)
- ☐ Gloves (leather or other material that will not melt to hot lights)
- ☐ Multi-tool, such as a Leatherman
- ☐ Mini traffic cones (for moving light focus)
- ☐ Welding glass/Gaffer's glass—used to protect eyes if looking directly into fixtures during focus (not recommended). Multiple cuts of saturate blue/indigo gel (like four cuts of R382 congo blue) or three primary gel cuts (red, green, and blue such as L106, R91, and R80 respectively) can also be used.
- ☐ Tape measures—preferably two (long lengths of 100'-0" or more and at least one that additionally measures in metric)
- ☐ Disto (laser distance measurer)

## PERSONAL ITEMS

- ☐ Business cards
- ☐ Pair of socks (for getting caught unexpectedly in the rain)
- ☐ Compact umbrella
- ☐ Mints—multiple flavors
- ☐ Chewing gum
- ☐ Toothpicks and dental floss
- ☐ Ibuprofen and aspirin
- ☐ Antacids and gas-relief medications
- ☐ Allergy relief medications
- ☐ Menstrual relief medications
- ☐ Feminine hygiene products
- ☐ Cough drops
- ☐ Eye drops
- ☐ Band-aids, antibiotic ointment, and alcohol wipes
- ☐ Hand sanitizer
- ☐ Wet wipes/hand sanitizing wipes
- ☐ Nail-clippers
- ☐ Deodorant (unused and sealed)
- ☐ Lip balm (unused and sealed)
- ☐ Sunscreen
- ☐ Kleenex—box for tech table and pocket-sized packs for individuals
- ☐ Tech table snacks
- ☐ Tea bags and sugar packets (assorted)
- ☐ Empty plastic bags
- ☐ Large plastic trash bags (large enough to cover your assistant's kit in case of rain)
- ☐ Roll of paper towels (for spills at the tech table)
- ☐ Disposable ear plugs—several pairs (for hearing protection—worn *under* headset during extremely loud concert-style productions)
- ☐ Bottle opener and corkscrew

# Electronic Folder Organization

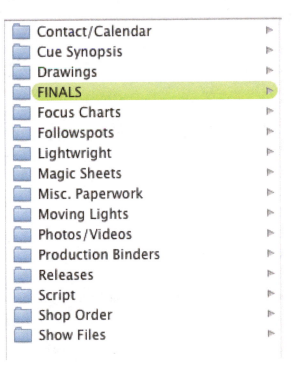

**Figure D.1** Electronic folder organization.

One possible way to organize your shared electronic listed folder is listed below. The indented items represent sub-folders within each directory. Always keep the most current file in the main directory and anything outdated in the "old" folder.

Build yourself a skeletal "sample show starter" folder that you can duplicate and rename each time you begin a production from scratch (if one is not provided from the design office).

- ☐ Contact/calendar
    - ☐ Old contact/calendar
- ☐ Cue synopsis
    - ☐ Old cue synopsis
- ☐ Drawings
    - ☐ Old drawings
    - ☐ Scenic drawings and renderings
        - ☐ Old scenic drawings and renderings
    - ☐ Theatre arch drawings
        - ☐ Old theatre arch drawings
- ☐ Final archives
    - ☐ Final PDF bible
    - ☐ Working PDF bible
- ☐ Focus charts
    - ☐ Focus chart photos
- ☐ Followspots
    - ☐ Old followspots
- ☐ Lightwright
    - ☐ Old Lightwright
- ☐ Magic sheets
    - ☐ Conventional magic sheets
        - ☐ Old conventional magic sheets
    - ☐ Moving light magic sheets
        - ☐ Old moving light magic sheets
- ☐ Misc. paperwork (to store groups list, scene breakdown, etc.)
    - ☐ Memos
    - ☐ Research
    - ☐ Literature

- ☐ Moving light info
  - ☐ ML focus charts and tracking
    - ☐ ML focus chart photos
    - ☐ Old ML focus charts and tracking
- ☐ Photos/videos
  - ☐ Model photos
  - ☐ Production photos
  - ☐ Site survey photos
- ☐ Production binders
  - ☐ Logos/images
- ☐ Releases (each folder dated and titled, such as "2014-03-05 For Bids" or "2014-04-06 Revision #1")
- ☐ Script
- ☐ Shop order
  - ☐ Bids
  - ☐ Old shop orders
  - ☐ Tech table drawing
- ☐ Show files
  - ☐ Old show files

APPENDIX E

# Site Survey Measurements

Recommended dimensions to be verified during a site survey:

☐ Proscenium opening—width and height (measure curve if applicable)

☐ Grid height

☐ Distance from 0,0 to the back wall of the theatre

☐ Distance to the wings SL and SR measured from CL

☐ Overall dimensions of wingspace SL and SR

☐ Distance from 0,0 to the orchestra pit

☐ Distance from 0,0 to the end of the apron, or edge of stage

☐ Location of permanent traps, if applicable

☐ Distance from 0,0 to the balcony rail. If the balcony rail curves, measure distances along the curve to 0,0

☐ Balcony rail overall length. Note if the balcony rail is enclosed or an exposed pipe. If enclosed, measure the interior dimension. (An enclosed balcony rail may limit the use of moving lights and may need to be altered.)

☐ Balcony rail height relative to stage height and audience height directly below it

☐ Distance from 0,0 to the booth

☐ Distance from 0,0 to the followspot platforms, if applicable

☐ Distance from 0,0 to the FOH lighting positions

☐ Placements of box booms and torm positions—both the distance from 0'-0" and from CL. Measure the length of the pipe and heights of any permanent mounting hardware. Confirm that SL and SR box booms reverse and repeat.

☐ Placement of FOH truss, if applicable—verify the length and width of the truss as well as its distance from 0,0. Confirm that it is centered on the CL. If possible, measure high and low trims to the bottom of the truss as relative to stage height and audience height. Note where the pick points for the motors are attached.

☐ Distance from stage height to audience floor level and curvature of the house

☐ House aisle and/or VOM placements

☐ Note and measure any additional permanently installed lighting positions and/or raceways. Confirm with house staff that they will remain during your production.

☐ Note and measure permanent features that may be hindrances, such as box seats, permanent catwalks, electrical boxes, or emergency egress restrictions.

☐ Note any permanently installed scenic items such as portals, travelers, and cyc (if applicable).

☐ If a permanent fly system exists, note any obstacles such as linesets out of service or blocked and rendered inoperable.

☐ Note orchestra pit height settings (if hydraulic or pneumatic) and any beauty wall surrounding the pit (if removable or not).

☐ Note any other conditions that seem unusual.

# Sample Shop Order

Use the shop order excerpt on the following pages as a guide for your next production. (Please note: personal information has been obscured.)

# ELECTRICAL EQUIPMENT LIST
## *"CHAPLIN"*
### *BARRYMORE THEATRE*
## <u>REVISED</u> JUNE 15, 2012

| | |
|---|---|
| Producer: | Hanwell Productions<br>contact info here |
| General Manager NY: | Roy Gabay<br>contact info here |
| Designer: | Ken Billington<br>contact info here |
| Assoc. LD | John Demous<br>contact info here |
| Production Supervisor: | Chris Smith<br>contact info here |
| Production Electrician: | Jimmy Fedigan<br>contact info here |
| Load In: | July 23, 2012<br>Barrymore Theatre<br>New York City |

**Figure F.1** *Chaplin* shop order
*Lighting By: Ken Billington*
*Assoc. LD: John Demous*

**"CHAPLIN"**
Barrymore Theatre, New York City

## IMPORTANT GENERAL NOTES

### PLEASE READ THIS – IT CONTAINS VERY IMPORTANT INFORMATION

✓ All units to be BLACK with quartz lamp, clamp, template slot safety, and BLACK color frame unless otherwise stated;

✓ All ColoRams to come complete with Safety Cables;

✓ All Automated Fixtures to come complete with Safety Cables;

✓ Any substitutions or revisions must be fully disclosed at the time of the bid, these substitutions or revisions are not accepted without permission of the Designer;

✓ Bidder assumes responsibility for any additional materials that are required on site due to rental shop oversight or error;

✓ Allow for ColoRam Color and Loading within bid – 21 Colors;

✓ Allow for Spare Units, ColoRams, Lamps, Dimmer Cards, Control Cards, Power Supplies, Fuses, etc.;

✓ See Conventional Section (Part A) and Automated Section (Part B) for additional notes;

✓ **We consider the definition of Shop Prep to mean that "all Equipment ordered either on this list or verbally added will be pulled, working, and available for the Prep Crew on the <u>first</u> day of prep when they arrive at your facility".**

---

**Figure F.1** *Chaplin* shop order
*Lighting By: Ken Billington*
*Assoc. LD: John Demous*

**"CHAPLIN"**
Barrymore Theatre, New York City

## PART A - CONVENTIONAL
## EQUIPMENT TOTALS

### CONVENTIONAL UNITS:

| | |
|---|---|
| 72 | Source 4 19° 575w (2 as Spare) |
| 65 | Source 4 26° 575w (2 as Spare) |
| 46 | Source 4 36° 575w (2 as Spare) |
| 1 | Altman 3.5" 21° Leko 500w |
| | |
| 56 | Source 4 Par NSP 575w (3 as Spare) |
| 13 | Source 4 Par MFL 575w (1 as Spare) |
| | |
| 18 | Wybron BP 2 750w |
| 4 | PAR 64 NSP 1000w |
| 12 | PAR 16 w/ 12v 75w EYC Lamp, Transformer (2 as Spare) |
| 2 | 10" Bambino Fresnel 5000w |
| | |
| 2 | 7'-6" 15 light R40 300w Flood Striplights w/ Hanging Irons |
| 12 | 5' 30 light MR11 35w FTH Striplights (6 w/ Hanging Irons. 6 w/ No Hanging Hardware) |
| 8 | Altman Q-Lites 300w No Barndoors w/ Safeties, Clamps (worklights) |
| 22 | Broad Cyc 500w |
| 1 | 3 Cell Far Cyc 1500w |
| 1 | GAM Stickup 150w (Spare) |
| | |
| 2 | Lycian 1290 2000w Xenon Followspots |

### SPECIAL EFFECTS:

| | |
|---|---|
| 14 | Wybron 4" ColoRam w/Fan Control w/Source 4 Std Plate Loaded w/21 Color Scrolls (2 Spare) |
| 67 | Wybron 7.5" ColoRam w/Fan Control w/Source 4-7.5" Std Plate Loaded w/21 Color Scrolls Includes Auto Yokes (3 Spare) |
| 5 | Wybron 24 Way Power Supplies  (1 spare ) |
| 7 | City Theatrical DMX Snow Machines |
| 2 | MDG Atmosphere w/DMX interface, remote, $CO_2$ regulator, transfer hose, 25' $CO_2$ hose |
| 2 | Martin GEM DMX Fans w/Hangers |

**Figure F.1** *Chaplin* shop order
    *Lighting By: Ken Billington*
    *Assoc. LD: John Demous*

**"CHAPLIN"**
Barrymore Theatre, New York City

## ACCESSORIES:

| | |
|---|---|
| 18 | Source 4 "A" Size Template Holders |
| 4 | Source 4 Iris |
| 10 | 6.25" Donut |
| 34 | 7.5" Top Hats |
| 4 | 7.5" Color Extender |
| 24 | Source 4 6.25" Tophats |
| 68 | Source 4 6.25"  Half Tophats |
| 19 | City Theatrical 2650 2" Short Top Hats for VL2500 Wash |
| 10 | City Theatrical Spill Rings for VL5B |
| 1 | City Theatrical Source 4 Follow Spot Handle |
| 2 | Adjustable 5' to 9' Rolling Stands |
| 2 | Heavy Duty Braced Adjustable 5' to 9' Rolling Stand (Studio Type) |

## CONTROL:

| | |
|---|---|
| 1 | ETC EOS 2048 outputs needed (Return after opening) |
| 2 | ETC ION Console's 2048 Outputs needed |
| 1 | iPod Touch w/ ETC IRFR Software |
| 3 | ETC Remote Video Interface (Return after opening) |
| | Network Switches as needed to provide a complete working system |
| | Net 3 Gateways w/ External Power Supply (4 x Female 5 Pin XLR Outputs) as per Production Elec |
| 1 | Wireless Router (10/100 Base T) |
| 6 | 19" Color LCD Touch Monitors (2 return after opening) |
| 7 | 19" Color LCD Monitors (1 as Spare) (Return after Opening) |

Cat 5 Cable as necessary

## DIMMERS / MISCELLANIOUS CONTROL:

| | |
|---|---|
| 2 | 96x2.4kw Sensor Dimmer Racks 400A/6Cir |
| 1 | 48x2.4kw Sensor Dimmer Racks 400A/6cir |
| 3 | Spare Sensor Control Module CEMs |
| 6 | Spare Dimmer Modules 2x2.4kw |
| | Opto Box 5-pin/ 6 Out Pathways w/ AC Cord (as per Prod Elec) |
| 2 | WDS Transmitter200mw (w/antenna and PN 5525 power supply) 5500 |
| 7 | WDS Personal Dimmer 5515 |
| 4 | WDS 12v 4A Autocharger 115v w/ Connectors 5540 |
| 4 | Twofer, Battery to Receiver and Dimmer 5550 |
| 8 | WDS 12v Rechargeable Battery w/ Connectors 5535 |
| 1 | A/B DMX Swithbox 1-4 Univ. |
| 2 | A/B Switch B.O. 5 pin Male X 4 |
| 1 | A/B Switch B.O. 5 pin Female X 4 |
| 3 | 6-way On/Off Switch Boxes (Stage Manager) |
| | NOTE: all like style and condition |
| 3 | UPS 120v. 1150 Best w/ Road Case |

**Figure F.1** *Chaplin* shop order
*Lighting By: Ken Billington*
*Assoc. LD: John Demous*

**"CHAPLIN"**
Barrymore Theatre, New York City

## IRON / RIGGING:

30    12" Sgl-Tee Sidearms
28    24" Dbl-Tee Sidearms
48    18" Stiffeners
20    1.5" Rigid Chesborough

8    38' 1 1/2" Schedule 40 Pipe
2    18' 1 1/2" Schedule 40 Pipe
2    8' 1 1/2" Schedule 40 Pipe
16    5' 1½" Schedule 40 Pipe (Ladder Stiffeners)
12    3' 1½" Schedule 40 Pipe

**Build the following as 8 two section Ladders**
8    6'-9" Open Face 28" x 24" Double Dance Tower TOP SECTIONS
8    6'-9" Open Face 28" x 24" Double Dance Tower MID SECTIONS OPEN BOTTOM

6    10' 20.5" Box Truss Painted Black
2    8'-0" 20.5" Box Truss Painted Black
     Black Span Sets and Shackles

## MISCELLANEOUS:

1    Personal Lift 36' w/Outriggers
1    Personal Lift 30' w/Outriggers
6    36' Zetex Black

**CABLE:**  Quantity and configuration per production electrician

     4 Pin Wybron Control Cable
     XLR Terminators
     5-Pin XLR
     6 Circuit Multi Cable
     Jumpers
     Breakouts
     Twofers -20A

---

**Figure F.1**  *Chaplin* shop order
          *Lighting By: Ken Billington*
          *Assoc. LD: John Demous*

**"CHAPLIN"**
Barrymore Theatre, New York City

## TECH TABLE EQUIPMENT TOTALS

**Note: The following is required for tech period – Specification will change based on current computer technology when shop order is awarded.**

| | |
|---|---|
| 8 | Production Tables 4x8 w/ Adjustable Legs |
| 16 | Sawhorses for Table Legs |
| 8 | Buttboards |

### PERISHABLES:

| | |
|---|---|
| 14 | Wybron 4" ColoRam 21 Color Scrolls |
| 63 | Wybron 10" ColoRam 21 Color Scrolls |

**Color . Gobos as per Prod. Electrician**

**Figure F.1** *Chaplin* shop order
*Lighting By: Ken Billington*
*Assoc. LD: John Demous*

**"CHAPLIN"**
Barrymore Theatre, New York City



## PART B - AUTOMATED
## EQUIPMENT TOTALS

5 Vari*Lite VL3500 Automated Fixture w/ Safeties, Clamps [1 Spare]
13 Vari*Lite VL3000 Automated Fixture w/ Safeties, Clamps [1 Spare]

**NOTE**: Please add high heat foil fix for the color bulkhead sensors, like the Ghost re-fit

19 Vari*Lite VL2500 Wash Automated Fixture w/Safeties, Clamps [2 Spare]
10 Vari*Lite VL5B 1200w Stipple Lens [ 2 Spare]
3 Smart Repeaters [1 Spare]
19 City Theatrical 2650 2" Short Top Hats for VL2500 Wash
10 City Theatrical Spill Rings for VL5B

7 City Theatrical Auto-Yokes w/ Wybron BP 2 750w [1 Spare]
5 City Theatrical Auto-Yokes w/ Source 4-14° 750w [1 Spare]
NOTE : All with Auto-Yoke Irises, Focus, Safeties, Mega Claw Clamps

Top Hats for Vari*Lites plus Scroller for Auto Yoke listed previously

**Note: All units must have less than 50 hours on the lamps when delivered**

Cable
DMX Cable
Power Distribution
Feeders

**MISC:**

1 Spare / Test Rack with complete parts inventory, test equipment, all tools required for unit maintenance - contained in road box(s)

**Figure F.1** *Chaplin* shop order
*Lighting By: Ken Billington*
*Assoc. LD: John Demous*

**"C H A P L I N"**
Barrymore Theatre, New York City

Page 8 of 22

**GOBOS FOR ALL AUTOMATIED FIXTURES**

**A = APOLLO, GA = GAM (INLIGHT), R = ROSCO, VL = VARI*LITE**

**VARI*LITE 2500 WASH COLOR INFO**

| | | Color | |
|---|---|---|---|
| AMT. | POS | # | Name |
| 38 | 0 | - | OPEN |
| | 1 | 0240 | LIGHT RED |
| | 2 | 0850 | DARK BLUE |
| | 3 | 0540 | YELLOW |
| | 4 | 0820 | LT. BLUE-GREEN |
| | 5 | 0150 | COOL PINK |
| | 6 | 0660 | GREEN |
| | 7 | 0020 | MAGENTA |
| | 8 | 0960 | DEEP LAVENDER |
| | 9 | 0320 | FLESH PINK |
| | 10 | 0440 | ORANGE |
| | 11 | 0990 | CONGO BLUE |

**Figure F.1** *Chaplin* shop order
*Lighting By: Ken Billington*
*Assoc. LD: John Demous*

**"CHAPLIN"**
Barrymore Theatre, New York City

Page 9 of 22

**GOBOS FOR ALL AUTOMATIED FIXTURES**

**A = APOLLO, GA = GAM (INLIGHT), R = ROSCO, VL = VARI*LITE**

**VARI*LITE 3000 GOBO LOAD**

| | | Rot.Gobo #1 | | | Rot.Gobo #2 | |
|---|---|---|---|---|---|---|
| **AMT.** | **POS** | **#** | **Name** | **POS** | **#** | **Name** |
| 24 | 0 | - | OPEN | 0 | - | OPEN |
| | 1 | VL 5002 | REAL CLOUD #2 (STOCK) | 1 | A 2201 | BEAMS 1 |
| | 2 | VL 7029 | ALPHA RAYS (STOCK) | 2 | A 2260 | DOTS MEDIUM |
| | 3 | R 7797 | THICKET | 3 | VL 7002 | PEBBLES (STOCK) |
| | 4 | VL 4211 | UNEVEN BARS (STOCK) | 4 | A 3552 | WILD PALMS |
| | 5 | A 2237 | BEAM SEARCHLIGHT | 5 | A 6029 | VENETIAN BLINDS |

| | Rot.Gobo #3 | |
|---|---|---|
| **POS** | **#** | **Name** |
| 0 | - | OPEN |
| 1 | STOCK | PRISM |
| 2 | A 2115 | SHUTTER |
| 3 | A 2116 | DOUBLE SHUTTER |
| 4 | R 77288 | INTERLOCKING BREAKUP |

| | Gobo/ Color | |
|---|---|---|
| **POS** | **#** | **Name** |
| 0 | - | OPEN |
| 1 | 30503 | CONGO BLUE (STOCK) |
| 2 | 30505 | ORANGE (STOCK) |
| 3 | 30502 | KELLY GREEN (STOCK) |
| 4 | 30506 | DARK FUSHIA (STOCK) |
| 5 | 30504 | MAGENTA (STOCK) |
| 6 | 30501 | DEEP RED (STOCK) |

**Figure F.1** *Chaplin* shop order
*Lighting By: Ken Billington*
*Assoc. LD: John Demous*

**"CHAPLIN"**
Barrymore Theatre, New York City

## VARI*LITE 3500 GOBO LOAD

| AMT. | POS | Rot.Gobo #1 # | Name | POS | Gobo #2 # | Name |
|---|---|---|---|---|---|---|
| 14 | 0 | - | OPEN | 0 | - | OPEN |
| | 1 | VL 5002 | REAL CLOUDS #2 (STOCK) | 1 | A 2104 | APERTURE ½" |
| | 2 | VL 7029 | ALPHA RAYS (STOCK) | 2 | A 7797 | THICKET |
| | 3 | A 2202 | BEAMS 2 | 3 | R 77288 | INTERLOCKING BREAKUP |
| | 4 | VL 4211 | UNEVEN BARS (STOCK) | 4 | A 3552 | WILD PALMS |
| | 5 | A 2237 | BEAM SEARCHLIGHT | 5 | VL 7002 | PEBBLES (STOCK) |
| | | | | 6 | VL 7014 | TRIANGLE BREAKUP (STOCK) |

| POS | Gobo/ Color # | Name |
|---|---|---|
| 0 | - | OPEN |
| 1 | 30503 | CONGO BLUE (STOCK) |
| 2 | 30505 | ORANGE (STOCK) |
| 3 | 30502 | KELLY GREEN (STOCK) |
| 4 | 30506 | DARK FUSHIA (STOCK) |
| 5 | 30504 | MAGENTA (STOCK) |
| 6 | 30501 | DEEP RED (STOCK) |

**Figure F.1** *Chaplin* shop order
*Lighting By: Ken Billington*
*Assoc. LD: John Demous*

**"CHAPLIN"**
Barrymore Theatre, New York City

Page 11 of 22

**Scroll Information:**

**ALL GEL STRINGS FROM WYBRON**

**Scroll (All Units):**

| | |
|---|---|
| 1. | L-130 |
| 2. | L-203 |
| 3. | L-202 |
| 4. | L-201 |
| 5. | G-325 |
| 6. | G-155 |
| 7. | L-110 |
| 8. | L-111 |
| 9. | L-136 |
| 10. | L-137 |
| 11. | L-180 |
| 12. | L-179 |
| 13. | L-128 |
| 14. | R-21 |
| 15. | L-116 |
| 16. | L-182 |
| 17. | L-161 |
| 18. | L-132 |
| 19. | R-83 |
| 20. | L-181 |
| 21. | L-117 |

**Figure F.1** *Chaplin* shop order
*Lighting By: Ken Billington*
*Assoc. LD: John Demous*

# Sample Cover Letter and Resume

Use the sample cover letter and theatrical resume found on the following pages as a guide for your own materials.

Thursday, September 12, 2013

Your Street Address
City, State, Zip Code
Your Cell Phone #
Your Email

(4 lines down)


Mr. / Ms. Contact Name
Company Name, if applicable
Street Address
City, State, Zip Code


Dear Mr. / Ms. Last Name:

**The opening paragraph should state why you are writing** and how you became attracted to this particular individual, company, or position. If you were referred by a friend or co-worker, mention them by name in the first or second sentence and point out that he or she suggested that you write. If you are applying to a job advertisement, name the specific job for which you are applying and the source in which you found the ad. Briefly mention specific characteristics about the individual or company that have impressed you and made you want to pursue this employment.

**In the second paragraph, draw attention to your qualifications** and/or experiences that are relevant to the potential employer. If you held a particular job or worked on a particular project that directly relates to the opportunity, highlight this experience. Convince your reader that this makes you the ideal candidate for the job. Do not reiterate the contents of your resume, but instead fill in any blanks that your resume leaves open and note any additional relevant qualifications not previously emphasized.

**The closing paragraph states what you will do next**, such as following up with a call to arrange an interview at the employer's convenience, or an assertive request, such as "I look forward to your call." The closing paragraph need only consist of a sentence or two.

Sincerely,


(Your Signature Here in Ink)

Your Name Typed


Enclosure

---

**Figure G.1**  Sample cover letter.[1]

# Your Name Here

**Assistant Lighting Designer**
Phone number, email address
Website, if applicable

---

**Assistant Experience:**

| | | | |
|---|---|---|---|
| Designer's Name (A) | *Show Name* | Theatre Name, Location | Year |
| | *Show Name* | Theatre Name, Location | Year |
| | *Show Name* | Theatre Name, Location | Year |
| | *Show Name* | Theatre Name, Location | Year |
| | *Show Name* | Theatre Name, Location | Year |
| | *Show Name* | Theatre Name, Location | Year |
| | *Show Name* | Theatre Name, Location | Year |
| | | | |
| Designer's Name (B) | *Show Name* | Theatre Name, Location | Year |
| | *Show Name* | Theatre Name, Location | Year |
| | *Show Name* | Theatre Name, Location | Year |
| | *Show Name* | Theatre Name, Location | Year |
| | *Show Name* | Theatre Name, Location | Year |
| | *Show Name* | Theatre Name, Location | Year |
| | | | |
| Designer's Name (C) | *Show Name* | Theatre Name, Location | Year |
| | *Show Name* | Theatre Name, Location | Year |
| | *Show Name* | Theatre Name, Location | Year |

**Related Experience:**

| | | | |
|---|---|---|---|
| Followspot Operator | *Show Name* | Theatre Name, Location | Year |
| | *Show Name* | Theatre Name, Location | Year |
| | *Show Name* | Theatre Name, Location | Year |
| | *Show Name* | Theatre Name, Location | Year |
| | *Show Name* | Theatre Name, Location | Year |
| | | | |
| Electrician | *Show Name* | Theatre Name, Location | Year |
| | *Show Name* | Theatre Name, Location | Year |

**Education:**

| | | | |
|---|---|---|---|
| MFA Lighting Design | University Name | Location | candidate Year |
| BFA Theatre Design | University Name | Location | achieved Year |

**Additional Skills:**

Software Skills: Vectorworks, Lightwright, AutoCAD, Adobe Photoshop, FileMaker Pro
Other skills: Musical Score reading, Basic Projection Design, Fluent in German
Lighting Design resume and portfolio available by request.

**References:**

| Reference's Name | Reference's Name | Reference's Name |
|---|---|---|
| 123-456-7890 cell | 123-456-7890 cell | 123-456-7890 cell |
| myreference@email.com | myreference@email.com | myreference@email.com |

---

**Figure G.2** Sample resume.

# Contributing Lighting Designers and Associates

## KEN BILLINGTON (KB ASSOCIATES, INC.)

Ken Billington (lighting designer) has 97 Broadway shows to his credit, including such theatre milestones as the original *Sweeney Todd* and *Chicago*, the longest running American musical ever. Many touring productions over the years including *Chicago* (Worldwide), *Riverdance* (lighting supervisor), *Fiddler on the Roof* (from 1976 till the present), *Annie* for almost as long, the seasonal *White Christmas*, as well as *9 to 5*, *High School Musical*, *The Drowsy Chaperone*, and *Doctor Doolittle* to name a few. Other projects include *Hugh Jackman Back on Broadway*, the Las Vegas spectacular, *Jubilee!*, for Seaworld Orlando, San Diego, and San Antonio *Shamu One Ocean* and *Shamu Rocks*, and from 1979 to 2006 the *Radio City Music Hall Christmas Spectacular*. Ken's many awards include the Tony, NY Drama Desk, and Outer Critics Awards as well as the Ace award for television lighting and the Lumen for his architectural work.

## CHRISTOPHER AKERLIND

Christopher Akerlind has designed lighting and sometimes scenery for over 600 productions at theatre and opera companies across the country and around the world. Broadway credits include: *End of the Rainbow*, *The Gershwins' Porgy and Bess* (Tony nom.), *Superior Donuts*,

*Top Girls*, *110 in the Shade* (Tony nom.), *Talk Radio, Shining City, Awake and Sing* (Tony nom.), *Well, Rabbit Hole, A Touch of the Poet, In My Life, The Light in the Piazza* (Drama Desk, Outer Critics, Tony Awards), *Reckless, The Tale of the Allergist's Wife, Seven Guitars* (Tony nom.), and *The Piano Lesson* among others. He is the recipient of the Obie Award for Sustained Excellence in Lighting Design, the Chicago area's Michael Merritt Award for Design and Collaboration, and numerous nominations for the Drama Desk, Lucille Lortel, Outer Critics Circle and Tony Awards among many others.

## F. MITCHELL DANA

F. Mitchell Dana has designed lighting for more than 600 shows for Broadway, Off-Broadway, LORT, opera, industrials, and dance. Broadway work includes: *The Suicide, Monday After the Miracle, Mass Appeal, Freedom of the City,* and *The Inspector General*. He has designed lighting for the NYC Opera, Royal Opera (Covent Garden and Wembley Arena), LA Opera, Washington National Opera, and numerous Regional Opera Companies. He has designed lighting for seven Pittsburgh Civic Light Opera seasons, over 30 for the Paper Mill Playhouse, and 10 seasons for the St. Louis MUNY. He has designed over 200 times for LORT theatres like the Mark Taper Forum, Seattle Rep, ACT, BAM, Roundabout, McCarter, PDG, Goodman, Stratford Ontario, NAC/Ottawa, and the Derby Playhouse in England. He is a professor at Rutgers University's Mason Gross School of the Arts.

## JOHN DEMOUS

Designer: *Motherhood the Musical*, Fort Lauderdale, Tampa, Rochester; *Les Misérables*, Theater Under the Stars, Houston; *Turn of the Screw*, Sacramento Opera; *Boheme*, Berkshire Opera; *Dardanus* and *Comte Ory*, Wolftrap Opera; *Cendrillon*, Manhattan School of Music; Seattle Opera Young Artist Program: *Cosi fan Tutte, La Casa Verde* and *Orpheus Sings of Love* and Immediate Theatre: *Woyzeck*, and *Blood Orange*.

Associate—for Ken Billington: Broadway: *An Evening with Jerry Herman, Ring of Fire, High Fidelity, Sondheim on Sondheim, The Scottsboro Boys, Hugh Jackman Back on Broadway, Don't Dress for Dinner, Chaplin. Chicago the Musical* since 2001: U.K. Tour, Düsseldorf, Mexico City, New York Ambassador, Sao Paulo, Moscow, Johannesburg, Paris, Milan, Dubai, Seoul, Copenhagen, Tokyo. *High School Musical*: U.S. Tour, U.K. Tour, London Hammersmith. He has also worked on the *Radio City Music Hall Christmas Spectacular*.

## BEVERLY EMMONS

Lighting design—Broadway: *Stick Fly, Annie Get Your Gun, Jekyll & Hyde, The Heiress, Passion, Amadeus* and *The Elephant Man*. Off-Broadway: Joseph Chaikin, Robert Wilson and Meridith Monk. Regionals: the Guthrie, Arena Stage, The Alley in Houston, Children's Theatre of Minneapolis. Dance: Martha Graham, Trisha Brown, Alvin Ailey, Merce Cunningham. Awards: one Tony award, seven Tony nominations, a 1976 Lumen, a 1980 Obie, Theatre Wing awards. Six years with the ERC.

## ERIN ERDMAN

Erin is the principal designer of eSquared Lighting Design. Since starting eSquared Lighting Design in 2003, Erin has designed and managed a wide variety of projects, including commercial, residential, retail, building facades, and exterior landscapes.

In addition to an accomplished commercial design portfolio, she has developed numerous residential projects treating the owner-clients to her comforting and efficient management style. Her residential design work ranges from ultra-modern to mountain lodge vernacular and is located throughout the west, including Los Angeles, Vail, Aspen, Telluride, and Steamboat Springs, Colorado.

## BRUCE FERRI

Principal Designer, Ferri Lighting Design & Associates (FLDA): Bruce Ferri, a SUNY Purchase alumnus, was at New York City Lites for 24 years, where his work was seen on ABC, NBC, CBS and FOX as well as many of the cable networks. For three consecutive years, Ferri received multiple Emmy nominations for his design work on ABC's *Who Wants to Be a Millionaire*. In 2004, he received a Sports Emmy nomination for ESPN's *SportsCenter* and designed the lighting for ESPN's new high-definition studios in Bristol, CT. One of his most memorable jobs was lighting live wraparounds in Kuwait right after Desert Storm for the History Channel. Ferri lit the last Pope, the previous President, and all of The Iron Chefs. Ferri won two Sports Emmy Awards; one for his work with the production design team for the MLB Network Studios and one shared with LD, Mick Smith, for *MLB Tonight* technical team work.

## MATT GORDON

Matt Gordon is a New York City-based freelance designer, lighting director, and assistant designer. He is a graduate from SUNY Purchase College Design/Technology Conservatory with a BFA with emphasis in lighting design. He has worked extensively in television, primarily with the team at Ferri Lighting Design and Associates. He has worked on projects such as *Iron Chef America*, *The Today Show*, *ESPN Sports Center*, CNBC, The Weather Channel HD, *Christmas in Rockefeller Center*, NBC Sports Network, *the NHL Fantasy Draft and All Star Game*, CBS Sports Network, and *the Heisman Awards Presentation*.

## ROB HALLIDAY

Rob has worked as a lighting designer and lighting programmer for the last 20 years.

Design work includes: *Sweeney Todd*, *Hello Dolly*, *Buried Child*, *Oliver!* and *West Side Story* at Leicester's Curve, *Goodbye Barcelona* at the Arcola, *The Wizard of Oz* at Madison Square Garden and on tour across the USA, *Daddy Cool* in London and Berlin, and more than a decade of musicals for London's Royal Academy of Music.

Programmer and associate work includes: the Tony Award-winning *Red*, *Evita*, *Equus*, *Hamlet*, *Mary Poppins* and *Oklahoma* in New York, shows including *Merrily We Roll Along*,

*Ragtime* and *The Coast of Utopia* in London, the film *My Week With Marilyn*, and other shows including *Les Misérables*, *Miss Saigon*, *Martin Guerre*, *The Witches of Eastwick* and Matthew Bourne's *Cinderella*.

Rob created FocusTrack and SpotTrack and is a regular contributor to a range of lighting-related publications, the best of these articles now collected together in the *Entertainment in Production* paper and e-books. www.robhalliday.com

### DONALD HOLDER

Broadway: *Golden Boy*, *Ragtime*, *A Streetcar Named Desire*, *Gem of The Ocean*, *Movin' Out*, *Juan Darien* (all Tony nominated), *South Pacific* (2008 Tony Award), *The Lion King* (Tony, Drama Desk, Outer Critics Circle Awards, Paris Moliere Award), *Spider-Man: Turn Off The Dark*, *Annie*, *The MotherF\*\*er With The Hat*, *Promises, Promises*, *Arcadia*, *Come Fly Away*, *Cyrano de Bergerac*, *Radio Golf*, *The Little Dog Laughed*, *Thoroughly Modern Millie*, *Prelude to a Kiss*, *The Boy From Oz*, and many others. Off-Broadway: *Blood and Gifts*, *The Blue Flower*, *Happiness*, *Yellowface*, *A Man of No Importance*, *Birdie Blue*, *Observe The Sons of Ulster...* (Lortel Award), *Jitney*, *Saturday Night*, *Three Days of Rain*, *All My Sons*, *The Most Fabulous Story Ever Told*, and many others. Television: *Smash*—Seasons One and Two: NBC-Dreamworks.

### VIVIEN LEONE

Vivien has been an associate lighting designer on Broadway for the last 25 years.

Credits include: *Spider-Man: Turn Off The Dark* and *Little Shop of Horrors* for Donald Holder; *Phantom of the Opera*, *Fosse*, and *Sunset Boulevard* for Andrew Bridge; *Lucky Guy* and *Caroline, Or Change* for Peggy Eisenhauer and Jules Fisher; *La Bohème* directed by Baz Luhrmann, lighting by Nigel Levings; *Titanic*, *Big*, and *Crazy For You* for Paul Gallo; and *Broadway Bound* for Tharon Musser. Vivien is also involved with The Lighting Archive.org and has guest lectured at LDI, The Broadway Lighting Master Classes, and various colleges on the topic of recording and preserving lighting design.

### JASON LYONS

Broadway: *Let It Be*, *Bring It On*, *Rock of Ages* (Vegas, Toronto, Australia, London and National Tours), *The Threepenny Opera*, *Barefoot In the Park*, *Good Vibrations*. Others: *Venice* (Public), *On The Town* (Barrington), *Hello Dolly* (Goodspeed), *All In The Timing* (Primary), *So You Think You Can Dance Tour 2011*, *White Noise* (Chicago), *Broke-ology* (LCT), *Uncle Vanya* (CSC), *Clay* (LCT), *2* by Pinter, *Scarcity* (Atlantic), *10 years* with The New Group. Faculty: Purchase College. www.jasonlyonsdesign.com

### ED McCARTHY

Lighting design: *Southern Comfort* at Barrington Stage Co., *Drop Dead Perfect* at Penguin Rep. Broadway: Adaptation of *Coram Boy* (2007 Tony nomination for Best Lighting of a Play);

the BC/EFA Benefit of *Once on This Island*; *Radio City Music Hall Christmas Spectacular*. Over 70 Off-Broadway and regional shows, including 17 for Rattlestick Playwright's Theater. Concerts: Florence Henderson, Judy Collins, Marvin Hamlisch. Guest Artist: University of Iowa 2005–13, Associate Lighting Designer for all companies of *Mamma Mia!* in the U.S., Canada, Mexico, Brazil, and Argentina; many others. Television: 7 Grammy Awards, 13 Kennedy Center Honors, the last 14 Tony Awards, more. *Lincoln Memorial Inaugural Concert*, 18 years of *Live from Lincoln Center*, *A Prairie Home Companion* Cinemacast; HBO telecast of *Thurgood*.

## JOHN MCKERNON

John McKernon has designed many Off-Broadway and regional shows, including *One Mo' Time* (Broadway), *Jelly Roll!* (New York and London), *The Piano Lesson*, *Further Mo'*, *Othello* (Roundabout), *Crazy for You*, *The Chalk Garden*, and *An Evening With Jerry Herman*. He has also designed extensively in dance and has lit more benefits than he can count.

For over 20 years he has also been an associate designer to Ken Billington, with whom he has worked on many prominent productions. Also, as an architectural lighting supervisor for KB Associates Inc., he was involved in the design of many outstanding restaurants and nightclubs from New York to Asia, many years of work with Tavern on the Green, and on the lighting design team for Sea World's Atlantis in Orlando.

John is a member of United Scenic Artists, Local 829, a graduate of the North Carolina School of the Arts, and is the creator of Lightwright.

## BRIAN MONAHAN

Lighting designer: *Magique: A Magic & Illusion Show* at the Eldorado Hotel in Reno; *South Street: A New Musical* at the Pasadena Playhouse; *The Disney Symphonic Legacy Concert* at Walt Disney Concert Hall; *Bear In The Big Blue House—Live!* (U.S. tour); *The Radio City Music Hall Christmas Spectacular* (Mexico City, Nashville) and *Disney's Steps In Time* (California Adventure). He co-designed the Broadway hit *The Drowsy Chaperone* (Tony Award nomination and LA Ovation Award nomination) and *The Woman in Black* (Old Globe, Off-Broadway). Brian design shows for the Holland America Line and Carnival Cruise Line. Concerts: Frank Sinatra (12 world tours); Ann-Margret (5 tours); and Charles Aznavour (Carnegie Hall, U.S. tour). Television: *Frank Sinatra's 75th Birthday Celebration* for CBS and *The Ultimate Event: Frank, Liza and Sammy* for Showtime for which he won a cable ACE Award. Brian has also worked on the Broadway and National Tour productions of *Stardust*, *Metro*, *Lettice & Lovage*, *Buddy: The Buddy Holly Story*, *Dream: The Johnny Mercer Musical*, and *Footloose*.

## RYAN O'GARA

(Lighting designer) U.S. tour—*The Little Prince*, NY; *Brazil Brazil*, *Knuckle Heads Zoo* and *Black Violin* at the New Victory Theatre; Michael Count's *Moses in Egypt* for New York City Opera; plus *THE RIDE*, Andrea Thome's *Pinkolandia*, Lourds Lane's *Chix 6*, John Maran's

*A Raw Space* and *A Strange and Separate People*, Stephen Stahl's *Straight to Hell* and *Norman Doesmen*, David Straussman's *Dummy* plus various designs for The Sonnet Repertory Company, Lincoln Center Festival, NYU/Playwrights Horizons, Westbeth Theatre Center.

On Broadway he has served as the associate lighting designer to Howell Binkley for: *A Christmas Story*, *Jesus Christ Superstar*, *Magic/Bird*, *How to Succeed...*, *Baby It's You*, *Long Story Short*, *Lombardi*, *Million Dollar Quartet*, *All About Me*, *West Side Story*, *To Be or Not To Be*, *Cry Baby*, *Gypsy*, *In the Heights*, *Xanadu*, *Love Musik* and *Avenue Q*. O'Gara is a graduate of the School of Design and Production from the University of North Carolina School of the Arts.

## JUSTIN A. PARTIER

Justin Partier is a New York City-based designer and assistant, who has worked in opera regionally and internationally as well as Off-Broadway and Broadway. He is a member of United Scenic Artsts, Local 829 and a MFA graduate of Mason Gross School of the Arts at Rutgers University.

## ANTHONY PEARSON

Associate lighting designer: (Broadway) *Porgy & Bess* (National Tour), *We Will Rock You* (National Tour), *Pippin*, *Kinky Boots*, *Shatner's World*, *Hugh Jackman Back on Broadway*, *Other Desert Cities*, *Little Miss Sunshine* (La Jolla), *9 to 5* (National Tour), *Chicago* (International), *Finian's Rainbow*, *Looped*, *Boeing Boeing*, *Bye Bye Birdie*, *Minsky's* (LA), *The Drowsy Chaperone* (National Tour and West End), *Rent* (Asia Tour). Assistant lighting designer: *Shrek* (Broadway and National Tour), *High School Musical 1 & 2* (U.S. and U.K. Tours), *White Christmas*, *High Fidelity*, *Spamalot* (Las Vegas), *...Spelling Bee* (National Tour), *The Drowsy Chaperone* (Broadway), *Princesses* (Seattle). Other projects include *Shamu One Ocean*, *Shamu Rocks*, and *O'Wondrous Night* at SeaWorld, *IllumiNights* and *Kinetix* at Busch Gardens, and New Year's Eve Celebrations from Times Square and his hometown of Sydney. Lighting designer: several projects in Australia as well as *Celtic Fyre* at Busch Gardens, *Hamlet* and *My Brilliant Divorce* at Asolo Rep.

## RICHARD PILBROW

Richard Pilbrow, Founder and Chairman Emeritus of Theatre Projects Consultants, is one of the world's leading theatre design consultants, a theatre, film and television producer, and an internationally known author and stage lighting designer.

Richard was honored as Lighting Designer of the Year (2005) by Lighting Dimensions magazine and named by LiveDesign as one of the ten visionaries among designers and artists, who were "the most influential people in the world of visual design for live events" (2005). Richard is the winner of the 2008 Wally Russell Lifetime Achievement Award, a pioneer of modern stage lighting in Britain, and his work has been seen in London, New York, Paris, Berlin, Vienna and Moscow.

Richard was conferred with Honorary Fellowship of the Hong Kong Academy for Performing Arts (2010), was honored with the 4th Knights of Illumination Lifetime Recognition Award (2011), awarded the Southeastern Theatre Conference 2012 Distinguished Career Award, and was conferred with Honorary Fellowship to the Royal Central School of Speech and Drama in London (2012).

## KENNETH POSNER

Kenneth Posner, lighting designer, has more than 50 Broadway play and musical theatre credits. He also designs extensively Off-Broadway, for resident theatres, and touring productions throughout the United States as well as internationally. Selected Broadway credits: *Wicked, Hairspray, Kinky Boots, Pippin, Dirty Rotten Scoundrels, Legally Blonde, The Coast of Utopia—Shipwrecked, Other Desert Cities, Harvey, The Best Man, The Merchant of Venice, The Royal Family, The Odd Couple, Glengarry Glen Ross, The Goat, Uncle Vanya, Side Man, The Little Foxes* and *The Rose Tattoo*. He is the recipient of the Tony, Drama Desk, Outer Critics' Circle and OBIE Awards.

## MICHAEL A. REESE

Michael Reese is the Executive Vice President at Barkley Kalpak Agency, a New York City based event design and production agency, collaborating with some of the world's most recognized brands to create award-winning live events all over the globe—from business meetings and conferences to product launches and press events to galas and awards shows. At BKA, Michael is the lead designer and heads up the creative and design departments overseeing creative direction, scenic and lighting design, technical direction, and graphic, web, and video design. Before joining BKA, Michael was a freelance lighting designer working in NYC, and across the United States. Since joining BKA, Michael has designed scenery and lighting across the globe, from theatre productions in Macau, China, to press launches at Radio City Music Hall. Michael lives with his wife and two children just north of New York City.

## PHILIP S. ROSENBERG

Lighting designer—Broadway: *A Gentleman's Guide to Love and Murder*. Off-Broadway: *The Explorers Club, Cactus Flower*. Regional credits include: Kennedy Center, La Jolla Playhouse, Ford's Theatre, The Guthrie Theater, The Old Globe, TheatreWorks, Hartford Stage, Huntington Theatre Company, Chicago Shakespeare Theatre, Shakespeare Theatre Company, Manhattan School of Music, Portland Stage Company, TACT, Barrington Stage Company, Williamstown Theatre Festival, Dorset Theatre Festival, Bay Street Theatre, Two River Theatre Company, George Street Playhouse, and Westport Country Playhouse. In years past, Philip has served as the associate lighting designer of over 35 Broadway plays and musicals.

## JARED A. SAYEG

Lighting design: International City Theatre: *Backwards in High Heels, Songs for a New World, Threepenny Opera, Bright Ideas, Facing East* and *The All Night Strut*.

Colony Theatre: *Educating Rita* and *TRYING* (Ovation Award Nomination). For Reprise Theatre Company: *Forum*, *They're Playing our Song* and *GIGI*, and *The Who's Tommy* (Ricardo Montalban Theatre). Other notable productions include: *Guys & Dolls* (Cabrillo Music Theatre), the Indie Rock Ballet's *The Question* (Ricardo Montalban Theatre) and the Intimate Opera's *Amahl & the Night Visitors* (Pasadena Playhouse).

West End: *Rolling with Laughter* at Her Majesty's Theatre and Nottingham playhouse as well as in Los Angeles. Broadway design credits include: *Bravo Bernstein and Gotham Glory*. U.S. assistant designer: (Broadway) *PRIMO* from London's National Theatre, Andrew Lloyd Webber's *The Woman in White* as well as the 2003 *Radio City Music Hall Christmas Spectacular*.

For three seasons Jared was in residence with LA Opera, has lit numerous industrial events, and his architectural designs are seen regularly in restaurants and exhibits.

### JEN SCHRIEVER

Selected lighting design: Broadway: John Leguizamo's *Ghetto Klown*. Opera: *Die Fledermaus* (MET Opera), *Faust*, *A Midsummer Night's Dream*—Russian Golden Mask award nominee (Mariinsky, Russia), *Pearl Fishers* (ENO, London). Off-Broadway: *The Other Josh Cohen* and *Triassic Parq* (Soho Playhouse), *A Bullet for Adolf* (New World Stages), *Mosaic & Whida Peru* (59E59), *Stuffed and UnStrung* (Union Square). Regional: *The Crucible* (IRT), *American Hero* (Williamstown), *Clybourne Park* (Asolo Rep), *The Taming of The Shrew* and *The Conference of the Birds* (Folger, DC), *The Gronholm Method* (Falcon, L.A.), *A Second Chance* (Signature, D.C.), *An Evening Without Monty Python* (L.A. and Town Hall). Associate design credits for Broadway include: *Betrayal*, *Death of A Salesman*, *The Mountaintop*, *The House of Blue Leaves*, *The Book of Mormon*, *Women on the Verge of a Nervous Breakdown*, *Fences*, *A Behanding in Spokane*, *Joe Turner's Come and Gone*, *You're Welcome America*, *American Buffalo*, *13—A New Musical*, *A Catered Affair*, *Cymbeline*, *The Vertical Hour*, *The Color Purple*, *The Threepenny Opera*. Adjunct Professor: Purchase College, BFA Purchase College. www.jenschriever.com

### HUGH VANSTONE

Hugh has designed lighting for plays, musicals, operas and ballets in London, New York and around the world. He is a recipient of three Olivier Awards for his work in London. New York credits include: *I'll Eat You Last: A Chat with Sue Mengers* (Booth); *Matilda* (Shubert—TONY Award for Best Lighting); *Ghost* (Lunt Fontanne - TONY nomination for Best Lighting); *La bête* (Music Box); *A Steady Rain* (Schoenfeld); *God of Carnage* (Jacobs); *Mary Stuart* (Broadhurst Theatre—Tony and Drama Desk nominations for Best Lighting); *Shrek* (Broadway); *Boeing-Boeing* (Longacre); *Spamalot* (Shubert—Tony nomination for Best Lighting).

### ANDREW VOLLER

Lighting designer, programmer and the creator of the Moving Lighting Assistant application. Andrew has worked as a programmer on large scale events such as the opening and closing ceremonies of the London 2012 Olympic/Paralympics, as well as West End and Broadway productions. He has also worked as an associate on productions for lighting designers Rick Fisher, Hugh Vanstone, and Howard Harrison. Andrew's own lighting designs span from opera to musicals in continental Europe. www.avld.com

## K. C. WILKERSON

K. C. Wilkerson is currently the senior lighting designer for Disney Parks and Resorts Creative Entertainment; overseeing the design, implementation, and programming of lighting and video content for live entertainment on the west coast. With Disney, he has designed hundreds of shows, projects, events, tours, parades, and themed environments all over the world. He also designs lighting and video for theatres across southern California. A longtime member of the Association of Lighting Designers, his work has been published in *Live Design, Stage Directions*, and *Lighting & Sound America*. Honors include Los Angeles Drama Critics Circle Awards (Best Lighting Design, Best Video Design), LA Stage Alliance Ovation Awards (Best Video Design), Backstage Garland Awards (Best Lighting Design), StageSceneLA Awards (Projection Designer of the Year, Lighting and Projection Design), and a THEA award. A passionate supporter of arts education, K. C. has spoken and/or conducted workshops at numerous theatre festivals, U.S.I.T.T., and L.D.I. He also speaks regularly to college and high school students about careers in the arts.

# Product Websites

Many products have been discussed throughout this text. For further information, please visit the websites listed on the following pages (shown in alphabetical order).

## 360 Panorama

www.occipital.com/360/app

## Adobe Acrobat

www.adobe.com/products/acrobat

## Adobe Photoshop

www.adobe.com/products/photoshop

## AutoPlotVW

www.autoplotvw.com

## BeamCalc

www.westsidesystems.com/f-pl/f-beam/beam.html

## Check Ninja

https://itunes.apple.com/us/app/check-ninja/id436959507?mt=8

## ClickBook

www.bluesquirrel.com/products/cbmac

*Dropbox*

www.dropbox.com

https://itunes.apple.com/us/app/dropbox/id327630330?mt=8

*DMX Calc*

www.westsidesystems.com/f-pl/f-dmx/dmx.html

*ESP Vision*

www.espvision.com

*Exit Strategy NYC*

www.exitstrategynyc.com

*FaceTime*

www.apple.com/ios/facetime

*FastFocus Pro*

www.mattpeel.com

*FeetInchesCalc*

www.feetinchescalculator.com/

*Flashlight*

www.i4software.com/iphone/flashlight

*FileMaker Pro*

www.filemaker.com

*Find My iPhone*

www.apple.com/icloud/find-my-iphone.html

*FocusTrack*

www.FocusTrack.co.uk

*Fusion*

www.vmware.com/products/fusion

*Gaffer's Glass*

www.gaffersglass.com

*Gel Swatch Library*

www.wybron.com/stage-lighting-accessories/iOS-apps/gel-swatch-library-iphone-app.html

*GoodNotes*

www.goodnotesapp.com

*Google Maps*

www.google.com/mobile/maps

*GraphicConverter*

www.lemkesoft.de/en/products

*Hangman*

www.optimesoftware.com/products/iphone/hangman_free/

*HopStop*

www.hopstop.com/mobile

*iAnnotate PDF*

www.branchfire.com/iannotate

*iConvert*

www.future-apps.net/app/iconvert

*iExit*

www.iexitapp.com

*iGobo*

www.apollodesign.net/igobo

*iPronunciation*

https://itunes.apple.com/us/app/60+-languages-translation+voice+pronunciation+ocr/
id345780733?mt=8

*iRFR and iRFR Preview*

www.etcconnect.com/product.overview.aspx?ID=22011

*iSquint*

www.isquint.net/iphone-app

*Jim on Light*

www.jimonlight.com/mobile

*Joshua Benghiat Lighting Design*

www.benghiatlighting.com/software

*JotNot Scanner Pro*

www.mobitech3000.com/applications.html

*LightCalc*

www.dhvproductions.com/lightcalc

*Lighting Calculator*

www.lightingappstore.com/?page_id=56

*The LightNetwork*

www.lightnetwork.com

*Lightwright*

www.mckernon.com

*Lightwright Touch*

www.westsidesystems.com/f-pl/f-lwtouch/lwtouch.html

*LX (Lighting) Handbook*

www.lightingappstore.com/?page_id=37

*Microsoft Office*

www.office.microsoft.com/en-us

*ML Finder PRO*

www.appato.com/michael-zinman/ml-finder-pro/

*Moiré*

www.wybron.com/stage-lighting-accessories/iOS-apps/moire-gobo-library-iphone-app.html

*Moving Light Assistant*

www.movinglightassistant.com

*MyGobo*

https://itunes.apple.com/us/app/mygobo/id320933772?mt=8

*My Voltage*

https://itunes.apple.com/us/app/my-voltage/id474205108?mt=8

*Nomad*

https://itunes.apple.com/us/app/nemetschek-vectorworks-nomad/id506706850?mt=8

*OpenTable*

https://itunes.apple.com/us/app/opentable/id296581815?mt=8

*Parallels*

www.parallels.com

*Pelican Case*

www.pelican.com

*PDF Compress*

www.metaobject.com/Products

*Photo Measures*

www.bigbluepixel.com/photo-measures

*Plugs World*

https://itunes.apple.com/tc/app/plugs-world/id454463063?mt=8

*PocketLD*

https://itunes.apple.com/us/app/pocketld/id292911261?mt=8

*Separate Checks*

www.tightapps.com/separatechecks.html

*Skype*

www.skype.com

*SoftSymbols*

www.fieldtemplate.com

*SpotTrack*

www.SpotTrack.co.uk

*Synchronize*

www.solv.tv/Synchronize

*Taxi Magic*

www.taximagic.com

*Theatre Words*

www.theatrewords.com

*TriangleCalc*

https://itunes.apple.com/us/app/trianglecalc/id326268526?mt=8

*Urbanspoon*

https://itunes.apple.com/us/app/urbanspoon/id284708449?mt=8

*Vectorworks*

www.vectorworks.net

*Viber*

www.viber.com

*Virtual Magic Sheet*

www.westsidesystems.com/vms/vms.html

*Where To?*

www.futuretap.com/apps/whereto

*Wikitude*

www.wikitude.com/app

*World Clock—Time Zones*

www.timeanddate.com/iphone/worldclock.html

*World Power Plug*

https://itunes.apple.com/us/app/world-power-plug/id401231243?mt=8

*Write 2*

www.writeapp.tumblr.com

*WYSIWYG*

www.cast-soft.com/wysiwyg

*Yahoo Weather*

mobile.yahoo.com/weather

*Yelp*

www.yelp.com/yelpmobile

*YouTube*

www.youtube.com/yt/devices

*Zagat*

www.zagat.com

# Notes

## CHAPTER 1

1. Robin, Natalie. "Light on the subject: Revisiting the roadmap." *Stage Directions*, October 2012. //www.stage-directions.com/current-issue/55-light-on-the-subject/4590-revisiting-the-roadmap-.html (accessed October 3, 2012).

2. Shelley, Steven Louis. *A practical guide to stage lighting*. 2nd ed. Oxford: Focal Press, 2009.

3. Riha, Michael J. *Starting your career as a theatrical designer: Insights and advice from leading Broadway designers*. New York: Allworth Press, 2012.

4. Kramer, Peter D. "Brian MacDevitt's Tony night." http://theater.lohudblogs.com/2009/06/17/brian-macdevitts-tony-night/ (accessed September 17, 2013).

5. Riha, Michael J. *Starting your career as a theatrical designer: Insights and advice from leading Broadway designers*. New York: Allworth Press, 2012.

6. Robin, Natalie. "Light on the subject: Revisiting the roadmap." *Stage Directions*, October 2012. www.stage-directions.com/current-issue/55-light-on-the-subject/4590-revisiting-the-roadmap-.html (accessed October 3, 2012).

7. Robin, Natalie. "Light on the subject: Revisiting the roadmap." *Stage Directions*, October 2012. www.stage-directions.com/current-issue/55-light-on-the-subject/4590-revisiting-the-roadmap-.html (accessed October 3, 2012).

8. Miller, Craig. "A guide for assistant lighting designers: Some modestly proffered notes." *Theatre Crafts*, January 1989, 21–27.

9. Shelley, Steven Louis. *A practical guide to stage lighting*. 2nd ed. Oxford: Focal Press, 2009.

10. Pilbrow, Richard. *Stage lighting design: The art, the craft, the life*. New York: By Design Press, 2008.

11. Miller, Craig. "A guide for assistant lighting designers: Some modestly proffered notes." *Theatre Crafts*, January 1989, 21–27.

12. Sandberg-Dierson, Marian. "Talking with Vivien Leone." *Live Design*, June 2004. http://livedesignonline.com/mag/talking-vivien-leone (accessed July 11, 2013).

13. Pilbrow, Richard. *Stage lighting design: The art, the craft, the life*. New York: By Design Press, 2008, p. 327.

14. Robin, Natalie. "Light on the subject: Revisiting the roadmap." *Stage Directions*, October 2012. www.stage-directions.com/current-issue/55-light-on-the-subject/4590-revisiting-the-roadmap-.html (accessed October 3, 2012).

15. Sandberg-Dierson, Marian. "Talking with Vivien Leone." *Live Design*, June 2004. http://livedesignonline.com/mag/talking-vivien-leone (accessed July 11, 2013).

16. Essig, Linda. *The speed of light: Dialogues on lighting design and technological change*. Portsmouth, N.H.: Heinemann, 2002.

17. Sonnenfeld, Sonny. "A genius for lighting: Jennifer Tipton looks back on her stellar career." *Lighting & Sound America*, September 2011, 79.

18. "Hit the books, hit on Broadway." *Stage Directions*. www.stage-directions.com/current-issue/81-training/3638-hit-the-books-hit-on-broadway.html (accessed September 17, 2013).

19. Robin, Natalie. "Light on the subject: Revisiting the roadmap." *Stage Directions*, October 2012. http://www.stage-directions.com/current-issue/55 light-on-the-subject/4590-revisiting-the-roadmap-.html (accessed October 3, 2012).

20. Pilbrow, Richard. *Stage lighting design: The art, the craft, the life*. New York: By Design Press, 2008.

## CHAPTER 3

1. Robin, Natalie. "Light on the subject: Revisiting the roadmap." *Stage Directions*, October 2012. http://www.stage-directions.com/current-issue/55-light-on-the-subject/4590-revisiting-the-roadmap-.html (accessed October 3, 2012).

2. Miller, Craig. "A guide for assistant lighting designers: Some modestly proffered notes." *Theatre Crafts*, January 1989, 21–27.

3. Miller, Craig. "A guide for assistant lighting designers: Some modestly proffered notes." *Theatre Crafts*, January 1989, 21–27.

## CHAPTER 4

1. "About the IATSE." IATSE Labor Union. www.iatse-intl.org/about-iatse (accessed July 11, 2013).

2. Stein, Tobie S., and Jessica Bathurst. *Performing arts management: A handbook of professional practices*. New York: Allworth Press, 2008.

## CHAPTER 5

1. Mumm, Robert C. *Photometrics handbook*. 2nd ed. Louisville, KY.: Broadway Press, 1997.

## CHAPTER 6

1. Miller, Craig. "A guide for assistant lighting designers: Some modestly proffered notes." *Theatre Crafts*, January 1989, 21–27.

2. Miller, Craig. "A guide for assistant lighting designers: Some modestly proffered notes." *Theatre Crafts*, January 1989, 21–27.

## CHAPTER 7

1. Miller, Craig. "A guide for assistant lighting designers: Some modestly proffered notes." *Theatre Crafts*, January 1989, 21–27.

2. Miller, Craig. "A guide for assistant lighting designers: Some modestly proffered notes." *Theatre Crafts*, January 1989, 21–27.

3. "Five questions for Jason Lyons, theatre lighting designer." *Live Design*, May 2006, 22–23.

## CHAPTER 8

1. Robin, Natalie. "Light on the subject: Revisiting the roadmap." *Stage Directions*, October 2012. http://www.stage-directions.com/current-issue/55-light-on-the-subject/4590-revisiting-the-roadmap-.html (accessed October 3, 2012).

## CHAPTER 9

1. "The Lighting Archive." The Lighting Archive. http://www.thelightingarchive.org/ (accessed September 10, 2013).

2. Courtesy of: KB Associates, Inc.

3. Courtesy of: KB Associates, Inc. and Brian MacDevitt

4. Sandberg-Dierson, Marian. "Talking with Vivien Leone." *Live Design*, June 2004. http://livedesignonline.com/mag/talking-vivien-leone (accessed July 11, 2013).

5. Winslow, Colin. *The handbook of set design*. Ramsbury, Marlborough, Wiltshire: Crowood Press, 2006, p. 72.

6. Courtesy of: KB Associates, Inc. and Brian MacDevitt.

7. Courtesy of: Ryan O'Gara and Howell Binkley.

8. Dialogue quoted from Frank Galati's play adaptation of John Steinbeck's classic novel, *The Grapes of Wrath*.

## CHAPTER 10

1. Sayer, Rob. "Colour correction filters." *On Stage Lighting*. www.onstagelighting.co.uk/lighting-design/colour-correction-filters-stage-lighting-gels/ (accessed July 11, 2013).

2. LEE Filters swatch book.

3. Miller, Craig. "A guide for assistant lighting designers: Some modestly proffered notes." *Theatre Crafts*, January 1989, 21–27.

## CHAPTER 11

1. Pilbrow, Richard. *Stage lighting design: The art, the craft, the life*. New York: By Design Press, 2008.

2. Stein, Tobie S., and Jessica Bathurst. *Performing arts management: A handbook of professional practices*. New York: Allworth Press, 2008. p. 37.

## CHAPTER 12

1. Winslow, Colin. *The handbook of set design*. Ramsbury, Marlborough, Wiltshire: Crowood Press, 2006.

2. Lampert-Greaux, Ellen. "Q&A: Neil Austin." *Live Design*, October 2010, 36–40.

3. "Society of London Theatre." Society of London Theatre. www.solt.co.uk/ (accessed July 11, 2013).

4. Pilbrow, Richard. *Stage lighting design: The art, the craft, the life*. New York: By Design Press, 2008.

5. Pilbrow, Richard. *Stage lighting design: The art, the craft, the life*. New York: By Design Press, 2008.

6. "Strikes and art: The role of unions in German theatre." Deutsch lernen, Kulturerleben – Â Goethe-Institut. http://www.goethe.de/kue/the/tst/en5221277.htm (accessed July 11, 2013).

7. "Strikes and art: The role of unions in German theatre." Deutsch lernen, Kulturerleben – Â Goethe-Institut. http://www.goethe.de/kue/the/tst/en5221277.htm (accessed July 11, 2013).

8. Excerpts from Söderberg, Olle. *New theatre words*. Amsterdam: Sttf, 1995.

9. Excerpts from Söderberg, Olle. *New theatre words*. Amsterdam: Sttf, 1995.

## CHAPTER 13

1. Riha, Michael J.. *Starting your career as a theatrical designer: Insights and advice from leading Broadway designers*. New York, NY: Allworth Press, 2012.

2. Box, Harry C. *Set lighting technician's handbook: Film lighting equipment, practice, and electrical distribution*. 3rd ed. Amsterdam: Focal Press, 2003.

3. Excerpts from Box, Harry C. *Set lighting technician's handbook*, 3rd ed. Amsterdam: Focal Press, 2003.

4. Bell, John. "Industrials: American business theatre in the '80s." *The Drama Review: TDR*, Winter 1987, 36–57.

## CHAPTER 14

1. Sandberg-Dierson, Marian. "Talking with Vivien Leone." *Live Design*, June 2004. http://livedesignonline.com/mag/talking-vivien-leone (accessed July 11, 2013).

2. Pilbrow, Richard. *Stage lighting design: The art, the craft, the life.* New York: By Design Press, 2008.

3. Riha, Michael J. *Starting your career as a theatrical designer: Insights and advice from leading Broadway designers.* New York: Allworth Press, 2012.

4. Essig, Linda. *The speed of light: Dialogues on lighting design and technological change.* Portsmouth, NH: Heinemann, 2002.

## APPENDIX G

1. Based on Millikin University Career Center's document: "The Elements of a Cover Letter."

# Bibliography

"AEA fogger guidelines." Actors' Equity. www.actorsequity.org/docs/safesan/TD_guidelines .pdf (accessed July 11, 2013).

"About the IATSE." IATSE Labor Union. www.iatse-intl.org/about-iatse (accessed July 11, 2013).

"Actors' Equity – Representing American actors and stage managers in the theatre." Actors' Equity. www.actorsequity.org/ (accessed July 11, 2013).

Alcorn, Steve. *Theme park design: behind the scenes with an engineer.* Orlando, FL: Theme Perks Inc., 2010.

"An interview with Dawn Chiang." *CityTheatrical.* www.citytheatrical.com/news_letter/ Dawn_Chiang_Interview.htm (accessed July 11, 2013).

"Associated Musicians of Greater New York." Associated Musicians of Greater New York. www.local802afm.org/ (accessed July 11, 2013).

"B'way 101: How a Broadway show 'Lights the lights'" – Video. Playbill.com. www .playbill.com/multimedia/video/4486/Bway-101-How-a-Broadway-Show-Lights-the-Lights (accessed July 11, 2013).

"BECTU." BECTU. www.bectu.org.uk (accessed July 11, 2013).

Barbour, David. "Rise above: Tracking Spider-Man's long and crooked road to Broadway success." *Lighting & Sound America*, September 2011, 58–75.

Beauvert, Thierry, Jacques Moatti, and Florian Kleinefenn. *Opera houses of the world.* New York, NY: Vendome Press, 1996.

Bell, John. "Industrials: American business theatre in the '80s." *The Drama Review: TDR*, Winter 1987, 36–57.

Box, Harry C. *Set lighting technician's handbook: Film lighting equipment, practice, and electrical distribution.* 3rd ed. Amsterdam: Focal Press, 2003.

Brault, Frank. "Making the most of Vectorworks spotlight." *PLSN: Projection, Lights, & Staging News*, March 2013, 54.

Cadena, Richard. *Automated lighting: The art and science of moving light in theatre, live performance, broadcast, and entertainment.* Amsterdam: Focal Press, 2006.

Choi, Christian. "John McKernon Software Lightwright 5." *Live Design*, September 2010, 50–60.

"CityTheatrical." CityTheatrical. www.citytheatrical.com/ (accessed July 11, 2013).

Coakley, Jacob. "An appreciation of Craig Miller." *Stage Directions*, October 2012. www.stage-directions.com/current-issue/55-light-on-the-subject/4582-an-appreciation-of-craig-miller.html (accessed July 11, 2013).

Conte, David M., and Stephen Langley. *Theatre management: Producing and managing the performing arts*. Hollywood, CA: EntertainmentPro, 2007.

Essig, Linda. *The speed of light: Dialogues on lighting design and technological change*. Portsmouth, NH: Heinemann, 2002.

Farber, Donald C. *Producing theatre: A comprehensive legal and business guide*. 3rd ed. Pompton Plains, NJ: Limelight Editions, 2006.

"Five questions for Jason Lyons, theatre lighting designer." *Live Design*, May 2006, 22–23.

"FocusTrack." FocusTrack. www.focustrack.co.uk/ (accessed July 11, 2013).

"FocusTrack 1.200." FocusTrack. www.focustrack.co.uk/news/news/FocusTrack1200.html (accessed July 11, 2013).

Gans, Andrew. "Believe it or not! Spider-Man Turn Off the Dark opens on Broadway June 14." Playbill.com. www.playbill.com/news/article/151764-Believe-It-or-Not-Spider-Man-Turn-Off-the-Dark-Opens-on-Broadway-June-14 (accessed July 11, 2013).

"Guide to standard paper sizes." WMW Reprographics, Ltd. www.wmw.ca/graphics/paper.gif (accessed July 11, 2013).

"Guide to buying the right lamp: Understanding light color temperature." My LED Lighting Guide. www.myledlightingguide.com/article.aspx?articleid=37 (accessed July 11, 2013).

Hardin, Terri. *Theatres & opera houses: masterpieces of architecture*. New York, NY: Todtri, 1999.

Healy, Patrick. "On Broadway, investors with shallow pockets." *The New York Times*. www.nytimes.com/2012/04/19/theater/for-godspell-on-broadway-crowd-sourced-producers.html?_r=1&pagewanted=all (accessed July 11, 2013).

"Hit the books, hit on Broadway." *Stage Directions*. www.stage-directions.com/current-issue/81-training/3638-hit-the-books-hit-on-broadway.html (accessed September 17, 2013).

"How to distinguish LED color temperature." EOSLED Limited. www.eosled.com/faqs/how-to-distinguish-led-color-temperature.html (accessed July 11, 2013).

"IATSE, Local One." IATSE, Local One. http://iatselocalone.org/Public/Home.aspx (accessed July 11, 2013).

"Illuminating a Broadway spider." *Revista-Backstage*. www.davidhbosboom.com/pdf/RevistaBackstage-September2011.pdf (accessed July 11, 2013).

"John McKernon Software." John McKernon Software. www.mckernon.com (accessed July 11, 2013).

Kenrick, John. "The making of a musical – Part V." Musicals101.com. www.musicals101.com/make5.htm (accessed July 11, 2013).

Kilburn, Mike. *London's theatres*. London: New Holland, 2002.

Kramer, Peter D. "Brian MacDevitt's Tony night." http://theater.lohudblogs.com/2009/06/17/brian-macdevitts-tony-night/ (accessed September 17, 2013).

Lampert-Greaux, Ellen. "Q&A: Neil Austin." *Live Design*, October 2010, 36–40.

Lang, Justin. "Moving Light Assistant." *PLSN: Projection, Lights, & Staging News*, March 2013, 53.

Lawler, Mike. "American theatre, December 2011." Theatre Communications Group. www .tcg.org/publications/at/jan12/technical.cfm (accessed August 28, 2012).

LeFurgy, Bill. "Insights interview with Beverly Emmons, lighting design preservation innovator." Library of Congress Blogs. http://blogs.loc.gov/digitalpreservation/2012/02/insights-interview-with-beverly-emmons-lighting-design-preservation-innovator/ (accessed September 16, 2013).

Maier, Marissa. "Will Boston become a Broadway outpost again?" Backstage.com. www .backstage.com/news/will-boston-become-broadway-outpost-again/ (accessed July 11, 2013).

Matson, John. "How to buy a better lightbulb." *Science News*. www.scientificamerican.com/article.cfm?id=buying-better-bulb (accessed July 11, 2013).

McMills, Anne E. 2001. *Thesis journal: Europe 2001*. MFA Thesis, Rutgers University, Mason Gross School of the Arts. New Brunswick: Unpublished.

Miller, Craig. "A guide for assistant lighting designers: Some modestly proffered notes." *Theatre Crafts*, January 1989, 21–27.

Moody, James L. *Concert lighting: Techniques, art, and business*. 3rd ed. Oxford: Focal Press, 2010.

"Moving Light Assistant." Moving Light Assistant. www.movinglightassistant.com (accessed July 11, 2013).

Mumm, Robert C. *Photometrics handbook*. 2nd ed. Louisville, KY: Broadway Press, 1997.

Newman, Mark A. "Q&A: Brian MacDevitt." *Live Design*, January 2006, 41.

Pennacchio, George. "'Spider-Man' musical opens: What critics said." ABC Owned Television Stations. http://abclocal.go.com/kabc/story?section=news/hollywood_wrap&id=8191203 (accessed July 11, 2013).

Pilat, Ben. "The assistant lighting designer's handbook: A reference for students and aspiring assistants." Instituto de Artes. www.iar.unicamp.br/lab/luz/ld/C%EAnica/Livros/assistent%20handbook.pdf (accessed July 11, 2013).

Pilbrow, Richard. *Stage lighting design: The art, the craft, the life*. New York, NY: By Design Press, 2008.

Riha, Michael J. *Starting your career as a theatrical designer: Insights and advice from leading Broadway designers*. New York, NY: Allworth Press, 2012.

Riley, Peter Jason. *The new tax guide for artists of every persuasion: Actors, directors, musicians, singers, and other show biz folk, visual artists and writers*. New York, NY: Limelight Editions, 2002.

Robin, Natalie. "Light on the subject: Revisiting the roadmap." *Stage Directions*, October 2012. www.stage-directions.com/current-issue/55-light-on-the-subject/4590-revisiting-the-roadmap-.html (accessed October 3, 2012).

Sandberg-Dierson, Marian. "Talking with Vivien Leone." *Live Design*, June 2004. http://live-designonline.com/mag/talking-vivien-leone (accessed July 11, 2013).

Sayer, Rob. "Colour correction filters." *On Stage Lighting*. www.onstagelighting.co.uk/lighting-design/colour-correction-filters-stage-lighting-gels/ (accessed July 11, 2013).

Scelfo, Julie. "Any other bright ideas?" *The New York Times*. www.nytimes.com/2008/01/10/garden/10lighting.html?pagewanted=all&_r=1& (accessed July 11, 2013).

Schiller, Brad. *The automated lighting programmer's handbook*. Oxford: Focal Press, 2004.

"Scotch broth." *Lighting & Sound*, October 2001, 55–56.

Shelley, Steven Louis. *A practical guide to stage lighting*. 2nd ed. Oxford: Focal Press, 2009.

Skalka, Anne, and Janice Beth Gregg. *Tax deductions A to Z for writers*. Lawrenceville, NJ: Boxed Books Inc., 2006.

"Society of London Theatre." Society of London Theatre. www.solt.co.uk/ (accessed July 11, 2013).

Sonnenfeld, Sonny. "A genius for lighting: Jennifer Tipton looks back on her stellar career." *Lighting & Sound America*, September 2011, 76–79.

Sonnenfeld, Sonny. "The insider: Vivien Leone, associate lighting designer, on a career that spans Phantom of the Opera to Spider-Man: Turn Off the Dark." *Lighting & Sound America*, November 2012, 74–78.

Söderberg, Olle. *New theatre words*. Amsterdam: Sttf, 1995.

"SpotTrack." SpotTrack. www.spottrack.co.uk/index.html (accessed July 11, 2013).

"SpotTrack 1.00 Released – Blue room technical forum." Blue Room technical forum. www.blue-room.org.uk/index.php?showtopic=37628 (accessed July 11, 2013).

Steffy, Gary R. *Architectural lighting design*. 2nd ed. New York, NY: John Wiley, 2002.

Stein, Tobie S., and Jessica Bathurst. *Performing arts management: A handbook of professional practices*. New York, NY: Allworth Press, 2008.

"Strikes and art: The role of unions in German theatre." Deutsch lernen, Kulturerleben – Â Goethe-Institut. www.goethe.de/kue/the/tst/en5221277.htm (accessed July 11, 2013).

Taub, Eric A. "LED lighting gaining acceptance (sort of)." NYTimes.com. http://bits.blogs.nytimes.com/2009/04/30/led-lighting-gaining-acceptance-sort-of/ (accessed July 11, 2013).

"Technical Paperwork." *Revista-Backstage*. www.davidhbosboom.com/pdf/RevistaBackstage-September2008.pdf (accessed July 11, 2013).

"The Broadway League." The Broadway League. www.broadwayleague.com/index.php?url_identifier=about-the-league-1 (accessed July 11, 2013).

"The element's of a cover letter." Millikin University Career Center. 1999. Out-of-print.

"The LD interview." The Hemsley Lighting Programs. www.hemsleylightingprograms.com/index.php/career/in-his-own-words/the-ld-interview/ (accessed July 11, 2013).

"The Lighting Archive." The Lighting Archive. www.thelightingarchive.org/ (accessed September 10, 2013).

"Theatrical Management Association." Theatrical Management Association. www.tmauk.org/ (accessed July 11, 2013).

"Top 10 best theaters in the world, amazing theatres." incastreasures on HubPages. http://incastreasures.hubpages.com/hub/Top-10-best-theaters-in-the-world (accessed July 11, 2013).

"Types of lanterns." Theatrecrafts.com – Entertainment Technology Resources. www
.theatrecrafts.com/page.php?id=803 (accessed July 11, 2013).

"United Scenic Artists, Local 829." United Scenic Artists, Local 829. www.usa829.org (accessed
July 11, 2013).

Winslow, Colin. *The handbook of set design*. Ramsbury, Marlborough, Wiltshire: Crowood
Press, 2006.

Zettl, Herbert. *Television production handbook*. 5th ed. Belmont, CA: Wadsworth Pub. Co., 1992.

# Index